Lecture Notes in Artificial Intelligence   5988

Edited by R. Goebel, J. Siekmann, and W. Wahlster

Subseries of Lecture Notes in Computer Science

Pedro Meseguer   Lawrence Mandow
Rafael M. Gasca (Eds.)

Current Topics in Artificial Intelligence

13th Conference of the Spanish Association
for Artificial Intelligence, CAEPIA 2009
Seville, Spain, November 9-13, 2009
Selected Papers

 Springer

Series Editors

Randy Goebel, University of Alberta, Edmonton, Canada
Jörg Siekmann, University of Saarland, Saarbrücken, Germany
Wolfgang Wahlster, DFKI and University of Saarland, Saarbrücken, Germany

Volume Editors

Pedro Meseguer
IIIA - CSIC
Campus UAB s/n
08193 Bellaterra, Spain
E-mail: pedro@iiia.csic.es

Lawrence Mandow
Universidad de Málaga
Campus de Teatinos
Dpto. Lenguajes y Ciencias de la Computación
29071 Malaga, Spain
E-mail: lawrence@lcc.uma.es

Rafael M. Gasca
Universidad de Sevilla
ETS de Ingeniería Informática
Dpto. Lenguajes y Sistemas Informáticos
41012 Seville, Spain
E-mail: gasca@us.es

Library of Congress Control Number: 2010929680

CR Subject Classification (1998): I.2, F.1, I.4, H.4, I.5, F.2

LNCS Sublibrary: SL 7 – Artificial Intelligence

ISSN   0302-9743

ISBN-10   3-642-14263-X Springer Berlin Heidelberg New York
ISBN-13   978-3-642-14263-5 Springer Berlin Heidelberg New York

springer.com

© Springer-Verlag Berlin Heidelberg 2010
Printed in Germany

Typesetting: Camera-ready by author, data conversion by Scientific Publishing Services, Chennai, India
Printed on acid-free paper   06/3180

Preface

This volume contains a selection of the papers accepted for oral presentation at the 13th Conference of the Spanish Association for Artificial Intelligence (CAEPIA 2009) and its associated Conference on Artificial Intelligence Technology Transfer (TTIA 2009), held in Seville, November 9–13, 2009. This was the 13th biennial conference in the CAEPIA series, which was started back in 1985. Previous editions took place in Madrid, Alicante, Málaga, Murcia, Gijón, Donostia, Santiago de Compostela and Salamanca.

With the permanent goal of making CAEPIA/TTIA a high-quality conference, and following the model of current demanding AI conferences, we organized the review process for CAEPIA and TTIA papers in the following way. The Scientific Committee was structured in two levels. In the first place, there was a Senior Program Committee, formed by 22 well-known members of the AI community affiliated to Spanish universities and research centers. Secondly, there was a Program Committee consisting of almost 100 members (30% affiliated to non-Spanish institutions). Each paper was assigned to three Program Committee members who made the reviews (following the double-blind model), and to two Senior Program Committee members, who supervised these reviews. Authors could read the reviews during three days, and then introduce some feedback. These replies to the reviews were added to the review process, papers were discussed again, and finally Senior Program Committee members made a proposal to the Scientific Committee Chair.

We received 125 submissions (107 CAEPIA and 18 TTIA). After the review process, 63 were accepted (54 CAEPIA and 9 TTIA) for oral presentation, in two modalities: 31 full papers (28 CAEPIA and 3 TTIA) and 32 short papers (26 CAEPIA and 6 TTIA). Only full papers were selected to be published in this volume.

We would like to acknowledge the work done by the Scientific Committee members in the review and discussion of the submissions, and by the authors to improve the quality of AI research. We would also like to thank the invited speakers and the professors in charge of the tutorials, for their participation in the conference. Last but not least, we would like to thank the Organizing Committee members for their hard work, the Universidad de Sevilla, our sponsors and AEPIA for their support.

March 2010

Pedro Meseguer González
Lawrence Mandow Andaluz
Rafael Martínez Gasca

Organization

CAEPIA/TTIA 2009 was organized by the Intelligent and Security Technologies in Information Systems (QUIVIR) Research Group of the Universidad de Sevilla, in cooperation with AEPIA, and the Universidad de Sevilla.

Executive Committee

Program Chair	Pedro Meseguer, IIIA - CSIC
Program Co-chair	Lawrence Mandow, Universidad de Málaga
Organization Chair	Rafael M. Gasca, Universidad de Sevilla
Workshop & Tutorial Chair	Vicent Botti, Universidad Politécnica de Valencia

Senior Program Committee

Enrique Alba, Spain
Daniel Borrajo, Spain
Hector Geffner, Spain
Asunción Gómez-Pérez, Spain
Francisco Herrera, Spain
Javier Larrosa, Spain
Roque Marín, Spain
Serafín Moral, Spain
José Luis Pérez de la Cruz, Spain
Carles Sierra, Spain
Felisa Verdejo, Spain

Federico Barber, Spain
Ricardo Conejo, Spain
Lluís Godo, Spain
Manuel Graña, Spain
Pedro Larrañaga, Spain
Carlos Linares, Spain
Lluís Màrquez, Spain
Juan Pavón, Spain
José Riquelme, Spain
Carme Torras, Spain
Jordi Vitrià, Spain

Program Committee

José Luis Alba, Spain
Carlos Alonso, Spain
José Luis Ambite, USA
Alessandro Antonucci, Switzerland
Jaume Bacardit, UK
Beatriz Barros, Spain
Salem Benferhat, France
Concha Bielza, Spain
Blai Bonet, Venezuela
Crescencio Bravo, Spain
Dídac Busquets, Spain
Xavier Carreras, USA
Juan Fernández Olivares, Spain
Carlo Combi, Italy
Oscar Corcho García, Spain

Amparo Alonso, Spain
Teresa Alsinet, Spain
Carlos Ansótegui, Spain
Luis Antunes, Portugal
Jorge Baier, Canada
Ramón Bejar, Spain
Jesús Bermúdez, Spain
Christian Blum, Spain
Juan Antonio Botía Blaya, Spain
Alberto Bugarín Diz, Spain
Andrés Cano, Spain
Gladys Castillo, Portugal
Carlos Chesñevar, Argentina
Juan Manuel Corchado Rodríguez, Spain
Oscar Cordón, Spain

Ulises Cortés, Spain

Alicia d'Anjou, Spain

María José del Jesús, Spain

Alvaro del Val, Spain

Carmelo del Valle, Spain

Arantza Díaz de Ilarraza, Spain

Carmel Domshlak, Israel

Richard Duro, Spain

Isabel Fernández, Spain

Fernando Fernández, Spain

Susana Fernández Arregui, Spain

Rubén Fuentes Fernández, Spain

Joao Gama, Portugal

José A. Gámez, Spain

Ana García Serrano, Spain

Raúl Giráldez, Spain

José Manuel Gómez-Pérez, Spain

José Manuel Gutiérrez, Spain

Malte Helmert, Germany

Gabriela P. Henning, Argentina

María Del Carmen Hernández Gómez, Spain

Pedro Isasi, Spain

Fernando Jiménez, Spain

Anders Jonsson, Spain

Manuel Lama Penín, Spain

Christian Lemaitre, Mexico

Karmele Lopez de Ipina, Spain

Beatriz López Ibáñez, Spain

José Antonio Lozano, Spain

Inés Lynce, Portugal

Jorge S. Marques, Portugal

David Martínez, Australia

Rafael Martínez Gasca, Spain

David Masip, Spain

Stan Matwin, Canada

Eduardo Mena, Spain

José del R. Millán, Switzerland

Manuel Montes, Mexico

Rafael Morales Gamboa, Mexico

Antonio Moreno, Spain

Lidia Moreno, Spain

José A. Moreno Pérez, Spain

Angelo Oddi, Italy

Manuel Ojeda Aciego, Spain

Eva Onaindía, Spain

Santi Ontañón, USA

Sascha Ossowski, Spain

José T. Palma, Spain

José Manuel Peña, Sweden

José Maria Peña, Spain

Bogdan Raducanu, Spain

Ramón Rizo, Spain

Horacio Rodríguez, Spain

Juan Antonio Rodríguez, Spain

Camino Rodríguez Vela, Spain

Roberto Ruiz, Spain

José Ruiz-Shulcloper, Cuba

Antonio Salmerón, Spain

Luciano Sánchez, Spain

Candelaria Sansores, Mexico

María J. Taboada, Spain

Valentina Tamma, UK

Basilio Sierra, Spain

Alicia Troncoso, Spain

Cristina Urdiales, Spain

Diego Zapata-Rivera, USA

Local Arrangements

Irene Barba	Diana Borrego	Rafael Ceballos	Fernando de la Rosa
Carmelo del Valle	Mayte Gómez	Pablo Neira	Luisa Parody
Sergio Pozo	Mari Carmen Romero	Carlos G. Vallejo	Angel Jesús Varela

Sponsors

Gobierno de España-Ministerio de Ciencia e Innovación
Junta de Andalucía
Universidad de Sevilla
Dynadec
Fidetia

Table of Contents

Diagnosis

Evolutive Algorithms and Neural Networks

Knowledge Representation and Engineering

Machine Learning

Multiagents

Natural Language

Planning

Tutoring Systems

Uncertainty: Bayesian Networks

Vision

Applications

Employing Test Suites for Verilog Fault Localization

Bernhard Peischl[1], Naveed Riaz[2], and Franz Wotawa[2,*]

[1] Münzgrabenstrasse 35/1
A-8010 Graz, Austria
[2] Inffeldgasse 16b/2
Technische Universität Graz
Institute for Software Technology
{peischl,nriaz,wotawa}@ist.tugraz.at

Abstract. This article briefly states the idea behind model-based diagnosis and its application to localizing faults in Verilog programs. Specifically this article outlines how to employ a test suite to further reduce the number of fault candidates. For this purpose, we propose the filtering approach and relate it to the concept of Ackermann constraints. Notably, our empirical results demonstrate that our novel technique considerably increases the diagnosis resolution even under presence of only a couple of test cases.

Keywords: model-based diagnosis, software debugging, debugging of hardware designs, multiple testcases.

1 Introduction

Detecting, localizing and fixing faults is a crucial issue in today's fast paced and error prone development process. In general, detecting and repairing misbehavior in an early stage of the development cycle reduces costs and development time considerably. In the area of hardware design, shrinking design windows, ever increasing design complexity, and expensive prototyping are pushing companies towards putting considerable efforts into design analysis, verification and debugging at the source code level.

Today's hardware manufacturers increasingly recognize that software engineering techniques have found their way into hardware design. Production use of source-code based methodology enables designers to create very complex systems on chip, thereby employing the source code as the basis for logic synthesis.

However, verification technology has to keep pace with this shift towards software engineering. Testing and debugging in such a setting resembles the test and debug process in software engineering and is inherently source-code centered. Furthermore, analysis in hardware design in naturally focused on source code, since hardware description

---

* Authors are listed in alphabetical order. The research herein is partially conducted within the competence network Softnet Austria (www.soft-net.at) and funded by the Austrian Federal Ministry of Economics (bm:wa), the province of Styria, the Steirische Wirtschaftsfrderungsgesellschaft mbH. (SFG), and the city of Vienna in terms of the center for innovation and technology (ZIT).

P. Meseguer, L. Mandow, and R.M. Gasca (Eds.): CAEPIA 2009, LNAI 5988, pp. 1–10, 2010.

languages (HDLs) also offer means of higher level specification, thus specification and implementation are somehow intermingled.

In this article we propose a novel model that directly relies on Verilog's trace semantics (in previous work the authors of [11] relied on the synthesized VHDL representation) and present novel empirical results with respect to leveraging multiple test cases. Notably our approach allows for employing error-revealing as well as passing test cases by means of filtering. We relate this technique to so called Ackermann constraints - and - in addition to the our work in [9] - we present novel empirical results on the filtering technique from the ISCAS'89 benchmarks. Thus our technique well integrates into the modern model- and simulation-driven development process.

Section 2 introduces the ideas behind model-based debugging and its relationship to fault-models. Section 3 discusses the novel extension that allows for taking advantage of error-revealing as well as passing test cases by incorporating Ackermann constraints. Notably this increases the diagnosis resolution considerably. Section 4 presents empirical results on the ISACS'89 benchmark suite and demonstrates the applicability of our solution in practice. In Section 5 we conclude the article.

2   Model-Based Debugging

Model-based diagnosis (MBD) is a proven technique for localizing faults in various kinds of systems and has successfully been applied to different areas. Its basic idea is to use the knowledge of the correct behavior of the system together with the system's structure and the given observations directly to locate erroneous components. The behavior and the structure of the system are expressed in terms of components and connections and build-up a (more or less abstract) model of the system. The components of the system are the parts that can either be correct or faulty.

For every component its correct behavior is specified, there is no need to specify possible faulty behaviors (so called fault modes). In the case that a component is assumed to be faulty, nothing in known about its behavior. The structure of the system is represented in terms of connections allowing the behavior of the whole system to be expressed by means of the behavior models of particular (diagnosable) components.

A model-based diagnosis engine [13] assumes that some components are faulty and others are not and checks whether the assumptions together with the model contradict the given observations (the test case). If there is no contradiction the assumption can be justified as correct and the assumed faulty components are a valid diagnosis of the system with respect to the given observations. In the area of design error diagnosis statements and expression correspond to components and variables and signals correspond to connections. Throughout the following discussion these terms are used interchangeably.

We borrowed the terms herein from model-based diagnosis terminology [13] but adapted them for design error diagnosis. To ease explanation, we use another small Verilog example program which represents an erroneous implementation of a 'XOR' gate in Listing 1.

To find an error in the design we need to have a (at least partial) specification of the design, e.g., a test case, and the design's behavior. The underlying behavior of the design is specified by the underlying programming language semantics. For example, if

```
1  module XOR(a:bit, b:bit, c:bit);
2    input a,b;
3    output c;
4    reg s1,s2:bit;
5    //procedure 1
6        s1 = a and (not(b));
7        s2 = b or (not(a));
8        // shall be s2 = b and (not(a))
9        c = s1 or s2;
10 endmodule;
```

Listing 1. Code snipped implementing the XOR gate

we know that a=b=′1′ and c=′0′ is a valid test case, then we can compute s1=′0′ from statement in line 6, s2=′1′ from statement in line 7, and finally, c=′1′ from statement in line 9 which contradicts the expected result. This computation only uses the semantics of the statements and the assumption that the statements are working as expected.

In arguing about this semantics we introduce a predicate $\neg AB(i)$ for a statement i, which stands for 'not abnormal'. A logical model for the program is stated by using the assumptions together with a logical representation of the statement. For example, the statements of the program XOR(behav) can be represented by $\neg AB(6) \rightarrow (s1 \leftrightarrow a \wedge \neg b)$, $\neg AB(7) \rightarrow (s2 \leftrightarrow b \vee \neg a)$, $\neg AB(9) \rightarrow (c \leftrightarrow s1 \vee s2)$.

The specification itself is represented by logical sentences. In our example the test case is specified by $a \wedge b \wedge \neg c$. In the following, we formally define the design error diagnosis problem which is a little bit more general than that in the previous discussion. Rather than assuming statements as possible sources of misbehavior, we allow statements as well as expressions to be erroneous.

Definition 1 (Design Error Diagnosis Problem). *A design error diagnosis problem is a tuple $(SD, STMNT, SPEC)$ where SD is the system description of a given design, $STMNT$ is a set of statements or expressions (also referred to as components) with associated assumptions in SD, and $SPEC$ is a logical sentence representing the (partial) specification.*

From the definition of design error diagnosis problem and the underlying concept of assumptions associated with statements and/or expressions, the definition of diagnosis follows immediately. A diagnosis shall comprise all parts of a program, i.e., statements or expressions, which might be responsible for misbehavior. In other words we are searching for program parts that, when assumed not to behave as expected, lead to a logical sentence that does not contradict the given specification.

Definition 2 (Diagnosis). *Let $(SD, STMNT, SPEC)$ be a design error diagnosis problem. A subset Δ of $STMNT$ is a diagnosis iff $SD \cup SPEC \cup \{AB(i)|i \in \Delta\} \cup \{\neg AB(i)|i \in STMNT \setminus \Delta\}$ can be satisfied thus does not lead to a contradiction.*

For example, the set $\{7\}$ is a diagnosis because assuming that the statements in line 6 and line 9 are correct and the statement in line 7 is not, leads to a satisfiable logical sentence. However, $\{6\}$ is no diagnosis, since we can derive a contradiction w.r.t.

the given specification solely from statements 7 and 9. The dual concept to diagnosis is the definition of a conflict. A conflict is itself a subset of $STMNT$ which, when assuming expressions and statements to work correctly, together with $SPEC$ leads to contradiction. For example, $\{7, 9\}$ is a conflict for program XOR(behav).

Definition 3 (Conflict). *Let $(SD, STMNT, SPEC)$ be a design error diagnosis problem. A set $C \subseteq STMNT$ is a conflict iff $SD \cup SPEC \cup \{\neg AB(i) | i \in C\}$ is contradictory, i.e., not satisfiable.*

Usually, we are only interested in minimal conflicts and minimal[1] diagnoses. The relationship between diagnosis and conflicts is discussed in [13].

Extensions to the introduced definitions can be found in [3] where fault modes (assumptions about the specific behavior of the faulty component, fault models) are used. Fault modes, like stuck-at-zero or stuck-at-one, often are used in design error diagnosis but exactly modeling defect behavior with fault modes remains elusive even with today's sophisticated approaches [2,5,15]. However, all kinds of fault modes can be handled with our approach with some slight modifications of the definitions given above. Details can for example be found in [18].

In our modeling approach the Verilog programs are mapped to a component-connection model. The components are objects with ports and specified behavior and connections are associated with ports. Using this component connection model, the received diagnoses can be mapped back to the associated parts of the program. For each component we provide a behavioral description, usually in first order logic. The $\neg ab$ predicate is used to state that the described behavior is only valid if the component is not faulty. This component-connection model forms the system description and is basically a Horn clause encoding of the design's structure and behavior. Notably our model is created fully automatically from the source code.

Verilog RTL hardware consists of combinational logic and flip-flops. In Verilog this is expressed in terms of a number of threads that are a combinational program plus a set of flip-flops of the form *always* @(*posedge clk*) S, where S denotes the statement block that might consist of assignments, sequencing blocks, conditionals and event controls.

Under the assumption that there is (1) a single input clock, (2) no inputs change when clock has a positive edge, and (3) no two distinct flip-flops drive the same output an RTL program can be partitioned into a number of threads that constitute a combinational program of the form *always* @(τ_i) $V_i := E_i$, where V_i is a denotes a vector of variables and E_i is a vector of expressions associated with the event control τ_i. Accordingly flip-flops are given by threads of the form *always* @(*posedge clk*) $V_i := E_i$ as every flip-flop is a single register with an input and an output that is clocked on the positive edge of clock - which according to our assumptions is distinct from the input and output.

It is thus clear that the effect of executing *always* @(*posedge clk*) $q := d$ is to update the value of q with the value on d for every point in time that triggers *posedge clk*. This happens at exactly those time instances where clk is high but was not high at the preceding time. According to [4], by letting $f(t)$ denote the value of input or variable f at simulation time t, the trace semantics of the thread above is given by

---

[1] Minimal refers to subset minimality, that is, no subset of a given diagnosis itself is a diagnosis.

```
1  module example(clk,in,out);
2    input in,clk
3    output out;
4    reg out,inter1,inter2,Q;
5    // thread 1
6      always @(posedge clk)
7      begin
8        inter1 <= out;
9        inter2 <= inter1;
10     end
11   // thread 2
12     always @(Q or inter2)
13     begin
14       out <= Q ^ inter2;
15     end
16   // thread 3
17     always @(in or inter1)
18     begin
19       Q <= in & inter1;
20     end
21 endmodule;
```

Listing 2. The Verilog design with three threads

$q(t+1) = if\ clk(t+1) = 1 \wedge clk(t) \neq 1$ then $d(t)$ else $q(t)$. By relying on this identity our model captures the quiescent states of any RTL Verilog design in terms of well-known modeling concepts [11,20]. For example, we can provide a model for $always\ @(posedge\ clk)\ q := d$ by relying on the if-then-else model and similar models for statements and expressions [14].

According to [4], to build up our semantic-based diagnosis model we start with those threads sensitive to *posedge clk* and continue with the remaining m threads sensitive to the conditions $\tau_1, \tau_2,...,\tau_m$. We employ a simple form of dependence analysis - logic levelization [17] - to associate a level to the individual threads triggered by $\tau_1,...,\tau_m$. According to these levels we determine the order the individual threads become executed and thus can obtain a model for a single clock cycle. By unfolding the model w.r.t. to simulation time we obtain the model for several clock cycles. To ease understanding, Listing 2 outlines a simple Verilog program comprising three threads, and Fig. 1 refers to the corresponding model including the unfolding for two cycles of clock.

3   Test Patterns for Improving the Diagnosis Resolution

Given an error-revealing test case and the model introduced previously allows one for coming up with a set of fault candidates. Depending on the structure of the model and the discrimination capability of the specific test case being used, the number of diagnosis candidates may vary considerably [11]. However, during development, a designer might be aware of further error-revealing test cases or also of test patterns that successfully pass. Most notably, model-based debugging allows for taking advantage of this in terms of increasing the diagnosis resolution.

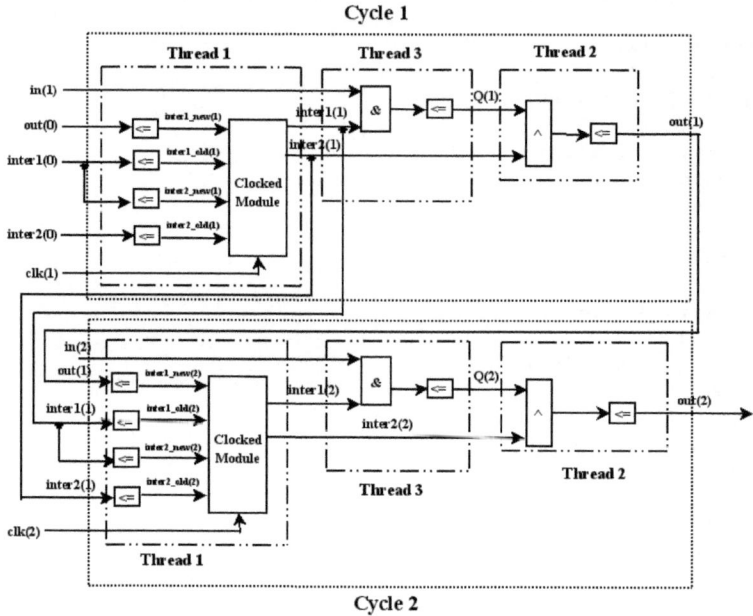

Fig. 1. The debugging model for the example program

Considering a set of test patterns, we have to distinguish between those patterns revealing misbehavior and the remaining one that do not identify the actual malfunctioning. According to Section 2, for every test pattern t_i revealing misbehavior, we obtain
a new conflict C_i. To leverage this for diagnosis we apply the hitting set computation
to the union of the conflicts $C = \bigcup C_i$ rather than to a single conflict. Note that due
to the increased number of conflicts, in general (and as demonstrated by the results in
the following section), the resolution of the diagnoses increases - that is at the cost of
further computation time the number of fault candidates being reported decreases. In
[8] we report on details regarding the iterative and efficient computation of hitting sets
for a number of conflicts.

In the following we assume that the set of test patterns $TC = TC_{incons} \cup TC_{cons}$ is
divided into error revealing ones TC_{incons} and passing test patterns TC_{cons}.

Definition 4 (Diagnosis Problem with Test Patterns). *Given a set of test pattern*
$TC = TC_1, TC_2, ..., TC_n$, *a system description* SD *and a set of components,*
the diagnosis problem considering all test cases in TC *is obtained as follows:*

- *for each* $TC_i \in TC$ *do*
    - *generate a new* SD_i, *where all components and connections are uniquely iden-*
    tified with a new index i
- *let* SD^* *be* $\bigcup_{i=1}^{k} SD_i \cup \{\neg AB(C) \rightarrow \neg AB(C_1) \wedge \neg AB(C_2) \wedge ... \wedge \neg AB(C_k) | C \in$
    $STMNT\}$, *where* C_j *denotes the corresponding components in* SD_i.
- *let* TC^* *be a renaming of* TC, *such that every test case is associated with connec-*
    tions in SD_i

The new diagnosis problem incorporating the test cases TC is given by the tuple
$(SD^*, STMNT, TC^*)$.

As the passing test cases do not yield to further conflicts, we capture their specific information on diagnoses in terms of SD_A, the system description with Ackermann constraints. Ackermann constraints capture the fact that all our components behave deterministically [1]. By adding these consistency constraints we incorporate that the same combination of input values applied to any component C results in the same output for every instance of C_i (e.g. there is one instance of C in every temporal unfolding).

Definition 5 (System Descr. with Ackermann constraints). *Given a set of consistent test cases TC_{cons}, we assume $in(C_i) = \{i^1_{c_i}, ..., i^m_{c_i}\}$ to denote the inputs of component C_i, and $out(C_i) = \{o^1_{c_i}, ..., o^n_{c_i}\}$ the outputs of component C_i. By extending the system description SD^* in terms of the Ackermann Constraints $\neg AB(C) \wedge CON_A = \{\forall^m_{l=1} i^l_{c_i} = i^l_{c_j}) \rightarrow \forall^n_{p=1}(o^p_{c_i} = o^p_{c_j})|i \neq j\}$, where i and j denote indices of test patterns, we obtain a diagnosis problem incorporating Ackermann constraints. The diagnosis problem is thus given in terms of the tuple $(SD^A, STMNT, TC^*_{cons})$ where $SD^A = SD^* \cup CON_A$ denotes the Ackermann constraint system description.*

To our best knowledge, the authors of [12] were the first to pursue a similar idea in allowing for non-intermittency assumptions at the gate level. Recently the authors of [16] moreover employed Ackerman constraints in the context of locating faults with a model checker. Whereas for small to medium-sized digital circuits [12] the complexity appears to be manageable, the author of [14] argues that the number of (Horn-like) rules increases exponentially with the number of inputs- and outputs of a component. Specifically, for a fine-grained debugging model incorporating expressions [7], where components often have several inputs and outputs, the number of rules becomes intractable. We thus followed an algorithmic approach called filtering [20].

Filtering refers to discarding certain diagnoses by taking advantage of further test patterns in dedicated post processing phase subsequently to diagnoses computation. We briefly sketch this technique in terms of the procedure filter($DIAGS,TC$), where $DIAGS$ denotes the set of diagnosis candidates and TC represents the test suite:

1. forall test cases $TC_i \in TC$ do
2. (a) forall $D \in DIAGS$ do
   (b) Let i_{d_i} denote the values at the input and o_{d_i} be the values at the output of component D
      obtained by assuming $AB(D) \wedge \{\neg AB(C)|C \in STMNT \setminus D\}$
   (c) if there exist indices $i, j, i \neq j$, such that $i_{d_i} = i_{d_j} \wedge o_{d_i} \neq o_{d_j}$
      (d) remove D from $DIAGS$
3. return $DIAGS$

Notably, as shown in [9], for single diagnosis filtering imposes Ackerman constraints on the set of diagnosis $DIAGS$.

4 Empirical Results

In this section we report on our empirical evaluation of the novel ideas outlined in the previous sections on the ISCAS'89 benchmark suite. The ISCAS89 suite comprises

Table 1. Empirical results, single-fault diagnoses

circ.	cycle no.	no. tc	diag. no.	faulty lines	% of reduction
s208	4	1	219	130	45.8
		2	105	64	73.3
		3	105	64	73.3
		4	75	50	78.9
		5	75	50	78.9
	8	1	219	130	45.8
		2	171	102	57.5
		3	134	80	66.6
		4	105	64	73.3
		5	83	50	78.9
s349	4	1	27	18	96.7
		2	27	18	96.7
		3	27	18	96.7
		4	27	18	96.7
		5	27	18	96.7
	8	1	139	82	85.1
		2	118	70	87.2
		3	107	64	88.4
		4	62	39	92.9
		5	41	26	95.3
s386	4	1	234	145	71.5
		2	31	20	96.1
		3	31	20	96.1
	8	1	252	156	71.5
		2	224	141	72.2
		3	151	96	81.1
		4	151	96	81.1
		5	54	35	93.1

Table 2. Empirical results for Filtering, single fault

cir.	c. no.	tc	diag. no.	f. lin.	%tot.red.	%filter.red.
s208	4	0	81	48	80.0	4.0
		1	67	43	82.1	14.0
		3	18	11	95.4	78.0
		5	18	11	95.4	78.0
	8	0	81	48	80.0	4.0
		1	67	43	82.1	14.0
		3	18	11	95.4	78.0
		5	18	11	95.4	78.0
s349	4	0	15	11	98.0	38.9
		1	5	4	99.3	77.7
		3	5	4	99.3	77.7
		5	4	3	99.5	83.3
	8	0	4	3	99.5	88.5
		1	4	3	99.5	88.5
		3	4	3	99.5	88.5
		5	4	3	99.5	88.5
s386	4	0	20	12	97.8	0.0
		1	13	7	98.7	41.7
		3	13	7	98.7	41.7
		5	13	7	98.7	41.7
	8	0	25	14	97.4	26.3
		1	25	14	97.4	26.3
		3	19	10	98.2	47.4
		5	19	10	98.2	47.4

sequential, synchronous circuits of various sizes with diverse structural properties. Most of them are real-world circuits and all circuits use only D-type flip flops. We have employed a Verilog-RTL representation of these circuits to evaluate the proposed approach. First we discuss novel results in employing several error-revealing test cases. Afterwards we stick to the empirical evaluation of the filtering approach.

In our experimental setting, we introduced a fault by randomly substituting a statement by another one, e.g., changing an *and* operator with an *or* operator. We obtained the error-revealing inputs by performing a circuit equivalence check with the model checker VIS. This input together with the faulty RTL circuit is the input to our prototypical debugger. The debugging tool returns a number of fault candidates at the expression level. For every circuit we checked that the faulty statement as well as the assignment statement assigning this statement's output to the left-hand side variable is among the fault candidates. Regarding our experiments in Table 1 and Table 2, this is always the case.

Table 1 outlines the obtained results for a number of circuits in the ISCAS89 benchmark: In column one the table lists the circuit name, column two shows the length of the error-revealing input sequence. Column three opens a sub-table which, for a number of test cases (ranging from one to five for every circuit), lists the number of fault candidates, the number of faulty lines (a single source line may correspond to several faults i.e. A faulty line may contain multiple fault candidates), and the percentage of reduction (last column) in terms of source code lines.

Table 2 further presents the results we obtained by applying the filtering technique after the computation of all single-fault diagnoses. In addition to Table 1, Table 2 outlines the amount of reduction accomplished by the filtering approach (last column). Note that we assumed that we solely are aware of the expected (quiescent) values for the primary outputs after 4 respectively 8 cycles. Considering these reasonable assumptions, the results indicate that under presence of a couple of test cases (5 error revealing test cases, 5 passing test cases) we manage to exclude more than 95 percent of the Verilog source from being faulty. Thus, considering our concrete results, a verification engineer can focus his/her attention to less than the remaining 5 percent of the code. As single-faults are more probable than multiple-faults we focused our evaluation to single diagnoses. However, basically the MBD framework allows for computing multiple-fault diagnoses as well (e.g. see [9] for details on dual-fault diagnoses).

5   Related Work and Conclusion

Our previous work in this area differs from the work presented herein in a couple of issues. Previous research focussed primarily on the VHDL hardware description language [19,20,11]. The semantic differences between Verilog and VHDL is discussed in [10]. The filtering technique has been introduced in [20], and the relationship between filtering and Ackermann contraints is discussed in [9].

Most of the work in HDL debugging focuses on the gate-level representation of a circuit and empoys particular fault models like stuck-at-zero or stuck-at-one (e.g. [6]). Model-based debugging allows for incorporating fault models [18], however, the malfunctioning of software components can hardy be captured by specific fault models. Details in the context of synthesize-able circuits and HDLs are discussed in [11].

In this article we briefly state the idea behind model-based diagnosis and its application to error location in RTL Verilog designs. In providing a scalable debugging model for the Verilog HDL we rely on trace semantics - a specific abstraction capturing those quiescent states holding at the end of a simulation cycle. We thereby overcome the inherent complexity issues of event-based Verilog and - in contrast to the majority of the approaches - do not rely on specific fault models. To leverage test patterns in context of our design error location technique we propose to incorporate Ackermann constraints and relate these constraints to an algorithmic post processing technique called filtering. Most notably, our empirical results on the ISCAS'89 benchmarks demonstrate the effectiveness and - due to the reasonable assumptions - the practical applicability of our novel technique.

References

1. Ackermann, W.: Solvable Cases of Decision Problems. North Holland, Amsterdam (1954)
2. Aitken, R.C.: Modeling the unmodelable: Algorithmic fault diagnosis. IEEE Test and Computes 97, 98–103 (1997)
3. de Kleer, J., Mackworth, A.K., Reiter, R.: Characterizing diagnosis and systems. Artificial Intelligence 56 (1992)
4. Gordon, M.J.C.: Relating event and trace semantics of hardware description languages. The Computer Journal 45(1), 27–36 (2002)

5. Holst, S., Wunderlich, H.-J.: Adaptive debug and diagnosis without fault dictionaries. In: ETS '07: Proceedings of the 12th IEEE European Test Symposium, Washington, DC, USA, pp. 7–12. IEEE Computer Society, Los Alamitos (2007)
6. Huang, S.-Y., Cheng, K.-T., Chen, K.-C., Lu, J.-Y.J.: Fault-simulation based design error diagnosis for sequential circuits. In: Proceedings of the 35th Design Automation Conference, San Francisco, CA (June 1998)
7. Peischl, B., Köb, D., Wotawa, F.: Debugging VHDL designs using temporal process instances. In: Chung, P.W.H., Hinde, C.J., Ali, M. (eds.) IEA/AIE 2003. LNCS (LNAI), vol. 2718, pp. 402–415. Springer, Heidelberg (2003)
8. Peischl, B., Riaz, N., Wotawa, F.: Advances in automated source-level debugging of verilog designs. Studies in Computational Intelligence. Springer, Heidelberg (2008)
9. Peischl, B., Riaz, N., Wotawa, F.: Model-based reasoning with multiple test cases and its application to debugging. In: 19th International Workshop on Principles of Diagnosis (September 2008)
10. Peischl, B., Riaz, N., Wotawa, F.: Test patterns for verilog design error localization. To appear in the Proceedings of the TAIC PART 2009, Windsor, UK (September 2009)
11. Peischl, B., Wotawa, F.: Automated source-level error localization in hardware designs. IEEE Design and Test 23(1), 8–19 (2006)
12. Raiman, O., de Kleer, J., Saraswat, V., Shirley, M.: Characterizing non-intermittent faults. In: Proceedings AAAI, Anaheim, July 1991, pp. 849–854. Morgan Kaufmann, San Francisco (1991)
13. Reiter, R.: A theory of diagnosis from first principles. Artificial Intelligence 32(1), 57–95 (1987)
14. Riaz, N.: Source-Level Debugging of Verilog Designs. PhD thesis, Technische Universität Graz (November 2008)
15. Rousset, A., Bosio, A., Girard, P., Landrault, C., Pravossoudovitch, S., Virazel, A.: Derric: A tool for unified logic diagnosis. In: ETS '07: Proceedings of the 12th IEEE European Test Symposium, Washington, DC, USA, pp. 13–20. IEEE Computer Society, Los Alamitos (2007)
16. Staber, S., Fey, G., Bloem, R., Drechsler, R.: Automatic fault localization for property checking. In: Second International Haifa Verification Conference, Haifa, October 2006, pp. 50–64 (2006)
17. Wang, L.-T., Hoover, N.E., Porter, E.H., Zasio, J.J.: Ssim: a software levelized compiled-code simulator. In: 24th ACM/IEEE conference proceedings on Design automation conference, pp. 2–8. ACM Press, New York (1987)
18. Wotawa, F.: Applying Model-Based Diagnosis to Software Debugging of Concurrent and Sequential Imperative Programming Languages. PhD thesis, Technische Universität Wien (1996)
19. Wotawa, F.: Debugging VHDL Designs using Model-Based Reasoning. Artificial Intelligence in Engineering 14(4), 331–351 (2000)
20. Wotawa, F.: Debugging hardware designs using a value-based Model. Applied Intelligence 16(1), 71–92 (2002)

Analyzing the Influence of Differential Constraints in Possible Conflict and ARR Computation

Belarmino Pulido, Aníbal Bregón, and Carlos J. Alonso-González

Dpto. de Informática. Universidad de Valladolid. Valladolid, Spain
{belar,anibal,calonso}@infor.uva.es

Abstract. Diagnosis of real world problems demands the integration of different techniques from several research fields. In Model-based Diagnosis, both Artificial Intelligence and Control Theory communities have provided different but complementary approaches. Recent works, known as BRIDGE proposal, provided a common framework for the integration of techniques for static systems.

This work proposes the extension of the BRIDGE framework for a specific class of dynamic systems, thus analyzing the influence of dynamic constraints in the behavior estimation capabilities for two Model-based Diagnosis techniques: Possible Conflicts and Analytical Redundancy Relations obtained through structural analysis. Results show the strong similarities between them, and provide new ways for integration of techniques from both areas. Additionally, algorithms computing Possible Conflicts provide the implicit structural model for state observer design with no extra knowledge added in the model. Results on a case study are provided, then compared and discussed against existing proposals.

Keywords: Model-based Diagnosis, Conflicts, Analytic Redundancy Relations, BRIDGE framework.

1 Introduction

Diagnosis of real world problems usually demands the integration of different techniques from several research fields. Just focusing on Model-based Diagnosis, MBD, two different research communities have approached dynamic systems diagnosis: Artificial Intelligence, known as DX approach, and Systems and Control Theory, known as FDI approach. Recently, a theoretical common framework, known as BRIDGE, has been established [1,2]. BRIDGE framework is based on the comparison between Consistency-based Diagnosis via conflicts [3], and Fault Detection and Isolation via Analytical Redundancy Relations –ARRs for short–, obtained through structural analysis [4]. The BRIDGE framework was established for static systems. Our proposal extends BRIDGE to a specific class of dynamic systems, analyzing the influence of temporal constraints in the models.

This work relies upon the Possible Conflict, PC, concept [5]. PCs are those subsytems capable to become conflicts, and they are computed off-line. The PC concept belongs to the BRIDGE framework, because it comes from the DX community but it is closely related to ARRs in the FDI community. Our goal is to use PCs, and their relation

P. Meseguer, L. Mandow, and R.M. Gasca (Eds.): CAEPIA 2009, LNAI 5988, pp. 11–21, 2010.

to ARRs, to establish clear links between FDI and DX approaches, concerning temporal issues, to make technique integration from both fields easier in a given diagnosis system.

The organization of this article is as follows. Next section summarizes diagnosis of dynamic systems in the DX and FDI approaches. Later on, a case study is introduced. Then, the inclusion and usage of dynamic information in PCs and ARRs is analyzed and compared. Finally, results on the comparison, and conclusions are given.

2 Model-Based Diagnosis of Dynamic Systems

2.1 Classical DX and FDI Approaches

The DX approach has a solid theoretical ground for static systems, being the GDE its computational paradigm [3]. However, there is no general framework for consistency-based diagnosis, CBD, of dynamic systems [6]; a wide variety of definitions and methods has been used by the DX community [7].

Main concern in DX has been the localization and identification stage in the diagnosis process. Uncertainties and disturbances in the models were solved by means of qualitative modeling. However, coupling qualitative models and GDE-like architectures generated several problems. One way to solve these problems was to avoid on-line dependency compilation with ATMS-like engines as performed by GDE. Propagation of qualitative values in temporal causal structures, and off-line dependency-compilation have emerged as suitable alternatives. This work is focused on this last trend, due to the strong similarity to structural analysis in the FDI approach.

The FDI approach [8,4], using mainly numerical analytical models, has standard specifications for dynamic aspects. Mathematical models can be expressed in a variety of ways: state-space, input-output, or even black-box models obtained through identification. In this community there are solid theoretical results for linear systems, while analysis of non-linear systems is a major research issue.

Main focus on FDI research is robust fault detection, generating a set of fault indicators, called residuals, which should be activated in presence of faults (a similar concept to conflict detection in DX). Residuals can be generated using parity equations, state observers, or parameter estimation. It has been demonstrated that these techniques are equivalent as far as linear models are concerned [8].

2.2 PCs, ARRs, and Conflicts in the BRIDGE Framework

Model-based FDI using ARRs. In the FDI approach, one way to obtain the set of residuals is to compute the set of Analytical Redundancy Relations, or ARRs, by means of structural analysis. It is is based on finding a unique canonical decomposition of the structural description of the system, then finding a complete matching for unknown variables (just-determined set of equations which can be solved). Afterwards, remaining equations are combined with the just-determined system to find structural redundancy. Each suitable combination is an ARR (this process is completely described in Blanke et al. [4]), which describes an expression that can be solved using only observations, thus providing a residual. Non-zero residuals can be used for diagnosis purposes.

It should be noticed that all the steps, except for residual computation, are done off-line. Hence, computing ARRs is a compilation technique in FDI.

Possible Conflicts: A dependency-compilation technique for consistency-based diagnosis. PCs are those sub-systems capable to become conflicts in CBD, i.e. *minimal subsets of equations with enough redundancy to perform fault diagnosis* [5].

PCs computation is performed on the abstract model for the set of equations in the system description. PCs are obtained off-line via two core concepts: *minimal evaluation chains*, MECs, and *minimal evaluation models*, MEMs. MECs are minimal over-constrained sets of relations, and they represent a necessary condition for a conflict to exist. MEMs describe how relations within a MEC can be solved using local propagation. Hence, each MEM describes an executable model which can be used to estimate the behaviour of one variable, which could be the source of a discrepancy. A Possible Conflict is a MEC with at least one MEM.

PCs fit in the BRIDGE framework, which was defined for static systems [2]. It has been demonstrated that PCs are equivalent to potential conflicts, the support[1] for minimal ARRs, and Minimal Structurally Overdetermined subsystems [5,9].

In this work we propose an extension of the BRIDGE framework for a specific class of dynamic systems. Concepts related to temporal constraints will be illustrated using the following system.

3   A Case Study

The plant shown in figure 1 resembles common features of industrial continuous processes. It is made up of four tanks $\{T_1, \ldots, T_4\}$, five pumps $\{P_1, \ldots, P_5\}$, and two PID controllers acting on pumps P_1, P_5 to keep level of $\{T_1, T_4\}$ close to their set points. To control temperature on tanks $\{T_2, T_3\}$ we use two resistors $\{R_2, R_3\}$, respectively. The plant can work on different situations, commanded through different operation modes. In the selected operation mode: R_2 is switched off, while R_3 is on. Also, $\{P_3, P_4\}$ are switched off; hence, just inflow $FT01$ is coming to tank T_1. In the plant there are eleven different measurements: levels of tanks T_1 and T_4 –$\{LT01, LT04\}$–, value of PID controllers on pumps $\{P_1, P_5\}$ –$\{LC01, LC04\}$–, in-flow in T_1 –$\{FT01\}$–, outflow from $\{T_2, T_3, T_4\}$ –$\{FT02, FT03, FT04\}$–, temperatures on $\{T_2, T_3, T_4\}$ –$\{TT02, TT03, TT04\}$–, and on-off control on pumps $\{P_2, P_3, P_4\}$, and resistors –$\{R_2, R_3\}$–. The behavior of the plant has been modelled using classical ODEs based on first principles, such as mass and energy balances in tanks, $-t_{dm}, t_{dE}, r_p-$, and flows from tanks through pumps or pipes, $-t_{fb}, t_f-$. Using these equations the set of Possible Conflicts in the plant can be seen in table 1. These PCs are minimal w.r.t. the set of constraints included in their MECs.

4   Dealing with Temporal Information in System Description

4.1   Inclusion of Time in PCs and ARRs Calculation

Both DX and FDI communities have included temporal information in the models in several ways, using different modeling approaches. To keep the comparison manageable,

---

[1] Support is the set of equations –components– used to derive an ARR.

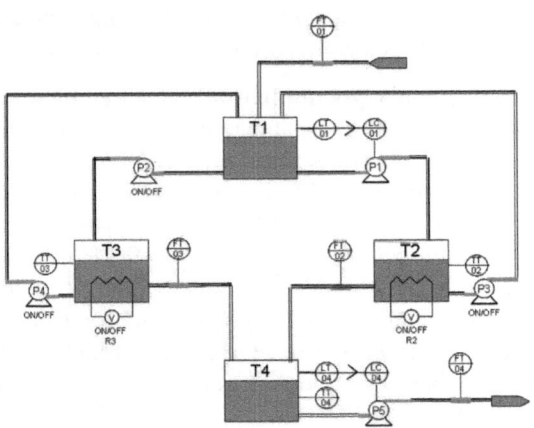

Fig. 1. Schema of the laboratory plant

Table 1. Possible Conflict/s found for the laboratory plant; constraints, components, and the estimated variable for each possible conflict, using integral causality

	$Constraints$	$Components(Support)$	$Estimate$	$Observer$
PC_1	$t1_{dm}, t1_{fb1}, t1_{fb2}$	T_1, P_1, P_2	$LT01$	yes
PC_2	$t1_{fb1}, t2_{dm}, t2_f$	T_1, T_2, P_1	$FT02$	yes
PC_3	$t1_{fb1}, t1_{dE}, t2_{dE}, t2_{dm}$	T_1, P_1, T_2	$TT02$	yes
PC_4	$t1_{fb2}, t3_{dm}, t3_f$	T_1, P_2, T_3	$FT03$	yes
PC_5	$t1_{fb2}, t1_{dE}, t3_{dm}, t3_{dE}, r3_p$	T_1, P_2, T_3, R_3	$TT03$	yes
PC_6	$t4_{dm}$	T_4	$LT04$	yes
PC_7	$t4_{fb}$	T_4, P_5	$FT04$	no

we have focused our discusion at the structural level, focusing on model descriptions made up of sets of Ordinary Differential Equations, ODEs, expressed in canonical form (only first-order derivatives are used)[2].

Modelling of temporal information gives rise to two kinds of constraints: *instantaneous* –also known as intra-state constraints, for static relations, and *differential* –also known as inter-state constraints, for dynamic behaviour [10]. Inter-state constraints just represent the relation between the state variable and its derivative.

Differential constraints can be used for behaviour estimation in two ways, depending on the causal interpretation given: the *derivative* approach ($\dot{x}(t) = \frac{dx}{dt}$ assumes the derivative can be computed based on present and past samples of x) –this is the preferred approach in FDI–, and the *integral* approach ($x(t) = x(t-1) + \int_{t-1}^{t} \dot{x}(t) \cdot dt$, assuming initial state $x(t-1)$ is known) –this is the preferred approach in DX–. It has been demonstrated that both approaches have equivalent behaviour estimation capabilities for numerical models, assuming adequate sampling rates and precise approximations for derivate computation are available, and assuming initial conditions are known [11].

---

[2] Using canonical notation we do not restrict the order of the derivatives to be used. Second order derivatives can be introduced by means of a differential constraint $(w_i, \frac{dw_i}{dt})$, being $w_i = \frac{dv_i}{dt}$, and so on.

PC calculation can easily handle temporal information in the models including both instantaneous and differential constraints. Both types can be easily represented in the model description (hypergraph). Using both integral and derivative approaches is allowed for PC calculation: each approach just represent a different causal assignment for a differential constraint in MEM computation.

Inclusion of temporal information in ARRs can be done in three different ways [12]. Difference between them comes from the way the relationship between an state variable, x, and its derivative, $\dot{x}$, is stated. These three methods have been compared in different works [12,13]. From these methods, the approach considering x and $\dot{x}$ as different variables, and linked by a constraint (eq_i x, $\dot{x}$), is equivalent to the DX approach used for PC computation. Our discussion will be focused in this last option, and ARR calculation algorithms based on the Lille method [4] – which were also used in the BRIDGE framework–.

Algorithms computing PCs or computing ARRs as in the Lille method can use differential constraints as expressed above. And both methods can include both types of causal interpretations [5,4]. Using integral or derivative causalities for each differential constraint provides different computable models for each MEM and ARRs, due to different causal matchings, but impose no restriction in the way MECs or ARRs are computed (see [14] for more details on this comparison).

These concepts are illustrated using the case study. Plant in figure 1 provides several examples of differential constraints, given by equations modelling mass or energy balances in tanks. Table 2 shows PCs found in the plant using derivative causality. It can be easily seen that fault isolation capabilities are lost w.r.t. results in table 1, which was computed using integral causality: faults in T_2, T_3, and R_3 can be neither detected nor isolated.

Table 2. Possible Conflict/s found for the laboratory plant;constraints, components, and the estimated variable for each possible conflict, using derivative causality

	$Constraints$	$Components(Support)$	$Estimate$	$Observer$
PC_1	$t1_{dm}, t1_{fb1}, t1_{fb2}$	T_1, P_1, P_2	$Deriv.T1\_h$	yes
PC_2	$t4_{dm}$	T_4	$Deriv.T4\_h$	yes
PC_3	$t4_{fb}$	T_4, P_5	$FT04$	no

Differential constraints in cyclical structures. The presence of cycles must be discussed. Cycles can halt local propagation for static systems while using GDE [15]; hence an inference engine able to solve algebraic loops is needed. Using off-line dependency-recording this step can be done off-line, once the set of PCs or ARRs are found [5,4]. Both methods, PCs and the Lille method for ARR computation, follow identical approaches, based on previous DX [10] and FDI [4] works, respectively.

Remaining cycles, containing both instantaneous and differential constraints, must be studied. First, using integral causality, loops containing differential constraints are not loops, but spirals, because x and $\dot{x}$ have different temporal indices [10]. Second, using derivative causality, no loop including x and $\dot{x}$ can be solved [4]. Hence, loops containing derivative constraints in ARRs or MEMs must be rejected.

Figure 2 shows the MEM for PC_2 in the case study, using integral causality: $FT02$, measurement for T_2 outflow, is compared against $LF4\_F$, which is obtained using

$T2\_H$, a state variable. $T2\_H$ is obtained by integration of $T2\_H'$ in the previous time step, which is obtained by mass balance of T_2 given $LF4\_F$ and $LF2\_F$. $LF2\_F$ is obtained given measured level on T_1, $LT01$, and the value of PI controller, PI_01_u. In this MEM, the initial condition $T2\_H(0)$, must be known for simulation purposes. Potential loop in the path $T2\_H(t) \rightarrow LF4\_F(t) \rightarrow T2\_H'(t) \rightarrow T2\_H(t+1)$ is broken, due to different time indices –integration step represented as dashed line or as an spiral–.

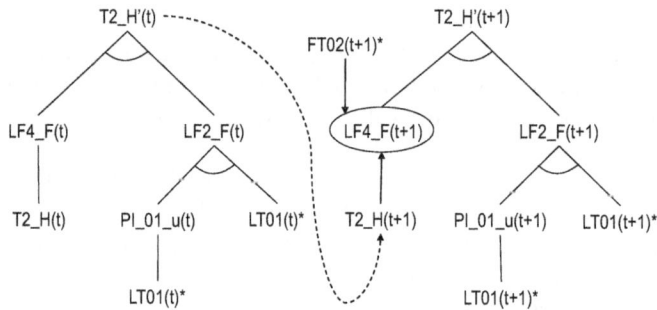

Fig. 2. A MEM for PC_2 using integral causality. Discrepancy node is represented as the difference between estimated $LF4\_F$ and measured $FT02$: the potential source of a conflict.

5   Comparing Temporal Issues in PC and ARR Calculation

5.1   PCs and ARRs for Dynamic Systems

Proposition 1. *Given equivalent system descriptions including differential constraints for PCs and ARR calculation, the sets of computed PCs and minimal ARRs have same isolation capabilities.*

Proof: The set of MEMs related to the set of PCs is complete because it is based on an exhaustive search for the set of minimal conflicts. Pulido et al. [5] have demonstrated that both approaches were equivalent for static systems, if algorithms used for ARR computation provided the complete set of minimal ARRs. Moreover, only differential constraints have been added, and they are used for propagation identically in both approaches. Finally, both approaches remove illegal cyclical structures. Therefore, both will provide same results in terms of fault isolability (structural information included).

   Previous results can be extended to minimal conflicts, ARRs, and the set of MEMs provided by the set of PCs, if the GDE inference engine is able to handle loops.

   Proposition 1 can not be directly extended for fault detection purposes (to fulfil the *d-completeness* property as stated by Cordier et al. [2]). For non-linear models, different MEMs for one MEC [5], and different ARRs for one support-set [2] can provide different evaluation results, thus leading to different fault detection outputs.

   Although assumptions in both fields are identical, main difference comes in practice. Most DX works have traditionally opted by the simulation approach, avoiding derivative estimation. Meanwhile, in FDI differentiation is preferred, focusing on estimation or observer schemes [4], thus avoiding initial state estimation for simulation.

Concerning DBC using PCs, they have been used in semi-closed loop simulation – one MEM for each PC is used for simulation during an established simulation period; if no discrepancy is found after that period, observed variables are used to settle the new initial conditions for simulation–. But PCs using derivatives can be easily obtained using just a different model description allowing derivative causality. And it seems quite obvious that ARRs containing integral causality could just be derived using the Lille algorithm, just introducing models allowing integral matchings.

Summarizing, both techniques provide identical structural descriptions of subsystems –PCs or ARRS– which can be used for Fault Detection and Isolation purposes, using simulation or estimation approaches, in the BRIDGE context. Therefore, by means of compilation techniques, DX and FDI approaches can profit from each other.

Based on these ideas this work will exploit structural equivalence between compilation techniques to easily design state observers in the PC framework.

5.2   Dependency-Compilation and State Observer Design

State-observer fundamentals. It was previously mentioned that algorithms for computing PCs provide a structural expression for the executable model related to a MEM, which can be implemented as a simulator or an estimator. Moreover, Chantler et al. [11] demonstrated the equivalence of the integral and derivative approaches. Additionally, in FDI there is evidence of the equivalence of the three main techniques –simulation, estimation, and state observers– for linear systems [8].

System description in state-space form could be also seen as[3]:

$$\dot{\hat{X}}(t) = A \cdot \hat{X}(t) + B \cdot U(t) + K \cdot (Y(t) - \hat{Y}(t)) \tag{1}$$
$$\hat{Y}(t) = C \cdot \hat{X}(t) \tag{2}$$

Depending on the selected value for the gain K, we obtain: from $K = 0$ for simulation (no state correction), to $A = K \cdot C$ for prediction (previous state is not used) [16].

State observers work with a system description described by equations 1 and 2. It is used to minimize the error, $e(t) = \hat{Y}(t) - \hat{Y}(t)$ -regarding some criteria- on the state estimation, using the set of available measurements. This step is independent of the type of observer -i.e. Luenberger, Extended Kalman Filter, etc.-. Observer gain, K, must be selected according to the desired expected behavior for the observer.

In the structural approach used by the Lille method, state observer design requires that three additional constraints, modelling $e(t)$ and the observer stability condition, are added to the model for each state equation. Is necessary to do the same process in Possible Conflict calculation?

State-observer design using PCs. The set of PCs is computed following the GDE approach for dependency-compilation [5]. Hence, each PC has at least one MEM which has exactly one discrepancy node in its associated and-or graph. Such node can be found as an estimation for a measured magnitude, or as a double estimation of a non-measured magnitude.

---

[3] Changes in the state of the system, $\dot{\hat{X}}$ depends upon previous state $\hat{X}$ and current input U. Depending on the value of K, the gain, there will be a correction proportional to error in output estimation. Outputs $\hat{Y}$ depend on values of state variables, via static relations.

When differential constraints are included, algorithms used to compute PCs provide an interesting side-result if integral causality is used [14]. A Minimal Evaluable Model may be implemented as a simulator or as a state observer, without extra constraints in the model if the following proposition holds:

Proposition 2. *Those MEMs containing a state variable, can provide the minimal structural description for a state observer, if there exists a path made only of instantaneous constraints from the estimated state variable to the observed variable.*

This result comes from the way the error $e(t)$ is introduced in a generalized state observer scheme in equation 1, which is implicit in the MEM:

$e(t) = Y(t) - \hat{Y}(t) = Y(t) - C \cdot \hat{X}(t)$, where $C \cdot \hat{X}(t)$ represents the direct estimation of observed variables $\hat{Y}$ given estimated state-variables $\hat{X}$.

In MEM computation, state variables $\hat{X}$ in t are estimated using differential arcs (integral approach in that case) from same state variable in $t - 1$. MEMs are minimal, hence a state-variable is the source of one discrepancy –i.e. $e(t)$– only if it is compared against an observed variable Y (using only instantaneous constraints), or against another estimation of the same variable. If the state variable is compared against its observed value, then $e(t)$ can be computed, and it could be used in a state observer to correct the estimation of the state variable in the next time step ($K \cdot e(t)$ in eq. 1).

Algorithms computing PCs are exhaustive, then they are capable to provide every estimation for a state variable. Hence, it is possible to trace backward in the and-or graph related to each MEM if there is a path made only of instantaneous constraints from the discrepancy node ($e(t)$) to the state variable.

No additional information is required in the model description to provide these results. We just need to include one step at the end of the algorithms used for analyzing cyclical structures in the MEMs (their and-or graphs) related to a Possible Conflict [14].

The case study will be used to illustrate these ideas.

5.3   Application to the Case Study

Using integral causality PCs shown in table 1 were found. Based on proposition 2 six of their MEMs can also be implemented as state observers. Using derivative causality, the set of PCs found is smaller as shown in table 2 (only $\{PC_1, PC_6, PC_7\}$ remains from table 1). Also, it has worst fault isolation capability. Moreover, only two of them can be implemented as observers.

Let's take PC_2 in table 1 as an example. Its related MEM was shown in figure 2. Outflow from T_2, $LF4\_F$, is estimated and compared against its measured value $FT02$. Using proposition 2, this MEM can be implemented as a state observer, because error related to $FT02$ estimation, $e(t)_{T2_H}$, is used to correct the estimation for state variable $T2\_H$ in the next time step. Figure 3 shows the structural model for the same MEM, but implemented as a state observer. The selection of gain K for the observer is done off-line afterwards, tunning its desired fault detection features.

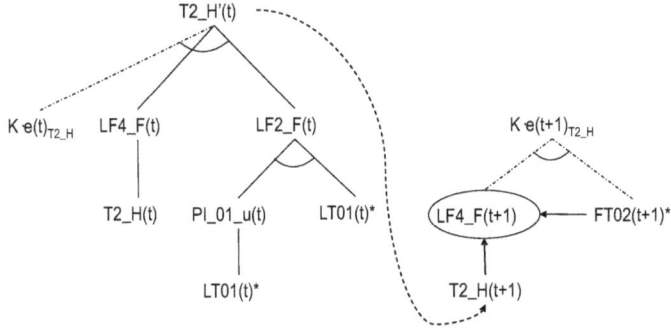

Fig. 3. MEM for PC_2 implemented as a state observer

6   Conclusions

PCs and ARRs provide almost identical approaches to fault isolation for static systems using compiled sets of analytical redundancy relations. Both approaches can find, off-line, those subsystems needed for conflict detection or residual evaluation purposes.

Inclusion of dynamic information in the models provides different approaches to behavior estimation as prediction, simulation, or state observers. Both approaches can again handle cyclical configurations, yielding similar results. But it must be noticed that using integral or derivative causality provides different sets of PCs, and consequently different fault detection and isolation capabilities as shown in the case study.

These results are consistent with ongoing work in the FDI field to automatically analyze the influence of differential constraints within structural analysis, allowing different representation for differential arcs [12,17]. Those works use different modelling approaches and algorithms, hence it is necessary additional research to provide further comparison.

Main advantage of PC computation is the ability to provide, using just integral causality, minimal structural descriptions for state observers design. In such sense, it is not necessary to include additional equations in the model as in the ARR approach [4].

It must be understood that there are two different stages in state observers design. First, finding the structural model for the observer (set of equations involved), and the set of faults related to them. Second, analyzing the observer convergence and robustness: computing gain, K, studying residual evaluation, etc. The proposal in this article is just linked to the first stage: providing the minimal structural expression for the state observer (because PCs are minimal w.r.t. set of constraints). Afterwards, proper values for the state observer gain must be computed following traditional FDI criteria.

ARRs and high-gain observers have been compared in [18]. That comparison is based on the analytical generation of the state observers. Our approach must be considered as a previous step for state observers design. Once the structural model is known, it can be analyzed to fulfill convergence, robustness or sensitivity criteria.

Main conclusion from this comparison is that dependency-compilation techniques from DX and FDI fields have approached diagnosis of dynamic systems almost identically in terms of simulation or prediction techniques. Differences come from the kind of models used to cope with uncertainty, noise, and disturbances.

Current work is focused on defining a framework for the integration of techniques from both fields for dynamic systems, following results on this article. Recently, we have proposed the integration of state observers following Proposition 2 to increase the robustness of consistency-based diagnosis using Possible Conflicts [19,20].

Acknowledgments. This work has been supported by regional grant JCyL VA005B09.

References

1. Biswas, G., Cordier, M., Lunze, J., Travé-Massuyès, L., Staroswiecki, M.: Diagnosis of complex systems: bridging the methodologies of the FDI and DX communities. IEEE Trans. on Syst., Man, and Cyb. Part B: Cybernetics 34(5), 2159–2162 (2004)
2. Cordier, M., Dague, P., Lévy, F., Montmain, J., Staroswiecki, M., Travé-Massuyès, L.: Conflicts versus Analytical Redundancy Relations: a comparative analysis of the Model-based Diagnosis approach from the Artificial Intelligence and Automatic Control perspectives. IEEE Trans. on Syst., Man, and Cyb. Part B: Cybernetics 34(5), 2163–2177 (2004)
3. Hamscher, W., Console, L., de Kleer, J. (eds.): Readings in Model based Diagnosis. Morgan-Kaufmann Pub., San Mateo (1992)
4. Blanke, M., Kinnaert, M., Lunze, J., Staroswiecki, M.: Diagnosis and Fault-Tolerant Control, 2nd edn. Springer, Heidelberg (2006)
5. Pulido, B., Alonso-González, C.: Possible conflicts: a compilation technique for consistency-based diagnosis. IEEE Trans. on Syst., Man, and Cyb. Part B: Cybernetics 34(5), 2192–2206 (2004)
6. de Kleer, J., Kurien, J.: Fundamentals of model-based diagnosis. In: Procs. of DX'03 (2003)
7. Brusoni, V., Console, L., Terenziani, P., Dupre, D.: A spectrum of definitions for temporal model-based diagnosis. In: Procs. of DX'96, Val Morin, Quebec, Canada, pp. 44–52 (1996)
8. Gertler, J.: Fault detection and diagnosis in Engineering Systems. Marcel Dekker, Inc., Basel (1998)
9. Armengol, J., Bregon, A., Escobet, T., Gelso, E., Krysander, M., Nyberg, M., Olive, X., Pulido, B., Travé-Massuyès, L.: Minimal structurally overdetermined sets for residual generation: A comparison of alternative approaches. In: Procs. of IFAC-Safeprocess'09, Barcelone, Spain (2009)
10. Dressler, O.: On-line diagnosis and monitoring of dynamic systems based on qualitative models and dependency-recording diagnosis engines. In: Procs. of ECAI'96, pp. 461–465 (1996)
11. Chantler, M., Daus, S., Vikatos, T., Coghill, G.: The use of quantitative dynamic models and dependency recording engines. In: Procs. of DX'96, Val Morin, Quebec, Canada, pp. 59–68 (1996)
12. Dustegör, D., Frisk, E., Coquempot, V., Krysander, M., Staroswiecki, M.: Structural analysis of fault isolability in the DAMADICS benchmark. Control Engineering Practice 14(6), 597–608 (2006)
13. Svärd, C., Nyberg, M.: A mixed causality approach to residual generation utilizing equation system solvers and differential-algebraic equation theory. In: Procs. of DX'08, Blue Mountains, Australia (September 2008)
14. Pulido, B., Alonso, C., Bregón, A., Puig, V., Escobet, T.: Analyzing the influence of temporal constraints in Possible Conflicts calculation for model-based diagnosis. In: Procs. of DX'07, Nashville, TN, USA (2007)

15. Katsillis, G., Chantler, M.: Can dependency-based diagnosis cope with simultaneous equations? In: Procs. of DX'97, Le Mont Saint Michel, France, pp. 51–59 (1997)
16. Puig, V., Quevedo, J., Escobet, T., Meseguer, J.: Toward a better integration of passive robust interval-based FDI algorithms. In: IFAC Safeprocess'06, China (2006)
17. Krysander, M., Åslund, J., Nyberg, M.: An efficient algorithm for finding minimal over-constrained sub-systems for model-based diagnosis. IEEE Trans. on Systems, Man, and Cybernetics – Part A: Systems and Humans 38(1) (2008)
18. Christophe, C., Cocquempot, V., Jiang, B.: Link between high-gain observer-based and parity space residuals for FDI. Trans. of the Institute of Measurement and Control 26(325) (2004)
19. Pulido, B., Bregón, A., Alonso, C.: Improving robustness in consistency-based diagnosis using Possible Conflicts. In: Procs. of ECAI'2008, Patras, Greece (2008)
20. Bregón, A., Pulido, B., Alonso-González, C.: Combination of simulation and state observers for consistency-based diagnosis. In: Procs. of the Annual Conference of the Prognostics and Health Management Society, PHM'09, San Diego, CA, USA (September 2009)

On the Complexity of Program Debugging Using Constraints for Modeling the Program's Syntax and Semantics

Franz Wotawa[1], Jörg Weber[1], Mihai Nica[1], and Rafael Ceballos[2,*]

[1] Institute for Software Technology
Graz University of Technology
[2] Computer Languages and Systems Department
University of Seville

Abstract. The use of model-based diagnosis for automated program debugging has been reported in several publications. The quality of the obtained results in terms of debugging accuracy is good. Unfortunately, most of the proposed models and techniques have very high computational needs. In this paper we focus on giving an explanation for the high computational needs of debugging. In particular, we propose a constraint representation of programs whose behavior is equivalent to the original programs. We further analyze the constraint representation to obtain its hypertree width, which is an indicator for the complexity of the corresponding constraint satisfaction problem. As constraint-based debugging is equivalent to constraint solving, the hypertree width is also an indicator for the debugging complexity. We further show that it is possible to construct arbitrarily complex programs such that their hypertree width is not bounded as indicated in previous literature.

1 Introduction

During programming and, even worse, during maintenance activities, locating and fixing faults in the source code is an arduous and difficult task, which is hardly automated in today's integrated development environments. One reason is the limited applicability of currently published approaches due to the underlying assumptions. E.g., approaches using frequency measures are only appropriate if a large test suite is available and if a tight integration of test case execution and debugging is given. Approaches that rely on the program's semantics provide good results even in cases where only one test case is available but they suffer from high computational requirements, which prevent them of being used for larger programs. Other approaches that are based on the program's structure can be used for larger programs but usually exhibit bad discrimination among possible fault candidates.

* This research has been funded in part by the Austrian Science Fund (FWF) under grant P20199-N15 and is partially conducted within the competence network Softnet Austria (www.soft-net.at) and funded by the Austrian Federal Ministry of Economics (bm:wa), the province of Styria, the Steirische Wirtschaftsförderungsgesellschaft mbH. (SFG), and the city of Vienna in terms of the center for innovation and technology (ZIT). Authors are listed in reverse alphabetical order.

P. Meseguer, L. Mandow, and R.M. Gasca (Eds.): CAEPIA 2009, LNAI 5988, pp. 22–31, 2010.

When considering the current state of research in debugging, should we conclude that current approaches to automated debugging have been not successful? The answer to this question is definitely no! There are many methods for automated debugging which prove that automation is possible and effectively helps focusing on those parts of a program which are more likely to be faulty. E.g., Peischl and Wotawa [12] provided empirical evidence that model-based diagnosis [14] can be effectively used to reduce the number of statements that someone has to consider during debugging. The published results indicated a median reduction of 97 percent for debugging sequential hardware designs. Mayer and colleagues [5] presented results on the use of model-based diagnosis for debugging of sequential programs. The work has been extended to handle object-oriented languages and the use of program abstraction; see Mayer's PhD thesis [9].

In this paper we tackle the problem of giving reasons for the high computational demands of automated debugging, in particular when using a model-based diagnosis approach which utilizes the complete semantics of the program in order to obtain precise diagnosis.

Obviously, in general model-based diagnosis itself requires a lot of computational resources, but a reduction is possible when focusing on single faults only. However, even in this case the debugging of larger programs using the complete semantics requires a lot of computing time. In this paper we explain why this is the case. By mapping programs to their equivalent constraint representation we reduce the debugging problem to a constraint satisfaction problem. Constraint representations of programs have been described in literature for different purposes like verification [13] and also for debugging [11]. In contrast to verification which deals with fault detection, debugging deals with fault localization and correction.

The tree width of the constraint satisfaction problem, which can be obtained from the hypertree representation, is an indicator of the complexity for computing solutions. The accuracy of this metric is especially high when the constraints are extensionally modeled. We show that it is possible to construct arbitrarily complex programs such that their hypertree width is not bounded. Moreover, we present experimental results that indicate a high tree width for debugging problems.

2   Representing Programs as Constraints

In this section we describe the conversion of programs into their constraint representation. We also show the equivalence of both with respect to a given test suite. In particular, we show that if a program computes an output O for a certain input I, then its constraint representation will also compute the same values for the corresponding output variables.

Our work addresses sequential programs with a syntax and semantics similar to well-known languages like Java, but without object-oriented constructs. For simplicity we do not consider procedure calls in this paper, but it should be noted that procedures can be straightforwardly integrated as shown in [10]. Our approach supports assignments statements, conditional statements, and loops.

Throughout the rest of this paper we use the program given in Fig. 1 as running example.

```
1.   i = 0;
2.   r = 0;
3.   while (i < x) {
4.       r = r + y;
5.       i = i + 1;
     }
```

```
1.   i = 0;
2.   r = 0;
3.   if (i < x) {
4.       r = r + y;
5.       i = i + 1;
     }
```

Fig. 1. A program for computing the product of two natural numbers

Fig. 2. Loop unrolling of the program from Fig. 1 for 1 iteration

The first step for obtaining a constraint representation of an arbitrary program is the conversion into a loop-free variant. The second step is to obtain a static single assignment form. The third step takes the static single assignment form and maps it to a constraint system. In order to prove that the conversion step does not change the program's behavior we have to define what we mean with program equivalence. First of all, converted program should compute the same outputs for the given inputs. Moreover, the names of the variables in the converted program may differ from the original program, but there is a correspondence between the variables, and so the corresponding variables must be compared. Since we want to use the representation for debugging, we restrict the program equivalence to the given test cases:

Definition 1. *Given a program Π and a program Π', an input environment $\omega_I \in ENV$, a set of relevant output variables $OUTPUT \subseteq VARS$, and a function $\sigma : VARS \mapsto VARS$ mapping variables from Π to the corresponding variables in Π'. We say that the programs Π and Π' behave equivalent if and only if for all relevant output variables $x \in OUTPUT$ the same values are computed, i.e., $\omega_O(x) = \omega'_O(\sigma(x))$, where $\omega_O = I(\Pi, \omega_I)$ and $\omega'_O = I(\Pi', \omega'_I)$ with $\omega'_I(\sigma(v)) = \omega_I(v)$ for all variables $v \in VARS$. We write $\Pi =_{\omega_I} \Pi'$.*

Note that all variables that are not specified in $OUTPUT$ might have different values after applying the interpretation function. We extend Def. 1 to a set of input environments of the available test suite:

Definition 2. *Two programs Π and Π' are equivalent if they are equivalent for all input environments ω_I, i.e., $\forall \omega_I : \Pi =_{\omega_I} \Pi'$. In this case we write $\Pi = \Pi'$.*

2.1 Loop-Free Programs

Since loops cannot be directly represented as a constraint system, we transform the original program to a loop-free variant and prove its equivalence.

If the body of a *while*-loop is executed at most once, then the behavior corresponds to the single execution of a conditional statement. In general, if a *while*-condition is fulfilled, the statements in the block are executed and afterwards the condition is evaluated again. Hence, programs can be compiled into their loop-free equivalent if the number of steps is known in advance. As we debug a program using a given test case, we can simply execute the program for this test case in order to determine the maximum number of iterations.

Example: The loop-free variant of the program from Fig. 1 is depicted in Fig. 2 for $n = 1$ iteration. It can be used for all cases where $x \in \{0, 1\}$ without leading to a different behavior compared to the original program.

Because of the loop unrolling the size (i.e., the number of statements) of the resulting loop-free program increases. The amount of increase depends on the time complexity of the original program. This results from the fact that the runtime of a program directly corresponds to the number of statement executions. The more iterations a program has, the more statements are executed. We summarize this finding in the following theorem:

Theorem 1. *Given a program Π with time complexity $O(f(\Sigma))$ where Σ denotes the size of the input. The corresponding loop-free program Π_{LF} has to have a size of $O(f(\Sigma_M))$ where Σ_M is the maximum input size to be considered.*

As a consequence, using this model directly for debugging is only feasible for programs which have a low time complexity or when using inputs of smaller size. Although the focus of this paper is on the complexity of debugging and not on the practicability of the approach, we briefly discuss how to tackle the challenge of feasibility. One way would be to compute the loop-free program in such a way that the number of nested if-statements does not exceed the number of iterations in the given test cases. Then it is guaranteed that the model captures the whole test suite. An improvement would be to consider only failing (negative) test cases and to further reduce the test suite to small test cases.

2.2 Static Single Assignment Form

The constraint representation requires that all left-side variables in the program have unique names. Hence, we use an intermediate representation of the program, the Static Single Assignment (SSA) form, which has the property that no two left-side variables share the same name [1]. Since all variables are defined only once, the SSA form allows for a clear representation of the dependencies that are established between different variables inside the corresponding program.

Unique variable names can be easily obtained by adding an index at the end of the name. However, although converting programs comprising only assignment statements is straightforward, it is more difficult to convert programs with loops or conditional statements. As we transform loops to nested if-statements, we only need to consider conditional statements.

The idea behind the conversion of conditional statements is as follows. The value of the condition is stored in a new unique variable. The if- and the $else$-branches are converted separately. In both cases the conversion starts using the indices of the variables already computed. Both conversions deliver back new indices of variables. In order to get a value for a variable we have to select the last definition of a variable from the if- and $else$-branch depending on how the if condition evaluates. This selection is done using a function phi. Hence, for every variable which is defined in the if- or the $else$-branch we have to introduce a selecting assignment statement which calls phi.

For example, the corresponding SSA form of the program fragment `if e { .. x = ..} else { .. x = ..}` is given as follows:

```
var_e = e; ...; x_i = ...; x_j = ...;
x_k = phi(x_i,x_j,var_e);
```

where the function `phi` is assumed to be part of the used data type and is defined as follows:

$$\text{phi}(x, y, b) = \begin{cases} x \text{ if } b = TRUE \\ y \text{ otherwise} \end{cases}$$

The SSA representation for the program from Fig. 1 is depicted in Fig. 3. For brevity, only one iteration is considered.

```
1.    i_0 = 0;
2.    r_0 = 0;
3.    var_e_4 = (i_0 < x_0);
4.    r_1 = r_0 + y_0;
5.    i_1 = i_0 + 1;
6.    r_2 = phi(r_1,r_0,var_e_4);
7.    i_2 = phi(i_1,i_0,var_e_4);
```

Fig. 3. The SSA form of the loop-free variant of the program from Fig. 1 (for one iteration)

Obviously the transformation of loop-free programs into their SSA form does not have an influence on the actual behavior (apart from the variable renaming), i.e., $\Pi_{LF} = \Pi_{SSA}$ without any restrictions.

Lemma 2. *Given a program Π, a number $n \in \mathbb{N}$, a set of relevant output variables $OUTPUT \subseteq VARS$, and a function σ, which is defined as follows: For all variables $x \in VARS \setminus OUTPUT$: $\sigma(x) = x\_0$. For all output variables $y \in OUTPUT$: $\sigma(y) = y\_M(y)$, where $M(y)$ is the largest index assigned to a variable y. The loop-free variant $\Pi_{LF} = \Gamma(\Pi, n)$ of Π behaves equivalent to its SSA form Π_{SSA}. I.e., for all input environments $\omega_I \in ENV$: $\Pi_{LF} =_{\omega_I} \Pi_{SSA}$.*

Note that in this lemma we implicitly assume, for simplicity, that output variables cannot be used as inputs for a program. This assumption does not contradict generality.

2.3   Constraint Representation

The final step of the conversion is the compilation to a constraint satisfaction problem (CSP). A CSP (V, D, CO) is characterized by a set of variables V, each variable having a set of domains D, and a set of constraints CO, where each constraint defines a relation R between variables. The variables occurring in a relation $R \in CO$ are called the scope S_R of the relation. A solution of a CSP is an assignment of values to all variables which does not contradict any given constraint. For more information regarding CSPs we refer to Dechter [2].

The *extensional modeling of a constraint* is the explicit representation of all allowed combinations of values for the variables of a constraint, within a certain domain. For example, if we have the boolean equation $z = y \wedge x$, $D_x = D_y = D_z = \{0, 1\}$, then the extensional representation of this constraint is given by the following tuples: $< 0, 0, 0 >, < 0, 0, 1 >, < 0, 1, 0 >, < 1, 1, 1 >$.

An extensionally modeled CSP has the advantage that it can be tractable based on its structure(i.e., hypergraph) rather than on the relations between its constraints. Based on the structural representation of the CSP, we can determine the complexity of finding its solution. Our framework implies such a modeling of the constraints.

The constraint representation of a program is extracted from its SSA representation.Let Π_{SSA} be a program in SSA form. Then the corresponding CSP $CSP(\Pi_{SSA})$ is constructed as follows:

- All variables in Π_{SSA} are variables of the CSP.
- The domain of the variables in the CSP is equivalent to the datatype.
- Every statement $x = e$ can be converted to a relation R where the scope $\{x_1, \ldots, x_n\}$ is equivalent to the set of variables used in expression e. The relation $R(x, x_1, \ldots, x_n)$ is defined as follows: For all $\omega \in ENV$ with $\omega(x_i) = v_i$: if $I(x = e, \omega) = \omega'$, then $R(\omega'(x), v_1, \ldots, v_n)$ is true, otherwise false.

Lemma 3. *Given a program Π_{SSA} in SSA form and its corresponding CSP representation $CSP(\Pi_{SSA})$. For all $\omega \in ENV$: $I(\Pi_{SSA}, \omega) = \omega'$ iff $\omega \cup \omega'$ is a solution of $CSP(\Pi_{SSA})$.*

Using this lemma we can finally conclude that the whole conversion process is correct:

Theorem 4. *Given a program Π and $n \in \mathbb{N}$, the loop-free representation for n iterations, the SSA form and the CSP representation of Π are equivalent under the given assumptions, i.e., $\Pi = \Pi_{LF} = \Pi_{SSA} = CSP(\Pi)$.*

This theorem follows directly from Lemma 1 to 3.

Example: From the SSA form which is depicted in Fig. 3 we extract the following CSP representation:

Variables: $V = V_N \cup V_B$ with
$V_N = \{x\_0, y\_0, i\_0, r\_0, r\_1, i\_1, r\_2, i\_2\}$ and
$V_B = \{var\_e\_4\}$
Domains: $D = \{D(x) = \mathbb{N} \mid x \in V_N\} \cup \{D(x) = \{TRUE, FALSE\} \mid x \in V_B\}$
Constraints:
$$CO = \left\{ \begin{array}{l} i\_0 = 0, r\_0 = 0, var\_e\_4 = (i\_0 < x\_0), r\_1 = r\_0 + y\_0, i\_1 = i\_0 + 1, \\ r\_2 = phi(r\_1, r\_0, var\_e\_4), i\_2 = phi(i\_1, i\_0, var\_e\_4) \end{array} \right\}$$

3   Constraint-Based Debugging

In the previous section we introduced a model that captures the syntax and semantics of an arbitrary program. The model itself is a constraint system which can be used for debugging by applying model-based diagnosis [14] techniques. For this purpose we introduce the predicate $AB(s_i)$, which means that statement s_i is abnormal. The constraints are changed to the form $\neg AB(s_i) \rightarrow C(s_i)$, where $C(s_i)$ is the original constraint corresponding to statement s_i. E.g., the constraint $(i\_0 = 0)$ is changed to $\neg AB(s_1) \rightarrow (i_0 = 0)$, where s_1 represents statement 1 in the SSA-form in Fig. 3.

Based on the debugging model we are able to compute diagnosis. Intuitively, a diagnosis is a subset of statements s.t. the assumption that those statements are abnormal and that all other statements are not abnormal does not contradict a given test case. Note that test cases are also represented as constraints (without the AB predicate).

Hence, debugging is reduced to CSP solving and so we can use techniques from CSP solving to classify the debugging complexity. It is well known that CSPs whose corresponding hypergraph is acyclic can be solved in polynomial time [2]. A hypergraph is a graph where edges connect an arbitrary number of vertices. The hypergraph for a CSP represents variables as vertices and the constraint scopes as edges. Moreover, a cyclic hypergraph can be decomposed into an acyclic one using available decomposition methods [3]. The resulting acyclic hypergraph is a tree structure where each vertex represents several constraints which have to be joined in order to solve the CSP. The maximum number of constraints to be joined is the tree width. When using the hypertree decomposition, which is the most general decomposition method [3], the width is called hypertree width. The hypertree width is a very good indicator for the complexity of solving a extensionally modeled CSPs: as stated in [3], any given CSP can be solved in $O(|\Sigma|^k * log|\Sigma|)$, where k is the hypertree width and Σ the input size of the CSP.

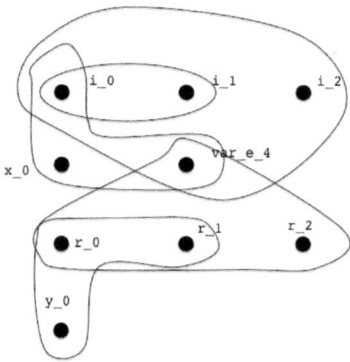

Fig. 4. The hypergraph of the debugging model for the program in Fig. 1

The hypergraph of the debugging model of the program in Fig. 1 is depicted in Fig. 4. In the following we discuss the consequences of the debugging model in terms of complexity. In particular we are interested whether the hypertree width is bounded for such a model or not. In [7] the author proved that structured programs have a hypertree width of 6 in the worst case. Unfortunately, the result is based on considering the control flow graph only but not the data flow, which is sufficient for some tasks to be solved in compiler construction. The following theorem shows that the result of [7] cannot be applied in the context of debugging where the control and data flow is of importance.

Theorem 5. *There is no constant upper-bound for the hypertree width of arbitrary programs.*

Proof: (Sketch) We prove this theorem indirectly. We assume that there is a constant value which serves as upper-bound for all programs and show that there is a class of programs where this assumption does not hold. Consider the class of programs that is obtained running the following algorithm for $n > 0$:

1. Let Π_n be a program comprising an empty block statement.
2. For $i = 1$ to n do:
   (a) For $j = i + 1$ to n do:
       i. Add the statement
          $$x_{j,i} = x_{i,i-1} + x_{j,i-1}$$
          at the end of the block statement of program Π_n.
3. Return Π_n.

In this class programs have n inputs and 1 output. Every variable depends on any other directly or indirectly via another variable. Hence, the hypertree width depends on the number of statements and there is no constant value, which contradicts our initial assumption.   □

Note that there is always an upper-bound of the hypertree width of a particular program, which is given by the number of statements. However, the above theorem states that there is no constant which serves as upper-bound for all programs. What is missing is a clarification whether the number of nested if-statements after loop-unrolling has an influence on the hypertree width. If the hypertree width of a program comprising a *while*-statement depended on the number of considered iterations, then the complexity of debugging would heavily depend on the used test cases. Fortunately this is not the case as stated in the following theorem.

Theorem 6. *Given an arbitrary program Π comprising at least one* while *statement. There always exists an upper bound on the hypertree width when the number of iterations increases.*

Proof: (Sketch) If we have a *while* statement, we obtain a sequence of block statements each block representing an iteration of the execution. These blocks are connected via variables defined in the block statement of the while and used in it. Hence, the sequence can be easily mapped to a tree where each node comprises all statements of the while's block statement. Hence, the hypertree width of this tree is bounded by the number of statements in the block statement. Variables that are defined outside the *while* statement and used by a statement inside do not increase the hypertree width because they are part of every node. Only the variables that are defined within the while's block statement have to be looked at more closely. These variables are summarized to a single variable using the phi functions. What we have to do is to add the corresponding constraint to each node. Because this has to be done only once per node the overall hypertree width of the resulting structure is bounded. Hence, the overall tree representing the *while* statement is bounded by the number of statements used in its block statement.   □

4   Experimental Results

As mentioned, the hypertree width is an important metric for the complexity of debugging based on a constraint representation. Complex debugging problems have a large hypertree width. In general, problems with a hypertree width of more than 5 are hard problems.

For computing the hypertree and the hypertree width we relied on an implementation provided by [6] which employs the Bucket Elimination algorithm [8]. Note that this algorithm is an approximation algorithm, i.e., it does not always generate the optimal hypertree decomposition with a minimal width. However, as reported in [8], the algorithm which performs the optimal decomposition is very time and space demanding and is therefore not suitable for practical use, and the Bucket Elimination algorithm in most cases provides better approximations than other known approximation algorithms.

The obtained results are summarized in Fig. 5. For each program the table comprises the lines of code (LOC) of the original program (column P) and of the corresponding SSA form (S), the number of $while$-statements ($\#W$), the number of if-statements ($\#I$), the max. number of considered iterations ($\#IS$) and the hypertree width (HW) with its minimum (min) and maximum (max) value. In min we depict the hypertree width for one iteration and in max the hypertree width for the max. number of iterations as stated in column $\#IS$.

	#LOC					HW	
Name	P	S	#W	#I	#IS	min	max
BinSearch	27	112	1	3	4	3	8
Binomial	76	1155	5	1	30	3	30
Hamming	27	989	5	1	10	2	14
ArithmeticOp	12	12	0	0	-	1	1
Huffman	64	342	4	1	20	2	12
Multiplication	10	350	1	0	50	2	5
whileTest	60	376	4	0	9	2	8
Permutation	24	119	3	1	7	3	6
ComplexHT	12	370	1	0	30	3	17
SumPowers	21	173	2	1	15	2	10
ATestCase	43	682	4	4	10	5	7
BM4bitPAV2_F1	21	21	0	0	-	2	2
BM4bitPAV2_F2	21	21	0	0	-	2	2
IscasC17_F3	6	6	0	0	-	2	2
IscasC17_F1	6	6	0	0	-	2	2
BM4bitAdder_F1	26	26	0	0	-	4	4
IscasC432_F1	160	160	0	0	-	9	9

Fig. 5. The hypertree width for different sequential programs

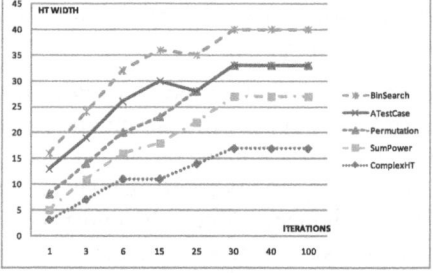

Fig. 6. The hypertree width as a function of the number of iterations when unrolling $while$-statements. For the sake of clarity we depict only 5 programs from the set of tested programs.

It can be seen that the hypertree width varies from 1 to more than 30. Although the obtained results are only for small programs they allow us to conclude that debugging programs is a very hard problem from the computational point of view.

The hypertree width obviously depends on the number of unrollings. We performed several experiments with a larger number of iterations. Fig. 6 depicts the hypertree evolutions of five different programs. It can be seen that in all of these cases the hypertree width reaches an upper bound, as indicated in Theorem 6.

5   Conclusion

Debugging is considered a computationally very hard problem. This is not surprising, given the fact that model-based diagnosis is NP-complete. However, more surprising is that debugging remains a hard problem even when considering single-faults only, at least when using models which utilize the entire semantics of the program in order to obtain precise results. In this paper we identified the hypertree width as an explanation. We have shown that it is possible to generate arbitrarily complex programs. So there is no constant upper bound for the hypertree width of programs. For programs with loops, the number of iterations to be considered for debugging has an impact on the hypertree width. This impact is limited by our finding that, for a given program, there is an upper bound on the hypertree width which is independent from the number of iterations.

We provided empirical results using small well-known programs like binary search. The computed values for the hypertree width varied from 1-30. Even the trivial Multiplication program, which has only 10 lines of code, has a hypertree width of 5 when considering 50 iterations. These values are very high, which explains why debugging is such a hard problem. A practical contribution of our work is the reduction of debugging to a constraint satisfaction problem, which allows for the use of standard CSP solvers for debugging.

References

1. Brandis, M.M., Mössenböck, H.: Single-pass generation of static assignment form for structured languages. ACM TOPLAS 16(6), 1684–1698 (1994)
2. Dechter, R.: Constraint Processing. Morgan Kaufmann, San Francisco (2003)
3. Gottlob, G., Leone, N., Scarcello, F.: A comparison of structural CSP decomposition methods. Artificial Intelligence 124(2), 243–282 (2000)
4. DeMillo, R.A., Pan, H., Spafford, E.H.: Critical slicing for software fault localization. In: International Symposium on Software Testing and Analysis (ISSTA), pp. 121–134 (1996)
5. Mayer, W., Stumptner, M., Wieland, D., Wotawa, F.: Can ai help to improve debugging substantially? debugging experiences with value-based models. In: Proceedings of the European Conference on Artificial Intelligence, Lyon, France, pp. 417–421 (2002)
6. http://www.dbai.tuwien.ac.at/proj/hypertree/index.html
7. Thorup, M.: All Structured Programs have Small tree width and Good Register Allocation. Information and Computation Journal
8. Dermaku, A., Ganzow, T., Gottlob, G., McMahan, B., Musliu, N., Samer, M.: Heuristic Methods for hypertree Decompositions, DBAI-TR-2005-53, Technische Universität Wien (2005)
9. Mayer, W.: Static and Hybrid Analysis in Model-based Debugging. PhD Thesis, School of Computer and Information Science, University of South Australia, Adelaide, Australia (2007)
10. Wotawa, F., Nica, M.: On the Compilation of Programs into their equivalent Constraint Representation. Informatica 32(4), 359–371 (2008)
11. Ceballos, R., Gasca, R.M., Del Valle, C., Borrego, D.: Diagnosing Errors in DbC Programs Using Constraint Programming. In: Marín, R., Onaindía, E., Bugarín, A., Santos, J. (eds.) CAEPIA 2005. LNCS (LNAI), vol. 4177, pp. 200–210. Springer, Heidelberg (2006)
12. Wotawa, F., Peischl, B.: Automated source level error localization in hardware designs. IEEE Design and Test of Computers 23(1), 8–19 (2006)
13. Collavizza, H., Rueher, M.: Exploring Different Constraint-Based Modelings for Program Verification. In: Bessière, C. (ed.) CP 2007. LNCS, vol. 4741, pp. 49–63. Springer, Heidelberg (2007)
14. Reiter, R.: A theory of diagnosis from first principles. Artificial Intelligence 32(1), 57–95 (1987)

An Analysis of Particle Properties on a Multi-swarm PSO for Dynamic Optimization Problems

Ignacio G. del Amo[1], David A. Pelta[1], Juan R. González[1], and Pavel Novoa[2]

[1] Models of Decision and Optimization (MODO) Research Group,
Dept. of Computer Sciences and Artificial Intelligence,
University of Granada
{ngdelamo,dpelta,jrgonzalez}@decsai.ugr.es
[2] University of Holguín, Holguín, Cuba
pnovoa@facinf.uho.edu.cu

Abstract. The particle swarm optimization (PSO) algorithm has successfully been applied to dynamic optimization problems with very competitive results. One of its best performing variants is the one based on the atomic model, with quantum and trajectory particles. However, there is no precise knowledge on how these particles contribute to the global behavior of the swarms during the optimization process. This work analyzes several aspects of each type of particle, including the best combination of them for different scenarios, and how many times do they contribute to the swarm's best. Results show that, for the Moving Peaks Benchmark (MPB), a higher number of trajectory particles than quantum particles is the best strategy. Quantum particles are most helpful immediately after a change in the environment has occurred, while trajectory particles lead the optimization in the final stages. Suggestions on how to use this knowledge for future developments are also provided.

1 Introduction

Particle Swarm Optimization (PSO) [11] is a population-based algorithm that has been successfully applied to solving a wide variety of static problems [14]. Its use for dynamic optimization problems (DOP) requires the canonical formulation of the PSO to be modified in order to obtain good performance.

Janson and Middendorf [10] propose a tree-like hierarchical organization of swarms (H-PSO), while Parrot and Li [13] adapt the speciation technique introduced for genetic algorithms by Li et al. [12] to the PSO. Some of the most successful proposals are based on features like multi-swarms, intra-swarm diversity or inter-swarm exclusion, most of them originally conceived by Blackwell and Branke [4, 2, 5, 3, 1]. Several of the previous variants have been tested using Scenario 2 of the Moving Peaks Benchmark (MPB) [6]. The best-performing configuration for this environment was a quantum multi-swarm approach (multi-QPSO) with 5 quantum and 5 trajectory (neutral) particles, having an equal number of peaks and swarms [3]. This last proposal is precisely the object of study of this work.

P. Meseguer, L. Mandow, and R.M. Gasca (Eds.): CAEPIA 2009, LNAI 5988, pp. 32–41, 2010.

Although these specific settings are known to produce good results for the test, no deep study has been reported on the influence of the number of particles of each type. The original work of Blackwell and Branke [3] only showed that the $(5t + 5q)$ was better than a $(0t + 10q)$ and a $(10t + 0q)$ configuration (i.e., only-quantum and only-trajectory, respectively). Understanding the influence of these particle types is not only of interest, but it also may lead to the design of more efficient techniques. The objective of this work is to study which is the best combination of each type of particle during the optimization process, as well as giving insights of their behavior during it, in order to obtain a deeper knowledge of their inner dynamics. Two variants of the previously referred Scenario 2 of the MPB have been used to perform the experiments.

The paper is structured as follows: first, the multi-QPSO used is presented in Sect. 2; then, a description of the MPB and the Scenario 2 is given in Sect. 3; computational experimentation and results are provided in Sect. 4; finally, conclusions and future work are commented in Sect. 5.

2   The Multi-QPSO

The multi-QPSO is a variant of the PSO that was firstly introduced in [3] by Blackwell and Branke, which specifically aims at DOP's.

A swarm in the multi-QPSO is formed by two types of particles:

- *Trajectory* particles (also known as *classical* or *neutral*). These are the particles used by the canonical PSO algorithm, which positions are updated following the usual movement equations:

$$\mathbf{a}(t+1) = \chi[\eta_1 c_1 \cdot (\mathbf{x}_{pbest} - \mathbf{x}(t)) + \eta_2 c_2 \cdot (\mathbf{x}_{gbest} - \mathbf{x}(t))] - (1 - \chi)\mathbf{v}(t) \quad (1)$$
$$\mathbf{v}(t+1) = \mathbf{v}(t) + \mathbf{a}(t+1) \quad (2)$$
$$\mathbf{x}(t+1) = \mathbf{x}(t) + \mathbf{v}(t+1) \quad (3)$$

where $\mathbf{x}$, $\mathbf{v}$ and $\mathbf{a}$ are position, velocity and acceleration respectively. $\mathbf{x}_{pbest}$ is the best so far position discovered by each particle, and $\mathbf{x}_{gbest}$ is the best so far position discovered by the whole swarm. Parameters $\eta_1, \eta_2 > 2$ are spring constants, and c_1 and c_2 are random numbers in the interval $[0.0, 1.0]$. Since particle movement must progressively contract in order to converge, a constriction factor χ, $\chi < 1$ is used, as defined by Clerc and Kennedy in [8]. This factor replaces other slowing approaches in the literature, such as inertial weight and velocity clamping [9].
- *Quantum* particles. These particles were newly introduced in the multi-QPSO algorithm, and aim at reaching a higher level of diversity by moving randomly within a hypersphere of radius $\mathbf{r}$ centered on $\mathbf{x}_{gbest}$. This random movement is performed according to a probability distribution over the hypersphere, in this case, a uniform distribution:

$$\mathbf{x}(t+1) = \mathbf{rand}_{hypersphere}(\mathbf{x}_{gbest}, \mathbf{r}) \quad (4)$$

Beside this, the general idea of the multi-QPSO is to use a set of multiple swarms that simultaneously explore the search space. This multi-swarm approach has the purpose of maintaining the diversity, in addition to the use of quantum particles. This is a key point for DOP's, since the optimum can change at any time, and the algorithm must be able to react and find a new optimum. In order to prevent several swarms from competing over the same area, an inter-swarm exclusion mechanism is also used, randomizing the worst swarm whenever two of them are closer than a certain distance.

3   The Moving Peaks Benchmark

The MPB is a test benchmark for DOP's originally proposed in [6]. Its current version, and the most updated source of information about it, is the webpage `http://www.aifb.uni-karlsruhe.de/~jbr/MovPeaks/`. Informally, the MPB consists on a set of **m** peaks, each of which has its own time-varying parameters height (**h**), width (**w**), and location ($\overrightarrow{\mathbf{p}}$).

Changes to a single peak are described by the following expressions:

$$\mathbf{h}_i(t+1) = \mathbf{h}_i(t) + \mathbf{h}_{severity} \cdot \mathbf{N}(0,1) \tag{5}$$

$$\mathbf{w}_i(t+1) = \mathbf{w}_i(t) + \mathbf{w}_{severity} \cdot \mathbf{N}(0,1) \tag{6}$$

$$\overrightarrow{\mathbf{p}}_i(t+1) = \overrightarrow{\mathbf{p}}_i(t) + \overrightarrow{\mathbf{v}}_i(t+1) \tag{7}$$

where the shift vector $\overrightarrow{\mathbf{v}}_i(t+1)$ is a linear combination of a random vector $\overrightarrow{\mathbf{r}}$ and the previous shift vector $\overrightarrow{\mathbf{v}}_i(t)$, normalized to length **s**, i.e.:

$$\overrightarrow{\mathbf{v}}_i(t+1) = \frac{\mathbf{s}}{|\overrightarrow{\mathbf{r}} + \overrightarrow{\mathbf{v}}_i(t)|}((1-\lambda)\overrightarrow{\mathbf{r}} + \lambda\overrightarrow{\mathbf{v}}_i(t)) \tag{8}$$

The random vector $\overrightarrow{\mathbf{r}}$ is created by drawing random numbers for each dimension and normalizing its length to **s**. Parameter **s** thus indicates the distance that a single peak moves when a change in the environment occurs (shift distance). Parameter **s** thus indicates the distance that a single peak moves when a change in the environment occurs (shift distance). Parameter λ indicates the linear correlation with respect to the previous shift, where a value of 1 indicates "total correlation" and a value of 0 "pure randomness".

The MPB has been widely used as a test suit for different algorithms under the presence of dynamism. One of the most used configurations for this purpose is Scenario 2, which is described in the web page of the MPB, and consists of the set of parameters indicated in table 1.

4   Computational Experiments

The multi-QPSO algorithm has been reported [3] to outperform other variants of the PSO under Scenario 2 of the MPB. Its superior performance can be attributed to two factors:

Table 1. Standard settings for the Scenario 2 of the Moving Peaks Benchmark

Parameter	Value
Number of peaks (m)	$\in [10, 200]$
Number of dimensions (d)	5
Peaks heights (h_i)	$\in [30, 70]$
Peaks widths (w_i)	$\in [1, 12]$
Change frequency (Δe)	5000
Height severity (h_s)	7.0
Width severity (w_s)	1.0
Shift distance (s)	$\in [0.0, 3.0]$
Correlation coefficient (λ)	$\in [0.0, 1.0]$

- a greater diversity, caused by the use of a multi-swarm scheme and the exclusion mechanism,
- the abilities of each swarm to converge to peaks, due to the trajectory particles, and to quickly react to changes due to the improved exploration capabilities of the quantum particles.

Blackwell and Branke conducted an exhaustive research work on the sensitivity of the multi-QPSO over variations on several parameters, like the number of swarms, the radius of the quantum particle's hypersphere, etc. Summarizing, the conclusions were that given a certain MPB configuration (for instance, Scenario 2), the best parameter settings for the multi-QPSO corresponded to one with the same number of swarms than peaks, and with quantum radius equal to the shift distance of the peaks. However, no deep study was reported on the influence of the number of particles of each type, and a $(5t + 5q)$ configuration was found to be the best compared to a $(0t + 10q)$ and a $(10t + 0q)$ configuration (i.e., only-quantum and only-trajectory, respectively).

In this work we perform a deeper analysis of the behavior of the algorithm with finer variations on the number of particles of each type.

4.1   Experimental Framework

For comparison purposes, the configurations for the MPB and the multi-QPSO were selected as close as possible to the ones used in [3]. However, there are some differences due to the nature of the experiment, and reasonable values, to the best of the authors' efforts, have been selected and justified bellow. The different configuration values are summarized in table 2.

All of the experiments have been performed using the Scenario 2 of the MPB (table 1) with some differences. The number of peaks of the MPB indicates the degree of multi-modality of the problem: the higher the number of peaks, the higher the difficulty and complexity of the problem. Thus, the number of peaks was also varied in the experiments conducted, in the range $[5, 10, ..., 95, 100]$, in order to give an idea of the behavior of the algorithm under increasingly difficult scenarios.

Table 2. Settings for the different experiments of the multi-QPSO on Scenario 2 of the MPB

Parameter	Value
Number of peaks	$\in [5, 100]$, stepsize 5
Change frequency	5000 (low freq.)
	200 (high freq.)
Number of swarms	5
Number of t-particles	$\in [0, 10]$, stepsize 1
Number of q-particles	$10 - t$
Number of changes	100
Number of runs (repetitions)	30

Regarding the multi-QPSO settings, each swarm has been set to contain a fixed number of particles, 10. Thus, all possible combinations of trajectory and quantum particles have been tested in the experiments, ranging from $0t10q$ to $10t0q$. As explained before, it has been reported that the best configuration for the multi-QPSO regarding the number of swarms is that of the same number as peaks (i.e., one swarm for covering each peak). However, this is a very strong *a priori* knowledge assumption, and, in general, it is not possible to know the number of local optima in a DOP scenario. Additionally, the higher the number of swarms, the bigger the number of evaluations required by the algorithm in each iteration, thus reducing the capacity of the multi-QPSO to converge to a peak. Because of all of this, it has been decided that the number of swarms would be fixed to 5, independently of the number of peaks, which implies a total of 50 particles for the algorithm.

The algorithm was run for 100 consecutive changes, and each run was independently repeated 30 times, with different random seeds. The performance measure used to evaluate the algorithm is the offline error [7], which is the average over the error of the best solution found by the algorithm since the last change, during the whole execution:

$$e_{offline} = \frac{1}{t} \cdot \sum_t e_t^{best} \tag{9}$$

where $e_t^{best} = max\{e_t^1, ..., e_t^n\}$ is the best value achieved by the algorithm at time (change number) t.

Finally, after an initial execution of the experiments with these settings, an additional variation of Scenario 2 has been tested to support the results obtained. This variation is designed to provide a rapidly changing scenario, with a very low number of function evaluations between changes (only 200, instead of the 5000 allowed originally). This second variation will be referred from now on as *high change-frequency*, in contraposition to the original scenario, which will be denominated as *low change-frequency*. Since the multi-QPSO contains 50 particles (50 function evaluations in every iteration), this implies that in the

Table 3. Mean values of the offline error for all the t-q configurations and number of peaks (**low change-frequency**). Values marked with (*) indicate the best (lowest) mean error. Values in bold-face indicate that no statistically significant difference exists with respect to the best value in the row.

Peaks	0t10q	1t9q	2t8q	3t7q	4t6q	5t5q	6t4q	7t3q	8t2q	9t1q	10t0q
5	4.395	3.738	2.911	2.594	2.274	**2.107***	**2.188**	**2.208**	**2.118**	2.492	2.529
10	7.322	6.384	5.816	5.452	4.984	4.954	4.864	**4.682***	**4.939**	**4.95**	5.114
15	8.1	7.353	6.554	6.078	6.239	**5.907**	6.17	**5.905***	**5.961**	6.314	6.48
20	8.832	7.97	7.02	7.005	6.515	**6.439**	**6.099***	6.345	6.908	**6.37**	6.894
25	8.453	8.087	7.557	7.212	6.685	**6.366***	**6.467**	6.367	**6.481**	7.14	7.061
30	8.908	8.533	7.98	7.284	7.542	6.99	**6.666***	**6.722**	**6.716**	7.282	7.164
35	9.194	8.188	8.296	7.861	7.289	**7.057**	**6.778***	**7.012**	**7.006**	**7.083**	7.536
40	8.538	8.294	7.632	7.703	7.542	**7.249**	**7.477**	**7.24**	**7.454**	**7.204***	**7.523**
45	8.593	8.52	7.514	**7.188**	7.248	**6.874***	**7.297**	**7.274**	7.533	7.612	7.796
50	8.403	7.761	7.77	6.871	7.071	7.129	**6.899**	**6.686***	7.194	7.082	8.014
55	8.792	8.533	7.777	7.206	7.603	**6.729***	7.302	7.18	**7.144**	**7.007**	7.563
60	8.705	8.523	8.059	7.238	7.67	7.38	**7.08***	**7.137**	7.343	**7.341**	7.773
65	8.588	7.77	7.705	7.51	7.46	**6.672***	7.248	7.112	7.495	7.581	8.162
70	8.515	8.179	7.983	7.231	**6.996***	7.306	7.138	7.075	7.286	**7.2**	8.087
75	8.554	7.899	7.764	**7.26**	**6.905***	7.016	7.384	7.185	7.135	7.257	7.7
80	8.266	8.082	7.153	**6.786**	6.941	**6.77**	**6.699***	6.967	6.913	7.1	7.206
85	8.781	8.145	7.235	7.516	7.24	7.376	7.092	**6.914***	**6.928**	**7.089**	7.577
90	8.557	8.051	7.088	7.045	6.883	6.771	7.204	**6.444***	**6.814**	7.098	7.587
95	8.434	7.963	7.72	7.271	**6.863**	**6.875**	**6.749***	6.807	**6.981**	**7.052**	7.878
100	8.443	7.571	6.89	6.966	6.67	**6.422***	**6.687**	**6.583**	**6.458**	6.99	7.635

low change-frequency scenario, the algorithm can run for 100 iterations before a change occurs, while in the high change-frequency scenario, this value is reduced to only 4 iterations.

After independently repeating each run 30 times, the average (mean) offline error was calculated, for each $t - q$ configuration, and for every number of peaks. The results for the low change-frequency scenario are shown in table 3, and the ones for the high change-frequency scenario are shown in table 4. For a given number of peaks, each table shows, by rows, the mean of the offline error values obtained by all the $t - q$ configurations. The best (lowest) value of a row is represented with a * symbol.

In order to assess the statistical significance of the results obtained, a non-parametric Mann-Whitney test was performed for every result, compared with respect to the best one in that row (p-$value = 0.05$). Values with no statistically significative difference respect to the best (i.e., *statistically* equal to the best) are shown in bold-face.

4.2 Analysis of the Results

The results in tables 3 and 4 show that the configurations that tend to obtain the best results (those in bold face) are the ones where the number of t-particles

Table 4. Mean values of the offline error for all the t-q configurations and number of peaks (**high change-frequency**). Values marked with (*) indicate the best (lowest) mean error. Values in bold-face indicate that no statistically significant difference exists with respect to the best value in the row.

Peaks	$0t10q$	$1t9q$	$2t8q$	$3t7q$	$4t6q$	$5t5q$	$6t4q$	$7t3q$	$8t2q$	$9t1q$	$10t0q$
5	19.804	18.953	18.723	18.764	19.881	19.67	**17.848***	**18.912**	25.495	29.471	52.622
10	19.654	19.489	18.386	17.981	18.355	**17.494**	**16.573***	**17.524**	17.896	**17.788**	29.239
15	19.677	18.226	17.583	17.06	16.36	16.049	15.771	16.543	**15.367***	**15.525**	18.207
20	19.467	19.175	18.162	17.619	17.575	16.740	16.674	**16.350**	16.291	**15.825***	16.851
25	18.294	17.795	17.018	16.973	16.051	16.057	15.927	**15.484**	**15.331**	**15.150***	17.086
30	19.970	18.985	18.045	17.733	16.675	16.048	15.987	15.978	**15.244***	**15.359**	17.577
35	19.351	18.659	18.159	17.827	17.355	16.779	15.993	**15.179***	**15.417**	16.032	**15.688**
40	17.891	18.071	16.539	16.776	16.763	15.654	15.112	**14.483**	15.013	15.179	**14.461***
45	17.975	17.477	16.572	16.858	15.925	15.805	**14.852**	**15.111**	15.366	15.567	**14.777***
50	18.647	17.979	17.393	16.519	16.156	15.841	15.482	15.227	**14.918**	**14.710***	14.993
55	18.208	17.568	17.152	16.433	16.351	15.87	16.171	15.312	**14.567***	14.988	14.809
60	17.407	16.374	16.057	16.158	15.868	**14.862**	15.323	15.041	**14.428***	14.547	14.748
65	18.353	17.330	16.178	16.536	16.630	15.950	15.697	**15.25**	14.982	**14.86***	14.929
70	17.339	17.508	16.425	16.216	16.521	15.443	16.259	15.725	15.342	**15.168**	**15.108***
75	17.762	17.893	16.492	16.559	16.621	15.613	**15.411**	15.682	**15.552**	**15.081***	15.996
80	16.968	15.994	15.942	15.595	15.822	15.142	15.082	**14.517***	16.062	15.043	15.159
85	16.781	16.699	16.394	15.309	15.014	15.332	15.151	**14.379***	14.703	14.756	14.865
90	17.342	16.842	16.133	16.178	**15.270**	15.719	**15.045**	14.891	14.995	**14.885***	15.326
95	17.569	16.842	16.571	15.806	15.573	15.253	15.291	15.265	**14.489***	14.827	14.821
100	16.796	15.709	15.505	15.777	14.840	14.246	15.464	14.645	14.625	**13.756***	14.401

is higher than the number of q-particles. This tendency is even more pronounced for the high change-frequency scenario, where the $10t0q$ configuration (i.e., no q-particles at all) obtains, in 10 experiments, the best result or one with no statistically significant difference with respect to the best.

Further support for these results can be obtained by observing the number of times that a particle of a certain type is the best of a swarm in an iteration. Figure 1 shows this in two histograms, where the distribution of each particle type's contribution to the best is depicted for every iteration in a change. The histograms where done using a $7t3q$ configuration for the 10 peak, low change-frequency scenario (100 iterations/change). However, histograms for the resting configurations, not presented here for space reasons, yield almost identical figures.

From the histograms, it can be seen that q-particles have their maximum impact on the swarm's best in the first iterations after a change in the environment, while t-particles, on the other hand, tend to contribute more often as time passes by. Also, it is clearly shown that, in total numbers, t-particles contribute very much oftener to the best of a swarm than q-particles.

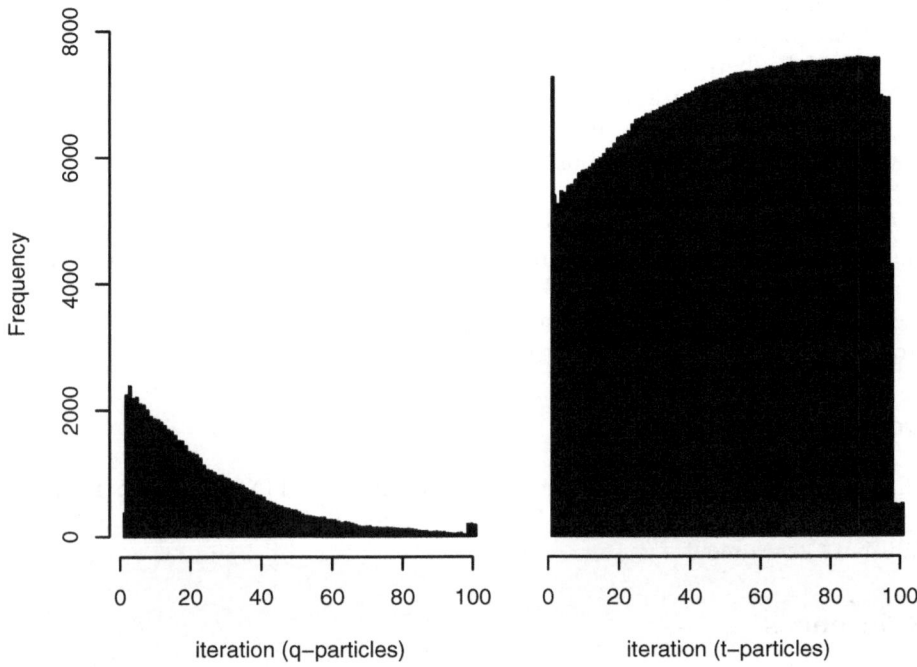

Fig. 1. Histogram representing the number of times each particle type contributed to its swarm's best, distributed over the 100 iterations of each change. Left panel shows q-particles distribution; right panel shows t-particle distribution.

5   Conclusions and Future Work

In this work we have presented an analysis of the properties of quantum and trajectory particles on a multi-QPSO algorithm. The objective was to determine how each type contributes to the evolution of the optimization process of a swarm, which would help in the design of more efficient techniques for the PSO. The experimentation has been conducted on two variants of the Scenario 2 of the Moving Peaks Benchmark, one with low change-frequency (5000 function evaluations between changes) and one with high change-frequency (200 function evaluations between changes).

The results obtained for each scenario suggest that an equal number of quantum and trajectory particles is not the best configuration, and those in which the number of t-particles is higher than the number of q-particles usually perform better. An analysis of the distribution of the best particle of a swarm, by particle types, also shows that t-particles contribute more oftener to the best. Only at the very first iterations after a change, q-particles may contribute more effectively. This supports the idea that q-particles are better suited for exploration (which is more necessary just after a change, where the conditions are no longer equal) and that t-particles behave better for intensification.

From the results, it can be concluded that a high number of q-particles yields to a waste of function evaluations in the middle and last iterations of a change, that could be better used by t-particles for converging to a peak. However, although the contribution of the q-particles is greatly overcame by t-particles performance, it cannot be dismissed, since their actions help to quickly find a new peak after a change, and usually give more stability to the overall behavior of the algorithm.

As future work, since quantum particles contribute mostly at the beginning of the search after a change has occurred, it seems reasonable to think that a good strategy would be to dynamically increase the number of quantum particles once a change in the environment is detected, and then gradually switch the proportion in favor of trajectory particles.

Acknowledgements

This work has been partially funded by the project TIN2008-01948 from the Spanish Ministry of Science and Technology, and P07-TIC-02970 from the Andalusian Government.

References

[1] Blackwell, T.: Particle swarm optimization in dynamic environments. In: Evolutionary Computation in Dynamic and Uncertain Environments, vol. 51, pp. 29–49. Springer, Heidelberg (2007)

[2] Blackwell, T., Branke, J.: Multi-swarm optimization in dynamic environments. In: Raidl, G.R., Cagnoni, S., Branke, J., Corne, D.W., Drechsler, R., Jin, Y., Johnson, C.G., Machado, P., Marchiori, E., Rothlauf, F., Smith, G.D., Squillero, G. (eds.) EvoWorkshops 2004. LNCS, vol. 3005, pp. 489–500. Springer, Heidelberg (2004)

[3] Blackwell, T., Branke, J.: Multiswarms, exclusion, and anti-convergence in dynamic environments. IEEE Transactions on Evolutionary Computation 10(4), 459–472 (2006)

[4] Blackwell, T.M.: Swarms in dynamic environments. In: Cantú-Paz, E., Foster, J.A., Deb, K., Davis, L., Roy, R., O'Reilly, U.-M., Beyer, H.-G., Kendall, G., Wilson, S.W., Harman, M., Wegener, J., Dasgupta, D., Potter, M.A., Schultz, A., Dowsland, K.A., Jonoska, N., Miller, J., Standish, R.K. (eds.) GECCO 2003. LNCS, vol. 2723. Springer, Heidelberg (2003)

[5] Blackwell, T.M.: Particle swarms and population diversity. Soft Computing 9(11), 793–802 (2005)

[6] Branke, J.: Memory enhanced evolutionary algorithms for changing optimization problems. In: Congress on Evolutionary Computation CEC'99, pp. 1875–1882. IEEE, Los Alamitos (1999)

[7] Branke, J., Schmeck, H.: Designing evolutionary algorithms for dynamic optimization problems. In: Advances in evolutionary computing: theory and applications, pp. 239–262 (2003)

[8] Clerc, M., Kennedy, J.: The particle swarm - explosion, stability, and convergence in a multidimensional complex space. IEEE Transactions on Evolutionary Computation 6(1), 58–73 (2002)

 [9] Eberhart, R.C., Shi, Y.: Comparing inertia weights and constriction factors in particle swarm optimization. In: Proceedings of the 2000 Congress on Evolutionary Computation, vol. 1, pp. 84–88 (2000)
[10] Janson, S., Middendorf, M.: A hierarchical particle swarm optimizer for dynamic optimization problems. In: Raidl, G.R., Cagnoni, S., Branke, J., Corne, D.W., Drechsler, R., Jin, Y., Johnson, C.G., Machado, P., Marchiori, E., Rothlauf, F., Smith, G.D., Squillero, G. (eds.) EvoWorkshops 2004. LNCS, vol. 3005, pp. 513–524. Springer, Heidelberg (2004)
[11] Kennedy, J., Eberhart, R.: Particle swarm optimization. In: Proceedings of IEEE International Conference on Neural Networks, vol. 4, pp. 1942–1948 (1995)
[12] Li, J.-P., Balazs, M.E., Parks, G.T., Clarkson, P.J.: A species conserving genetic algorithm for multimodal function optimization. Evol. Comput. 10(3), 207–234 (2002)
[13] Parrott, D., Li, X.: A particle swarm model for tracking multiple peaks in a dynamic environment using speciation. In: Proceedings of the 2004 Congress on Evolutionary Computation, CEC 2004, vol. 1, pp. 98–103 (2004)
[14] Parsopoulos, K.E., Vrahatis, M.N.: Recent approaches to global optimization problems through particle swarm optimization. Natural Computing 1, 235–306 (2002)

An Incremental Learning Method for Neural Networks Based on Sensitivity Analysis

Beatriz Pérez-Sánchez, Oscar Fontenla-Romero, and Bertha Guijarro-Berdiñas

Department of Computer Science
Faculty of Informatics, University of A Coruña
Campus de Elviña s/n, 15071, A Coruña, Spain
{bperezs,ofontenla,cibertha}@udc.es

Abstract. The Sensitivity-Based Linear Learning Method (SBLLM) is a learning method for two-layer feedforward neural networks based on sensitivity analysis that calculates the weights by solving a linear system of equations. Therefore, there is an important saving in computational time which significantly enhances the behavior of this method as compared to other batch learning algorithms. The SBLLM works in batch mode; however, there exist several reasons that justify the need for an on-line version of this algorithm. Among them, it can be mentioned the need for real time learning for many environments in which the information is not available at the outset but rather, is continually acquired, or in those situations in which large databases have to be managed but the computing resources are limited. In this paper an incremental version of the SBLLM is presented. The theoretical basis for the method is given and its performance is illustrated by comparing the results obtained by the on-line and batch mode versions of the algorithm.

1 Introduction

Many algorithms for training neural networks can be found in the literature. In the case of feedforward multilayer neural networks, most of them are based on the classical gradient descent method proposed by Rumelhart et al. [1]. This approach can be very slow, particularly for multilayered networks where the cost surface is typically non-quadratic, non-convex, and highly dimensional with many local minima and/ or flat regions. Moreover, there is no formula to guarantee that:

- the network will converge to a good solution,
- convergence is swift, or
- convergence even occurs at all.

In order to alleviate as far as possible, these problems, several variations of the classical gradient descent algorithm and new methods have been proposed, such as, adaptive step size, appropriate weights initialization, rescaling of variables, or even second order methods and methods based on linear least-squares. In [2] we find a description of the Sensitivity-Based Linear Learning Method (SBLLM),

P. Meseguer, L. Mandow, and R.M. Gasca (Eds.): CAEPIA 2009, LNAI 5988, pp. 42–50, 2010.

a novel supervised learning method for two-layer feedforward neural networks. This method is based on sensitivity analysis and it consists in using a linear training algorithm for each of the two layers. Its main innovations are: 1) the cost function that is minimized is based on the sensitivities of each layer's parameter with respect to its inputs and outputs and 2) the weights of each layer of the network are calculated by solving a linear system of equations. As a result, the method reaches a minimum error in few epochs of training and exhibits a higher speed when compared to other classical methods, as demonstrated in [2].

This learning algorithm is a batch method, since during the learning process the complete set of samples is provided in each iteration or epoch, so the weights changes depend on the whole set of learning examples. Nevertheless, there exists several learning environments in which the information is not available at the outset but rather is continually received and the learning algorithm must allow real-time learning. Therefore, the main difference between on-line and batch methods is that in on-line learning [6,7,8], samples are provided to the network on a one by one basis or in small packages (mini-batches) and these reduced sets are used sequentially in order to change the weights. Another situation in which on-line learning is also useful occurs when the available data sets are very large, so that its complete management would be unwieldy for those methods when the computer resources are limited.

Summarizing, some of the most important advantages that the on-line learning presents with respect to batch learning, are [8]

1. Often decreases the convergence time, particularly when data sets are large and contain redundant information.
2. An incremental learning system updates its hypotheses as a new instance arrives without reexamining old instances.
3. It is both spatially and temporally economical since it does not need to store and reprocess old instances.
4. It is crucial for a learning system which continually receives inputs and must process it in a real-time manner.
5. It can be used for tracking changes.

For the reasons cited above, and considering the profitable characteristics of the original algorithm previously mentioned, an incremental version of the SBLLM is presented. The paper is structured as follows. In Section 2 the on-line learning method for the SBLLM is described and the incorporated modifications for the algorithm to work in on-line mode are indicated. Section 3 contains some experimental results using several classification data sets in order to check the performance of the method when it works in batch and on-line mode. Finally, in Section 4 some conclusions are given.

2   On-Line Sensitivity Learning Algorithm

Consider the feedforward neural network illustrated in Fig.1. S being the size of the training data set, with I inputs, x_{is}, and J desired outputs, d_{js}. During the learning process samples can be provided to the network on a one by one basis or in small packages (mini-batches) unlike batch learning where the complete set of samples is provided in each iteration.

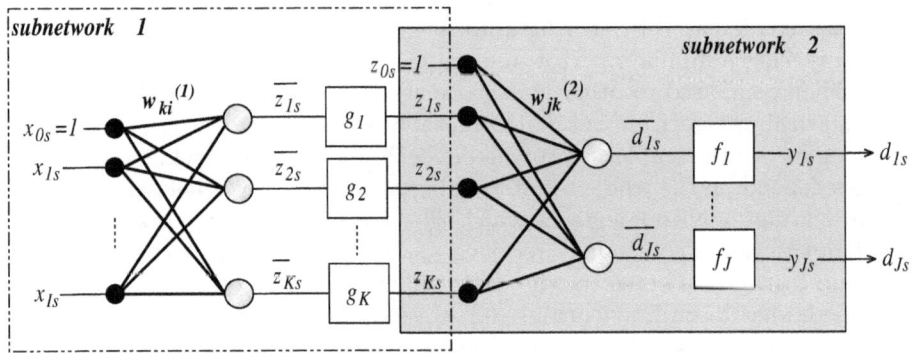

Fig. 1. Two-layer feedforward neural network

The proposed learning method considers this network as composed of two subnetworks (see Fig. 1). The novelty of the SBLLM is that the weights of layers 1 and 2 are calculated independently by minimizing for each layer l a loss function, $Q^{(l)}$. This function measures the training error that is usually based on the mean squared error. The SBLLM considers Q as the sum of squared errors *before* the nonlinear activation functions (g_k and f_j) instead of *after* them as is normally the case. Therefore, z_{ks} being the desired output for hidden neuron z and $\bar{z}_{ks} = g_k^{-1}(z_{ks})$, the alternative loss function used for solving subnetwork 1 can be written as

$$Q^{(1)} = \sum_{s=1}^{S} \sum_{k=1}^{K} \left(\sum_{i=0}^{I} w_{ki}^{(1)} x_{is} - \bar{z}_{ks} \right)^2, \tag{1}$$

Analogously, the loss function for the subnetwork 2 is defined,

$$Q^{(2)} = \sum_{s=1}^{S} \sum_{j=1}^{J} \left(\sum_{k=0}^{K} w_{jk}^{(2)} z_{ks} - \bar{d}_{js} \right)^2, \tag{2}$$

where $\bar{d}_{js} = f_j^{-1}(d_{js})$, d_{js} being the desired output for output neuron j. This loss function, that measures the error before the nonlinearity, was proposed in [3,4,5]. In these previous works it was shown that the optimum of this alternative loss function, up to first order of a Taylor series, is the same as that of the loss function that is obtained when the sum of squared errors *after* the nonlinear activation functions is employed. The advantage of the presented loss function is that the optimum set of weights, for each layer, can be easily calculated by solving a system of linear equations that are obtained deriving $Q^{(1)}$ and $Q^{(2)}$

with respect to the weights and equating to zero. Considering the ideas previously commented upon, the proposed learning method is described.

Step 0: Initialization. Initialize the outputs of the intermediate layer as the outputs associated with some random weights $\mathbf{w}^{(1)}(0)$ plus a small random error,

$$z_{ks} = g_k \left(\sum_{i=0}^{I} w_{ki}^{(1)}(0)x_{is} \right) + \epsilon_{ks}; \quad \epsilon_{ks} \sim U(-\eta, \eta); k = 1, \ldots, K; s = 1, \ldots, S,$$

where η is a small number.

For every available mini-batch of samples the algorithm performs the following steps,

Step 1: Subproblem solution. The weights of layers 1 and 2 are calculated independently by minimizing for each layer l its loss function, by solving the system of linear equations that are obtained deriving $Q^{(1)}$ and $Q^{(2)}$ with respect to the weights and equating to zero. That is:

$$\sum_{i=0}^{I} A_{pi}^{(1)} w_{ki}^{(1)} = b_{pk}^{(1)}; \quad p = 0, 1, \ldots, I; \quad k = 1, \ldots, K$$

$$\sum_{k=0}^{K} A_{qk}^{(2)} w_{jk}^{(2)} = b_{qj}^{(2)}; \quad q = 0, \ldots, K; \quad j = 1, \ldots, J,$$

with $A_{pi}^{(1)} = \hat{A}_{pi}^{(1)} + \sum_{s=1}^{M} x_{is}x_{ps}; \quad b_{pk}^{(1)} = \hat{b}_{pk}^{(1)} + \sum_{s=1}^{M} \bar{z}_{ks}x_{ps}; \quad \bar{z}_{ks} = g_k^{-1}(z_{ks})$

and $A_{qk}^{(2)} = \hat{A}_{qk}^{(2)} + \sum_{s=1}^{M} z_{ks}z_{qs}; \quad b_{qj}^{(2)} = \hat{b}_{qj}^{(2)} + \sum_{s=1}^{M} \bar{d}_{js}z_{qs}; \quad \bar{d}_{js} = f_j^{-1}(d_{js})$

M being the size of the mini-batch that is being considered in the current iteration, and $\hat{A}^{(l)}$ and $\hat{b}^{(l)}(l = 1, 2)$ are the matrices that store the coefficients obtained in previous epochs to calculate the values of the weights. This is the main difference with respect to the original algorithm as these old coefficients are further used in order to calculate the new weights in the current iteration. Therefore, this permits handling the knowledge previously acquired and using it to progressively approach the optimum value of the weights. In this way, we convert the original learning algorithm into an on-line method that is updating its knowledge depending on the information that is acquired over time. In the initial epoch of the process the matrices $\hat{A}^{(l)}$ and $\hat{b}^{(l)}$ contain values equal to zero. This is due to the fact that the learning process begins without any type of previous knowledge.

Step 2: Evaluate the sum of squared errors. Using the new weights obtained in the previous step, the MSE is evaluated for the entire network and also the new cost function defined as $Q(\mathbf{z}) = Q^{(1)}(\mathbf{z}) + Q^{(2)}(\mathbf{z})$. This cost function measures the global error of the network as the sum of the errors of each layer but *before* the nonlinearities, as opposed to the MSE. Later on, based on this cost function, the new values of the $\mathbf{z}$ will be obtained.

Step 3: Convergence checking. If $|Q - Q_{previous}| < \gamma$ or $|MSE_{previous} - MSE| < \gamma'$ stop and return the weights and the sensitivities. Otherwise, continue with Step 4. Initially, the values of $Q_{previous}$ and $MSE_{previous}$ will be arbitrary large numbers.

Step 4: Check improvement of Q. If $Q > Q_{previous}$ reduce the value of ρ, and restore the weights, $\mathbf{z} = \mathbf{z}_{previous}$, $Q = Q_{previous}$ and go to Step 5. Otherwise, store the values $Q_{previous} = Q$, $MSE_{previous} = MSE$ and $\mathbf{z}_{previous} = \mathbf{z}$ and obtain the sensitivities of the cost function Q with respect to the output $\mathbf{z}$ of the hidden layer,

$$\frac{\partial Q}{\partial z_{ks}} = \frac{\partial Q^{(1)}}{\partial z_{ks}} + \frac{\partial Q^{(2)}}{\partial z_{ks}}$$

where, $\dfrac{\partial Q^{(1)}}{\partial z_{ks}}$ and $\dfrac{\partial Q^{(2)}}{\partial z_{ks}}$ are defined as,

$$\frac{\partial Q^{(1)}}{\partial z_{ks}} = \frac{-2\left(\sum_{i=0}^{I} w_{ki}^{(1)} x_{is} - g_k^{-1}(z_{ks})\right)}{g_k(z_{ks})}$$

$$\frac{\partial Q^{(2)}}{\partial z_{ks}} = 2\sum_{j=1}^{J}\left(\sum_{r=0}^{K} w_{jr}^{(2)} z_{rs} - f_j^{-1}(d_{js})\right) w_{jk}^{(2)}$$

being $\bar{z}_{ks} = g_k^{-1}(z_{ks})$, $\bar{d}_{js} = f^{-1}(d_{js})$, $k = 1, ..., K; j = 1, ..., J$ and $z_{0s} = 1, \forall s$.

Step 5: Update intermediate outputs. Using the Taylor series approximation over the cost function,

$$Q(\mathbf{z} + \Delta\mathbf{z}) = Q(\mathbf{z}) + \sum_{k=0}^{K}\sum_{s=1}^{S} \frac{\partial Q(\mathbf{z})}{\partial z_{ks}} \Delta z_{ks} \approx 0,$$

the following increments are calculated to update the desired outputs of the hidden neurons $\Delta\mathbf{z} = -\rho\dfrac{Q(\mathbf{z})}{||\nabla Q||^2}\nabla Q$, where ρ is a relaxation factor or step size. This procedure continues from Step 1 using the next mini-batch until a convergence condition is achieved.

3   Experimental Results

In this section we want to check the performance of the SBLLM algorithm when it operates in batch and on-line mode. The aim is to verify that the on-line method does not degrade the performance of the batch learning. If the results obtained are similar, the SBLLM can be applied properly to environments that have to work in a real-time manner.

For this reason, the on-line version of the learning algorithm is illustrated by its application to several binary classification problems. We have chosen several data sets and network sizes in order to verify the performance in different situations. These data sets were obtained from two on-line standard repositories. Housing and Forest CoverType data sets were obtained from the UCI Machine Learning Repository [10] whereas Dim and Mushroom data sets from the Data Mining Institute of the University of Wisconsin [11]. The conditions of the experiments are summarized in table 1, regarding the number of attributes, number of samples of each data sets and the topology of the neural network. The topology column indicates the number of units used for the input, hidden and output layers.

For the experimentation, we use the original databases facilitated in the references for the Housing, Dim and Mushroom data sets. However in the case of Forest CoverType, a variation of the initial data set is used, for the following reason. The original database contains data describing the wilderness areas and soil types for 30x30 meter cells obtained from US Forest Service Region 2 Resource Information System data. It is a real classification problem whose goal is to determine the forest cover type from 54 input variables. Firstly, the problem considers 7 cover classes, although for this paper we have employed the 2-class version of the problem that consist of distinguishing the most frequent class from the other six [9]. This database contains 500,000 examples from which we built a training set of 101,241 examples, a validation set of 10,123 and a test set of 50,620 examples. These sets preserve the same proportion of samples of the seven classes as in the original data set.

Table 1. Characteristics of the classification data sets

Data Set	Attributes	Instances	Topology
Dim data	14	4,192	14–40–2
Mush data	22	8,124	22–40–2
Housing data	13	506	13–30–2
Forest CoverType	54	101,241	54–100–2

We have run the learning algorithm operating in different modes. The experimental results show the performance obtained by the algorithm when working in, 1) batch mode (original learning algorithm), 2) with mini-batches (10, 50 and 100 packages of samples of the whole data set) and 3) on-line mode. In order to be comparable, all versions of the SBLLM were run under the same following conditions:

- The input data set was normalized (in the interval [-0.95,0.95]).
- The arctan and logsig functions were used for hidden and output neurons respectively. Regarding the number of hidden units of the networks it is

important to remark that the aim was not to investigate the optimal one for each data set, however, the topology of the network in each problem is determined by the dimension of the input and output data.
- Step size equal to 0.2.
- In order to obtain statistically significant results, 10 (for housing, dim and mushroom) or 5 simulations (forest data set) were performed using for each one a different initial set of values for **z**, which were randomly generated from a normal distribution $N(0.5, 0.01)$ and subsequently normalized in the interval [-0.95,0.95] to be in the output range of the activation functions. Also for each simulation the performance was calculated using 10-fold cross validation for all data sets except the Forest Covertype. This last database is already divided into three sets (training, test and validation) and consequently we did not apply the cross validation.
- Dim, Mushroom and Housing data sets were run on an Intel Core Quad 2.40Ghz processor and 4GB of memory. For the Forest CoverType data set the execution was carried out on an Intel Xeon MP 3.16GHz processor and 29GB of memory.

Tables 2, 3, 4 and 5 display the performance measures obtained for the Dim, Mushroom, Housing and Forest CoverType data sets respectively. The first column in these tables indicates the number of samples which are managed by the algorithm in each epoch of the learning process. The second and third columns show the mean classification accuracy and the corresponding standard deviations for the training and test data sets. Finally, the last column indicates the mean and standard deviation CPU time per epoch, in seconds, needed by each version of the learning algorithm. In the case of the Forest CoverType data set (see Table 5) an additional column for the results of the validation data set is shown. This database contains a large number of examples, it makes possible to have an independent validation set, as previously mentioned.

Table 2. Performance Measures for Dim data set

$Samples/epoch$	$Train_{mean\pm std}$	$Test_{mean\pm std}$	$Tepoch_{mean\pm std}$
Batch	$95.086 \pm 7.318 \times 10^{-2}$	94.810 ± 0.128	$1.791 \times 10^{-1} \pm 3.966 \times 10^{-3}$
419	$93.450 \pm 1.291 \times 10^{-1}$	93.387 ± 0.195	$2.550 \times 10^{-2} \pm 5.384 \times 10^{-4}$
84	$93.484 \pm 7.839 \times 10^{-1}$	93.249 ± 0.201	$2.709 \times 10^{-2} \pm 8.402 \times 10^{-4}$
42	$94.685 \pm 8.233 \times 10^{-2}$	94.407 ± 0.206	$3.835 \times 10^{-2} \pm 1.555 \times 10^{-3}$
On-line	$95.034 \pm 1.105 \times 10^{-1}$	94.824 ± 0.276	$2.886 \times 10^{-2} \pm 3.390 \times 10^{-3}$

As can be observed in all data sets the performance obtained by the on-line method is similar to that reached by the batch version. This supposes that the on-line learning does not entail degradation in the performance of the algorithm. Moreover, the last column of the tables shows that the on-line method requires less time per epoch, this result is evident because the algorithm treats a minor number of samples per epoch. Nevertheless, this fact allows optimizing the use of the available computer resources. A sample of this is the Forest Covertype

Table 3. Performance Measures for Mushroom data set

Samples/epoch	$Train_{mean\pm std}$	$Test_{mean\pm std}$	$Tepoch_{mean\pm std}$
Batch	83.173 ± 0.579	82.985 ± 0.531	$4.297 \times 10^{-1} \pm 7.375 \times 10^{-3}$
812	82.731 ± 0.618	82.712 ± 0.765	$6.323 \times 10^{-2} \pm 1.906 \times 10^{-3}$
162	82.323 ± 0.529	82.164 ± 0.418	$4.004 \times 10^{-2} \pm 4.004 \times 10^{-2}$
81	81.928 ± 0.521	81.797 ± 0.645	$3.615 \times 10^{-2} \pm 3.615 \times 10^{-2}$
On-line	83.177 ± 0.662	82.913 ± 0.776	$3.019 \times 10^{-2} \pm 3.019 \times 10^{-2}$

Table 4. Performance Measures for the Housing data set

Samples/epoch	$Train_{mean\pm std}$	$Test_{mean\pm std}$	$Tepoch_{mean\pm std}$
Batch	87.084 ± 0.218	85.294 ± 1.124	$3.309 \times 10^{-2} \pm 2.062 \times 10^{-3}$
50	85.709 ± 0.208	84.121 ± 1.075	$2.064 \times 10^{-2} \pm 1.224 \times 10^{-3}$
10	81.222 ± 0.648	78.219 ± 1.276	$2.332 \times 10^{-2} \pm 2.189 \times 10^{-3}$
5	86.447 ± 0.288	84.155 ± 0.933	$2.309 \times 10^{-2} \pm 2.579 \times 10^{-3}$
On-line	87.323 ± 0.221	84.607 ± 0.497	$2.332 \times 10^{-2} \pm 2.738 \times 10^{-3}$

Table 5. Performance Measures for Forest CoverType data set

Samples/epoch	$Train_{mean\pm std}$	$Test_{mean\pm std}$	$Valid_{mean\pm std}$	$Tepoch_{mean\pm std}$
Batch	75.443 ± 0.028	75.664 ± 0.017	75.462 ± 0.014	1009.90 ± 1.635
10,124	75.139 ± 0.011	75.390 ± 0.021	75.151 ± 0.007	89.533 ± 0.317
2,024	75.424 ± 0.038	75.669 ± 0.036	75.467 ± 0.049	8.068 ± 0.071
1,012	75.013 ± 0.054	75.337 ± 0.074	75.195 ± 0.014	3.475 ± 0.052
On-line	75.549 ± 0.027	75.885 ± 0.198	75.654 ± 0.132	0.489 ± 0.045

database. In this case, the batch method is unapproachable for an Intel Core Quad 2.40Ghz processor and 4GB of memory, whereas employing whether the on-line mode or mini-batches, the execution can be carried out without any type of problem.

4   Conclusions

A well designed on-line learning algorithm learns just as fast as any batch algorithm in terms of the number of samples. Furthermore, on-line learning algorithms require less computing resources per example, and thus are able to process more examples for a given amount of computing resources. Incremental (on-line) learning is a feasible learning strategy for machine learning problems specially if the network does not possess sufficient initial knowledge, as the network could start with little knowledge and later on achieve a satisfactory result. In this paper, we have developed an on-line method for the learning algorithm SBLLM. The experimental results have demonstrated that no degradation in the performance of the algorithm exists when it operates in on-line mode rather than employing the whole data set in each iteration of the process. This approach allows its use in a real time environment as well as working with large data sets since it permits an optimum employment of the available computer resources.

Acknowledgements

We would like to acknowledge support for this work from the Xunta de Galicia (project 08TIC012105PR) and the Ministerio de Ciencia e Innovación, Spain (project TIN2009-104748 and TIN2006-02402, partially supported by the European Union ERDF).

References

1. Rumelhart, D.E., Hinton, G.E., Willian, R.J.: Learning Representations of Back-Propagation Errors. Nature 323, 533–536 (1986)
2. Castillo, E., Guijarro-Berdiñas, B., Fontenla-Romero, O., Alonso-Betanzos, A.: A very fast learning method for Neural Networks Based on Sensitivity Analysis. Journal of Machine Learning Research 7, 1159–1182 (2006)
3. Castillo, E., Fontenla-Romero, O., Alonso-Betanzos, A., Guijarro-Berdiñas, B.: A Global Optimum Approach for One-Layer Neural Networks. Neural Computation 14(6), 1429–1449 (2002)
4. Erdogmus, D., Fontenla-Romero, O., Principe, J.C., Alonso-Betanzos, A., Castillo, E.: Linear-Least-Squares Initialization of Multilayer Perceptrons Through Backpropagation of the Desired Response. IEEE Transactions on Neural Network 16(2), 325–337 (2005)
5. Fontenla-Romero, O., Erdogmus, D., Principe, J.C., Alonso-Betanzos, A., Castillo, E.: Linear least-squares based methods for neural networks learning. In: Kaynak, O., Alpaydın, E., Oja, E., Xu, L. (eds.) ICANN 2003 and ICONIP 2003. LNCS, vol. 2714, pp. 84–91. Springer, Heidelberg (2003)
6. Bottou, L.: Stochastic Learning. In: Bousquet, O., von Luxburg, U., Rätsch, G. (eds.) Machine Learning 2003. LNCS (LNAI), vol. 3176, pp. 146–168. Springer, Heidelberg (2004)
7. Moller, M.: Supervised learning on large redundant training sets. Neural Networks for Signal Processing II, 79–89 (1992)
8. LeCun, Y.A., Bottou, L., Orr, G.B., Müller, K.-R.: Efficient backProp. In: Orr, G.B., Müller, K.-R. (eds.) NIPS-WS 1996. LNCS, vol. 1524, p. 9. Springer, Heidelberg (1998)
9. Collobert, R., Bengio, Y., Bengio, S.: Scaling large learning problems with hard parallel mixtures. International Journal of Pattern Recognition and Artificial Intelligence 17(3), 349–365 (2003)
10. Newman, D., Hettich, S., Blake, C., Merz, C.: UCI repository of machine learning databases (1998), http://www.ics.uci.edu/~mlearn/MLRepository.html
11. Mangasarian, O.L., Ramakrishnan, R.: Data Mining Intitute, Computer Sciences Department, University of Wisconsin (1999), http://www.cs.wisc.edu/dmi

A Multi-objective Neuro-evolutionary Algorithm to Obtain Interpretable Fuzzy Models

Gracia Sánchez, Fernando Jiménez, José F. Sánchez, and José M. Alcaraz

Department of Ingeniería de la Información y las Comunicaciones – University of Murcia
{gracia,fernan}@um.es, jsanchez@ditec.um.es, josem.alcaraz@carm.es

Abstract. In this paper, a multi-objective constrained optimization model is proposed to improve interpretability of TSK fuzzy models. This approach allows
a linguistic approximation of the fuzzy models. A multi-objective evolutionary
algorithm is implemented with three different selection and generational replace-
ments schemata (Niched Preselection, NSGA-II and ENORA) to generate fuzzy
models in the proposed optimization context. The results clearly show a real ability and effectiveness of the proposed approach to find accurate and interpretable
TSK fuzzy models. These schemata have been compared in terms of accuracy, interpretability and compactness by using three test problems studied in literature.
Statistical tests have also been used with optimality and diversity multi-objective
metrics to compare the schemata.

Keywords: TSK Fuzzy Models, Multi-objective Evolutionary Algorithms, RBF
Neural Networks.

1 Introduction

Evolutionary Algorithms (EA) [6] have been successfully applied to learn fuzzy models
[10]. EAs have been also combined with other techniques like fuzzy clustering [7] and
neural networks [12]. This has resulted in many complex algorithms and, as recognized
in [18] and [15], often interpretability of the resulting rule base is not considered to
be of importance. In such cases, the fuzzy model becomes a black-box, and one can
question the rationale for applying fuzzy modeling instead of other techniques.

On the other hand, EAs have been recognized as appropriate techniques for multi-
objective optimization because they perform a search for multiple solutions in parallel [3,5]. Current evolutionary approaches for multi-objective optimization consist of
multi-objective EAs based on the Pareto optimality notion, in which all objectives are
optimized simultaneously to find multiple non-dominated solutions in a single run of
the EA. The decision maker can then choose the most appropriate solution according
to the current decision environment at the end of the EA run. Moreover, if the decision
environment changes, it is not always necessary to run the EA again. Another solution
may be chosen out of the set of non-dominated solutions that has already been obtained.

The multi-objective evolutionary approach can be considered from the fuzzy modeling perspective [9]. Current research lines in fuzzy modeling mostly tackle improving
accuracy in descriptive models, and improving interpretability in approximative models

P. Meseguer, L. Mandow, and R.M. Gasca (Eds.): CAEPIA 2009, LNAI 5988, pp. 51–60, 2010.

[2]. This paper deals with the second issue approaching the problem by means of multi-objective optimization in which accuracy and compactness criteria are simultaneously optimized while interpretability is reached by means of similarity constraints imposed to the fuzzy sets.

In this paper, we propose a neuro-evolutionary multi-objective optimization approach to generate TSK fuzzy models considering accuracy, interpretability and compactness criteria. A multi-objective constrained optimization model is proposed. Three different selection and generational replacement schemata have been implemented: Niched pre-selection, NSGA-II and ENORA. Section 2 describes the TSK type rule-based fuzzy model, and criteria taken into account for fuzzy modeling. Section 3 shows the main components of the three implemented neuro-evolutionary multi-objective algorithms. Section 4 shows the experiments performed and the results obtained for three test problem studied in literature. Finally, section 5 concludes the paper.

2   Improving Interpretability in TSK Fuzzy Models

2.1   Fuzzy Models Identification

We consider Takagi-Sugeno-Kang (TSK) type rule-based models [17] where rule consequents are taken to be linear functions of the inputs. The rules have, therefore, the following expression:

$$R_i : \textbf{If } x_1 \text{ is } A_{i1} \textbf{ and } \ldots \textbf{ and } x_n \text{ is } A_{in} \textbf{ then } y_i = \theta_{i1}x_1 + \ldots + \theta_{in}x_n + \theta_{i(n+1)}$$

where $i = 1,\ldots,M$, M is the number of rules, $\boldsymbol{x} = (x_1,\ldots,x_n)$, $x_i \in [l_i,u_i] \subset \mathfrak{R}$, is the input vector, $\theta_{ij} \in [l,u] \subset \mathfrak{R}$ are the consequent parameters, y_i is the output of the ith rule, A_{ij} are fuzzy sets defined in the antecedent space by membership functions $\mu_{A_{ij}} : \mathcal{X}_j \to [0,1]$, being $\mathcal{X}_j$ the domain of the input variable x_j. The total output of the model is computed by aggregating the individual contributions of each rule: $y = \sum_{i=1}^{M} \mu_i(\boldsymbol{x})y_i / \sum_{i=1}^{M} \mu_i(\boldsymbol{x})$ where $\mu_i(\boldsymbol{x}) = \prod_{j=1}^{n} \mu_{A_{ij}}(x_j)$ is the normalized firing strength of the ith rule and each fuzzy set A_{ij} is described by a gaussian membership function:

$$\mu_{A_{ij}}(x_j) = \exp\left[-\frac{1}{2}\left(\frac{x_j - a_{ij}}{\sigma_{ij}}\right)^2\right]$$

where $a_{ij} \in [l_j,u_j]$ is the center, and $\sigma_{ij} > 0$ is the variance. This fuzzy model can be defined by a radial basis function neural network. The number of neurons in the hidden layer of an RBF neural network is equal to the number of rules in the fuzzy model. The firing strength of the ith neuron in the hidden layer matches the firing strength of the ith rule in the fuzzy model. We apply a gaussian membership function defined by two parameters, (a_{ij},σ_{ij}): the center a_{ij} and variance σ_{ij}. Therefore, each neuron in the hidden layer has these two parameters that define its firing strength value.

The neurons in the output layer perform the computations for the first order linear function described in the consequents of the fuzzy model, therefore, the ith neuron of the output layer has the parameters $\boldsymbol{\theta}_i = \left(\theta_{i1},\ldots,\theta_{i(n+1)}\right)$ that correspond to the linear function defined in the ith rule of the fuzzy model.

Criteria for Fuzzy Modeling. We consider three main criteria: accuracy, transparency, and compactness. It is necessary to define quantitative measures for these criteria by means of appropriate objective functions which define the complete fuzzy model identification.

(1) *Accuracy.* The accuracy of a model can be measured with the *mean squared error*:

$$MSE = \frac{1}{N} \sum_{k=1}^{N} (y_k - t_k)^2 \tag{1}$$

where y_k is the model output for the kth input vector, t_k is the desired output for the kth input vector, and N is the number of data samples.

(2) *Transparency.* For transparency, there are many possible measures, however we consider one of the most used, the *similarity* [14]. The similarity S among distinct fuzzy sets in each variable can be expressed as $S = \max \{ S(A_{ij}, A_{kj}) \}$, where similarity between two different fuzzy sets A and B can be measured using different criteria. In our case we use the following measure:

$$S(A,B) = \max \left\{ \frac{|A \cap B|}{|A|}, \frac{|A \cap B|}{|B|} \right\} \tag{2}$$

(3) *Compactness.* Measures for compactness are the number of rules (M), and the number of different fuzzy sets (L) of the fuzzy model. It is assumed that models with a small number of rules and fuzzy sets are compact.

An Optimization Model for Fuzzy Modeling. According to the previous remarks, we propose the following multi-objective constrained optimization model:

$$\begin{aligned} &Minimize \quad f_1 = MSE \\ &Minimize \quad f_2 = M \\ &Subject \ to \ S < g_s \end{aligned} \tag{3}$$

where $g_s \in [0,1]$ is a threshold for similarity defined by the decision maker (we use $g_s = 0.35$).

An "a posteriori" articulation of preferences applied to the non-dominated solutions of the problem is used to obtain the final compromise solution.

3   Multi-objective Neuro-evolutionary Algorithms

We propose an hybrid learning system to find multiple Pareto-optimal solutions simultaneously, considering accuracy, transparency and compactness criteria. We study different multi-objective evolutionary algorithms to evolve the structure and parameters of TSK-type rule sets, together with gradient-based learning to train rule consequents. Additionally, a rule set simplification operator is used to encourage rule base transparency and compactness. This method may be applied to a wide variety of classification and control problems.

Considering the multi-objective constrained optimization model (3), we use three Pareto-based multi-objective evolutionary algorithms: Niched Preselection , ENORA and NSGA-II. Niched Preselection and ENORA are algorithms proposed by authors in [8], and [13] respectively, while NSGA-II is the well-known MOEA proposed by Deb in [5].

Representation of Solutions. The EAs have a variable-length, real-coded representation using a Pittsburgh approach. Each individual of a population contains a variable number of rules between 1 and *max*, where *max* is defined by a decision maker. Fuzzy numbers in the antecedents and parameters in the consequent are coded by floating-point numbers a_{ij}, $b_{ij} = 2\sigma_{ij}^2$ and $c_{ij} = \theta_{ij}$. In order to carry out adaptive crosses and mutations, each individual has two discrete parameters $d \in (0, \delta)$ and $e \in (0, \varepsilon)$ associated to the crossing and mutation, where δ is the number of crossing operators and ε is the number of mutation operators. It has, also, four real parameters: $\eta \in [\eta_{min}, \eta_{max}]$ that define the training rate (we use $\eta_{min} = 1E-5$ and $\eta_{max} = 1E-2$) and $e_c, e_v, e_p \in [0,1]$ that respectively define the amplitude of the mutation of the centers and variances of the fuzzy sets and parameter consequents.

Initial Population. The population is initialized by generating individuals with different numbers of rules. Each individual is generated randomly with a uniform distribution within the boundaries of the search space, defined by the learning data and trained with the gradient technique described forward.

Training of the RBF Neural Networks. In RBF neural networks, each neuron in the hidden layer can be associated with a fuzzy rule, therefore RBF neural networks are suitable to describe fuzzy models. The RBF neural networks associated with the fuzzy models can be trained with a gradient method to obtain more accuracy. However, in order to maintain the transparency and compactness of the fuzzy sets, only the consequent parameters are trained. The training algorithm incrementally updates the parameters based on the currently presented training pattern. The network parameters are updated by applying the gradient descent method to the *MSE* error function. The error function for the *i*th training pattern is given by the *MSE* function error defined in equation (1).

Constraint-Handling. The EAs use the following constraint-handling rule proposed in [11]. This rule considers that an individual I is better than an individual J if any of the following conditions is true: (1) I is feasible and J is not, (2) I and J are both unfeasible, but $S_I < S_J$. (S_I and S_J are similarity of I and J), or (3) I and J are feasible and I dominates J.

Rule Set Simplification Technique. Automated approaches to fuzzy modeling often introduce redundancy in terms of several similar fuzzy sets and fuzzy rules that describe almost the same region in the domain of some variable. An iterative process merges or separates two similar fuzzy sets according to some similarity measure. Similarity between two fuzzy sets, $S(A,B)$ is measure using the expression in equation (2). Those sets with $\eta_2 < S(A_{ij}, A_{kj})$ are merged and those with $\eta_1 < S(A_{ij}, A_{kj}) < \eta_2$ are separated. The values η_1 and η_2 are the threshold to perform the merging or the separation and must be $0 < \eta_1 < \eta_2 < 1$. We use the values $\eta_1 = 0.6$ and $\eta_2 = 0.9$. This merging-separation process is repeated until fuzzy sets for each model variable are not similar. Finally, this simplification may results in several identical rules, which must be removed from the rule set.

Variation Operators. In order to achieve an appropriate exploitation and exploration of the potential solutions in the search space, variation operators working in the different levels of the individuals are necessary. In this way, we define consider three levels

Table 1. Non dominated solutions according to the optimization model described obtained with the algorithms in the last populations for the different problems. Final chosen solutions are shown in bold.

Problem	Algorithm	M	L	MSE training	MSE evaluation	S
Wang	Niched Preselection	1	2	0.041685	0.043931	0.000000
		2	3	0.005547	0.006112	0.172085
		3	4	0.002129	0.002465	0.223785
		4	**4**	**0.000134**	**0.000156**	**0.257242**
	NSGA-II	1	2	0.041685	0.043933	0.000000
		2	4	0.013197	0.014154	0.240398
		3	4	0.002180	0.002527	0.241200
		4	**4**	**0.000158**	**0.000175**	**0.276168**
	ENORA	1	2	0.041685	0.043934	0.000000
		2	3	0.005612	0.006235	0.114939
		3	4	0.002155	0.002515	0.232097
		4	4	0.000157	0.000185	0.267967
		6	**5**	**0.000075**	**0.000142**	**0.235043**
Pressure	Niched Preselection	1	2	0.019734	0.018571	0.000000
		2	**3**	**0.000442**	**0.000519**	**0.216647**
	NSGA-II	1	2	0.019625	–	0.000000
		2	**3**	**0.000304**	**0.000323**	**0.252506**
	ENORA	1	2	0.019764	0.018633	0.000000
		2	3	0.000251	0.000258	0.267134
		4	4	0.000224	0.000294	0.267134
		5	5	0.000216	0.000283	0.267134
		6	**5**	**0.000215**	**0.000282**	**0.267134**
Sugeno	Niched Preselection	1	2	61.969782	64.988395	0.000000
		2	3	27.919187	30.227530	0.033833
		3	4	13.164426	16.095176	0.077420
		4	5	6.330606	6.994414	0.177380
		5	**6**	**3.285726**	**4.702785**	**0.309893**
	NSGA-II	1	2	62.012734	65.386962	0.000000
		2	3	27.295529	29.357669	0.098393
		3	4	11.225574	11.936249	0.224915
		4	**5**	**5.164989**	**5.382990**	**0.230075**
	ENORA	1	2	61.911668	65.201351	0.000000
		2	3	27.303031	29.153356	0.205611
		3	4	11.658130	12.017913	0.170365
		4	5	5.749831	6.056454	0.205401
		6	**6**	**2.780846**	**3.125010**	**0.229598**

Table 2. Statistical Values for the Hypervolume obtained with 100 runs

	Wang Problem			Babuska Problem			Sugeno Problem		
	Niched Preselection	NSGA-II	ENORA	Niched Preselection	NSGA-II	ENORA	Niched Preselection	NSGA-II	ENORA
Minimum	0.3015	0.3778	0.3029	0.5355	0.4197	0.3596	0.7151	0.7582	0.7379
Maximum	0.6124	1.0000	0.5070	1.0000	1.0000	0.9201	1.0000	1.0000	1.0000
Medium	0.3474	0.6145	0.3599	0.9443	0.9942	0.4120	0.8557	0.9194	0.8012
S.D.	0.0714	0.3001	0.0381	0.1134	0.0580	0.1022	0.0664	0.0725	0.0577
C.I Lower	0.3332	0.5550	0.3524	0.9218	0.9827	0.3917	0.8425	0.9050	0.7897
C.I Upper	0.3616	0.6741	0.3675	0.9668	1.0057	0.4323	0.8688	0.9338	0.8126

S.D = Standard Deviation for the Medium
C.I = Confidence Interval for the Medium (90%)

of variation operators: rule set level, rule level and parameter level. Different variation operators are defined for each level and applied in adaptive way with a variation probability p_v defined by the user (we use $p_v = 0.1$).

Fuzzy Set Crossover. Exchange two random fuzzy sets.
Fuzzy Rule Crossover. Exchange two random fuzzy rules.

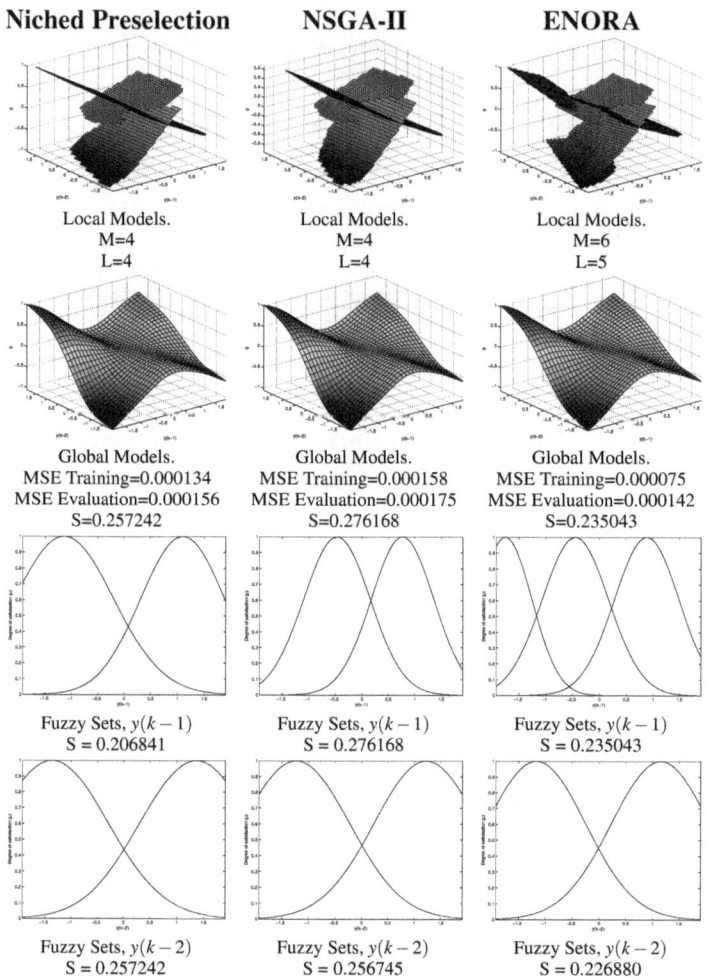

Fig. 1. Final solutions obtained by algorithms for Wang problem

Fuzzy Rule Incremental Crossover. Add to each individual a random fuzzy rule from the other individual.
Fuzzy Set Center Mutation. Mutate the center of a random number of fuzzy sets.
Fuzzy Set Variance Mutation. Mutate the variance of a random number of fuzzy sets.
Fuzzy Set Mutation. Change a random fuzzy set by another random fuzzy set.
Fuzzy Rule Incremental Mutation. Add a new random fuzzy rule.

4   Experiments and Results

The multi-objective neuro-evolutionary algorithm has been executed 100 times for each selection and generational replacement technique (Niched Preselection, NSGA-II and ENORA). Size Population is $N = 100$, number of function evaluations is 10^5 and rule

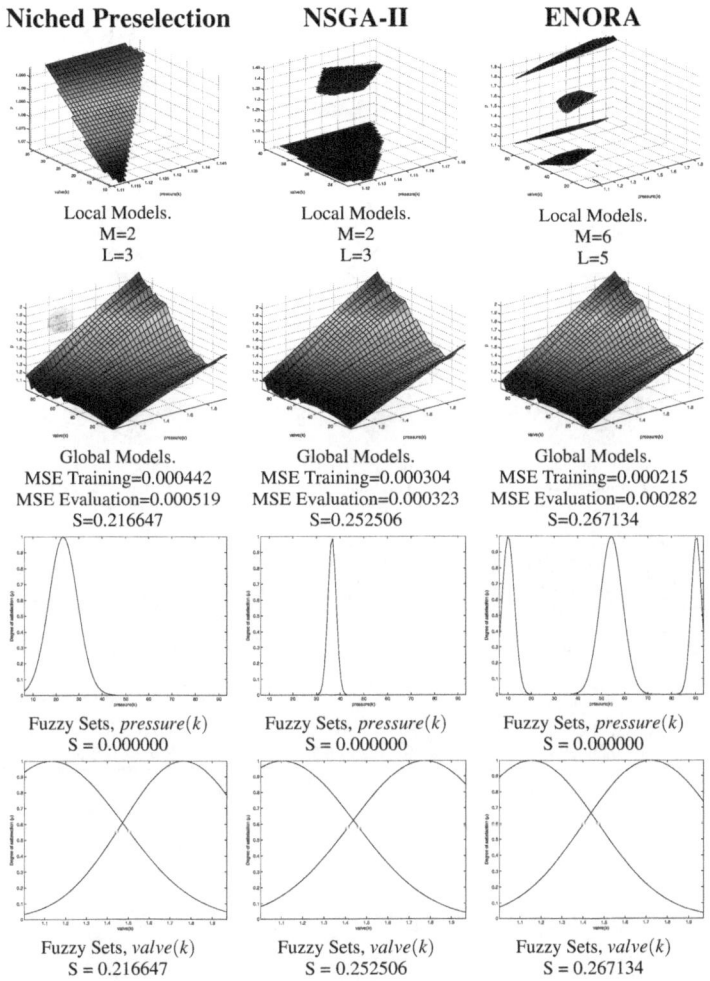

Niched Preselection   **NSGA-II**   **ENORA**

Fig. 2. Final solutions obtained by algorithms for Babuska problem

numbers is between 1 and $max = 6$. For Niched Preselection technique, the lower and upper number of individuals in each niche is 5 and 35 respectively.

We consider three test problems: Second Order Non Lineal Plant studied by Wang and Yen in [19,20]; Fermentor Pressure Dynamic described by Babuska and Verbruggen [1] and Rule Base Model given by Sugeno in [16].

Table 1 shows the non dominated solutions obtained by algorithms in the last populations. In this table, eventually chosen solutions are shown in bold. Local models for each rule, global model surface and fuzzy sets for each input variable are shown, for each test problem, in figures 1, 2 and 3.

Results show that the finally chosen solutions obtained by ENORA has a lower training and evaluation error than the solutions obtained by Niched Preseletion and NSGA-II. Table 2 and figure 4 show the statistical values for the hypervolume and boxplots.

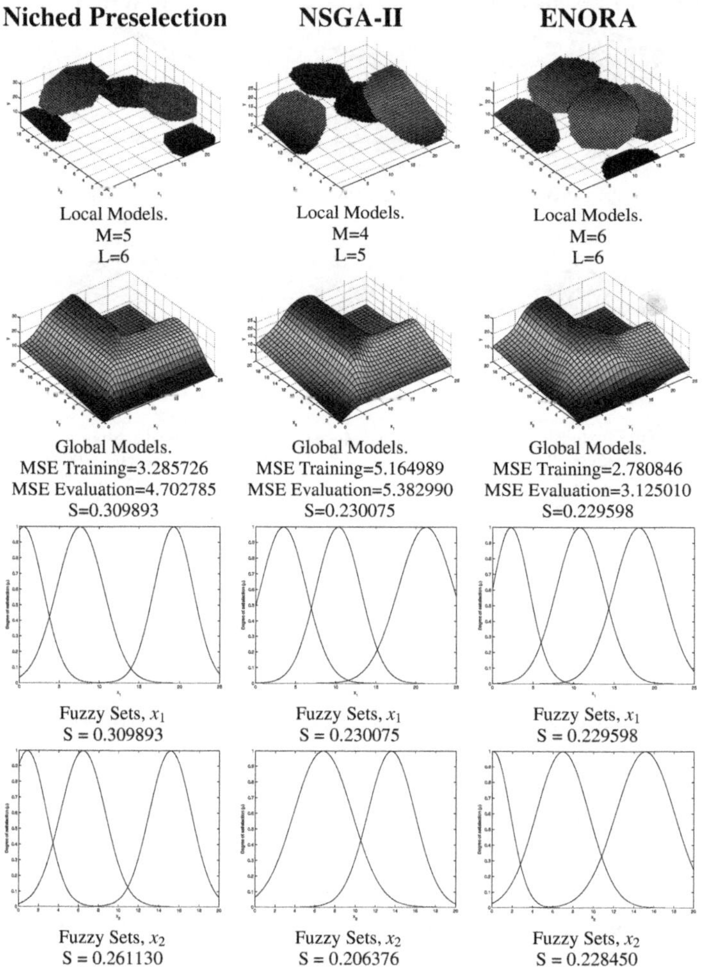
Niched Preselection
NSGA-II
ENORA
Local Models.
M=5
L=6
Local Models.
M=4
L=5
Local Models.
M=6
L=6
Global Models.
MSE Training=3.285726
MSE Evaluation=4.702785
S=0.309893
Global Models.
MSE Training=5.164989
MSE Evaluation=5.382990
S=0.230075
Global Models.
MSE Training=2.780846
MSE Evaluation=3.125010
S=0.229598
Fuzzy Sets, x_1
S = 0.309893
Fuzzy Sets, x_1
S = 0.230075
Fuzzy Sets, x_1
S = 0.229598
Fuzzy Sets, x_2
S = 0.261130
Fuzzy Sets, x_2
S = 0.206376
Fuzzy Sets, x_2
S = 0.228450

Fig. 3. Final solutions obtained by algorithms for Sugeno problem

Wang Problem
Babuska Problem
Sugeno Problem

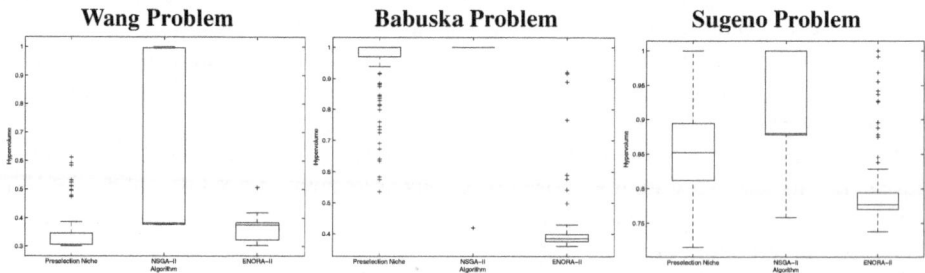

Fig. 4. Boxplots for the Hypervolume obtained with 100 runs

Taking into account these values, we can assert that NSGA-II obtains the worst results in the three problems, ENORA obtain the best results for Babuska and Sugeno problems and for the Wang problem, ENORA and Preselection are statistically similar.

5 Conclusions

This paper remarks on some results in the combination of Pareto-based multi-objective evolutionary algorithms, neural networks and fuzzy modeling. A multi-objective constrained optimization model is proposed in which criteria such as accuracy, transparency and compactness have been taken into account. Three multi-objective evolutionary algorithms (Niched Preselection, ENORA and NSGA-II) have been implemented in combination with neural network based and rule simplification techniques. The results obtained improve on other more complex techniques reported in literature, with the advantage that the proposed technique identifies a set of alternative solutions. Statistical tests have been performed over the hypervolume quality indicator values to compare the algorithms and it has shown that, for the test problem studied, ENORA obtains better results than Niched Preselection and NSGA-II algorithms.

Acknowledgements

Research supported by MEC under projects "Modelos de optimización fuzzy y computación evolutiva y de simulación de los procesos de planificación de la producción y del transporte en una cadena de suministro. Propuesta de planificación colaborativa soportada por sistemas multi-agente. Integración en un sistema de decisión. Aplicaciones" (Ref. DPI2007-65501, PAID-05-08, www.cigip.upv.es/evolution) and PET2007 0033.

References

1. Babuska, R., Verbruggen, H.B.: Applied fuzzy modeling. In: IFAC Symposium on Artificial Intelligence in Real time Control, Valencia, Spain, pp. 61–68 (1994)
2. Casillas, J., Cordón, O., Herrera, F., Magdalena, L.: Interpretability improvements to find the balance interpretability-accuracy in fuzzy modeling: an overview. In: Casillas, J., Cordón, O., Herrera, F., Magdalena, L. (eds.) Interpretability Issues in Fuzzy Modeling, Studies in Fuzziness and Soft Computing, pp. 3–22. Springer, Heidelberg (2003)
3. Coello, C.A., Veldhuizen, D.V., Lamont, G.B.: Evolutionary Algorithms for Solving Multi-Objective Problems. Kluwer Academic/Plenum publishers, New York (2002)
4. Deb, K., Agrawal, S., Pratap, A., Meyarivan, T.: A fast elitist non-dominated sorting genetic algorithm for multi-objective optimization: NSGA-II. In: Deb, K., Rudolph, G., Lutton, E., Merelo, J.J., Schoenauer, M., Schwefel, H.-P., Yao, X. (eds.) PPSN 2000. LNCS, vol. 1917, pp. 849–858. Springer, Heidelberg (2000)
5. Deb, K.: Multi-Objective Optimization using Evolutionary Algorithms. John Wiley and Sons, Ltd, Chichester (2001)
6. Goldberg, D.E.: Genetic Algorithms in Search, Optimization, and Machine Learning. Addison-Wesley, Reading (1989)
7. Gómez-Skarmeta, A.F., Jiménez, F.: Fuzzy modeling with hybrid systems. Fuzzy Sets and Systems 104, 199–208 (1999)

8. Gómez-Skarmeta, A.F., Jiménez, F., Sánchez, G.: Improving Interpretability in Approximative Fuzzy Models via Multiobjective Evolutionary Algorithms. International Journal of Intelligent Systems 22, 943–969 (2007)
9. Ishibuchi, H., Murata, T., Türksen, I.: Single-objective and two-objective genetic algorithms for selecting linguistic rules for pattern classification problems. Fuzzy Sets and Systems 89, 135–150 (1997)
10. Ishibuchi, H., Nakashima, T., Murata, T.: Performance evaluation of fuzzy classifier systems for multidimensional pattern classification problems. IEEE Transactions on Systems, Man, and Cubernetics - Part B: Cybernetics 29(5), 601–618 (1999)
11. Jiménez, F., Gómez-Skarmeta, A.F., Sánchez, G., Deb, K.: An evolutionary algorithm for constrained multi-objective optimization. In: Proceedings IEEE World Congress on Evolutionary Computation (2002)
12. Russo., M.: FuGeNeSys - a fuzzy genetic neural system for fuzzy modeling. IEEE Transactions on Fuzzy Systems 6(3), 373–388 (1998)
13. Sánchez, G., Jiménez, J., Vasant, P.: Fuzzy Optimization with Multi-Objective Evolutionary Algorithms: a Case Study. In: IEEE Symposium of Computational Intelligence in Multicriteria Decision Making (MCDM), Honolulu, Hawaii (2007)
14. Setnes, M.: Fuzzy Rule Base Simplification Using Similarity Measures. M.Sc. thesis, Delft University of Technology, Delft, the Netherlands (1995)
15. Setnes, M., Babuska, R., Verbruggen, H.B.: Rule-based modeling: Precision and transparency. IEEE Transactions on Systems, Man and Cybernetics, Part C: Applications & Reviews 28, 165–169 (1998)
16. Sugeno, M., Kang, G.T.: Structure identification of fuzzy model. Fuzzy Sets and Systems 28, 15–23 (1998)
17. Takagi, T., Sugeno, M.: Fuzzy identification of systems and its application to modeling and control. IEEE Transactions on Systems, Man and Cybernetics 15, 116–132 (1985)
18. Valente de Oliveira, J.: Semantic constraints for membership function optimization. IEEE Transactions on Fuzzy Systems 19(1), 128–138 (1999)
19. Wang, L., Yen, J.: Extracting fuzzy rules for system modeling using a hybrid of genetic algorithms and Kalman filter. Fuzzy Sets and Systems 101, 353–362 (1999)
20. Yen, J., Wang, L.: Application of statistical information criteria for optimal fuzzy model construction. IEEE Transactions on Fuzzy Systems 6(3), 362–371 (1998)

Improving Isolated Handwritten Word Recognition Using a Specialized Classifier for Short Words

Francisco Zamora-Martínez[1], María José Castro-Bleda[2],
Salvador España-Boquera[2], and Jorge Gorbe[2]

[1] Departamento de Ciencias Físicas, Matemáticas y de la Computación
Universidad CEU-Cardenal Herrera
46115 Alfara del Patriarca (Valencia), Spain
[2] Departamento de Sistemas Informáticos y Computación
Universidad Politécnica de Valencia
46022 Valencia, Spain
{fzamora,mcastro,sespana,jgorbe}@dsic.upv.es

Abstract. The aim of this work is to improve the performance of off-line handwritten text recognition systems based on hidden Markov models (HMM) and hybrid Markov models with neural networks (HMM/ANN). In order to study the systems without the influence of the language model, an isolated word recognition task has been performed. The analysis of the influence of word lengths on the error rates of the recognizers has lead to combine those classifiers with another one specialized in short words. To this end, various multilayer perceptrons have been trained to classify a subset of the vocabulary in a holistic manner. Combining the classifiers by means of a variation of the Borda count voting method achieves very satisfying results.

1 Introduction

Handwritten text recognition is one of the most active areas of research in computer science [1,2,3,4], and it is inherently difficult because of the high variability of writing styles. Works in this area can be divided into two large blocks according to the handwriting acquisition means: on-line recognition, in which information is captured while the text is being written, obtaining spatial (stroke coordinates) and temporal (stroke speeds, sequences, numbers and directions) information, and off-line recognition, in which the input data is extracted from previously scanned text images. The latter is more difficult as there is less available information (an on-line recognition problem can be reduced to an off-line one by using the data about the strokes to generate a static image of the text).

In this work, two off-line handwriting recognition systems have been analyzed, centering our attention on grapheme modelling. One recognizer is based on hidden Markov models and the other one is based on hybrid Markov models with neural networks. An isolated word recognition task has been performed [1,2,5] in order to avoid the influence of language models.

P. Meseguer, L. Mandow, and R.M. Gasca (Eds.): CAEPIA 2009, LNAI 5988, pp. 61–70, 2010.

The analysis of the influence of word lengths on the performance of the recognizers has suggested the convenience of building a classifier ensemble which includes a new classifier specialized in short words and based on multilayer perceptrons. The different classifiers have been combined using a variant of the "Borda count" voting system [6,7,8] giving promising results.

The next section describes the recognition systems used in the experiments. Section 3 introduces the experimental framework describing the task from the IAM handwriting database [9,10], and the preprocessing steps applied to the images. The actual experiments and their results are presented in sections 4 and 5. The work concludes with an analysis of the obtained results.

2   Recognition Systems

2.1   Hidden Markov Models

Hidden Markov models (HMMs) are a powerful tool frequently used in handwritten text recognition [2,11], and also in other fields related to pattern recognition and computational linguistics, like speech recognition, machine translation, Parts-Of-Speech tagging, information retrieval, etc.

When HMMs are used for off-line handwriting recognition, the image containing the handwritten text is usually interpreted as a sequence of columns to be generated by the model from left to right. Models can be created for individual graphemes or for complete words, and transition and emission probabilities are estimated by expectation-maximization over a training corpus. Recognition is achieved by finding the state sequence with a maximum probability given the input sequence of feature vectors using the Viterbi algorithm. This process requires also a dictionary and a language model (typically an n-gram model) [12].

2.2   Hybrid HMM/ANN Models

Hidden Markov models can be used in combination with neural networks which are used to compute the emission probabilities for each state of the model [13]. We have used a multilayer perceptron (MLP) to estimate the posterior probability $P(q|x)$ of every state q given the frame x if each output of the MLP is associated with a state and it is trained as a classifier [14].

Markov models need the conditional probability $P(x|q)$ so, in order to integrate the MLPs into the statistical framework of HMMs, Bayes' theorem can be applied to use the probabilities computed by the MLP:

$$P(x|q) = \frac{P(q|x)P(x)}{P(q)}$$

The probability of the state, $P(q)$, can be estimated by counting and the probability of the frame, $P(x)$, can be ignored resulting in scaled values.

The advantages of this approach are that the training criteria is discriminative (each class is trained with all the training samples, those which belong to the class and those which do not), and the fact that it is not necessary to assume an *a priori* distribution for the data.

Another advantage of this kind of hybrid HMM/ANN models is the lower computational cost compared to Gaussian mixtures, since a single forward evaluation of a unique MLP generates the values for all HMM states whereas a different Gaussian mixture is needed for each type of HMM state.

2.3   Multilayer Perceptrons

Multilayer perceptrons can be used as holistic classifiers, processing each word as a whole instead of segmenting it into smaller units [15,16,17]. The input to the neural network consists of features obtained from the image or even the pixel values. The output comprises a score for each possible word of the lexicon.

The MLPs used in this work receives as input the pixels of the word image after being centered and rescaled to a fixed size (60 × 30 pixels). This approach is only feasible when the input layer and the lexicon are small. Otherwise, the variability of the inputs and the huge number of parameters of the model would require too many training samples. Despite these limitations, this approach is adequate to our objectives, as we will see in the following sections.

3   Experimental Framework

3.1   IAM Corpus

The recognition experiments described in this work have been carried out over a subset of the IAM Handwriting Database version 3.0 [9,10]. This database consists of 1,539 images of scanned pages of English handwritten text and their corresponding transcriptions. A total of 5,685 sentences from the LOB corpus [18] containing approximately 115,000 words have been written by 657 different writers, with no restrictions of style or writing tool. In addition to the form images, the database is segmented in sentences, lines and words. This database is freely available to download for non-commercial research use.

The subset used in our experiments is the same as used in [19] (6,161 training lines, 920 validation lines and 2,781 test lines), split into individual words and removing the punctuation marks, for a total of 41,763 training words, 6,313 validation words and 17,477 test words. The size of the lexicon is 10,199 words. Figure 1 shows a pair of sample word images from the corpus.

3.2   Preprocessing

The individual word images have been preprocessed using the method described in [19,20]. Neural networks have been used to estimate the slope and slant angles, and also to find the main body area of the text line in order to perform size normalization.

A set of local extrema from the text contours of the image are extracted and then processed by a multilayer perceptron (Normalize-MLP) which receives, for a

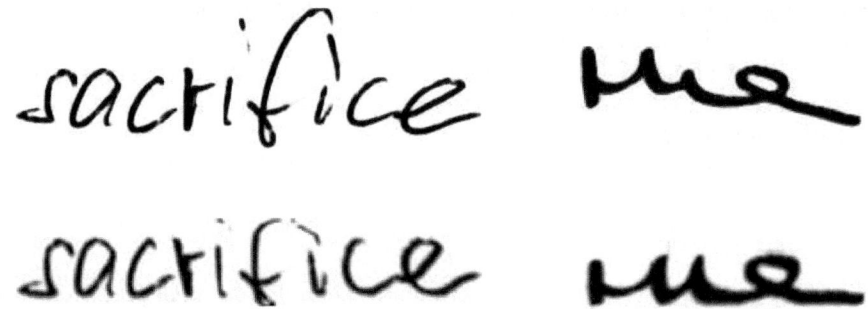

Fig. 1. Sample word images from the corpus (*top*) and result of applying the preprocess to these words (*bottom*)

given local extremum, a window of the image around that point. The Normalize-MLP classifies the point into 5 classes: 'ascender', 'descender', 'lower baseline', 'upper baseline' and 'other'. Using this information, the sizes of ascenders, descenders and main body areas are normalized. Moreover, the same method can be used to estimate the lower baseline which is useful to correct the slope. In this case, a specialized MLP (Slope-MLP) is used to detect only this baseline.

A non-uniform slant correction based on a multilayer perceptron (Slant-MLP) is also performed. Instead of trying to estimate the slant angle, the Slant-MLP only detects whether a fragment of an image is slanted or not. For each angle in a given range, the input image is slanted, and the Slant-MLP gives a score to each pair (angle, column) of the original image. Finally, a dynamic programming algorithm is used to find the maximum-score path across all the columns of the image which satisfies a smoothness constraint, to avoid abrupt slant changes. This path is an estimation of the local slant angle for each column of the image. Figure 1 shows a pair of words from the corpus before and after preprocessing.

The feature extraction method is the same described in [3]. A grid of square cells is applied over the image and three values are extracted from each cell: normalized gray level, horizontal derivative of the gray level and vertical derivative of the gray level. Gray levels are weighted with a Gaussian which gives more importance to the pixels in the center of the cell and tends to zero in the borders. In all of the experiments a grid with 20 rows has been used.

4   Experiments

All experiments have been performed using the same grapheme HMM and hybrid HMM/ANN models used in [19]:

- Continuous left-to-right HMMs using mixtures of 64 Gaussians to estimate the emission probabilities of the states, trained with HTK [21].
- HMM/ANN models with a multilayer perceptron which estimates the emission probabilities for all states, trained with our own software [22].

Table 1. Validation WER (%) with the initial HMMs (left) and with the initial hybrid HMM/ANN models (right)

HMM	Validation (%)
6 states	37.5
7 states	35.7
8 states	33.1
9 states	**32.1**
10 states	33.3
11 states	36.0
12 states	37.7

HMM/ANN	Validation (%)
6 states, MLP 192-128	26.2
7 states, MLP 192-128	24.5
8 states, MLP 384-128	**21.9**
9 states, MLP 384-128	22.7

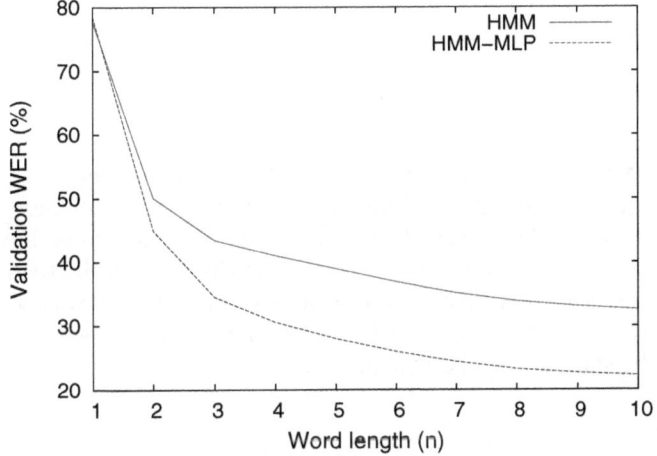

Fig. 2. WER for words in the validation set with length $\leq n$

As can be observed in Table 1, the best word error rate (WER) achieved for the validation set is 21.9%, with a 8-state HMM/ANN using two hidden layers of sizes 384 and 128 for the MLP, and 32.1% with a 9-state HMM.

The analysis of the results of these recognizers revealed that many errors were caused by short words. In order to confirm this observation, the validation WER for words containing between 1 and n characters has been obtained and plotted in Figure 2, showing that shorter words have an error rate far greater than the global error rate shown in Table 1.

A possible way to tackle this problem is to train a classifier specialized for short words and to combine it with the initial recognizers, which should improve the system performance. A holistic connectionist classification approach for short words is possible by using MLPs. Two kinds of inputs have been studied: the original and the preprocessed word images. The purpose of using different representations is twofold. On the one hand, using the original images makes the system more robust against possible preprocessing errors, given that the preprocessing method was devised to deal with whole lines instead of individual words. On the other hand, using different inputs can be useful to make the classifiers less correlated so that they can also be combined.

In order to obtain a reduced lexicon for the holistic classifiers, only words with three or less characters with a minimum of 40 occurrences in the training set were considered, resulting in a lexicon of 56 words.

During recognition, the word class is unknown, so the criterion needed to decide whether an image is to be classified by the holistic MLP must rely uniquely on image features. An experimental study on the training set has shown that selecting the images whose width is lower than or equal to 150 pixels accepts a reasonable percentage of short words while accepting a very low number of words outside the reduced lexicon, which should be rejected by the classifier.

5   Experimental Results

5.1   Holistic Models

The holistic models used in our experiments are based on MLPs using the softmax activation function at the output layer, therefore estimating the probability of each class given an input word image [14]. The purpose of these models is to recognize a reduced subset of the lexicon and therefore they must have the ability to reject word images outside that subset. For this reason, instead of trying to minimize the error rate (which would be achieved in a trivial way by rejecting all the inputs), the training process tries to maximize the harmonic mean between precision and recall, known as F-measure:

$$P = \frac{\text{correct}}{\text{total accepted}} \qquad R = \frac{\text{correct}}{\text{correct+incorrectly rejected}} \qquad F = \frac{2 \cdot P \cdot R}{P + R}$$

In order to control overfitting during the MLP training, the validation set has been split into two subsets, one for stopping the MLP training, and another one for choosing the best network topology and training parameters. Since the F-measure is used as stopping criterion, the rejection of samples must be fixed a priori and used during training and recognition: an input sample is accepted if the most probable outputs have a combined probability mass greater than or equal to a given threshold. A threshold of 0.7 for the sum of the probabilities of the two most probable words has been selected after some previous experiments.

Two different kinds of MLP have been trained, differing only in their inputs (original images or preprocessed images). In both cases, the input image is centered and rescaled to a fixed size of 60 × 30 pixels. In this way, every MLP has 1,800 neurons in the input layer. The backpropagation algorithm with momentum term has been used to train the MLPs, shuffling the training samples in each epoch. The following parameters have been tested:

- Number of neurons in the hidden layers: (256, 128), (192, 128), (192, 192), (256, 192), (128, 128) and (128, 64). All the considered topologies had two hidden layers using the hyperbolic tangent as the activation function.

- Learning rate and momentum term pairs: (0.0075, 0.004), (0.01, 0.002), (0.05, 0.01) and (0.005, 0.0001).
- Connection weights and neuron biases have been initialized using random values in the interval $[-0.08, 0.08]$.

The output layer uses the softmax activation function. There is not any output neuron representing the unknown word, so the images of words not belonging to the reduced lexicon have been used to train the MLPs setting their target output to $1/|classes|$ for each output neuron, because the softmax activation function requires that all outputs sum to 1. This is consistent with the rejection criterion based on the probability of the two most probable classes.

For each combination of parameters, an MLP was trained until the best F-measure for the first validation subset did not improve for 200 epochs. Once all the MLPs were trained, the MLP which achieved the best F-measure for the second validation subset was selected. The results achieved for the best holistic classifier of each input type (original and preprocessed images) on the validation set are shown in Table 2.

Table 2. Precision (P), recall (R) and F-measure (F) of the holistic classifiers for validation (%)

Input image	Validation 1			Validation 2		
	P	R	F	P	R	F
Original	76.3	67.5	71.6	79.1	64.7	71.1
Preprocessed	77.3	73.0	**75.1**	76.5	77.0	**76.8**

5.2   Classifier Ensembles

Given an input image, the following method has been used to combine the HMM-based recognizers with the holistic recognizers:

1. The ordered list of the N most probable words is obtained from the general recognizers (HMM or HMM/ANN).
2. When the image width is smaller than 150 pixels, the image is also classified with the holistic MLPs. For each MLP which accepts the sample, the ordered list of the N most probable words is obtained.
3. All previous recognizer outputs are combined by means of the Borda voting method [6,7]: each word is assigned a score based on the output order (N points for the most probable word, 1 point for the least probable one), and then the words are sorted according to their total score.

In order to be able to vary the relative importance of the recognizers, an extension of the Borda count method has been considered which uses two additional parameters per recognizer:

- a constant value which is added to the scores assigned by the recognizer, and
- a weight that multiplies the previous result.

Table 3. Validation WER combining HMM-based and holistic recognizers

Model	Validation WER (%)
HMM	32.1
HMM + holistic (orig)	27.4
HMM + holistic (prep)	27.9
HMM + holistic (both)	**25.5**
HMM/ANN	21.9
HMM/ANN + holistic (orig)	18.1
HMM/ANN + holistic (prep)	18.9
HMM/ANN + holistic (both)	**17.1**
HMM + HMM/ANN + holistic (both)	22.6

Table 4. Test WER (%) combining the recognizers with the holistic classifiers

Model	Test WER (%)
HMM	38.6
HMM + holistic (both)	32.1
HMM/ANN	27.6
HMM/ANN + holistic (both)	22.1

After some experiments with this approach it was observed that the best results for the validation corpus were obtained adding the recognizer scores without any weighting. These results are shown in Table 3.

Taking into account the good results obtained by the ensembles, another ensemble containing all the classifiers was tested. Unfortunately, the results were worse than the HMM/ANN by itself (22.6% WER for the validation set using the unmodified Borda count).

Finally, the test set recognition error has been computed for the best classifier ensemble on validation, as well as for the original classifiers (see Table 4). The combination of the holistic recognizers with the original ones achieves a significant improvement, between 5 and 6 absolute points, of the word error rate. The best result obtained is 22.1% WER for the test set, with the HMM/ANN and both holistic classifiers.

6   Conclusions

The use of a holistic classifier specialized in short words significantly improves the best results achieved by both HMMs and hybrid HMM/ANNs. However, the combination of all three recognizers does not outperform even the HMM/ANN alone, probably because the HMM and HMM/ANN classifiers are very correlated each other.

The next step is the integration of holistic models specialized in short words in a continuous handwriting recognition system, which is not a trivial task given the discriminative nature of the holistic MLPs, and to obtain other models with low correlation among them to improve the ensemble performance.

Acknowledgements

This work has been partially supported by the Spanish Ministerio de Educación y Ciencia (TIN2006-12767 and TIN2008-06856-C05-02), and the research grant BFPI06/250 from the Conselleria de Empresa, Universidad y Ciencia of Generalitat Valenciana.

References

1. Plamondon, R., Srihari, S.N.: On-line and off-line handwritting recognition: a comprehensive survey. IEEE Trans. pattern Anal. Mach. Intell. 22(1), 63–84 (2000)
2. Bunke, H.: Recognition of Cursive Roman Handwriting – Past, Present and Future. In: Proc. 7th International Conference on Document Analysis and Recognition, Edinburgh, Scotland, vol. 1, pp. 448–459 (2003)
3. Toselli, A.H., Juan, A., González, J., Salvador, I., Vidal, E., Casacuberta, F., Keysers, D., Ney, H.: Integrated Handwriting Recognition and Interpretation using Finite-State Models. Integrated Handwriting Recognition and Interpretation using Finite-State Models 18(4), 519–539 (2004)
4. Vinciarelli, A., Bengio, S., Bunke, H.: Offline Recognition of Unconstrained Handwritten Texts Using HMMs and Statistical Language Models. IEEE Trans. pattern Anal. Mach. Intell. 26(6), 709–720 (2004)
5. Vinciarelli, A.: A survey on off-line cursive word recognition. Pattern Recognition 35(7), 1433–1446 (2002)
6. de Borda, J.: Mémoire sur les élections au scrutin in the Histoire de l'Académie Royale des Sciences, Paris, France (1781)
7. Verma, B., Gader, P., Chen, W.: Fusion of multiple handwritten word recognition techniques. Pattern Recognition Letters 22(9), 991–998 (2001)
8. Wang, W., Brakensiek, A., Rigoll, G.: Combination of multiple classifiers for handwritten word recognition. In: 8th International Workshop on Frontiers in Handwriting Recognition, pp. 157–162 (2002)
9. Marti, U., Bunke, H.: A full English sentence database for off-line handwriting recognition. In: Proc. 5th International Conference on Document Analysis and Recognition, Bangalore, pp. 705–708 (1999)
10. Marti, U.V., Bunke, H.: The IAM-database: an English sentence database for offline handwriting recognition. International Journal of Document Analysis and Recognition 5, 39–46 (2002)
11. Marti, U., Bunke, H.: Handwritten sentence recognition. In: Proc. of 15th International Conference on Pattern Recognition, Barcelona, Spain, vol. 3, pp. 467–470 (2000)
12. Jelinek, F.: Statistical Methods for Speech Recognition. The MIT Press, Cambridge (1998)
13. Bourlard, H., Morgan, N.: Connectionist speech recognition—A hybrid approach. Series in engineering and computer science, vol. 247. Kluwer Academic, Dordrecht (1994)
14. Bishop, C.M.: Neural networks for pattern recognition. Oxford University Press, Oxford (1995)
15. Madhvanath, S., Govindaraju, V.: The role of holistic paradigms in handwritten word recognition. IEEE Trans. Pattern Anal. Mach. Intell. 23(2), 149–164 (2001)

16. Castro, M., et al.: A Holistic Classification System for Check Amounts Based on Neural Networks with Rejection. In: Pal, S.K., Bandyopadhyay, S., Biswas, S. (eds.) PReMI 2005. LNCS, vol. 3776, pp. 310–314. Springer, Heidelberg (2005)
17. Ruiz-Pinales, J., Jaime-Rivas, R., Castro-Bleda, M.J.: Holistic cursive word recognition based on perceptual features. Pattern Recognition Letters 28(13), 1600–1609 (2007)
18. Johansson, S., Atwell, E., Garside, R., Leech, G.: The Tagged LOB Corpus: User's Manual. Technical report, Norwegian Computing Centre for the Humanities, Bergen, Norway (1986)
19. España-Boquera, S., Castro-Bleda, M., Gorbe-Moya, J., Zamora-Martínez, F.: Improving Offline Handwritten Text Recognition with Hybrid HMM/ANN Models. Technical report, Departamento de Sistemas Informáticos y Computación, Universidad Politécnica de Valencia, Valencia, Spain (2009)
20. Gorbe-Moya, J., España-Boquera, S., Zamora-Martínez, F., Castro-Bleda, M.J.: Handwritten Text Normalization by using Local Extrema Classification. In: Proc. 8th International Workshop on Pattern Recognition in Information Systems, pp. 164–172. INSTICC Press (2008)
21. Young, S.J., Woodland, P.C., Byrne, W.J.: HTK: Hidden Markov Model Toolkit V1.5. Technical report, Cambridge University Engineering Department Speech Group and Entropic Research Laboratories Inc (1993)
22. España-Boquera, S., Zamora-Martínez, F., Castro-Bleda, M.J., Gorbe-Moya, J.: Efficient BP algorithms for general feedforward neural networks. In: Mira, J., Álvarez, J.R. (eds.) IWINAC 2007. LNCS, vol. 4527, pp. 327–336. Springer, Heidelberg (2007)

Closeness and Distance Relations in Order of Magnitude Qualitative Reasoning via PDL*

Alfredo Burrieza[1], Emilio Muñoz-Velasco[2], and Manuel Ojeda-Aciego[2]

[1] Dept. Filosofía. Universidad de Málaga., Spain
burrieza@uma.es
[2] Dept. Matemática Aplicada. Universidad de Málaga., Spain
{emilio,aciego}@ctima.uma.es

Abstract. The syntax, semantics and an axiom system for an extension of Propositional Dynamic Logic (PDL) for order of magnitude qualitative reasoning which formalizes the concepts of closeness and distance is introduced in this paper. In doing this, we use some of the advantages of PDL: firstly, we exploit the possibility of constructing complex relations from simpler ones for defining the concept of closeness and other programming commands such as *while ... do* and *repeat ... until*; secondly, we employ its theoretical support in order to show that the satisfiability problem is decidable and the completeness of our system. Moreover, the specific axioms of our logic have been obtained from the *minimal* set of formulas needed in our definition of qualitative sum of small, medium and large numbers. We also present some of the advantages of our approach on the basis of an example.

1 Introduction

The area of research within Artificial Intelligence that automates reasoning and problem solving about the physical world is called Qualitative Reasoning (QR). It creates non-numerical descriptions of systems and their behaviour, preserving important behavioural properties and qualitative distinctions. Successful application areas include autonomous spacecraft support, failure analysis and on-board diagnosis of vehicle systems, automated generation of control software for photocopiers, conceptual knowledge capture in ecology, and intelligent aids for human learning. Order of magnitude reasoning is a part of QR which stratifies values according to some notion of scale [19, 11, 20, 17].

There are different approaches in the literature [2, 23, 12] for using logic in QR that face the problem about the soundness of the reasoning supported by the formalism, and try to give some answers about the efficiency of its use. In particular, multimodal logics dealing with order of magnitude reasoning have been developed in [9, 8] defining different qualitative relations (*order of magnitude, negligibility, non-closeness,* etc.) on the basis of qualitative classes obtained by dividing the real line in intervals [22].

---

* Partially supported by projects TIN2006-15455-C03-01 and P6-FQM-02049.

P. Meseguer, L. Mandow, and R.M. Gasca (Eds.): CAEPIA 2009, LNAI 5988, pp. 71–80, 2010.
© Springer-Verlag Berlin Heidelberg 2010

The syntax, semantics and an axiom system for a logic which formalizes the concepts of closeness and distance are introduced in this paper. To do this, we use the advantages of Propositional Dynamic Logic [14, 16, 4], mainly the possibility of constructing complex relations from simpler ones. Some recent applications of PDL in AI can be seen in [3, 15, 6, 5]. In our case, we define the concept of closeness as a program obtained by the union of the sum of classes representing zero, positive and negative small numbers. Moreover, we introduce some nominals in order to represent the different qualitative classes, for this reason we can say that our logic is a part of Combinatory PDL [1, 18].

This work continues the line of [7] about using PDL in the framework of order of magnitude reasoning, however it introduces some differences, for example, here we use constants to represent the qualitative classes instead of the milestones which divide them, introducing an ordering only in the set of qualitative classes. This makes the approach more heavily founded on quantitativeness. Furthermore, this paper is an step forward in the formalization for two main reasons. Firstly, it gives a syntactic approach by presenting an axiom system where the specific axioms have been obtained from the *minimal* set of formulas needed in our definition of qualitative sum of small, medium and large numbers. Secondly, we have used the theoretical support of PDL in order to prove the decidability of the satisfiability problem and the completeness of this logic.

The paper is organized as follows. In Section 2, the syntax and semantics of the proposed logic is introduced, together with an example of application of our logic. In Section 3, we give an axiom system for our logic and in Section 4 the decidability of the problem of satisfiability and the completeness are proved. Finally, some conclusions and future works are discussed in Section 5.

2   Syntax and Semantics

In order to introduce the language of our logic, we consider a set of formulas Φ and a set of programs Π, which are defined recursively on disjoint sets Φ_0 and Π_0, respectively. Φ_0 is called the set of *atomic formulas* which can be thought as abstractions of properties of states. Similarly, Π_0 is called the set of *atomic programs* which are intended to represent basic instructions.

Formulas:

- $\Phi_0 = \mathbb{V} \cup \mathbb{C}$, where $\mathbb{V}$ is a denumerable set of propositional variables and $\mathbb{C} = \{\mathsf{nl}, \mathsf{nm}, \mathsf{ns}, \mathsf{0}, \mathsf{ps}, \mathsf{pm}, \mathsf{pl}\}$. The elements of $\mathbb{C}$ are intended to represent, respectively the qualitative classes of "negative large", "negative medium", "negative small", "zero", "positive small", "positive medium", and "positive large" numbers.
- If φ and ψ are formulas and a is a program, then $\varphi \to \psi$ (propositional implication), $\bot$ (propositional falsity) and $[a]\varphi$ (program necessity) are also formulas. As usual, $\vee$ and $\wedge$ represent logical disjunction and conjunction, respectively; while $\langle a \rangle$ represents the program posibility.

Programs:

- $\Pi_0 = \{+_\star \mid \star \in \mathbb{C}\}$.
- If a and b are programs and φ is a formula, then $(a;b)$ ("do a followed by b"), $a \cup b$ ("do either a or b, nondeterministically"), a^* ("repeat a a nondeterministically chosen finite number of times") and φ? ("proceed if φ is true, else fail") are also programs.

As an example of programs, we can consider $+_{ps} \cup +_{ns}$ and $ns?; +_{pl}$ in order to represent, respectively, the intuitive meanings of adding a (positive or negative) small number and adding a positive large number to a negative small number.

The possibility of construction complex programs from simpler ones allow us to define programming commands such as *while ... do* and *repeat ... until* as follows. If φ is a formula and a is a program, the program **while** φ **do** a is defined by $(\varphi?; a)^*; \neg\varphi?$ and the program **repeat** a **until** φ is given by $a; (\neg\varphi?; a)^*; \varphi?$.

We now define the *semantics* of our logic. A *model* $\mathcal{M}$ is a tuple (W, m), where W is a non-empty set divided in 7 qualitative classes, chosen depending on the context [21], denoted also [1] by $\{nl, nm, ns, 0, ps, pm, pl\}$, and m is a meaning function such that $m(p) \subseteq W$, for every propositional variable, $m(\star) = \star$, for every $\star \in \mathbb{C}$ and $m(a) \subseteq W \times W$, for all program a. Moreover, for every formula φ and ψ and for all programs a, b, we have:

- $m(\varphi \to \psi) = (W \setminus m(\varphi)) \cup m(\psi)$
- $m(\bot) = \varnothing$
- $m([a]\varphi) = \{w \in W : \text{for all } v \in W, \text{ if } (w,v) \in m(a) \text{ then } v \in m(\varphi)\}$
- $m(a \cup b) = m(a) \cup m(b)$
- $m(a;b) = m(a); m(b)$ (composition of relations $m(a)$ and $m(b)$)
- $m(a^*) = m(a)^*$ (reflexive and transitive closure of relation $m(a)$).
- $m(\varphi?) = \{(w, w) : w \in m(\varphi)\}$

The following properties are required for our atomic programs:

- $m(+_{ps})$ is a relation on W such that:

1. $m(+_{ps})(nl) \subseteq nl \cup nm$
2. $m(+_{ps})(nm) \subseteq nm \cup ns$
3. $m(+_{ps})(ns) \subseteq ns \cup 0 \cup ps$

4. $m(+_{ps})(ps) \subseteq ps \cup pm$
5. $m(+_{ps})(pm) \subseteq pm \cup pl$
6. $m(+_{ps})(pl) \subseteq pl$

- $m(+_{pm})$ is a relation on W such that:

1. $m(+_{pm})(nl) \subseteq nl \cup nm \cup ns$
2. $m(+_{pm})(nm) \subseteq nm \cup ns \cup 0 \cup ps \cup pm$
3. $m(+_{pm})(ns) \subseteq ps \cup pm$

4. $m(+_{pm})(ps) \subseteq pm \cup pl$
5. $m(+_{pm})(pm) \subseteq pm \cup pl$
6. $m(+_{pm})(pl) \subseteq pl$

---

[1] By abuse of notation, we will use the same symbols to represent the qualitative classes and its corresponding formulas.

- $m(+_{pl})$ is a relation on W such that:

1. $m(+_{pl})(nm) \subseteq ps \cup pm \cup pl$
2. $m(+_{pl})(ns) \subseteq pm \cup pl$
3. $m(+_{pl})(ps) \subseteq pl$

4. $m(+_{pl})(pm) \subseteq pl$

5. $m(+_{pl})(pl) \subseteq pl$

- $m(+_{ns})$, $m(+_{nm})$ and $m(+_{nl})$ are given similarly and $m(+_0)$ is defined such that $m(+_0) = \{(w, w) \mid w \in W\}$.

Notice that the properties required for the specific atomic programs are intended to reflect intuitive properties of qualitative sum. For example, $m(+_{ps})(pl) \subseteq pl$ means that the sum of a positive small number plus a positive large number has to be a positive large number, and similarly for the rest of properties.

Given a model $\mathcal{M} = (W, m)$, a formula φ is *true* in $u \in W$ whenever we have that $u \in m(\varphi)$. We say that φ is satisfiable if there exists $u \in W$ such as φ is true in u. Moreover, φ is *valid in a model* $\mathcal{M} = (W, m)$ if φ is true in all $u \in W$, that is, if $m(\varphi) = W$. Finally, φ is *valid* if φ is valid in all models.

The informal meaning of some of our formulas is given as follows:

- $\langle +_{ps} \rangle \varphi$ is true in u iff there exists u', obtained by adding a positive small number to u, such that φ is true in u'.
- $\langle nl? \rangle \varphi$ is true in u iff u is a negative large number and φ is true in u.
- $\langle +_{ps}^* \rangle \varphi$ is true in u iff there exists u', obtained by adding a finitely many small positive numbers to u, such that φ is true in u'.
- $[+_{ps} \cup +_{nm}]\varphi$ is true in u iff for every u', obtained by adding either a positive small number or a negative medium number to u, φ is true in u'.

As stated above, one of the main advantages of using PDL is the possibility of constructing complex programs from basic ones. As a consequence, following the ideas presented in [7], we can use our connectives in order to represent the relations of *closeness* and *distance*. Thus, for any formula φ, we define the modal connectives [c] and [d] as follows:

$$[c]\,\varphi = [+_{ns} \cup +_0 \cup +_{ps}]\varphi \qquad [d]\,\varphi = [+_{nl} \cup +_{pl}]\varphi$$

The intuitive interpretation of the closeness relation is that x is close to y if, and only if, y is obtained from x by adding a small number. On the other hand, x is distant from y if and only if y is obtained from x by adding a large number.

The following example was presented in [8] for a multimodal logic. In this case, the use of PDL gives us many advantages, such as the possibility of expressing not only closeness and distance, but also the programming commands *while... do* and *repeat... until* defined above.

Example 1. Let us suppose that we want to specify the behaviour of a device to automatically control the temperature, for example, in a museum, subject to have some specific conditions. If we have to maintain the temperature close to some limit T, for practical purposes any value of the interval $[T-\epsilon, T+\epsilon]$ for small ϵ is admissible. This interval can be considered as ns $\cup$ 0 $\cup$ ps in our approach. Moreover, assume that if the temperature is out of this interval (for example, because the number of people inside the museum is changing), it is necessary to put into operation either some *heating* or *cooling* system. We also assume that, when the normal system of *cooling* or *heating* is operating, a system to maintain the humidity is needed, and when the extra system is operating, we also need an extra system of humidification. As a consequence, the qualitative classes nl, nm, ns $\cup$ 0 $\cup$ ps, pm and pl can be interpreted by the formulas: VERY_COLD, COLD, OK, HOT and VERY_HOT, respectively.

We consider that program $+_0$ means that the system is *off*; moreover $+_{ps}$ $\cup$ $+_{pm}$ and $+_{pl}$, mean that a system for *heating* and *extra heating* are operating, respectively. Similarly, the programs $+_{nm}$ $\cup$ $+_{ns}$ and $+_{nl}$ represent *cooling* and *extra cooling* operations, respectively.

Some consequences of the previous specification are the following:

1. HOT $\rightarrow$ $([+_{pl}]$VERY_HOT $\wedge \langle(+_{nm} \cup +_{ns})^*\rangle$OK$)$
2. $[(\neg$OK?$; +_{Sys})^*; $OK?$]$OK, being $+_{Sys} = +_{nl} \cup +_{nm} \cup +_{ns} \cup +_{ps} \cup +_{pm} \cup +_{pl}$
3. VERY_HOT $\rightarrow [(+_{nl}; (\neg$OK?$; +_{nl})^*; $OK?$]$OK
4. 0 $\rightarrow [$c$]$ OK
5. OK $\rightarrow [$d$]$ (VERY_COLD $\vee$ COLD $\vee$ HOT $\vee$ VERY_HOT)

We give now the intuitive meanings for the previous formulae.

- Formula 1 means that, if the temperature is hot and the extra heating system is put into operation, then the temperature will be very hot. Moreover, if the temperature is hot, the temperature becomes OK after finitely many applications of the cooling system.
- Formula 2 says that *while* the temperature is not OK, the system has to be operating, as a consequence, we will obtain the desired temperature.
- Formula 3 is interpreted as if the temperature is very hot, *repeat* the application of the extra cooling system *until* the temperature is OK.
- Formula 4 means that every value close to the desired temperature is considered OK.
- Formula 5 can be read in this way: if the temperature is OK, for every distant value, the temperature will be either very cold or cold or hot or very hot.

Assume now that the system is more efficient (in terms of energy saving) if the temperature is close to the desired value and if the temperature is distant to these values, the system is wasting very much energy. The following formula must be true: OK $\rightarrow$ $([$c$]$ *efficient* $\wedge [$d$]$ *warning*), which means that for every temperature close to OK, the system is running efficiently and if the temperature is distant to OK, the system is wasting very much energy.

3   Axiom System

We introduce here the axiom system for our logic.

Axiom schemata for PDL:

A1 All instances of tautologies of the propositional calculus.
A2 $[a](\varphi \to \psi) \to ([a]\varphi \to [a]\psi)$
A3 $[a](\varphi \wedge \psi) \leftrightarrow ([a]\varphi \wedge [a]\psi)$
A4 $[a \cup b]\varphi \leftrightarrow ([a]\varphi \vee [b]\varphi)$
A5 $[a; b]\varphi \leftrightarrow [a][b]\varphi$
A6 $[\varphi?]\psi \leftrightarrow (\varphi \to \psi)$
A7 $(\varphi \wedge [a][a^*]\varphi) \leftrightarrow [a^*]\varphi$
A8 $(\varphi \wedge [a^*](\varphi \to [a]\varphi)) \to [a^*]\varphi$ (induction axiom)

Axiom schemata for qualitative classes:

QE nl $\vee$ nm $\vee$ ns $\vee$ 0 $\vee$ ps $\vee$ pm $\vee$ pl
QU $\star \to \neg\#$ for every $\star \in \mathbb{C}$ and $\# \in \mathbb{C} - \{\star\}$

QO1 nl $\to \langle +_{ps}^* \rangle$ nm   **QO4** 0 $\to \langle +_{ps}^* \rangle$ ps
QO2 nm $\to \langle +_{ps}^* \rangle$ ns   **QO5** ps $\to \langle +_{ps}^* \rangle$ pm
QO3 ns $\to \langle +_{ps}^* \rangle$ 0   **QO6** pm $\to \langle +_{ps}^* \rangle$ pl

Axiom schemata for specific programs:

PS1 nl $\to [+_{ps}]$ (nl $\vee$ nm)   **PS4** ps $\to [+_{ps}]$ (ps $\vee$ pm)
PS2 nm $\to [+_{ps}]$ (nm $\vee$ ns)   **PS5** pm $\to [+_{ps}]$ (pm $\vee$ pl)
PS3 ns $\to [+_{ps}]$ (ns $\vee$ 0 $\vee$ ps)   **PS6** pl $\to [+_{ps}]$ pl

PM1 nl $\to [+_{pm}]$ (ns $\vee$ nm $\vee$ nl)   **PM4** ps $\to [+_{pm}]$ (pm $\vee$ pl)
PM2 nm $\to [+_{pm}]$ (nm$\vee$ns$\vee$0$\vee$ps$\vee$pm)   **PM5** pm $\to [+_{pm}]$ (pm $\vee$ pl)
PM3 ns $\to [+_{pm}]$ (ps $\vee$ pm)   **PM6** pl $\to [+_{pm}]$ pl

PL1 nm $\to [+_{pl}]$ (ps $\vee$ pm $\vee$ pl)   **PL4** pm $\to [+_{pl}]$ pl
PL2 ns $\to [+_{pl}]$ (pm $\vee$ pl)
PL3 ps $\to [+_{pl}]$ pl   **PL5** pl $\to [+_{pl}]$ pl

We also consider as axioms **NS1...NS6**; **NM1...NM6** and **NL1...NL5** by changing in the previous axioms every appearance of p by n and vice versa.

Z1 $\langle +_0 \rangle \varphi \to [+_0] \varphi$ **Z2** $[+_0] \varphi \to \varphi$

Inference Rules:
(MP) $\varphi, \varphi \to \psi \vdash \psi$ *(Modus Ponens)*   **(G)** $\varphi \vdash [a]\varphi$ (generalization)

Notice that axioms **A1... A8** are classical for this type of logics. The rest ones have the following intuitive meaning:

- **QE** and **QU** mean the existence and uniqueness of the qualitative classes, respectively. **Q01–Q06** represent the ordering of these qualitative classes.

- **PS1–PS6, PM1–PM6** and **PL1–PL5**; the respective ones for negative numbers and **O1–O6** represent the desired properties of our atomic specific programs.

It is straightforward that all the previous axioms are valid formulas and that the inference rules preserve validity. For this reason, we can conclude that our system is *sound*, that is, every theorem is a valid formula.

4 Decidability and Completeness

In order to obtain the decidability of the satisfiability problem, we prove the *small model property*. This property says that if a formula φ is satisfiable, then it is satisfied in a model with no more than $2^{|\varphi|}$ elements, where $|\varphi|$ is the number of symbols of φ. This result can be obtained by the technique of *filtrations* used in modal logic. However, while in modal logic it is used the concept of subformula, in PDL we have to rely on the Fisher-Lander Closure. All the results in this section can be proved in a standard way. For more details, see [14].

First of all, we define by simultaneous induction the following two functions, being Φ the set of formulas, Π the set of programs of our logic and for every $\varphi, \psi \in \Phi$, $a, b \in \Pi$:

$$FL : \Phi \to 2^{\Phi}; \qquad FL^{\square} : \{[a]\varphi \mid a \in \Pi, \varphi \in \Phi\} \to 2^{\Phi}$$

(a) $FL(p) = \{p\}$, for every propositional variable p.
(b) $FL(\star) = \star$, for all $\star \in \mathbb{C}$.
(c) $FL(\varphi \to \psi) = \{\varphi \to \psi\} \sqcup FL(\varphi) \sqcup FL(\psi)$
(d) $FL(\bot) = \{\bot\}$
(e) $FL([a]\varphi) = FL^{\square}([a]\varphi) \cup FL(\varphi)$
(f) $FL^{\square}([a]\varphi) = \{[a]\varphi\}$, being a an atomic program.
(g) $FL^{\square}([a \cup b]\varphi) = \{[a \cup b]\varphi\} \cup FL^{\square}([a]\varphi) \cup FL^{\square}([b]\varphi)$
(h) $FL^{\square}([a;b]\varphi) = \{[a;b]\varphi\} \cup FL^{\square}([a][b]\varphi) \cup FL^{\square}([b]\varphi)$
(i) $FL^{\square}([a^*]\varphi) = \{[a^*]\varphi\} \cup FL^{\square}([a][a^*]\varphi)$
(j) $FL^{\square}([\psi?]\varphi) = \{[\psi?]\varphi\} \cup FL(\psi)$

$FL(\varphi)$ is called the *Fisher-Lander closure* of formula φ.

The following result bounds the number of elements of $FL(\varphi)$, denoted by $|FL(\varphi)|$, in terms of $|\varphi|$. It is proved by simultaneous induction following the ideas presented in [14], taking into account our specific definition of $FL(\star) = \star$, for all $\star \in \mathbb{C}$, in the basis case of this induction.

Lemma 1.

(a) *For any formula φ, $|FL(\varphi)| \leq |\varphi|$.*
(b) *For any formula $[a]\varphi$, $|FL^{\square}([a]\varphi)| \leq |a|$, being $|a|$ the number of symbols of program a.*

We now define the concept of filtration. First of all, given a formula φ and a model (W, m), we define the following equivalence relation on W:

$$u \equiv v \overset{\text{def}}{\Longleftrightarrow} \forall \psi \in FL(\varphi)[u \in m(\psi) \text{ iff } v \in m(\psi)]$$

The filtration structure $(\overline{W}, \overline{m})$ of (W, m) by $FL(\varphi)$ is defined on the quotient set $W/\equiv$, denoted by $\overline{W}$, and the qualitative classes in $\overline{W}$ are defined, for every $\star \in \mathbb{C}$, by $\overline{\star} = \{\overline{u} \mid u \in \star\}$. Furthermore, the map $\overline{m}$ is defined as follows:

1. $\overline{m}(p) = \{\overline{u} \mid u \in m(p)\}$, for every propositional, variable p.
2. $\overline{m}(\star) = m(\star) = \star$, for all $\star \in \mathbb{C}$.
3. $\overline{m}(a) = \{(\overline{u}, \overline{v}) \mid \exists u' \in \overline{u} \text{ and } \exists v' \in \overline{v} \text{ such that } (u', v') \in m(a)\}$, for every atomic program a.

$\overline{m}$ is extended inductively to compound propositions and programs as described previously in the definition of model.

The following two Lemmas are the key of this section and are proved following also the ideas presented in [14]. To do this, we have to take into account that our definition of Fisher-Lander closure includes the qualitative classes and that the properties required in our models for atomic programs, such as $m(+_{\mathsf{ps}})(\mathsf{nl}) \subseteq \mathsf{nl} \cup \mathsf{nm}$, are maintained in the filtration structure, as a direct consequence of our previous definitions.

Lemma 2. $(\overline{W}, \overline{m})$ *is a finite model.*

Lemma 3 (Filtration Lemma). *Let (W, m) be a model and $(\overline{W}, \overline{m})$ defined as previously from a formula φ. Consider $u, v \in W$.*

1. *For all $\psi \in FL(\varphi)$, $u \in m(\psi)$ iff $\overline{u} \in \overline{m}(\psi)$.*
2. *For all $[a]\psi \in FL(\varphi)$,*
   (a) if $(u, v) \in m(a)$ then $(\overline{u}, \overline{v}) \in \overline{m}(a)$;
   (b) if $(\overline{u}, \overline{v}) \in \overline{m}(a)$ and $u \in m([a]\psi)$, then $v \in m(\psi)$.

As a consequence or the previous Lemmas, we can give the following result.

Theorem 1 (Small Model Theorem). *Let φ a satisfiable formula, then φ is satisfied in a model with no more than $2^{|\varphi|}$ states.*

Proof. If φ is satisfiable, then there exists a model (W, m) and $u \in W$ such that $u \in m(\varphi)$. Let us consider $FL(\varphi)$ the Fisher-Lander closure of φ and the filtration model $(\overline{W}, \overline{m})$ of (W, m) by $FL(\varphi)$ defined previously. From Lemma 2, $(\overline{W}, \overline{m})$ is a finite model and by Lemma 3 (Filtration Lemma), we have that $\overline{u} \in \overline{m}(\varphi)$. As a consequence, φ is satisfied in a finite model. Moreover, $\overline{W}$ has no more elements as the truth assignments to formulas in $FL(\varphi)$, which by Lemma 1 is at most $2^{|\varphi|}$.

In order to get the completeness of our system, we construct a *nonstandard model* from maximal consistent sets of formulas and we use a filtration lemma for nonstandard models to collapse it to a finite *standard* model. For lack of space, we present only an sketch of this proof. For more details, see [14].

A *nonstandard model* is any structure $\mathcal{N} = (N, m_{\mathcal{N}})$ such as it is a model in the sense of Section 2 in every respect, except that, for every program a, $m_{\mathcal{N}}(a^*)$ need not to be the reflexive and transitive closure of $m_{\mathcal{N}}(a)$, but only a reflexive and transitive relation which contains $m_{\mathcal{N}}(a)$. Given a nonstandard model $(N, m_{\mathcal{N}})$ and a formula φ, we can construct the filtration model $(\overline{N}, \overline{m}_{\mathcal{N}})$ as above, and the Filtration Lemma (Lemma 3) also holds in this case.

As said before, to obtain completeness, we define a nonstandard model $(N, m_{\mathcal{N}})$ as follows: N contains all the maximal consistent sets of formulas of our logic and $m_{\mathcal{N}}$ is defined, for every formula φ and every program a, by:

$$m_{\mathcal{N}}(\varphi) = \{u \mid \varphi \in u\}; \quad m_{\mathcal{N}}(a) = \{(u, v) \mid \text{for all } \varphi, \text{ if } [a]\varphi \in u \text{ then } \varphi \in v\}$$

It is easy to prove that with the previous definition, all the properties for nonstandard models are satisfied, even the ones for our specific atomic programs. Now, we can give the following completeness result.

Theorem 2. *For every formula φ, if φ is valid then φ is a theorem.*

Proof. We need to prove that if φ is consistent, then it is satisfied. If φ is consistent, it is contained in a maximal consistent set u, which is a state of the nonstandard model constructed above. By the Filtration Lemma for nonstandard models, φ is satisfied in the state $\overline{u}$ of the filtration model $(\overline{N}, \overline{m}_{\mathcal{N}})$.

5   Conclusions and Future Work

A PDL for order of magnitude reasoning has been introduced which deals with qualitative relations as closeness and distance. An axiom system for this logic has been defined by including as axioms the formulas which express syntactically the needed properties. Moreover, we have shown the decidability of the satisfiability problem of our logic. As a future work, we are trying to extend this approach for more relations such as a linear order and negligibility, by maintaining decidability and completeness. Finally, we have planned to give a relational proof system based on dual tableaux for this logic in the line of [10, 13].

References

1. Areces, C., ten Cate, B.: Hybrid Logics. In: Blackburn, P., Van Benthem, J., Wolter, F. (eds.) Handbook of Modal Logic. Studies in Logic and Practical Reasoning, vol. 3, pp. 821–868. Elsevier, Amsterdam (2007)
2. Bennett, B., Cohn, A.G., Wolter, F., Zakharyaschev, M.: Multi-Dimensional Modal Logic as a Framework for Spatio-Temporal Reasoning. Applied Intelligence 17(3), 239–251 (2002)
3. Benthem, J., Eijck, J., Kooi, B.: Logics of communication and change. Information and Computation 204(11), 1620–1662 (2006)
4. Blackburn, P., Van Benthem, J.: Modal Logic: A semantic perspective. In: Blackburn, P., Van Benthem, J., Wolter, F. (eds.) Handbook of Modal Logic. Studies in Logic and Practical Reasoning, vol. 3, pp. 58–61. Elsevier, Amsterdam (2007)
5. Bollig, B., Kuske, D., Meinecke, I.: Propositional dynamic logic for message-passing systems. In: Arvind, V., Prasad, S. (eds.) FSTTCS 2007. LNCS, vol. 4855, pp. 303–315. Springer, Heidelberg (2007)

6. Bugaychenko, D., Soloviev, I.: MASL: A logic for the specification of multiagent real-time systems. In: Burkhard, H.-D., Lindemann, G., Verbrugge, R., Varga, L.Z. (eds.) CEEMAS 2007. LNCS (LNAI), vol. 4696, pp. 183–192. Springer, Heidelberg (2007)
7. Burrieza, A., Muñoz-Velasco, E., Ojeda-Aciego, M.: A Propositional Dynamic Logic Approach for Order of Magnitude Reasoning. In: Geffner, H., Prada, R., Machado Alexandre, I., David, N. (eds.) IBERAMIA 2008. LNCS (LNAI), vol. 5290, pp. 11–20. Springer, Heidelberg (2008)
8. Burrieza, A., Muñoz-Velasco, E., Ojeda-Aciego, M.: A logic for order of magnitude reasoning with negligibility, non-closeness and distance. In: Borrajo, D., Castillo, L., Corchado, J.M. (eds.) CAEPIA 2007. LNCS (LNAI), vol. 4788, pp. 210–219. Springer, Heidelberg (2007)
9. Burrieza, A., Ojeda-Aciego, M.: A multimodal logic approach to order of magnitude qualitative reasoning with comparability and negligibility relations. Fundamenta Informaticae 68, 21–46 (2005)
10. Burrieza, A., Ojeda-Aciego, M., Orłowska, E.: Relational approach to order-of-magnitude reasoning. In: de Swart, H., Orłowska, E., Schmidt, G., Roubens, M. (eds.) TARSKI 2006. LNCS (LNAI), vol. 4342, pp. 105–124. Springer, Heidelberg (2006)
11. Dague, P.: Symbolic reasoning with relative orders of magnitude. In: Proc. 13th Intl. Joint Conference on Artificial Intelligence, pp. 1509–1515. Morgan Kaufmann, San Francisco (1993)
12. Duckham, M., Lingham, J., Mason, K., Worboys, M.: Qualitative reasoning about consistency in geographic information. Information Sciences 176(6, 22), 601–627 (2006)
13. Golińska-Pilarek, J., Muñoz-Velasco, E.: Relational approach for a logic for order of magnitude qualitative reasoning with negligibility, non-closeness and distance. International Journal of Computer Mathematics (to appear, 2009)
14. Harel, D., Kozen, D.: Dynamic Logic. MIT Press, Cambridge (2000)
15. Heinemann, B.: A PDL-like logic of knowledge acquisition. In: Diekert, V., Volkov, M.V., Voronkov, A. (eds.) CSR 2007. LNCS, vol. 4649, pp. 146–157. Springer, Heidelberg (2007)
16. Mirkowska, C., Salwicki, A.: Algorithmic Logic. Kluwer Academic Publishers, Norwell (1987)
17. Nayak, P.: Causal Approximations. Artificial Intelligence 70, 277–334 (1994)
18. Passy, S., Tinchev, T.: An essay in combinatory dynamic logic. Information and Computation 93(2), 263–332 (1991)
19. Raiman, O.: Order of magnitude reasoning. Artificial Intelligence 51, 11–38 (1991)
20. Sanchez, M., Prats, F., Piera, N.: Una formalización de relaciones de comparabilidad en modelos cualitativos. Boletín de la AEPIA (Bulletin of the Spanish Association for AI) 6, 15–22 (1996)
21. Travé-Massuyès, L., Ironi, L., Dague, P.: Mathematical Foundations of Qualitative Reasoning. AI Magazine, American Asociation for Artificial Intelligence, 91–106 (2003)
22. Travé-Massuyès, L., Prats, F., Sánchez, M., Agell, N.: Relative and absolute order-of-magnitude models unified. Annals of Mathematics and Artificial Intelligence 45, 323–341 (2005)
23. Wolter, F., Zakharyaschev, M.: Qualitative spatio-temporal representation and reasoning: a computational perspective. In: Lakemeyer, G., Nebel, B. (eds.) Exploring Artificial Intelligence in the New Millenium. Morgan Kaufmann, San Francisco (2002)

Base Belief Change
for Finitary Monotonic Logics

Pere Pardo[1], Pilar Dellunde[1,2], and Lluís Godo[1]

[1] Institut d'Investigació en Intel·ligència Artificial (IIIA - CSIC)
08193 Bellaterra, Spain
[2] Universitat Autònoma de Barcelona (UAB) 08193 Bellaterra, Spain

Abstract. We slightly improve on characterization results already in the literature for base revision. We show that consistency-based partial meet revision operators can be axiomatized for any sentential logic $\mathcal{S}$ satisfying finitarity and monotonicity conditions (neither the deduction theorem nor supraclassicality are required to hold in $\mathcal{S}$). A characterization of limiting cases of revision operators, full meet and maxichoice, is also offered. In the second part of the paper, as a particular case, we focus on the class of graded fuzzy logics and distinguish two types of bases, naturally arising in that context, exhibiting different behavior.

1 Introduction

This paper is about (multiple) base belief change, in particular our results are mainly about base revision, which is characterized for a broad class of logics. The original framework of Alchourrón, Gärdenfors and Makinson (AGM) [1] deals with belief change operators on deductively closed theories. This framework was generalized by Hansson [9,10] to deal with *bases*, i.e. arbitrary set of formulas, the original requirement of logical closure being dropped. Hansson characterized revision and contraction operators in, essentially, monotonic compact logics with the deduction theorem property. These results were improved in [11] by Hansson and Wassermann: while for contraction ([11, Theorem 3.8]) it is shown that finitarity and monotony of the underlying logic suffice, for revision (Theorem [11, Theorem 3.17]) their proof depends on a further condition, *Non-contravention*: for all sentences φ, if $\neg\varphi \in \mathrm{Cn}_{\mathcal{S}}(T \cup \{\varphi\})$, then $\neg\varphi \in \mathrm{Cn}_{\mathcal{S}}(T)$.

In this paper we provide a further improvement of Hansson and Wassermann's results by proving a characterization theorem for base revision in any finitary monotonic logic. Namely, in the context of partial meet base revision, we show that *Non-contravention* can be dropped in the characterization of revision if we replace the notion of unprovability (remainders) by consistency in the definition of partial meet, taking inspiration from [4]. This is the main contribution of the paper, together with its extension to the characterization of the revision

P. Meseguer, L. Mandow, and R.M. Gasca (Eds.): CAEPIA 2009, LNAI 5988, pp. 81–90, 2010.

operators corresponding to limiting cases of selection functions, i.e. full meet and maxichoice revision operators.

In the second part of the paper, as a particular class of finitary monotonic logics, we focus on graded fuzzy logics. We introduce there a distinction in basehood and observe some differences in the behavior of the corresponding base revision operators.

This paper is structured as follows. First we introduce in Section 2 the necessary background material on logic and partial meet base belief change. Then in Section 3 we set out the main characterization results for base revision, including full meet and maxichoice revision operators. Finally in Section 4 we briefly introduce fuzzy graded logics, present a natural distinction between bases in these logics (whether or not they are taken to be closed under truth-degrees) and compare both kinds of bases.

2   Preliminaries on Theory and Base Belief Change

We introduce in this section the concepts and results needed later. Following [6], we define a logic S as a finitary and structural consequence relation $\vdash_S \subseteq \mathcal{P}(\mathbf{Fm}) \times \mathbf{Fm}$, for some algebra of formulas $\mathbf{Fm}$[1].

Belief change is the study of how some theory T (non-necessarily closed, as we use the term) in a given language L can adapt to new incoming information $\varphi \in L$ (inconsistent with T, in the interesting case). The main operations are: *revision*, where the new input must follow from the revised theory, which is to be consistent, and *contraction* where the input must not follow from the contracted theory. In the classical paper [1], by Alchourrón, Gärdenfors and Makinson, partial meet revision and contraction operations were characterized for closed theories in, essentially, monotonic compact logics with the deduction property[2]. Their work put in solid grounds this newly established area of research, opening the way for other formal studies involving new objects of change, operations (see [14] for a comprehensive list) or logics. We follow [1] and define change operators by using partial meet: *Partial meet* consists in (i) generating all logically maximal ways to adapt T to the new sentence (those subtheories of T making further information loss logically unnecessary), (ii) selecting some of these possibilities, (iii) forming their meet, and, optionally, (iv) performing additional steps (if required by the operation). Then a set of axioms is provided to capture these partial meet operators, by showing equivalence between satisfaction of these

---

[1] That is, S satisfies (1) If $\varphi \in \Gamma$ then $\Gamma \vdash_S \varphi$, (2) If $\Gamma \vdash_S \varphi$ and $\Gamma \subseteq \Delta$ then $\Delta \vdash_S \varphi$, (3) If $\Gamma \vdash_S \varphi$ and for every $\psi \in \Gamma$, $\Delta \vdash_S \psi$ then $\Delta \vdash_S \varphi$ (*consequence relation*); (4) If $\Gamma \vdash_S \varphi$ then for some finite $\Gamma_0 \subseteq \Gamma$ we have $\Gamma_0 \vdash_S \varphi$ (*finitarity*); (5) If $\Gamma \vdash_S \varphi$ then $e[\Gamma] \vdash_S e(\varphi)$ for all substitutions $e \in Hom(\mathbf{Fm}, \mathbf{Fm})$ (*structurality*). We will use throughout the paper relational $\vdash_S$ and functional Cn_S notation indistinctively, where Cn_S is the consequence operator induced by S. We will further assume the language of S contains symbols for conditional $\rightarrow$ and *falsum* $\bar{0}$.

[2] That is, logics satisfying the Deduction Theorem: $\varphi \vdash_S \psi$ iff $\vdash_S \varphi \rightarrow \psi$.

axioms and being a partial meet operator[3]. In addition, new axioms may be introduced to characterize the limiting cases of selection in step (ii), full meet and maxichoice selection types. Finally, results showing the different operation types can be defined each other are usually provided too.

A *base* is an arbitrary set of formulas, the original requirement of logical closure being dropped. Base belief change, for the same logical framework than AGM, was characterized by Hansson (see [9], [10]). The results for contraction and revision were improved in [11] (by Hansson and Wassermann): for contraction ([11, Theorem 3.8]) it is shown that finitarity and monotony suffice, while for revision ([11, Theorem 3.17]) their proof depends on a further condition, *Non-contravention*: for all sentences φ, if $\neg\varphi \in \mathrm{Cn}_S(T \cup \{\varphi\})$, then $\neg\varphi \in \mathrm{Cn}_S(T)$. Observe this condition holds in logics having (i) the deduction property and (ii) the structural axiom of Contraction[4]. We show *Non-contravention* can be dropped in the characterization of revision if we replace unprovability (remainders) by consistency in the definition of partial meet.

The main difference between base and theory revision is syntax-sensitivity (see [12] and [3] for a discussion): two equivalent bases may output different solutions under a fixed revision operator and input (compare e.g. $T = \{p, q\}$ and $T' = \{p \wedge q\}$ under revision by $\neg p$, which give $\{\neg p, q\}$ and $\{\neg p\}$ respectively). Another difference lies in maxichoice operations: for theory revision it was proved in [2] that: non-trivial revision maxichoice operations $T \circledast \varphi$ output complete theories, even if T is far from being complete. This was seen as an argument against maxichoice. For base belief change, in contrast, the previous fact is not the case, so maxichoice operators may be simply seen as modeling optimal knowledge situations for a given belief change problem.

3   Multiple Base Revision for Finitary Monotonic Logics

Partial meet was originally defined in terms of unprovability of the contraction input sentences: *remainders* are maximal subsets of T failing to imply φ. This works fine for logics with the deduction theorem, where remainders and their consistency-based counterparts (defined below) coincide. But, for the general case, remainder-based revision does not grant consistency and it is necessary to adopt the consistency-based approach. Observe we also generalize revision operators to the *multiple* case, where the input of revision is allowed to be a base, rather than just a single sentence.

---

[3] Other known formal mechanisms defining change operators can be classified into two broad classes: *selection*-based mechanisms include selection functions on remainder sets and incision functions on kernels; *ranking*-based mechanisms include entrenchments and systems of spheres. For the logical framework assumed in the original developments (compact -and monotonic- closure operators satisfying the deduction property), all these methods are equivalent (see [14] for a comparison). These equivalences between methods need not be preserved in more general class of logics.

[4] If $T \cup \{\varphi\} \vdash_S \varphi \rightarrow \bar{0}$, then by the deduction property $T \vdash_S \varphi \rightarrow (\varphi \rightarrow \bar{0})$; i.e. $T \vdash_S (\varphi \& \varphi) \rightarrow \bar{0}$. Finally, by transitivity and the axiom of contraction, $\vdash_S \varphi \rightarrow \varphi \& \varphi$, we obtain $T \vdash_S \varphi \rightarrow \bar{0}$.

Definition 1. ([15], [4]) *Given some monotonic logic* $\vdash_S$, *let* T_0, T_1 *be theories. We say* T_0 *is* consistent *if* $T_0 \nvdash_S \bar{0}$, *and define the set* $\mathrm{Con}(T_0, T_1)$ *of subsets of* T_0 *maximally consistent with* T_1 *as follows:* $X \in \mathrm{Con}(T_0, T_1)$ *iff:*

(i) $X \subseteq T_0$,
(ii) $X \cup T_1$ *is consistent, and*
(iii) For any X' *such that* $X \subsetneq X' \subset T_0$, *we have* $X' \cup T_1$ *is inconsistent*

Now we prove some properties[5] of $\mathrm{Con}(\cdot, \cdot)$ which will be helpful for the characterization theorems of base belief change operators for arbitrary finitary monotonic logics.

Lemma 1. *Let* S *be some finitary logic and* T_0 *a theory. For any* $X \subseteq T_0$, *if* $X \cup T_1$ *is consistent, then* X *can be extended to some* Y *with* $Y \in \mathrm{Con}(T_0, T_1)$.

Proof. Let $X \subseteq T_0$ with $X \cup T_1 \nvdash_S \bar{0}$. Consider the poset $(T^*, \subseteq)$, where $T^* = \{Y \subseteq T_0 : X \subseteq Y \text{ and } Y \cup T_1 \nvdash_S \bar{0}\}$. Let $\{Y_i\}_{i \in I}$ be a chain in $(T^*, \subseteq)$; that is, each Y_i is a subset of T_0 and consistent with T_1. Hence, $\bigcup_{i \in I} Y_i \subseteq T_0$; since S is finitary, $\bigcup_{i \in I} Y_i$ is also consistent with T_1 and hence is an upper bound for the chain. Applying Zorn's Lemma, we obtain an element Z in the poset with the next properties: $X \subseteq Z \subseteq T$ and Z maximal w.r.t. $Z \cup \{\varphi\} \nvdash_S \bar{0}$. Thus $X \subseteq Z \in \mathrm{Con}(T, \varphi)$.

Remark 1. Considering $X = \emptyset$ in the preceding lemma, we infer: if T_1 is consistent, then $\mathrm{Con}(T_0, T_1) \neq \emptyset$.

For simplicity, we assume that the input base T_1 (to revise T_0 by) is consistent. Now, the original definition of selection functions is modified according to the consistency-based approach.

Definition 2. *Let* T_0 *be a theory. A* selection function *for* T_0 *is a function*

$$\gamma : \mathcal{P}(\mathcal{P}(\mathbf{Fm})) \setminus \{\emptyset\} \longrightarrow \mathcal{P}(\mathcal{P}(\mathbf{Fm})) \setminus \{\emptyset\}$$

such that for all $T_1 \subseteq \mathbf{Fm}$, $\gamma(\mathrm{Con}(T_0, T_1)) \subseteq \mathrm{Con}(T_0, T_1)$ *and* $\gamma(\mathrm{Con}(T_0, T_1))$ *is non-empty.*

Thus, selection functions and revision operators are defined relative to some fixed base T_0. Although, instead of writing $\circledast^{T_0} T_1$, we use the traditional infix notation $T_0 \circledast T_1$ for the operation of revising base T_0 by T_1.

3.1   Base Belief Revision

The axioms we propose (inspired by [4]) to characterize (multiple) base revision operators for finitary monotonic logics S are the following, for arbitrary sets T_0, T_1:

---

[5] Note that $\mathrm{Con}(T_0, T_1)$ cannot be empty, since if input T_1 is consistent, then in the worst case, we will have $\emptyset \subseteq T_0$ to be consistent with T_1.

(F1) $T_1 \subseteq T_0 \circledast T_1$ (Success)

(F2) If T_1 is consistent, then $T_0 \circledast T_1$ is also consistent. (Consistency)

(F3) $T_0 \circledast T_1 \subseteq T_0 \cup T_1$ (Inclusion)

(F4) For all $\psi \in \mathbf{Fm}$, if $\psi \in T_0 - T_0 \circledast T_1$ then,
there exists T' with $T_0 \circledast T_1 \subseteq T' \subseteq T_0 \cup T_1$
and such that $T' \nvdash_{\mathcal{S}} \bar{0}$ but $T' \cup \{\psi\} \vdash_{\mathcal{S}} \bar{0})$ (Relevance)

(F5) If for all $T' \subseteq T_0$ $(T' \cup T_1 \nvdash_{\mathcal{S}} \bar{0} \Leftrightarrow T' \cup T_2 \nvdash_{\mathcal{S}} \bar{0})$
then $T_0 \cap (T_0 \circledast T_1) = T_0 \cap (T_0 \circledast T_2)$ (Uniformity)

Given some theory $T_0 \subseteq \mathbf{Fm}$ and selection function γ for T_0, we define the partial meet revision operator $\circledast_\gamma$ for T_0 by $T_1 \subseteq \mathbf{Fm}$ as follows:

$$T_0 \circledast_\gamma T_1 = \bigcap \gamma(\mathrm{Con}(T_0, T_1)) \cup T_1$$

Definition 3. *Let $\mathcal{S}$ be some finitary logic, and T_0 a theory. Then $\circledast : \mathcal{P}(\mathbf{Fm}) \to \mathcal{P}(\mathbf{Fm})$ is a revision operator for T_0 iff for any $T_1 \subseteq \mathbf{Fm}$, $T_0 \circledast T_1 = T_0 \circledast_\gamma T_1$ for some selection function γ for T_0.*

Lemma 2. *The condition $\mathrm{Con}(T_0, T_1) = \mathrm{Con}(T_0, T_2)$ is equivalent to the antecedent of Axiom (F5)*

$$\forall T' \subseteq T_0 \ (T' \cup T_1 \nvdash_{\mathcal{S}} \bar{0} \Leftrightarrow T' \cup T_2 \nvdash_{\mathcal{S}} \bar{0})$$

Proof. (If-then) Assume $\mathrm{Con}(T_0, T_1) = \mathrm{Con}(T_0, T_2)$ and let $T' \subseteq T_0$ with $T' \cup T_1 \nvdash_{\mathcal{S}} \bar{0}$. By Lemma 1, T' can be extended to $X \in \mathrm{Con}(T_0, T_1)$. Hence, by assumption we get $T' \subseteq X \in \mathrm{Con}(T_0, T_2)$ so that $T' \cup T_2 \nvdash_{\mathcal{S}} \bar{0}$ follows. The other direction is similar. (Only if) This direction follows from the definition of $\mathrm{Con}(T_0, \cdot)$.

Finally, we are in conditions to prove the main characterization result for partial meet revision.

Theorem 1. *Let $\mathcal{S}$ be a finitary monotonic logic. For any $T_0 \subseteq \mathbf{Fm}$ and function $\circledast : \mathcal{P}(\mathbf{Fm}) \to \mathcal{P}(\mathbf{Fm})$:*

$\circledast$ *satisfies* (F1) − (F5) *iff* $\circledast$ *is a revision operator for* T_0

Proof. (Soundness) Given some partial meet revision operator $\circledast_\gamma$ for T_0, we prove $\circledast_\gamma$ satisfies (F1) − (F5).

(F1) − (F3) hold by definition of $\circledast_\gamma$. (F4) Let $\psi \in T_0 - T_0 \circledast_\gamma T_1$. Hence, $\psi \notin T_1$ and for some $X \in \gamma(\mathrm{Con}(T_0, T_1))$, $\psi \notin X$. Simply put $T' = X \cup T_1$: by definitions of $\circledast_\gamma$ and Con we have (i) $T_0 \circledast_\gamma T_1 \subseteq T' \subseteq T_0 \cup T_1$ and (ii) T' is consistent (since T_1 is). We also have (iii) $T' \cup \{\psi\}$ is inconsistent (otherwise $\psi \in X$ would follow from maximality of X and $\psi \in T_0$, hence contradicting our previous step $\psi \notin X$). (F5) We have to show, assuming the antecedent of (F5), that $T_0 \cap (T_0 \circledast_\gamma T_1) = T_0 \cap (T_0 \circledast_\gamma T_2)$. We prove the $\subseteq$ direction only since the other is similar. Assume, then, for all $T' \subseteq T_0$,

$$T' \cup T_1 \nvdash_{\mathcal{S}} \bar{0} \Leftrightarrow T' \cup T_2 \nvdash_{\mathcal{S}} \bar{0}$$

and let $\psi \in T_0 \cap (T_0 \circledast_\gamma T_1)$. This set is just $T_0 \cap (\bigcap \gamma(Con(T_0, T_1)) \cup T_1)$ which can be transformed into $(T_0 \cap \bigcap \gamma(Con(T_0, T_1))) \cup (T_0 \cup T_1)$, i.e. $\bigcap \gamma(Con(T_0, T_1)) \cup (T_0 \cup T_1)$ (since $\bigcap \gamma(Con(T_0, T_1)) \subseteq T_0$). <u>Case</u> $\psi \in \bigcap \gamma(Con(T_0, T_1))$. Then we use Lemma 2 upon the assumption to obtain $\bigcap \gamma(Con(T_0, T_1)) = \bigcap \gamma(Con(T_0, T_2))$, since γ is a function. <u>Case</u> $\psi \in T_0 \cap T_1$. Then $\psi \in X$ for all $X \in \gamma(Con(T_0, T_1))$, by maximality of X. Hence, $\psi \in \bigcap \gamma(Con(T_0, T_1))$. Using the same argument than in the former case, $\psi \in \bigcap \gamma(Con(T_0, T_2))$. Since we also assumed $\psi \in T_0$, we obtain $\psi \in T_0 \cap (T_0 \circledast_\gamma T_2)$.

(<u>Completeness</u>) Let $\circledast$ satisfy (F1) $-$ (F5). We have to show that for some selection function γ and any T_1, $T_0 \circledast T_1 = T \circledast_\gamma T_1$. We define first

$$\gamma(\mathrm{Con}(T_0, T_1)) = \{X \in \mathrm{Con}(T_0, T_1) : X \supseteq T_0 \cap (T_0 \circledast T_1)\}$$

We prove that (1) γ is well-defined, (2) γ is a selection function and (3) $T_0 \circledast T_1 = T \circledast_\gamma T_1$.

(1) Assume (i) $\mathrm{Con}(T_0, T_1) = \mathrm{Con}(T_0, T_2)$; we prove that $\gamma(\mathrm{Con}(T_0, T_1)) = \gamma(\mathrm{Con}(T_0, T_2))$. Applying Lemma 2 to (i) we obtain the antecedent of (F5). Since $\circledast$ satisfies this axiom, we have (ii) $T_0 \cap (T_0 \circledast T_1) = T_0 \cap (T_0 \circledast T_2)$. By the above definition of γ, $\gamma(\mathrm{Con}(T_0, T_1)) = \gamma(\mathrm{Con}(T_0, T_2))$ follows from (i) and (ii).

(2) Since T_1 is consistent, by Remark 1 we obtain $\mathrm{Con}(T_0, T_1)$ is not empty; we have to show that $\gamma(\mathrm{Con}(T_0, T_1))$ is not empty either (since the other condition $\gamma(\mathrm{Con}(T_0, T_1)) \subseteq \mathrm{Con}(T_0, T_1)$ is met by the above definition of γ). We have $T_0 \cap T_0 \circledast T_1 \subseteq T_0 \circledast T_1$; the latter is consistent and contains T_1, by (F2) and (F1), respectively; thus, $(T_0 \cap T_0 \circledast T_1) \cup T_1$ is consistent; from this and $T_0 \cap T_0 \circledast T_1 \subseteq T_0$, we deduce by Lemma 1 that $T_0 \cap T_0 \circledast T_1$ is extensible to some $X \in \mathrm{Con}(T_0, T_1)$. Thus, exists some $X \in \mathrm{Con}(T_0, T_1)$ such that $X \supseteq T_0 \cap T_0 \circledast T_1$. In consequence, $X \in \gamma(\mathrm{Con}(T_0, T_1)) \neq \emptyset$.

For (3), we prove first $T_0 \circledast T_1 \subseteq T_0 \circledast_\gamma T_1$. Let $\psi \in T_0 \circledast T_1$. By (F3), $\psi \in T_0 \cup T_1$. <u>Case</u> $\psi \in T_1$: then trivially $\psi \in T_0 \circledast_\gamma T_1$ <u>Case</u> $\psi \in T_0$. Then $\psi \in T_0 \cap T_0 \circledast T_1$. In consequence, for any $X \in \mathrm{Con}(T_0, T_1)$, if $X \supseteq T_0 \cap T_0 \circledast T_1$ then $\psi \in X$. This implies, by definition of γ above, that for all $X \in \gamma(\mathrm{Con}(T_0, T_1))$ we have $\psi \in X$, so that $\psi \in \bigcap \gamma(\mathrm{Con}(T_0, T_1)) \subseteq T_0 \circledast_\gamma T_1$. In both cases, we obtain $\psi \in T_0 \circledast_\gamma T_1$.

Now, for the other direction: $T_0 \circledast_\gamma T_1 \subseteq T_0 \circledast T_1$. Let $\psi \in \bigcap \gamma(\mathrm{Con}(T_0, T_1)) \cup T_1$. By (F1), we have $T_1 \in T_0 \circledast T_1$; then, in case $\psi \in T_1$ we are done. So we may assume $\psi \in \bigcap \gamma(\mathrm{Con}(T_0, T_1))$. Now, in order to apply (F4), let X be arbitrary with $T \circledast T_1 \subseteq X \subseteq T_0 \cup T_1$ and X consistent. Consider $X \cap T_0$: since $T_1 \subseteq T_0 \circledast T_1 \subseteq X$ implies $X = X \cup T_1$ is consistent, so is $(X \cap T_0) \cup T_1$. Together with $X \cap T_0 \subseteq T_0$, by Lemma 1 there is $Y \in \mathrm{Con}(T_0, T_1)$ with $X \cap T_0 \subseteq Y$. In addition, since $T_0 \circledast T_1 \subseteq X$ implies $T_0 \circledast T_1 \cap T_0 \subseteq X \cap T_0 \subseteq Y$, we obtain $Y \in \gamma(\mathrm{Con}(T_0, T_1))$, by the definition of γ above. Condition $X \cap T_0 \subseteq Y$ also implies $(X \cap T_0) \cup T_1 \subseteq Y \cup T_1$. Observe that from $X \subseteq X \cup T_1$ and $X \subseteq T_0 \cup T_1$ we infer that $X \subseteq (X \cup T_1) \cap (T_0 \cup T_1)$. From the latter being identical to $(X \cap T_0) \cup T_1$ and the fact that $(X \cap T_0) \cup T_1 \subseteq Y \cup T_1$, we obtain that $X \subseteq Y \cup T_1$. Since $\psi \in Y \in \mathrm{Con}(T_0, T_1)$, we have $Y \cup T_1$ is consistent with ψ, so its subset X is also consistent with ψ. Finally, we may apply *modus tollens* on Axiom (F4) to obtain that $\psi \notin T_0 - T_0 \circledast T_1$, i.e. $\psi \notin T_0$ or $\psi \in T_0 \circledast T_1$. But since the former is false, the latter must be the case.

Full meet and maxichoice base revision operators. The previous result can be extended to limiting cases of selection functions formally defined next.

Definition 4. *A revision operator for T_0 is* full meet *if it is generated by the identity selection function* $\gamma_{\mathrm{fm}} = \mathsf{Id}$: $\gamma_{\mathrm{fm}}(\mathrm{Con}(T_0, T_1)) = \mathrm{Con}(T_0, T_1)$; *that is,*

$$T_0 \circledast_{\mathrm{fm}} T_1 = (\bigcap \mathrm{Con}(T_0, T_1)) \cup T_1$$

A revision operator for T_0 is maxichoice *if it is generated by a selection function of type* $\gamma_{\mathrm{mc}}(\mathrm{Con}(T_0, T_1)) = \{X\}$, *for some $X \in \mathrm{Con}(T_0, T_1)$, and in that case* $T_0 \circledast_{\gamma_{\mathrm{mc}}} T_1 = X \cup T_1$.

To characterize *full meet* and *maxichoice* revision operators for some theory T_0 in any finitary logic, we define the next additional axioms:

(FM)   For any $X \subseteq \mathbf{Fm}$ with $T_1 \subseteq X \subseteq T_0 \cup T_1$
  $X \nvdash_S \overline{0}$ implies $X \cup (T_0 \circledast T_1) \nvdash_S \overline{0}$
(MC) For all $\psi \in \mathbf{Fm}$ with $\psi \in T_0 - T_0 \circledast T_1$ we have
  $T_0 \circledast T_1 \cup \{\psi\} \vdash_S \overline{0}$

Theorem 2. *Let $T_0 \subseteq \mathbf{Fm}$ and $\circledast$ be a function $\circledast : \mathcal{P}(\mathbf{Fm})^2 \to \mathcal{P}(\mathbf{Fm})$. Then the following hold:*

(fm) $\circledast$ *satisfies* (F1) $-$ (F5) *and* (FM)   iff $\circledast = \circledast_{\gamma_{\mathrm{fm}}}$
(mc) $\circledast$ *satisfies* (F1) $-$ (F5) *and* (MC)   iff $\circledast = \circledast_{\gamma_{\mathrm{mc}}}$

Proof. We prove (fm) first. (Soundness): We know $\circledast_{\gamma_{\mathrm{fm}}}$ satisfies (F1) $-$ (F5) so it remains to be proved that (FM) holds. Let X be such that $T_1 \subseteq X \subseteq T_0 \cup T_1$ and $X \nvdash_S \overline{0}$. From the latter and $X - T_1 \subseteq (T_0 \cup T_1) - T_1 \subseteq T_0$ we infer by Lemma 1 that $X - T_1 \subseteq Y \in \mathrm{Con}(T_0, T_1)$, for some Y. Notice $X = X' \cup T_1$ and that for any $X'' \in \mathrm{Con}(T_0, T_1)$ $X'' \cup T_1$ is consistent and

$$T_0 \circledast_{\gamma_{\mathrm{fm}}} T_1 = (\bigcap \mathrm{Con}(T_0, T_1)) \cup T_1 \subseteq X' \subseteq X''$$

Hence $X \subseteq X''$, so that $T_0 \circledast_{\gamma_{\mathrm{fm}}} T_1 \cup X \subseteq X''$. Since the latter is consistent, $T_0 \circledast_{\mathrm{fm}} T_1 \cup X \nvdash_S \overline{0}$. (Completeness) Let $\circledast$ satisfy (F1) $-$ (F5) and (FM). It suffices to prove that $X \in \gamma(\mathrm{Con}(T_0, T_1)) \Leftrightarrow X \in \mathrm{Con}(T_0, T_1)$; but we already know that $\circledast = \circledast_\gamma$, for selection function γ (for T_0) defined by: $X \in \gamma(\mathrm{Con}(T_0, T_1)) \Leftrightarrow T_0 \cap T_0 \circledast T_1 \subseteq X$. It is enough to prove, then, that $X \in \mathrm{Con}(T_0, T_1)$ implies $X \supseteq T_0 \cap T_0 \circledast T_1$. Let $X \in \mathrm{Con}(T_0, T_1)$ and let $\psi \in T_0 \cap T_0 \circledast T_1$. Since $\psi \in T_0$ and $X \in \mathrm{Con}(T_0, T_1)$, we have by maximality of X that either $X \cup \{\psi\} \vdash_S \overline{0}$ or $\psi \in X$. We prove the former case to be impossible: assuming it we would have $T_1 \subseteq X \cup T_1 \subseteq T_0 \cup T_1$. By (FM), $X \cup T_1 \cup (T_0 \circledast T_1) \nvdash_S \overline{0}$. Since $\psi \in T_0 \circledast T_1$, we would obtain $X \cup \{\psi\} \nvdash_S \overline{0}$, hence contradicting the case assumption; since the former case is not possible, we have $\psi \in X$. Since X was arbitrary, $X \in \mathrm{Con}(T_0, T_1)$ implies $X \subseteq T_0 \cap T_0 \circledast T_1$ and we are done.

For (mc): (Soundness) We prove (MC), since (F1) − (F5) follow from $\circledast_{\gamma_{mc}}$ being a partial meet revision operator. Let $X \in \mathrm{Con}(T_0, T_1)$ be such that $T_0 \circledast_{\gamma_{mc}} \varphi = X \cup T_1$ and let $\psi \in T_0 - T_0 \circledast_{\gamma_{mc}} T_1$. We have $\psi \notin X \cup T_1 = T_0 \circledast T_1$. Since $\psi \in T_0$ and $X \in \mathrm{Con}(T_0, T_1)$, $X \cup \{\psi\} \vdash_S \bar{0}$. Finally $T_0 \circledast T_1 \cup \{\psi\} \vdash_S \bar{0}$. (Completeness) Let $\circledast$ satisfy (F1) − (F5) and (MC). We must prove $\circledast = \circledast_{\gamma_{mc}}$, for some maxichoice selection function γ_{mc}. Let $X, Y \in \mathrm{Con}(T_0, T_1)$; we have to prove $X = Y$. In search of a contradiction, assume the contrary, i.e. $\psi \in X - Y$. We have $\psi \notin \bigcap \gamma(\mathrm{Con}(T_0, T_1))$ and $\psi \in X \subseteq T_0$. By MC, $T_0 \circledast T_1 \cup \{\psi\} \vdash_S \bar{0}$. Since $T_0 \circledast T_1 \subseteq X$, we obtain $X \cup \{\psi\}$ is also inconsistent, contradicting previous $\psi \in X \nvdash_S \bar{0}$. Thus $X = Y$ which makes $\circledast = \circledast_{\gamma_{mc}}$, for some maxichoice selection function γ_{mc}.

4   The Case of Graded Fuzzy Logics

The characterization results for base revision operators from the previous section required weak assumptions (monotony and finitarity) upon the consequence relation $\vdash_S$. In particular these results hold for a wide family of systems of mathematical fuzzy logic. The distinctive feature of these logics is that they cope with graded truth in a compositional manner (see [8]). Graded truth may be dealt implicitly, by means of comparative statements, or explicitly, by introducing truth-degrees in the language. Here we will focus on a particular kind of fuzzy logical languages allowing for explicit representation of truth-degrees, that will be referred as *graded fuzzy logics*, and which are expansions of t-norm logics with countable sets of truth-constants, see e.g. [5]. These logics allow for occurrences of truth-degrees, represented as new propositional atoms $\bar{r}$ (one for each $r \in C$) in any part of a formula. These truth-constants and propositional variables can be combined arbitrarily using connectives to obtain new formulas. The graded language obtained in this way will be denoted as $\mathbf{Fm}(C)$. A prominent example of a logic over a graded language is Hájek's Rational Pavelka Logic $\mathbf{RPL}$ [8], an extension of Łukasiewicz logic with rational truth-constants in $[0, 1]$; for other graded extensions of t-norm based fuzzy logics see e.g. [5]. In t-norm based fuzzy logics, due to the fact that the implication is residuated, a formula $\bar{r} \to \varphi$ gets value 1 under a given interpretation e iff $r \leq e(\varphi)$. In what follows, we will also use the signed language notation (φ, r) to denote the formula $\bar{r} \to \varphi$.

If S denotes a given t-norm logic, let us denote by $S(C)$ the corresponding expansion with truth-constants from a suitable countable set C such that $\{0, 1\} \subset C \subseteq [0, 1]$. For instance if S is Łukasiewicz logic and $C = \mathbb{Q} \cap [0, 1]$, then $S(C)$ would refer to $\mathbf{RPL}$. For these graded fuzzy logics, besides the original definition of a base as simply a set of formulas, it makes sense to consider another natural notion of basehood, where bases are closed by lower bounds of truth-degrees. We call them C-closed bases.

Definition 5. *(Adapted from [9]) Given some (monotonic) t-norm fuzzy logic S with language $\mathbf{Fm}$ and a countable set $C \subset [0, 1]$ of truth-constants, let $T \subseteq \mathbf{Fm}(C)$ be a base in $S(C)$. We define $\mathrm{Cn}_C(T) = \{(\varphi, r') : (\varphi, r) \in T, \text{ for } r, r' \in C \text{ with } r \geq r'\}$. A base $T \subseteq \mathbf{Fm}(C)$ is called C-closed when $T = \mathrm{Cn}_C(T)$.*

Notice that, using Gerla's framework of abstract fuzzy logic [7], Booth and Richther [4] define revision operators for bases which are closed with respect to truth-values in some complete lattice W.

The following results prove $\circledast_\gamma$ operators preserve $\mathcal{C}$-closure, thus making $\mathcal{C}$-closed revision a particular case of base revision under Theorem 1.

Proposition 1. *If T_0, T_1 are $\mathcal{C}$-closed graded bases, for any partial meet revision operator $\circledast_\gamma$, $T_0 \circledast_\gamma T_1$ is also a $\mathcal{C}$-closed graded base.*

Proof. Since T_0 is $\mathcal{C}$-closed, by maximality of $X \in \gamma(\mathrm{Con}(T_0, T_1))$ we have X is also $\mathcal{C}$-closed, for any such X. Let $(\psi, s) \in \bigcap \gamma(\mathrm{Con}(T_0, T_1))$ and $s' <_\mathcal{C} s$ for some $s' \in \mathcal{C}$. Then $(\psi, s) \in X$ for any $X \in \gamma(\mathrm{Con}(T_0, T_1))$ implies $(\psi, s') \in X$ for any such X. Hence $\bigcap \gamma(\mathrm{Con}(T_0, T_1))$ is $\mathcal{C}$-closed. Finally, since T_1 is $\mathcal{C}$-closed, we deduce $\bigcap \gamma(\mathrm{Con}(T_0, T_1)) \cup T_1$ is also $\mathcal{C}$-closed.

Let $\mathcal{P}_\mathcal{C}(\mathbf{Fm})$ be the set of $\mathcal{C}$-closed sets of $\mathbf{Fm}$ sentences. We introduce an additional axiom (F0) for revision of $\mathcal{C}$-closed bases by $\mathcal{C}$-closed inputs:

$$\text{(F0)} \quad T_0 \circledast T_1 \text{ is } \mathcal{C}\text{-closed, if } T_0, T_1 \text{ are}$$

Corollary 1. *Assume $\mathcal{S}$ and $\mathcal{C}$ are as before and let $\circledast : \mathcal{P}_\mathcal{C}(\mathbf{Fm}) \to \mathcal{P}(\mathbf{Fm})$. Then, $\circledast$ satisfies (F0) − (F5) iff for some selection function γ, $T_0 \circledast T_1 = T_0 \circledast_\gamma T_1$ for every $T_1 \in \mathcal{P}_\mathcal{C}(\mathbf{Fm})$.*

As shown in the next example, $\mathcal{C}$-closed revision makes a big difference[6] in **RPL**. (Recall that **RPL** negation function, defined in $[0, 1]$, is $n(x) = 1 - x$.)

Example 1. (In **RPL**) Let $\mathcal{C} = \mathbb{Q} \cap [0, 1]$, base $T = \{(p, 0.9), (p \to q, 0.9)\}$ and input $T' = \{(\neg q, 0.4)\}$.

1. (No $\mathcal{C}$-closure.) In this case, we have two maxichoice revision outputs: $\{(p, 0.9), (\neg q, 0.4)\}$, and $\{(p \to q, 0.9), (\neg q, 0.4)\}$; the remaining revision is full meet: $T \circledast_{fm} T' = T'$.
2. (Rational $\mathcal{C}$-closure) Consider base $T_0 = \mathrm{Cn}_\mathcal{C}(T)$ and input $T_1 = \mathrm{Cn}_\mathcal{C}(T')$. Maxichoice revisions $T_0 \circledast_{mc} T_1$ are of form: $T_0 \circledast_{mc} T_1 = \mathrm{Cn}_\mathcal{C}(\{(p, r), (p \to q, s), (\neg q, 0.4)\})$ for any r, s such that $r + s - 1 = 0.6$ and $r, s \le 0.9$.
3. (Finite $\mathcal{C}$-closure) Under the finite set of truth-constants $\mathcal{C} = \{\frac{k}{10} : k \le 10\}$ (i.e. with constants for $0, 0.1, \ldots, 0.9, 1$), $\mathcal{C}$-closure gives three maxichoice revisions: $r = 0.9, s = 0.7$; $r = s = 0.8$; and $r = 0.7, s = 0.9$ (for sets $T_0 \circledast_{mc} T_1$ defined above); the remaining operators are obtained by combining two maxichoice selections, giving $r = 0.8, s = 0.7$; $r = 0.7, s = 0.8$; and (full meet) $r = s = 0.7$.

---

[6] Examples on syntax-sensitivity show that in base revision it is natural to prefer bases without conjunctive formulas, i.e. to prefer $\{\ldots, \varphi, \psi, \ldots\}$ rather than $\{\ldots, \varphi \wedge \psi, \ldots\}$. This is also the case for **RPL** conjunction &: we should rephrase $\varphi \equiv \bar{r}$ as the two formulas $\bar{r} \to \varphi$, $\overline{1 - r} \to \neg \varphi$, instead of the original definition in [8] of $\equiv$, which would give $(\bar{r} \to \varphi \,\&\, \varphi \to \bar{r})$. This way, we obtain $\mathrm{Cn}_\mathcal{C}(\{\varphi \equiv \overline{0.5}\}) \circledast \mathrm{Cn}_\mathcal{C}(\{\overline{0.7} \to \varphi\}) \vdash_{\mathbf{RPL}} \overline{0.7} \equiv \varphi$.

5 Conclusions

We improved Hansson and Wassermann characterization of revision operators
in a class of logics without the deduction property. Apart from the general theorem, standard results for full meet and maxichoice revision operators are also
provided. Then we moved to the field of graded fuzzy logics, in contradistinction
to the approach by Booth and Richter in [4]; their work inspired us to prove similar results for a more general logical framework, including t-norm based fuzzy
logics from Hájek. Finally, we observed the differences between revision for bases
if they are assumed to be closed under truth-degrees.

Acknowledgements

The authors acknowledge partial support of the Spanish MICINN Consolider
project AT (CSD2007-022), the Generalitat de Catalunya grant 2009-SGR-1434
and the MICINN project FFI2008-03126-E/FILO related to Eurocores-LogICCC
Project LoMoReVI (FP006).

References

1. Alchourrón, C., Gärdenfors, P., Makinson, D.: On the Logic of Theory Change: Partial Meet Contraction and Revision Functions. The Journal of Symbolic Logic 50,
   510–530 (1985)
2. Alchourrón, C., Makinson, D.: On the Logic of Theory Change: Contraction functions and their associated revision functions. Theoria 48, 14–37 (1982)
3. Benferhat, S., Dubois, D., Prade, H.: Some syntactic approaches to the Handling
   of Inconsistent Knowledge Bases: A Comparative Study. Studia Logica 58, 17–45
   (1997)
4. Booth, R., Richter, E.: On Revising Fuzzy Belief Bases. Studia Logica 80, 29–61
   (2005)
5. Esteva, F., Gispert, J., Godo, L., Noguera, C.: Adding truth-constants to logics
   of continuous t-norms: axiomatization and completeness results. Fuzzy Sets and
   Systems 185, 597–618 (2007)
6. Font, J.M., Jansana, R.: A General Algebraic Semantics for Sentential Logics.
   Lecture Notes in Logic, vol. 7. Springer, Heidelberg (1996)
7. Gerla, G.: Fuzzy Logic: Mathematical Tools for Approximate Reasoning. In: Trends
   in Logic, vol. 11, Kluwer, Dordrecht (2001)
8. Hájek, P.: Metamathematics of Fuzzy Logic. In: Trends in Logic, vol. 4, Kluwer,
   Dordrecht (1998)
9. Hansson, S.: Reversing the Levi Identity. J. of Phil. Logic 22, 637–699 (1993)
10. Hansson, S.: A Textbook of Belief Dynamics. Kluwer, Dordrecht (1999)
11. Hansson, S., Wassermann, R.: Local change. Studia Logica 70, 49–76 (2002)
12. Nebel, B.: Base Revision Operations and Schemes: Semantics, Representation and
    Complexity. In: 11th European Conference on Artificial Intelligence, ECAI (1994)
13. Pavelka, J.: On fuzzy logic I, II, III. Zeitschrift für Mathematische Logik und
    Grundlagen der Mathematik 25, 45–52, 119–134, 447–464 (1979)
14. Peppas, P.: Belief Revision. In: van Harmelen, F., Lifschitz, V., Porter, B. (eds.)
    Handbook of Knowledge Representation. Elsevier, Amsterdam (2007)
15. Zhang, D., Foo, N.: Infinitary Belief Revision. J. of Phil. Logic 30, 525–570 (2001)

Common Pitfalls in Ontology Development

María Poveda, Mari Carmen Suárez-Figueroa, and Asunción Gómez-Pérez

Ontology Engineering Group. Departamento de Inteligencia Artificial
Facultad de Informática, Universidad Politécnica de Madrid
Campus de Montegancedo s/n
28660 Boadilla del Monte. Madrid. Spain
mpoveda@delicias.dia.fi.upm.es, {mcsuarez,asun}@fi.upm.es

Abstract. The so-called Ontology Design Patterns (ODPs), which have been defined as solutions to ontological design problems, are of great help to developers when modelling ontologies since these patterns provide a development guide and improve the quality of the resulting ontologies. However, it has been demonstrated that, in many cases, developers encounter difficulties when they have to reuse the correct design patterns and include errors in the modelling. Thus, to avoid pitfalls in ontology modelling, this paper proposes classifying errors into two types: (1) errors related to existing ODPs, called anti-patterns, and (2) errors not related to existing ODPs, called pitfalls. This classification is the result of analysing a set of ontologies. This paper is focused on the pitfalls identified during the analysis. In addition the paper presents a classification of the pitfalls found and a set of pitfall examples.

Keywords: patterns, anti-patterns, pitfalls, ontology.

1 Introduction

Modelling ontologies has become one of the main topics of research within ontological engineering because of the difficulties it involves. In recent years, the emergence of Ontology Design Patterns (ODPs), which are defined as solutions to design problems [4], has supposed a great help to developers when modelling ontologies.

Some experiments [3] carried out in ontology engineering have demonstrated that design patterns are perceived as an aid to modelling ontologies, a development guide, and a way to improve the quality of the resulting ontologies. However, it is well known that [3, 1], in some cases, ontology developers experience difficulties when reusing the patterns during modelling, and include errors in the modelling. Therefore, in order to understand and use correctly ODPs, we need a better support that prevents the emergence of modelling errors.

Thus, to avoid the appearance of pitfalls in ontology development, we are working on the creation of a new set of methodological guides. These guides, based on the identification and classification of modelling errors, classify errors into two types: (1) errors related to ODPs, called *anti-patterns*; and (2) errors not related to ODPs, called *pitfalls*. In this paper, both types are presented. The paper is focused on the pitfalls identified during the analysis. In addition, we include a classification of the pitfalls identified and a set of examples of such pitfalls.

P. Meseguer, L. Mandow, and R.M. Gasca (Eds.): CAEPIA 2009, LNAI 5988, pp. 91–100, 2010.
© Springer-Verlag Berlin Heidelberg 2010

The remainder of the article is structured as follows: Section 2 presents the state of the art of patterns and anti-patterns in ontological engineering. Section 3 describes the analysis carried out in 11 ontologies, which shows the presence of ODPs and describes anti-patterns, and pitfalls. Section 4 includes a template where the pitfalls are described as well as the classification of the pitfalls found and a set of examples of pitfalls. Finally, Section 5 includes the conclusions drawn and future lines of work.

2   State of the Art: Patterns and Anti-Patterns

The term "pattern" [4] appeared in the XIV century and derives from the Latin term "patronus", which, among other meanings, stands for an item that can be imitated. In the 1970s Christopher Alexander introduced the term design pattern [2] to refer to those shared guides that help solve modelling problems.

In ontology engineering, the ontology design patterns can be considered as modelling solutions to problems widely known in the area. These solutions are based on good practices and solve modelling problems.

In the ODPs field, we can distinguish between logical patterns and conceptual patterns [4]. With regard to logical patterns, the W3C work team, known as *"Semantic Web Best Practices and Deployment* (SWBPD)[1], has established that in order to provide support to developers and users of the Semantic Web, a set of good practices is required. To that purpose, this group proposes patterns that solve design problems in the OWL[2] language, independently of the particular conceptualization, which solve logical problems. Regarding conceptual patterns [4], the author proposes patterns (in OWL or any other logical language) that solve design problems for specific domains, which solve content problems.

In addition to the distinction mentioned above, in [6] the authors propose the classification shown in Fig.1.

The work described in [6] is focused on content patterns and provides guidelines on how to apply content ODPs using import, specialization, composition and expansion functions. In the same work, the content ontology anti-pattern concept is defined as a design that is different from a content pattern in that the former codes the solution to a problem in a wrong way.

However, we have observed that none of the papers analyzed have carried out a thorough study on the use of any type of ODPs and their corresponding anti-patterns. We have also observed that there is no previous work focused on identifying and preventing to model errors not related to any existing ODP.

It is worth mentioning that ODPs can be found in on-line libraries that include both the description and the OWL code associated to the patterns as, for example, "the *Ontology Design Pattern* Wiki"[3], or they can be obtained from the work team *"Semantic Web Best Practices and Deployment"*. Some other libraries [6, 7] do not provide the pattern code, but they store descriptions of a great number of ODPs. These libraries, which follow a software engineering approach, use a template for describing the patterns included in the catalogue.

---

[1] http://www.w3.org/2001/sw/BestPractices/
[2] http://www.w3.org/TR/2004/REC-owl-guide-20040210/
[3] http://ontologydesignpatterns.org/

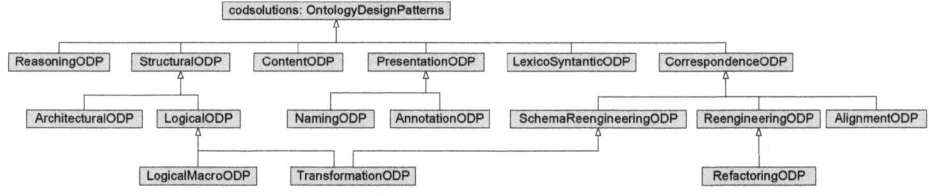

Fig. 1. Ontology Design Pattern types [6]

3 Identification of Patterns, Anti-Patterns and Pitfalls

With the aim of identifying the types of errors normally made when developing ontologies, we have analyzed 11 ontologies that tackle different aspects (art, architecture, geography, tastes and likings, and community services) of the domain of Saint James's Way. These ontologies were developed by Master students as a practical assignment on the "Ontologies and the Semantic Web" subject at the *Universidad Politécnica de Madrid*, during the 2007-2008 academic year. Due to the provenance of the ontologies, most of them were developed in Spanish. The students did not have any previous notion of ODPs; therefore, it did not make sense to focus our study on the correctly or incorrectly reuse of ODPs. Instead, we focused our work on examining whether ODPs, anti-patterns and pitfalls could be detected in the resulting ontologies. The approach adopted in the analysis was based on the manual search of ODPs in ontologies and on the manual identification of two types of modelling errors: (1) those related to ODPs, called *anti-patterns;* and those not related to ODPs, called *pitfalls.*

Taking into account the problem that each ontology intended to solve, the manual analysis of each ontology was centered on the search of ontology modules that corresponded to some of the following scenarios:

- Designs that match solutions proposed in some ODP within those available in libraries [6, 7].
- Design problems that could be solved by reusing some ODP within those available in libraries [6, 7].
- Non appropriate solutions for the design problems under consideration.

As a result of the analysis carried out, we have identified the possibilities shown in the tree of Fig. 2. In that tree, we can distinguish two main branches: the first one, whose nodes are linked by arrows in a continuous line, represents whether an ODP or an anti-pattern has been observed; the second one, whose nodes are linked by arrows in a discontinuous line, represents that no ODP has been observed, but where it is possible to apply some ODPs from the libraries.

The tree in Fig.2 classifies each of the scenarios found in some of the four leaf nodes and determines if such scenario matches a pattern identification, an anti-pattern identification, or a pitfall identification in the following way:

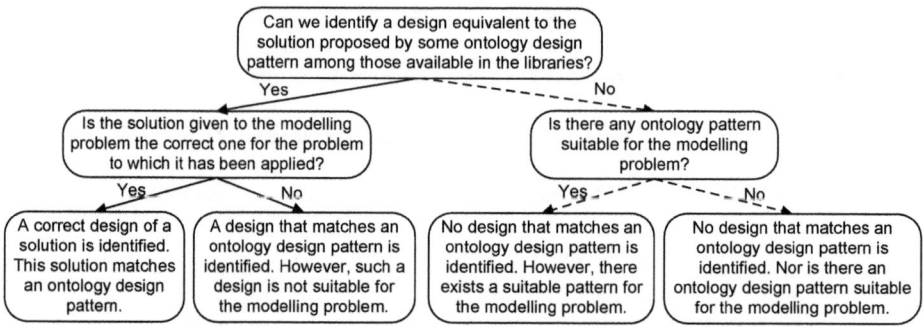

Fig. 2. Decision tree for classifying patterns, anti-patterns, and pitfalls

1. *Identification of an ontology design pattern.* (1st leaf from the left) We have identified some cases that have a correct design for the modelling problem; such a design
   matches an ODP of those in the available libraries.
2. *Identification of an anti-pattern.* (2nd and 3rd leaf) In some cases we have identified a design that matches an ODP but this design is not a suitable solution to the
   modelling problem. In some other cases we have not identified a design that could
   match an ODP in a suitable solution to the modelling problem; however, there is a
   suitable pattern that could have been applied if we had known the ODPs.
3. *Identification of a pitfall.* (4th leaf) In some other cases we have observed that
   there is an unsuitable solution to the modelling problem whereas there is not an
   ODP suitable for the modeling problem. Most of these cases have been treated as
   pitfalls; however, a few set of cases could have been solved by means of adapting
   or combining existing ODPs.

As a result of the analysis performed with 11 ontologies, we have found 208 cases in
which we have identified a correct design of a solution that matches an ODP. We
have also found 117 cases of anti-patterns, of which 83 correspond to situations in
which the solution matches the modelling proposed in some ODP. However, such a
solution is not suitable for the design problem intended to solve. Besides, we have
found 34 cases in which we were unable to identify a design solution matching an
ODP though a suitable ODP exists. Finally, we have come across a set of pitfalls, that
is, solutions unsuitable for the design problem in the domain of the ontologies studied
for such design problem; such pitfalls do not have an ODP associated. These pitfalls
are described in Section 4.

4   Pitfalls: Description, Classification and Examples

As can be seen in Section 3, we have identified a set of pitfalls for solving a modelling problem for which there is no an available ODP.

To describe the pitfalls found, we propose the template shown in Table 1 that includes, among other fields, a series of recommendations to avoid pitfalls.

In addition, we have classified the pitfalls identified in the ontologies studied bear-
ing in mind the types of ODPs proposed in Fig.1. Each pitfall is associated to the
type(s) of ODP to which a pattern created to avoid such a pitfall could belong.

Table 1. Template describing possible pitfalls during ontology development

Name	Representative name of the pitfall intended to avoid.
Description	
This field can include a general description of the pitfall. It can also include the possible inconveniences that its use may imply and the different cases in which the pitfall can appear.	
Recommendation	
This field provides some guidelines or recommendations to avoid the use of the pitfall.	
Example[4]	
Description of a representative example of the application of the pitfall. In the "Not Recommended" field we can see a graphical representation of the example where the pitfall has been identified. In the "Recommended" field we can see a possible design for the problem proposed in the example; such a design tries to avoid the pitfall.	
Not Recommended	**Recommended**
Graphic representation: Protégé screenshots.	Graphic representation: Protégé screenshots.
Comments	
This optional field includes possible comments on the pitfall or the associate recommendation.	

As can be observed in the pitfalls classification appearing in Fig.3, the types of pitfalls identified are the following:

- *Annotation pitfall.* It refers to the ontology usability from the user's point of view. Therefore, it means additional information in the form of annotations included in the ontology. These annotations should improve the user's understanding of the ontology and its elements.
- *Reasoning pitfall.* It refers to the implicit knowledge derived from the ontology when reasoning procedures are applied to such an ontology.
- *Naming pitfall.* It refers to the ontology usability from the user's point of view and, specifically, to the naming of the ontology elements. It is important to note that the naming of the elements should provide the users with a better understanding of the ontology.
- *Logical pitfall.* It refers to the solution to design problems in which the primitives of the representation language used do not provide support.
- *Content pitfall.* It refers to the solution to design problems related to the ontology domain.

Below we provide a brief description and an example of each pitfall classified. Some examples are provided both in Spanish and English.

- **Synonyms as classes.** This pitfall consists both in creating several classes whose identifiers are synonyms and in defining them as equivalent.
- **Label vs. Comment and other annotations.** This pitfall consists in interchanging the contents of the annotations of the types "label" and "comment" and in not including any annotation of the type "label" and "comment".
- **Inverse relationships that are not inverse.** This pitfall consists in defining two relationships as inverse when, in fact, they are not.

---

[4] Some examples found in Spanish have been translated into English to facilitate the reading.

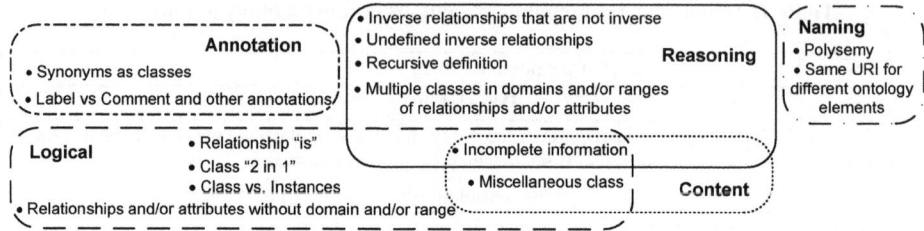

Fig. 3. Classification of the pitfalls identified

- **Undefined inverse relationships.** This pitfall consists in having inverse relationships in the ontology, but they are not defined as such.
- **Recursive definition.** This pitfall entails using an ontology element in its own definition.
- **Multiple classes in domains and/or ranges of relationships and/or attributes.** This pitfall consists in defining the ranges and/or domains of the relationships and/or attributes by intersecting several classes in cases in which they should be the union of such classes.
- **Polysemy.** This pitfall entails using an ontology element to represent concepts different from the domain under consideration.
- **Same URI for different ontology elements.** This pitfall entails assigning the same URI to two different ontology elements.
- **Relationship *"is"*.** This pitfall entails confusing the subclass relationship (*subclassOf*), the membership to a class (*instanceOf*), or the equality between instances *(sameIndividual)* with an ad hoc relation called "is".
- **Class 2 in 1.** This pitfall entails creating a class whose name is "Class1AndClass2".
- **Classes vs. Instances.** This pitfall consists in deepening into a hierarchy so that the more specific classes do not have instances since such classes become class instances of the upper level of the hierarchy.
- **Relationship and/or attributes without domain or range.** This pitfall consists in not specifying the domain or range in the relationships/attributes.
- **Incomplete information.** This pitfall entails not representing all the knowledge that could be included in the ontology.
- **Miscellaneous class.** This pitfall consists in creating an artificial miscellaneous class to classify in a certain level the instances not belonging to any of the sibling classes of this level.

In section 4.1 we present a set of pitfalls, related among them, that have appeared very frequently in the ontologies analyzed. These pitfalls are related among them in Section 4.2.

4.1   Pitfalls in Relationship Modelling

This section presents three examples of pitfalls, identified in the ontologies we have analyzed, that would affect the relationship modelling. The two first ones are related to reasoning patterns (Undefined inverse[5] relationships (Table 2) and Inverse relationships that are not inverse (Table 3)), and the last one is related to logical patterns (Relationships and/or attributes without domain and/or range (Table 4)).

Table 2. Pitfall referring to "Undefined inverse relationships"

Name	Undefined inverse relationships
Description	
The pitfall consists in having inverse relationships in the ontology but not defining them as such. This implies that when reasoning we obtain less information than that we could infer.	
Recommendation	
• When creating a new relationship, verify whether by putting the verb into the passive voice its inverse relationship can also be created; verify also whether this new relationship makes sense. • Define the relationships by establishing, if possible, the domains and ranges. If two relationships have the domains and ranges inverted, that is, the domain of one is the range of the other and vice versa, it is probable that both are in inverse relation. Then, analyze their meanings.	
Example	
In the non-recommended scenario, within the ontology on architecture, we can observe how the relationships "isLocatedAt" and "isLocationOf" have been created without defining them as inverse. With this modelling, if we have that "building1 isLocatedAt site3", then, when we activate a reasoner, we will not obtain that in "site3 isLocationOf building1". In the recommendation we have added the domain and range that the relationship "isLocatedAt" could have.	

Not Recommended		Recommended
Description: isLocatedAt Domains (intersection) Ranges (intersection) Equivalent object properties Super properties Inverse properties	Description: isLocationOf Domains (intersection) Ranges (intersection) Equivalent object properties Super properties Inverse properties	Description: isLocatedAt Domains (intersection) ● **Building OR ArchitecturalElement** Ranges (intersection) ● **Place** Equivalent object properties Super properties Inverse properties ▬ **isLocationOf**

4.2 Relationships among Pitfalls

During the analysis of the ontologies we have observed that the pitfalls can be related through different types of relationships. For instance, some pitfalls can be specific cases of a more general pitfall, or a pitfall can occur as a consequence of other pitfall that has taken place previously.

With regard to the pitfalls presented in Section 4.1, it should be noted that the "Inverse relationships that are not inverse" and "Not defined inverse relationships" pitfalls are inverse. That is, in the first case, not valid knowledge is represented, whereas in the second case knowledge is omitted although is valid. In addition, these two pitfalls can be a consequence of the "Relationships and/or attributes without domain and/or range" pitfall, since in the case of "Not defined inverse relationships" pitfall,

---

[5] If a relationship P1 is defined as inverse to other relationship P2, then for all x and y is satisfied that $P1(x,y) \leftrightarrow P2(y,x)$.

two inverse relationships may not be defined as such because their ranges and domains have not been defined.

Table 3. Pitfall referring to "Inverse relationships that are not inverse"

Name	Inverse relationships that are not inverse

Description
This pitfall consists in defining two relationships as inverse when, in fact, they are not.
As a consequence of this pitfall, undesired knowledge is probably obtained when a reasoner is applied to the ontology. This is because if we have one of the instanced relationships, then the reasoner will conclude the inverse relationship, which could be incorrect in the domain.
Some possible situations where these mistake can appear
▪ Confuse two complementary relationships with inverse relationships.
▪ Do not check the bidirectional implication of the definition of the inverse relationships in both directions. That is, we want define the relationships A and B as inverse, and we know that whenever A occurs B occurs, but we do not check if whenever B occurs, A occurs necessarily.

Recommendation
▪ Check that if the verb from a relationship is put in passive the verb of the other relationship is obtained.
▪ Check that the domain of one of the relationships matches the range of the other, and vice versa. This is one of the reasons why we recommend to set the domain and range of the relationships whenever possible.
▪ Check that whenever a relationship between two individuals exists, the inverse relationship necessarily exists.

Example
In this example we can see the result of considering two complementary relationships, "toSell" and "toBuy", as inverse.
In the non-recommended scenario and within the ontology on art, we can observe how the relationships "isSoldIn" and "isBoughtIn" are defined as inverse. This fact could cause an error at the semantic level, since if we have that "object1 isSoldIn place3", then the reasoner will infer that "place3 isBoughtIn object1".
In the recommended scenario, the relationship "isBoughtIn" has been changed to "isPointOfSale". In this way, the semantic error above commented disappears, since if "object1 isSoldIn place3", then the reasoner will infer that "place3 isPointOfSale object1".
It has been added in the recommendation the domain and range that could have the relationship "isSoldIn".

Not Recommended	Recommended

Comments
It is possible that sold and buy are inverse relationships; for example, if the relationship refers to the people involved in buying and selling, then it can been said that "buyTo" (buy something to) is inverse of "sellTo" (sell something to). That is, if "company1 buysTo company2", it will be correct to infer that "company2 sellsTo company1".

Table 4. Pitfall referring to "Relationships and/or attributes without domain and/or range"

Name	Relationships and/or attributes without domain and/or range
Description	
This pitfall entails not specifying the domain and/or range in the relationships/attributes.	
Recommendation	
It is recommended to specify, if possible, the domains and/or ranges in the properties and/or attributes.	
Additionally, annotations in the "comment" fields should be added. These annotations should describe what we wish to represent with the Property and/or attribute; for instance, if the property or attribute forms part of an n-ary pattern.	
Example	
We can observe in the not recommended scenario, how the relationship "isLocatedAt" has been defined without specifying its domain or range, whereas in the recommended scenario, the relationship "isLocatedAt" has been defined by specifying its domain and range.	

Not Recommended	Recommended
Description: isLocatedAt Domains (intersection) ⊕ Ranges (intersection) ⊕	Description: isLocatedAt Domains (intersection) ⊕ ● **Building OR ArchitecturalElement** Ranges (intersection) ⊕ ● **Place**

We think that the relationships between the pitfalls can be very useful during the development of the methodological guides to avoid pitfalls. Therefore, we are now analyzing the existence and types of relationships.

5   Conclusions and Future Work

This paper presents the analysis carried out on 11 ontologies with the aim of identifying a series of patterns and anti-patterns. During the analysis we have also found a set of pitfalls that may appear during the ontology development.

The pitfalls identified have been classified according to a subset of the types of ODPs found in the literature with which they could be related. The paper also provides a template in which the pitfalls and some of their examples are described.

However, even though it is possible to find relationships among the different pitfalls, we have not studied all the possible relationships. Therefore, as a future line of work we propose the identification of the relationships between the different pitfalls. It would be interesting to identify the groups of pitfalls that usually appear simultaneously so that, once the concurrence of a pitfall is identified, the other pitfalls that could appear could also be identified.

We also propose to analyze the existence of pitfalls and their relationships in domains other than those represented in the ontologies studied in this paper.

Another interesting work could be to carry out the analysis described in this paper but modifying the ontology development process followed by the students. In this new process we propose to include notions about ODPs in order to compare the resulting ontologies with and without notions about OPDs and analyze to what extent the pitfalls do not appear.

Finally, as we have already mentioned, the pitfalls identified are not related to any ODP present in the current libraries; therefore, we are investigating the creation of new design patterns with the objective of avoiding the use of such pitfalls.

Acknowledgments. This work has been partially supported by the European Commission project NeOn (FP6-027595) and the Spanish project GeoBuddies (TSI2007-65677-C02). We are very grateful to Rosario Plaza for her English revisions and comments.

References

1. Aguado De Cea, G., Gómez-Pérez, A., Montiel-Ponsoda, E., Suárez-Figueroa, M.C.: Natural Language-Based Approach for Helping in the Reuse of Ontology Design Patterns. In: Gangemi, A., Euzenat, J. (eds.) EKAW 2008. LNCS (LNAI), vol. 5268, pp. 32–47. Springer, Heidelberg (2008)
2. Alexander, C.: The timeless way of building. Oxford University Press, New York (1979)
3. Blomqvist, E., Gangemi, A., Presutti, V.: Experiments on Pattern-based Ontology Design. In: Proceedings of the Fifth International Conference on Knowledge Capture (K-CAP), pp. 41–48 (2009)
4. Gangemi, A.: Ontology Design Patterns for Semantic Web Content. In: Gil, Y., Motta, E., Benjamins, V.R., Musen, M.A. (eds.) ISWC 2005. LNCS, vol. 3729, pp. 262–276. Springer, Heidelberg (2005)
5. Gangemi, A., Presutti, V.: Ontology Design Patterns. In: Staab, S., Studer, R. (eds.) Handbook on Ontologies, 2nd edn. International Handbooks on Information Systems. Springer, Heidelberg (2009)
6. Presutti, V., Gangemi, A., David, S., Aguado de Cea, G., Suárez-Figueroa, M.C., Montiel-Ponsoda, E., Poveda, M.: NeOn D2.5.1: A Library of Ontology Design Patterns: reusable solutions for collaborative design of networked ontologies. NeOn project (2008), http://www.neon-project.org
7. Suárez-Figueroa, M.C., Brockmans, S., Gangemi, A., Gómez-Pérez, A., Lehmann, J., Lewen, H., Presutti, V., Sabou, M.: NeOn D5.1.1: NeOn Modelling Components. NeOn project (2007), http://www.neon-project.org

Obtaining Optimal Class Distribution for Decision Trees: Comparative Analysis of CTC and C4.5

Iñaki Albisua, Olatz Arbelaitz, Ibai Gurrutxaga, José I. Martín, Javier Muguerza, Jesús M. Pérez, and Iñigo Perona

Dept. of Computer Architecture and Technology, University of the Basque Country
M. Lardizabal, 1, 20018 Donostia, Spain
{inaki.albisua,olatz.arbelaitz,i.gurrutxaga,j.muguerza,j.martin,
txus.perez,inigo.perona}@ehu.es
http://www.sc.ehu.es/aldapa

Abstract. When using machine learning to solve real world problems, the class distribution used in the training set is important; not only in highly unbalanced data sets but in every data set. Weiss and Provost suggested that each domain has an optimal class distribution to be used for training. The aim of this work was to analyze the truthfulness of this hypothesis in the context of decision tree learners. With this aim we found the optimal class distribution for 30 databases and two decision tree learners, C4.5 and Consolidated Tree Construction algorithm (CTC), taking into account pruned and unpruned trees and based on two measures for evaluating discriminating capacity: AUC and error. The results confirmed that changes in the class distribution of the training samples improve the performance (AUC and error) of the classifiers. Therefore, the experimentation showed that there is an optimal class distribution for each database and this distribution depends on the used learning algorithm, whether the trees are pruned or not and the used evaluation criteria. Besides, results showed that CTC algorithm combined with optimal class distribution samples achieves more accurate learners, than any of the options of C4.5 and CTC with original distribution, with statistically significant differences.

Keywords: class imbalance, decision trees, optimal class distribution.

1 Introduction

Nowadays, advances in technology give business companies the opportunity to store large amounts of data. Data mining processes try to obtain knowledge from the stored data. When using machine learning to solve real world problems, the researches usually build the model from data where the proportion of each class in the training set matches the proportion found in reality. This can be a problem if the class distribution is very unbalanced since it is easy to obtain high accuracy predicting always the majority class. As a consequence many efforts have been made to face it [9][8][3][6][12]. However, the class distribution used in the training set is not only important in highly unbalanced datasets but in every dataset. Weiss and Provost [16] suggested that each domain has an optimal class distribution to be used for training.

P. Meseguer, L. Mandow, and R.M. Gasca (Eds.): CAEPIA 2009, LNAI 5988, pp. 101–110, 2010.

They showed that it is mostly preferable to use a distribution other than the one appearing in the dataset.

In general, any machine learning algorithm builds a classifier based on a sample with a particular distribution. The distribution of the sample can be changed hoping that better results will be achieved, using two strategies: oversampling or undersampling. Even if the direct consequence of undersampling is that some examples are ignored, in general, undersampling techniques obtain better results than oversampling techniques (repeating some examples) [5].

Weiss and Provost worked in this context and presented an experimentation where they found the optimal class distribution for 26 real world databases (20 from the UCI and 6 from their environment). They worked with C4.5 algorithm and undersampled the training data to experiment with different class distributions. They only presented results for unpruned trees.

Based on Weiss and Provost work, Perez et al showed in [14] that CTC algorithm was able to combine the information in several samples in an efficient way and improve C4.5 with samples generated using the optimal class distribution proposed in [16]. In order to analyze where the improvement in performance came from, the algorithm itself or the new class distributions they built two kinds of samples, both with the same size. Samples with the original class distribution and samples with the optimal class distribution Weiss and Provost proposed. Results showed that in general CTC achieved greater discriminating capacity than C4.5 in every situation: samples with original and optimal class distribution and pruned and unpruned trees. Besides, this happened for two performance evaluation criteria: error and AUC. Nevertheless they pointed that the use of samples with the optimal distribution proposed by Weiss and Provost, independently of the algorithm, CTC or C4.5, not always produced improvement. From our point of view these results required a further analysis.

The two works had different characteristics: on the one hand, the size of the subsamples used in [14] was larger (around 73.7% of the training sample in average) than the one Weiss and Provost used (around 27.17% in average). Nevertheless the latter affirmed that the optimal distribution for one database was independent of the size of the samples. This is crucial for the "budget-sensitive progressive sampling algorithm for selecting training data" they propose. On the other hand, the number of classifiers used to make the estimation was also different in both works. Perez et al used 5,000 C4.5 trees for each value of class distribution whereas Weiss and Provost only used 30. Obviously conclusions obtained with 5,000 observations seem to be sounder.

The work of Perez et al was based on Weiss and Provost assertions "since the role that class distribution plays in learning is not specific to decision tree learners, one would expect other learners to behave similarly" and they used the optimal distribution proposed for the C4.5 in CTC algorithm. But for some of the databases the results compared to the original distribution did not improve, and this suggested that the optimal distribution might not be the same for both algorithms.

Similarly, Perez et al used the optimal distribution proposed for unpruned trees also for pruned trees. In the case of pruned trees, the use of the optimal distribution produced improvement for the classifiers, C4.5 and CTC, only in 5 databases out of 10. This makes us suspect that whether the trees are pruned or not also affects to the optimal class distribution.

This work tries to clarify all the previous points. We made a wide experimentation with 30 two-class real problems and 14 different class distributions. We used these samples to build CT trees based on different sets and, C4.5 trees with each of them (pruned and unpruned) and find the optimal class distribution for each database and algorithm. To estimate the generalization capacity of the classifiers, we used a 10 fold cross-validation methodology five times. Although AUC (Area Under the ROC curve) is a better measurement than error in comparing learning algorithms [10][11][2] we performed the analysis for both: the AUC and the error. Finally we applied statistical tests [4][7] to evaluate the statistical significance of the results.

The paper proceeds describing how a single tree can be built from several subsamples, CTC algorithm, in Section 2. The characteristics of the databases used in the experimentation and details about the experimental methodology are described in Section 3. In Section 4 an analysis of the optimal distributions obtained under different conditions and quality of results for CTC and C4.5 is presented. Finally Section 5 is devoted to show the conclusions and further work.

2   The CTC Algorithm

In this work we evaluated two algorithms: the well known C4.5 [15] and the CTC (Consolidated Tree Construction) algorithm [13]. The CTC algorithm uses the main idea of bagging: voting. In bagging a set of classifiers is built, and then, voting is used to classify new examples. Nevertheless, the CTC algorithm uses a voting process to decide the variable that will be used to split the node at each step of the tree's building process. The decision is made based on a set of samples. The repetition of this process in every node leads to the construction of a single tree. In order to make the CTC comparable to the C4.5, the split function used is the gain ratio criterion used by Quinlan in the C4.5 [15]. This idea is kept in the different steps of the algorithm and the default parameters of the C4.5 used. Algorithm 1 describes the iterative process.

The algorithm starts extracting a set of samples (S^i, $1 \leq i \leq Number\_Samples$ or N_S) from the original training set, based on the desired resampling technique (*Resampling_Mode* or *R_M*). For example, changing the class distribution. During the process, LS^i contains a list with all the data partitions created from each sample S^i. At the beginning, the only existing partitions are the initial samples.

CurrentConsolidatedNode guides the construction of the CT tree during the whole process. In the first iteration, it will be the root node of the consolidated tree (*RootConsolidatedNode*) —the node representing all the root nodes related to each of the samples S^i. During the remaining iterations, *CurrentConsolidatedNode* points to the node returned by the function *NextNodeToConsolidate()*. This function returns the next node to be treated and covers the tree in pre-order as it is done in the C4.5. Analogously, *CurrentS^i* points to the next data partition (related to one node) of S^i to be treated in the building process of the i-th tree.

Each node of the CT tree is consolidated based on the information coming from N_S samples. The pair $(X,B)^i$ represents the split proposal for the first data partition in LS^i. X is the feature selected to split and B indicates the proposed branches or criteria to divide the data in the current node. In the consolidation step, X_c and B_c are the feature and branches selected after a voting process based on all the proposals.

The process is repeated while LS^i is not empty for all i. The Consolidated Tree's generation process finishes when, in the last data partition in all LS^i, most of the proposals are not to split it, so, to become a leaf node (stopping criteria).

The a posteriori probabilities of the leaves are calculated by averaging the a posteriori obtained from the data partitions related to that node in all the samples (similar to *measurement level* classifiers [17]).

Algorithm 1. The CTC Algorithm

Inputs:
S training set
C4.5 algorithms' criteria used to split nodes
N_S (*Number_Samples*) number of subsamples to generate
R_M (*Resampling_Mode*) method used to generate subsamples

Procedure CTC (S, $C4.5$, N_S, R_M)

for $i := 1$ to N_S
    Let S^i be a sample extracted from S using R_M method
    $LS^i := \{S^i\}$ // initialise LS^i with S^i
end for

$CurrentConsolidatedNode := RootConsolidatedNode$

repeat
    for $i := 1$ to N_S
        $CurrentS^i := First(LS^i)$ // obtain the first element of the list
        $LS^i := LS^i - CurrentS^i$
        Induce the best split $(X,B)^i$ for $CurrentS^i$
    end for
    Obtain the consolidated pair (X_c,B_c) based on $(X,B)^i$, $1 \leq i \leq N\_S$
    if $(X_c,B_c) \neq Not\_Split$
        Split $CurrenConsolidatedtNode$ based on (X_c,B_c)
        for $i := 1$ to N_S
            Divide $CurrentS^i$ based on (X_c,B_c) to obtain n subsamples $\{S_1^i, ..., S_n^i\}$
            $LS^i := \{S_1^i, ..., S_n^i\} \cup LS^i$
        end for
    else consolidate $CurrentConsolidatedNode$ as a leaf
    end if
    $CurrentConsolidatedNode := NextNodeToConsolidate()$
until $\forall i$, LS^i is empty

---

3 Experimental Methodology

In order to answer the research questions of this work, we performed experimentation with 30 two-class real problems: Breast-W, Credit-g, Bands, Ks-vs-kp, Optdigits, Car, Abalone, Solar_flare, Yeast, Splice_junction, Heart-C, Hypo, Liver, Credit-a, Breast-y, Voting, Heart-H, Hepatitis, Sick_euthyroid, Kddcup, Spam, Pima, Lymph, Vehicle, Iris, Glass, Soybean-Large, Segment210, Segment2310 and Fraud. 29 databases are from the UCI Repository benchmark [1] and one, Fraud, a fraud detection problem in car insurance companies, from our environment. The characteristics of the databases vary from 148 examples to 108,000, 4 features to 64 features and 2 classes to 29 classes. And the minority class distribution goes from 1.35 to 47.8.

We used a 10-fold cross-validation methodology five times (5x10CV) to estimate the generalization capacity of the classifiers. As a consequence, we obtained 50 pairs of training and test samples for each database. From each training sample, we further generated 100 sub-samples, with each of the 14 different class distributions: 2%, 5%, 10%, 20%, 30%, 40%, 50%, 60%, 70%, 80%, 90%, 95%, 98% and the original. Figure 1 represents the sample generation process for a database. Thus, in this experiment, we sed 5x10x14x100 samples per database. All the samples generated in one database had identical size: the number of examples of the minority class [16]. If we take into account the 30 databases, the average size of the generated samples is 26.96% of the training samples.

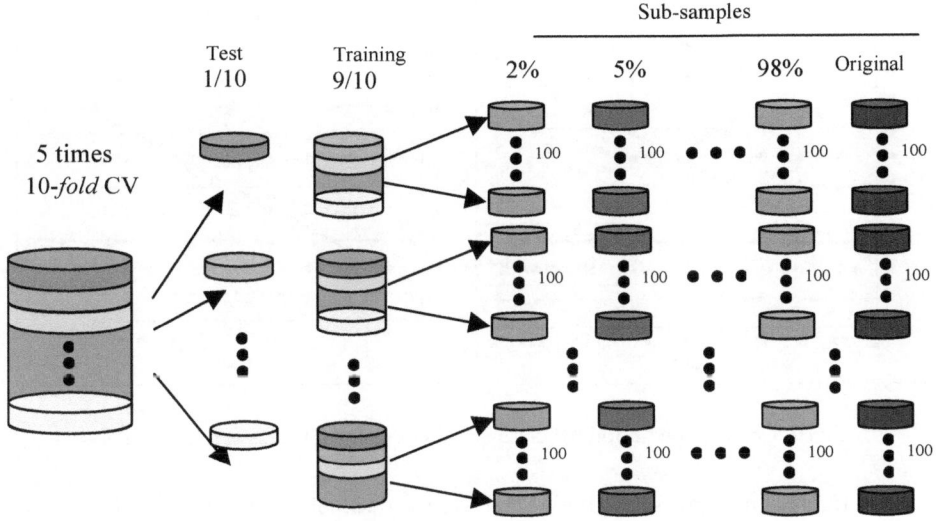

Fig. 1. Schema repeated in each database for sample generation

We used these samples to build C4.5 and CTC classifiers. In each fold with each one of the 1400 samples (14 class distributions x 100 samples) we built two C4.5 trees, one pruned and another unpruned,. On the other hand, we used the 100 samples generated for each database, class distribution and fold to build all the possible CT trees, with disjoint sets of 5, 10, 20, 30, 40 and 50 samples (42 pruned and 42 unpruned). Thus taking into account the 30 databases we experimented with 4,200,000 C4.5 trees and 1,764,000 CT trees.

In order to determine to what extent the optimal class distribution for a database is independent or it depends on the classifier and its parameters as well as on the efficiency measure, we tested the built trees with the test sample in each fold and we measured the obtained AUC, Area Under the ROC curve, and the error. In addition we used the non-parametric statistical tests proposed by Demsär [4] to evaluate the statistical significance of the results, combined with a recent proposal of García and Herrera [7].

4   Experimental Results

As described in the experimental setup section, we performed an extensive experimentation. We calculated the optimal class distribution for each database, algorithm, pruned and unpruned option, and evaluation criteria. Then, we used the obtained results to determine to what extent the optimal class distribution for a database is independent or it depends on the analyzed options. Furthermore, we also used the experimentation to compare the discriminating capacity of C4.5 trees and CT trees and evaluate the performance of the two algorithms.

To start with the analysis we present in Figure 2 the relationship of the optimal class distribution of CT trees and C4.5 trees,calculated based on error and AUC. We present results for pruned trees (left) and unpruned trees (right).

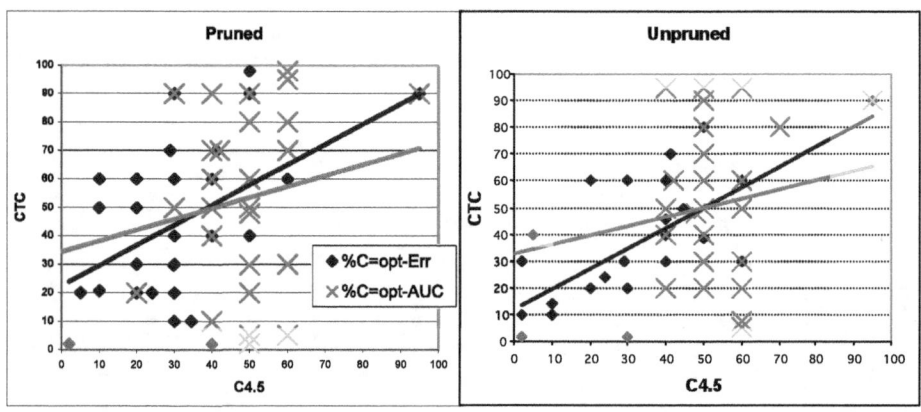

Fig. 2. Comparison of optimal class distributions for CT trees and C4.5 trees

Each figure represents in the horizontal axe the optimal distributions for C4.5 algorithm and in the vertical axe the optimal distributions for CTC algorithm obtained for each database. If the optimal distributions would not be algorithm or efficiency measure dependent, we would expect the points in the graphic to be located in the diagonal and to be exactly the same for the error and the AUC.

The mass of points we obtain and their corresponding regression curves, added just as a visual tool, show that in general, the optimal distribution for each database does not coincide for the two algorithms and neither from the error or the AUC point of view.

Looking to the points and regression lines it seems that if the evaluation criteria is the error (diamonds), although still different, the optimal distributions obtained for the C4.5 and the CTC are more similar, since the corresponding regression line (the dark one) is nearer the diagonal.

We can observe that the points corresponding to the optimal distribution for C4.5 algorithm based on AUC are concentrated in the central area (columns) of the figure. This means that for most of the databases (26 for pruned and 28 for unpruned) the optimal distributions are in the central values: among 40% and 60%. This confirms one of the conclusions of Weiss and Provost; they concluded that using AUC, the optimal distribution is near 50%. Nevertheless, for CTC algorithm the optimal values appear dispersed along the whole range of distributions (rows): from 2% to 98%. Nevertheless, as we will show later, it achieves higher quality results for both evaluation criteria: AUC and error.

On the other hand, although they are not exactly the same, the conclusions obtained from the graphics corresponding to pruned trees are similar to the ones we could obtain from the graphics corresponding to unpruend trees. The comparison from this point of view could be next step, that is, to observe how pruning or not pruning the trees affects in each algorithm to the selection of the optimal class distribution. We show this analysis for C4.5 trees (left) and CT trees (right) in Figure 3.

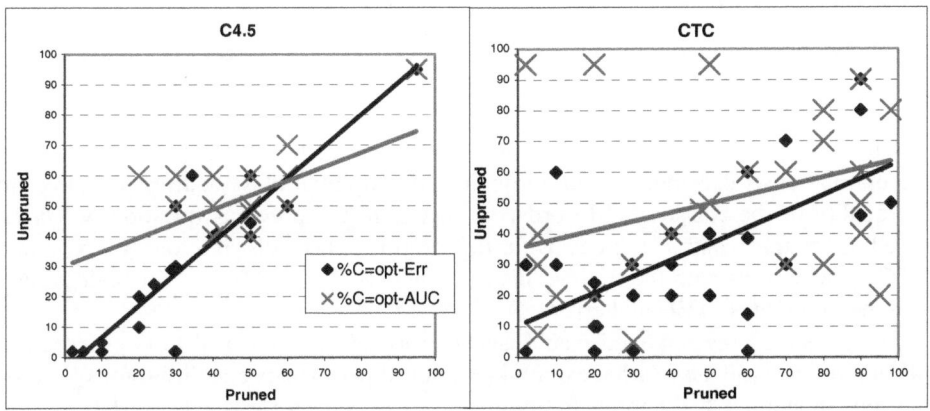

Fig. 3. Comparison of optimal class distributions for pruned and unpruned trees

Each figure represents in axe X the optimal distributions for pruned trees and in axe Y the optimal distributions for unpruned trees. Again, if the optimal distributions would not be pruning or efficiency measure dependent, we would expect the points in the graphics to be located in the diagonal and to be exactly the same for the error and the AUC.

The graphics show that pruning affects in a different way to the optimal distributions for C4.5 and CT trees. In the case of C4.5 and error, the optimal distributions for pruned and unpruned trees are similar since most of the points appear near the diagonal. If we allow a margin of ± 10%, the optimal distribution coincides in 26 databases for the two measures: error and AUC. On the contrary, in the case of CT trees, the points appear very disperse and this means that optimal distributions for pruned and unprunet trees are different. Again, if we allow a margin of ± 10%, the optimal distribution only coincides in 17 databases for the AUC and 16 for the error.

From the previous analysis we could state that, opposite to the assertion made in Weiss and Provost's paper, the optimal class distribution for a database is classifier dependent and furthermore, it can also depend on the pruning process used in decision trees.

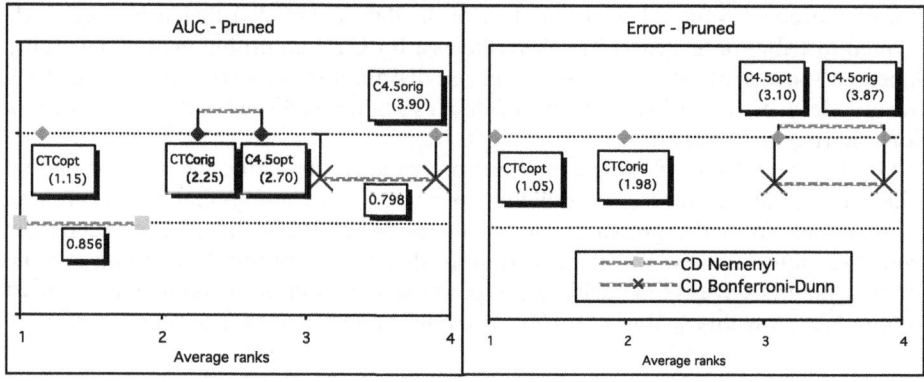

Fig. 4. CD diagrams to show results of the analysis of statistically significant differences for AUC and error for pruned trees

Up to this point we analyzed how the different parameters affect to the selection of the optimal class distribution. But, how does this optimal class distribution affect to the quality of the classifiers? In order to answer to the previous question, we compared C4.5 trees and CT trees with the original class distribution (C4.5$_{orig}$ and CTC$_{orig}$) with trees with the optimal distribution (C4.5$_{opt}$ and CTC$_{opt}$) for both evaluation measurements: AUC and error.

We compared the obtained results and performed the statistical tests proposed in [4] in order to evaluate to what extent the achieved performance is different. We show the corresponding CD diagrams in Figure 4. The left side corresponds to AUC evaluation whereas the figure in the right corresponds to the error evaluation. Friedman test showed that there were significant differences between the compared classifiers at more than 99%. Therefore, we performed Nemenyi –all vs. all– and Bonferoni-Dunn –C4.5$_{orig}$ vs. the rest– tests to determine where those differences happened. Average rank values for each one of the compared algorithms appear on the corresponding boxes. In the left figure, the line on the left most part of the horizontal axe (marked as CD Nemenyi in the legend) represents the maximum distance (0.8563) two algorithms can have based on Nemenyi's test so that there are not significant differences between them. On the other hand, the line on the right most part of the horizontal axe (marked as CD Bonferroni-Dunn in the legend) represents the maximum distance (0.7980) two algorithms can have based on the Bonferroni-Dunn test so that there are not significant differences between them.

Both graphics show that trees built with the optimal class distribution always perform better than the ones built with the original class distribution. In every case, there are statistically significant differences between CTC$_{opt}$ and CTC$_{orig}$ and C4.5$_{opt}$ and C4.5$_{orig}$. In the case of the error, although significant differences between the two options of C4.5 do not appear in the graphic they appeared using the more powerful tests proposed by García and Herrera [7] –Holm, Shaffer and Bergmann. Furthermore, CTC combines the subsamples in an adequate manner and it does it better if they have optimal class distribution. For both performance measures, CTC$_{opt}$ achieved better results than the rest with statistically significant differences. Besides, in the case of the error, both versions of CTC had also statistically significant differences with the two options of C4.5. In the other case, although the order was maintained, not statistically significant differences appeared between CTC_{orig} and $C4.5_{opt}$ (neither with the most powerful test –Bergmann–proposed in [7]).

5 Conclusions and Further Work

The aim of this work was to analyze if the optimal class distribution to build classifiers from a database depends on the selected learning algorithm. In a previous work Weiss and Provost [16] made next assertion: "since the role that class distribution plays in learning is not specific to decision tree learners, one would expect other learners to behave similarly". However, the work of Perez et al [14] showed that this assertion might not always be satisfied. With this aim we found and compared the optimal class distribution for 30 databases and two decision tree learners: C4.5 and CTC. We worked with pruned and unpruned trees and performed the evaluation of the discriminating capacity based on two measures: AUC and error.

The experimentation confirmed one of the outcomes of Weiss and Provost: changes in the class distribution of the training samples improve the performance (AUC and error) of the classifiers. Therefore there is an optimal class distribution for each database. However, results showed that, opposite to other of the Weiss and Provost assertions, this distribution depends on the used learning algorithm, even if they are decision tree learners using the same split criteria (C4.5 and CTC). Weiss and Provost only showed results for unpruned trees. Nevertheless, the results obtained in this work showed that the optimal distribution not always coincides for pruned and unpruned trees. This happened more often for CTC algorithm. The optimal distribution was not the same when the evaluation criteria changed (AUC or error).

Another assertion of Weiss a Provost confirmed in this work, is that the optimal distributions for C4.5 trees based on AUC are mostly balanced (around 50%). However, for CTC algorithm the optimal distribution takes a wide range of values. In spite of this, it is worth finding the optimal distribution for CTC algorithm, since it achieves more accurate learners, than any of the options of C4.5 and CTC with original distribution, with statistically significant differences.

This work opens some new lines. From a practical point of view, when trying to solve new real problems, it would be interesting to introduce a mechanism to determine the optimal parameters to be used to generate samples. This should be a process based on an optimization algorithm.

Acknowledgments

This work was funded by the University of the Basque Country, DAMISI project (EHU 08/39), the Diputacin Foral de Gipuzkoa and the E.U.

References

1. Asuncion, A., Newman, D.J.: UCI Machine Learning Repository. University of California, School of Information and Computer Science, Irvine, CA (2007), http://www.ics.uci.edu/~mlearn/MLRepository.html
2. Chawla, N.V., Bowyer, K.W., Kegelmeyer, W.P.: SMOTE: Synthetic Minority Over-sampling Technique. Journal of Artificial Intelligence Research 16, 321–357 (2002)
3. Chawla, N.V.: C4.5 and Imbalanced Data sets: Investigating the effect of sampling method, probabilistic estimate, and decision tree structure. In: Proc. of the Workshop on Learning from Imbalanced Data Sets, ICML, Washington DC (2003)
4. Demšar, J.: Statistical Comparisons of Classifiers over Multiple Data Sets. Journal of Machine Learning Research 7, 1–30 (2006)
5. Drummond, C., Holte, R.C.: Exploiting the Cost (In)sensitivity of Decision Tree Splitting Criteria. In: Proc. of the 17th Int. Conf. on Machine Learning, pp. 239–246 (2000)
6. Estabrooks, A., Jo, T.J., Japkowicz, N.: A Multiple Resampling Method for Learning from Imbalanced Data Sets. Computational Intelligence 20(1), 18–36 (2004)
7. García, S., Herrera, F.: An Extension on Statistical Comparisons of Classifiers over Multiple Data Sets for all Pairwise Comparisons. JMLR 9, 2677–2694 (2008)
8. Japkowicz, N., Stephen, S.: The Class Imbalance Problem: A Systematic Study. Intelligent Data Analysis Journal 6(5) (2002)
9. Kennedy, R.L., Lee, Y., Van Roy, B., Reed, C.D., Lippmann, R.P.: Solving Data Mining Problems through Pattern Recognition. Prentice-Hall, Englewood Cliffs (1998)
10. Ling, C.X., Huang, J., Zhang, H.: AUC: a better measure than accuracy in comparing learning algorithms. In: Xiang, Y., Chaib-draa, B. (eds.) Canadian AI 2003. LNCS (LNAI), vol. 2671, pp. 329–341. Springer, Heidelberg (2003)
11. Marrocco, C., Duin, R.P.W., Tortorella, F.: Maximizing the area under the ROC curve by pairwise feature combination. Pattern Recognition 41(6), 1961–1974 (2008)
12. Orriols-Puig, A., Bernadó-Mansilla, E.: Evolutionary rule-based systems for imbalanced data sets. Soft Comput. 13, 213–225 (2009)
13. Pérez, J.M., Muguerza, J., Arbelaitz, O., Gurrutxaga, I.: A New Algorithm to Build Consolidated Trees: Study of the Error Rate and Steadiness. In: Advances in Soft Computing, Proc. of the International Intelligent Information Processing and Web Mining Conference (IIS: IIPWM'04). Zakopane, Poland, pp. 79–88 (2004)
14. Pérez, J.M., Muguerza, J., Arbelaitz, O., Gurrutxaga, I., Martín, J.I.: Combining multiple class distribution modified subsamples in a single tree. Pattern Recognition Letters 28(4), 414–422 (2007)
15. Quinlan, J.R.: C4.5: Programs for Machine Learning. In: Morgan Kaufmann Publishers Inc. (eds.), San Mateo, (1993)
16. Weiss, G.M., Provost, F.: Learning when Training Data are Costly: The Effect of Class Distribution on Tree Induction. JAIR 19, 315–354 (2003)
17. Xu, L., Krzyzak, A., Suen, C.Y.: Methods of Combining Multiple Classifiers and Their Applications to Handwriting Recognition. IEEE Transactions on Systems, Man and Cybernetics SMC-22(3), 418–435 (1992)

Selecting Few Genes for Microarray Gene Expression Classification

Carlos J. Alonso-González, Q. Isaac Moro,
Oscar J. Prieto, and M. Aránzazu Simón

Intelligent Systems Group (GSI), Department of Computer Science,
E.T.S.I Informática, University of Valladolid, Valladolid, Spain

Abstract. Due to the high number of gene expressions contained on microarray data, feature extraction techniques are usually applied before inducing classifiers. A common criterion to decide on the number of selected genes is minimizing the classifier error. However, considering the risk of overfitting due to the small sample size, and the fact that the number of selected genes is usually larger than the suspected number of discriminating genes, this work proposes relaxing the minimum error rate criterion. The paper shows that from a small number of feature selection and classification methods, it is possible to find configurations that select few genes without significantly worsening the error rate of the best classifier. Average ranking for 10 to 40 genes shows that SVM-RFE with Naïve Bayes and FCBF with SVM behave consistently well.

Keywords: Microarray Gene Expression Data, Feature Extraction, Few Genes Selection.

1 Introduction

The application of machine learning methods to DNA microarray gene expression data allows for systematic and high throughput analysis procedures, compared to histological and other methods [18]. Microarray classification is used to discover discriminating genes that allow identifying tissue types and it has been intensively applied to cancer diagnosis. However, microarray data classification is a challenging issue because of its high dimensionality and the small samples sizes. Typical values are around 10.000 gene expressions and a hundred or less tissue samples. To tackle this problem, the need to reduce dimensionality was soon recognized and the use of feature selection techniques has become customary [15]. An equally important reason to decrease dimensionality is to help biologist to identify the underlying mechanism that relates gene expression to diseases.

Previous studies [18,1,10] indicate that best classification results are obtained selecting in the range of 100-500 gene expressions. However, this conclusion is solely based on the criterion on minimizing the classifiers error rates. For a two class cancer classification, 50 informative genes are usually enough [6]. And there are studies suggesting that only a few genes are sufficient [11,21].

P. Meseguer, L. Mandow, and R.M. Gasca (Eds.): CAEPIA 2009, LNAI 5988, pp. 111–120, 2010.

In this work we examine the possibility of finding, from a small number of feature selection and classification methods, configurations that allow identifying a small number of attributes, without a significant penalty on the classifier performance. Hypothesis testing, for specific data sets, is applied looking for these configurations. We also compare the performance of these methods against a simple random attribute selection, to check that the extremely high redundancy found in microarray data does not make trivial the feature selection method. Additionally, we study the average behavior of the combined feature selection and classification methods looking for general recommendations to orient the novel practitioner.

Next section of the paper introduces the feature selection and classification methods. After describing the experimental methodology, results based on errors for best configurations with few genes on particular data sets are presented. Finally, general behavior based on average rankings is discussed.

2 Feature Selection and Classification Techniques

There are two main approaches to feature selection techniques, filter and wrapper, with the embedded approach somewhere in between [15]. Filtering methods rely on intrinsic properties of data; they are independent of the classifier used and are fast and scalable to high dimension data sets. Wrapper techniques search subsets of features that are evaluated by the performance of the intended classification method. Although wrapper methods model feature dependencies, they depend on the classifier, risk overfitting and have a higher computational complexity than filter methods. Embedded methods use classifier parameters to select, usually iteratively, subsets of features; they offer a good tradeoff between filters and wrapper approaches, being more computationally effective than wrappers and modeling feature dependencies. We have opted for two filtering methods, ReliefF and FCBF, and an embedded one, SVM-RFE, on the basis of their higher computationally efficiency and smaller overfitting risk than wrappers. Additionally, a Random attribute selection has been considered as a base line to contrast the effectiveness of the aforementioned methods.

ReliefF feature selection algorithm is based on original Relief algorithm [8] that could only be used for binary classification problems. The key idea of Relief is to estimate the relevance of features according to how well their values distinguish between the instances of the same and different classes that are near each other [22]. Original algorithm was extended by Kononenko [9] so that it can deal with multi-class problems and missing values. Later it was further improved by Robnik-Sikonja and Kononenko [16] so that it is suitable for noisy data and can also be used for regression problems. ReliefF is claimed [17] to behave well when few attributes are selected.

ReliefF, as many other filter methods, selects features that are deemed relevant to the class concept, even though many of them were highly correlated to each other [8]. Several authors [4,12] suggest that feature selection algorithms must reject both irrelevant and redundant features. Fast Correlation Based

Filter, FCBF, [22] is a computationally efficient algorithm designed to identify both irrelevant and redundant features. FCBF uses symmetrical uncertainty to evaluate individual attributes and the concept of predominant correlation to heuristically remove redundant features.

SVM combined with Recursive Feature Elimination, SVM-RFE, was introduced to gene selection in bioinformatics by Guyon et al. [7]. SVM-RFE is an embedded method based on linear SVM. On each cycle, less weighted attributes, which have the smallest effect on classification, are discarded. Although more computationally expensive than filter methods, SVM-RFE is recognized as a very effective algorithm for microarray gene expression classification task [19,15].

We have considered three classification methods: 3 Nearest Neighbor (3-NN), Naïve Bayes (NB), and Support Vector Machines with linear kernel (SVM). SVM is regarded as an effective classification method in this domain by several authors [17,19,18]. Naïve Bayes is a classic and simple method that behaves surprisingly well on many application domains. Preliminary work on the considered data sets showed that 3-NN generally behaves better than Decision Trees, 1-NN and 5-NN.

3 Experimental Setting

Experiments were performed on 10 genomic and proteomic data sets, whose basic properties are summarized in Table 1. All data sets are publicly available at Kent Ridge Biomedical Data Set Repository [14].

Except for MLL and ALL, the data sets are related with binary classification problems. MLL is a three class problem, and it is used as it is. ALL comprises seven different classes of pediatric acute lymphoblastic leukemia (BCR-ABL, E2A-PBX1, Hyperdiploid>50, MLL, T-ALL, TEL-AML1, and a group labeled as "other"); we transformed these seven types in a two class problem.

Table 1. Data set description. All of them are free to download in [14].

Data Set and original work reference		Samp.	Attrib.	Items in each class		
				C1	C2	C3
ALL-AML	Golub et al. (1999)	72	7129	47 (65.2%)	25 (34.8%)	-
ALL	Yeoh et al. (2002)	327	12558	43 (13.1%)	284 (86.9%)	-
Breast	Van't Veer (2002)	97	24481	46 (47.4%)	51 (52.6%)	-
CNS	Mukherjee et al. (2002)	60	7129	21 (35.0%)	39 (65.0%)	-
Colon	Alon et al. (1999)	62	2000	22 (35.4%)	40 (64.6%)	-
DLBCL	Alizadeh et al. (2000)	47	4026	24 (51.0%)	23 (49.0%)	-
Lung	Gordon et al. (2002)	181	12533	31 (17.1%)	150 (82.9%)	-
MLL	Armstrong et al. (2001)	72	12582	24 (33.3%)	20 (27.7%)	28 (38.8%)
Ovarian	Petricoin et al. (2002)	253	15154	162 (64.0%)	91 (36.0%)	-
Prostate	Singh et al. (2002)	136	12600	77 (56.6%)	59 (43.4%)	-

The combination of 4 attribute selection algorithms and 3 classification techniques produces 12 basic methods that are named joining their acronym by '+'. Hence, FCBF+NB indicates that NB is applied to data sets filtered with FCBF.

Feature selection algorithms are invoked to obtain a specific number of features, given by an additional parameter. Since we are interested on the behavior of the methods when few attributes are selected, we have covered the range [10,250] in steps of 10. Consequently, we had a total of 300 ($4 \times 3 \times 25$) different configurations.

For each data set, error rates have been obtained with Nadeau and Bengio methodology that proposes the corrected resampled t-test for hypothesis testing. It provides an acceptable type I error (finding differences when there are none) and a small type II error (failing to find genuine differences) [13]. This method requires 15 repetitions of training and test, where 90% randomly selected instances are used for training and the remaining 10% for testing. Feature selection techniques were applied internally to each training set to provide a honest evaluation.

All experiments were performed on the data mining framework Weka [20], with default values for all parameters, except for SVM-RFE: we set to 5% the number of features eliminated by the algorithm in each cycle. Rankings and Friedman test where performed with a Spreadsheet. For additional test on rankings we used the publicly available software facilitated in [5].

Due to space limitation, we do not include results for the average error rate of each basic method. Graphical representations (not included) are similar to those published elsewhere [17,18], with classifiers average accuracy increasing from 10 genes on, reaching a maximum value with 200 or less genes and obtaining similar precision from 200 to 250 genes. Averaging error rates on different data sets is not adequate to obtain general conclusions on the behavior of the basic methods, because error rates on different data sets are not directly comparable. Moreover, it may hide the behavior of particularly good configurations with few genes on some data set. For those reasons, we proceed to compare the behavior of different configurations based on error on each data set, looking for good configurations with a small number of genes, resorting to average rankings to compare different configurations on all data sets.

4   Configurations for Individual Data Sets Based on Error

Table 2, column 'Best', shows the configuration (attribute selection+classifier and number of attributes) with highest accuracy on each data set. In case of ties, the configuration with less attributes is shown. Except for data sets DL-BCL and Prostate, there is a configuration with 100 or less attributes that provides the best result. Nevertheless, 100 attributes is still a very high number to find a biomedical interpretation [3]. This task is simplified when the algorithms select a smaller number of attributes. Of course, using a smaller number of attributes than the specified for the best configuration reduces the precision of the classifiers. To check to what extent it is possible to find configurations with a smaller number of attributes without significantly worst precision, we have used the following procedure for each data set:

1. Apply resampled t-test with $\alpha = 0.05$ to compare the best configuration with configurations that use fewer attributes, discarding those significantly worse.

2. Select, from the surviving configurations, the 10 with better accuracy.

Table 2, column '10 next best with less attributes', shows out 3 of the 10 best configurations: the configuration with the minimum number of attributes, the configuration with the best precision, and the configuration with the worst precision. Notice that there are some singular cases:

- When there are not significantly next best configurations with less attributes. In our experiments it only happened when the best configuration selected 10 attributes. This is indicated by *none* in the table.
- When there are several configurations with the same error rate. This is indicated as '*' in the table.

Table 2. Best results for each data set. Contents are described on section 4.

	Best			10 next best with less attributes			
Data set	% hit	Algorithm	Attrib.		% hit	Algorithm	Attrib.
ALL-AML	100.00	SVM-RFE+3-NN	90	Min. attr.	98.21	SVM-RFE+NB	10
				Best %	99.17	SVM-RFE+3-NN	70
				Worst %	97.10	SVM-RFE+SVM	80
ALL	100.00	*	10	Min. attr.		none	
				Best %		none	
				Worst %		none	
Breast	70.52	ReliefF+SVM	50	Min. attr.	68.07	ReliefF+NB	10
				Best %	68.48	SVM-RFE+3-NN	30
				Worst %	64.89	ReliefF+SVM	20
CNS	75.49	SVM-RFE+SVM	100	Min. attr.	71.21	SVM-RFE+NB	50
				Best %	74.38	SVM-RFE+SVM	90
				Worst %	70.19	Random+3-NN	60
Colon	88.41	Random+SVM	60	Min. attr.	86.08	ReliefF+SVM	10
				Best %	87.30	ReliefF+NB	50
				Worst %	84.29	Relief+NB	10
DLBCL	98.67	ReliefF+NB	120	Min. attr.	97.56	FCBF+NB	20
				Best %	97.56	*	*
				Worst %	97.56	*	*
Lung	99.63	SVM-RFE+NB	100	Min. attr.	99.26	FCBF+NB	40
				Best %	99.26	*	*
				Worst %	99.26	*	*
MLL	98.21	SVM-RFE+3-NN	100	Min. attr.	97.26	SVM-RFE+*	40
				Best %	97.26	*	*
				Worst %	95.48	FCBF+SVM	90
Ovarian	100.00	SVM-RFE+3-NN	10	Min. attr.		none	
				Best %		none	
				Worst %		none	
Prostate	95.39	SVM-RFE+SVM	180	Min. attr.	94.79	ReliefF+3-NN	10
				Best %	94.79	ReliefF+3-NN	10
				Worst %	93.52	ReliefF+NB	10

Table 2 shows that for the 10 data sets, it is always possible to find a configuration with 50 or less attributes that is not significantly worse than the best configuration. Moreover, for 6 data sets it is possible to find configurations of 10 genes with the same property.

5 Overall Behavior Based on Rankings

Ranking is a popular method to compare the behavior of different classifiers across several data sets. Ranking orders classifiers on each data set according to some merit figure, assigning average values in case of ties. The average ranking of the classifiers over all data sets is usually a better performance index that the averages of the original merit figure, which may be not directly comparable between different data sets. In this work we resort to average rankings based on accuracy rates. Hence, if a classifier obtains an average ranking of 1, then this classifier is the most accurate on all data sets, which is rarely the case.

5.1 Average Rankings for All the Algorithms from 10 to 250 Genes

Average rankings have been computed for the twelve algorithms, resulting of combining the three classification techniques with the four attribute selection methods, on the ten data sets. Given that we want to compare the behavior of the algorithms for a given number of selected genes, rankings have been obtained for each value of this parameter. Figure 1 a), b) and c) shows the rankings, grouped by classifiers. As it is expected, worst rankings are obtained by each classifier when genes are randomly selected. Best rankings vary with the number of genes. For 100 genes or more, SVM with ReliefF or SVM-RFE provides the best rankings. For 40 or less genes, best rankings are obtained by SVM with FCBF or NB with SVM-RFE. Between 50 and 90 genes 3-NN also obtains good rankings. All the rankings succeed Friedman, and Iman and Davenport tests indicating that rankings are significantly different ($\alpha = 0.05$) from the mean rank, 6.5. Nemenyi Critical Distance, CD, for a significant level of 0.05 is CD=5.19. This value identifies differences between 3-NN and NB with Random attribute selection and nearly all the other algorithms with a non random attribute selection method. However, it does not find differences between Random+SVM and any other method. Similar results are obtained applying Holm or Shafer tests for a pairwise comparison [5].

To observe any significant difference between standard attribute selection methods and Random+SVM, we have to resort to $1 \times (k-1)$ comparison methods, where 1 base line algorithm is compared against the rest. Based on the previous results, we have disregarded 3-NN and NB with random selection, maintaining Random+SVM as the base line. For these tests, ranking are based on error rates. Consequently, if a classifier obtains an average ranking of 1, then this classifier obtains the largest error rate on all data set. Table 3 shows the results of Holm's test for 60 genes, where the minimum difference between the first and the last ranked algorithm is found. The best ranked, and consequently worst algorithm

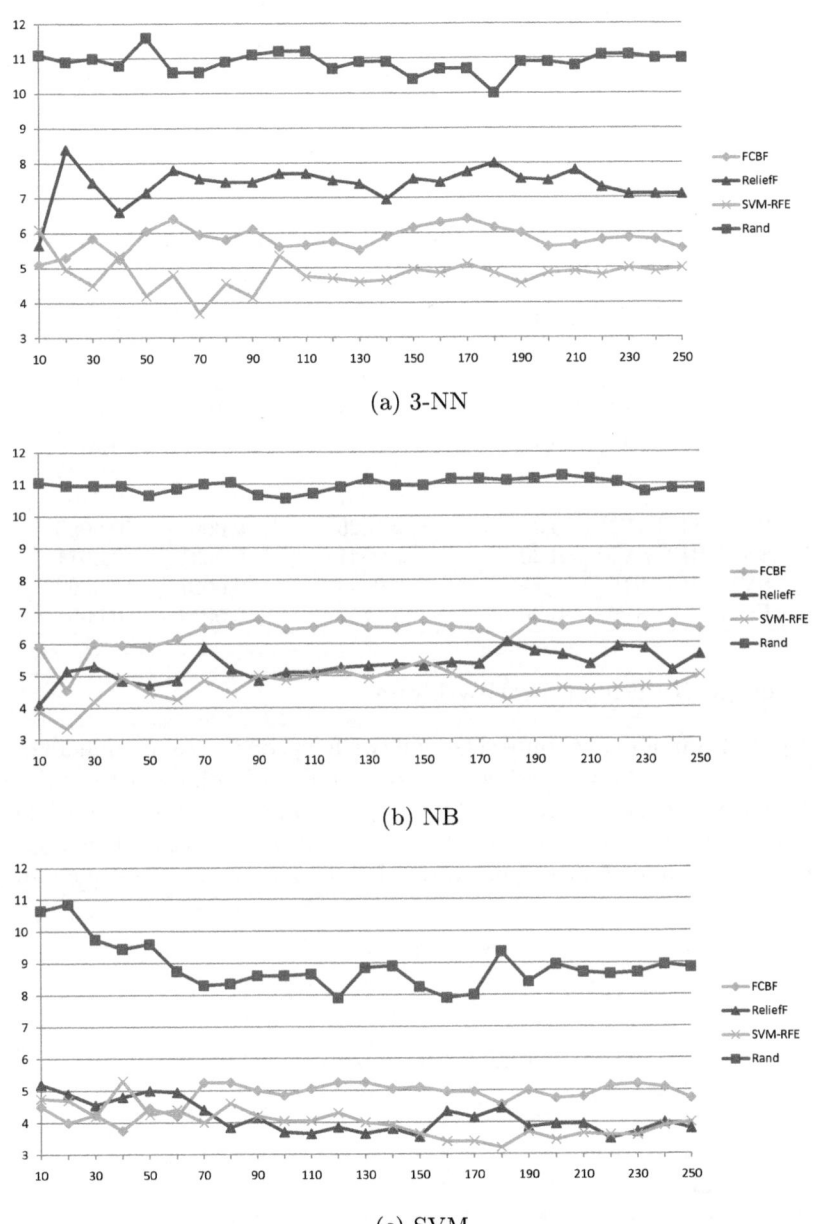

(a) 3-NN

(b) NB

(c) SVM

Fig. 1. Average ranking over all the data sets, grouped by the classifier method. In horizontal is expressed the number of attributes, in vertical is the average ranking position. Smaller ranking values reflects better average performance.

for 60 genes is Random-SVM. Holm's procedure rejects those methods with a p-value ≤ 0.0166, that is, all but FCBF+3-NN and Relief+3-NN. Similar results are obtained for the range from 10 to 100 genes. In the extreme case of 10 and 20 genes, where differences on error rates are wider, Bonferroni-Dun test find that Random-SVM is significantly worse than any other method. Hence, we can conclude that we can find algorithms that perform better than random attribute selection.

Table 3. Holm Table (α=0.05) selecting 60 genes. Smaller rankings reflects worse performance.

i	Algorithm		Ranking	$z = (R_0 - R_i)/SE$	p	Holm
0	Random	SVM	2.60	-	-	-
1	ReliefF	3NN	3.5	0.6646	0.5062	0.0500
2	FCBF	3NN	4.80	1.6248	0.1042	0.0250
3	FCBF	NB	5.15	1.8832	0.0596	0.0166
4	ReliefF	SVM	6.15	2.6218	0.0087	0.0125
5	ReliefF	NB	6.25	2.6957	0.0070	0.0100
6	SVM-RFE	3NN	6.30	2.7326	0.0062	0.0083
7	SVM-RFE	SVM	6.60	2.9541	0.0031	0.0071
8	SVM-RFE	NB	6.75	3.0649	0.0021	0.0062
9	FCBF	SVM	6.90	3.1757	0.0014	0.0055

5.2   Average Rankings for Few Genes

Once rejected Random attribute selection, we focus on the remaining algorithms from 10 to 40 genes. Now, rankings are not significantly different from the mean rank. Major differences are observed for 30 genes when Friedman, and Iman and Davenport statistics are 12.17 and 1.16 respectively, far from their significant threshold (15.50 and 2,33 respectively). Even in this case, average rankings,

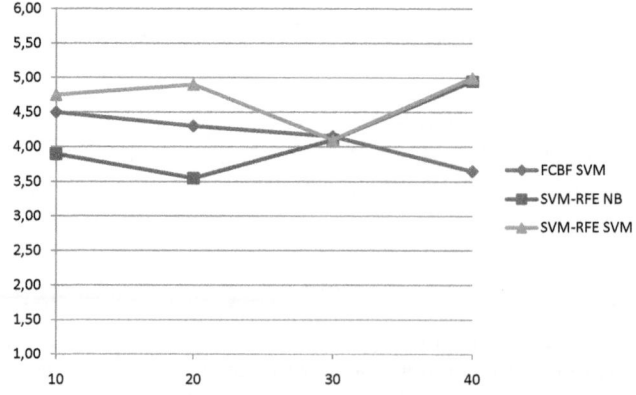

Fig. 2. Algorithms with rankings systematically smaller than mean rank (5)

by themselves, provide a fair comparison of the classifiers [2]. Fig 2 shows the rankings of the algorithms that systematically obtain a ranking below the mean value of 5. NB combined with SVM-RFE attribute selection obtains the best rankings for 10-20 genes. SVM behaves well both with FCBF and SVM-RFE. Except for 30 genes, where the three algorithms nearly tie, SVM with FCBF outperforms SVM with SVM-RFE. This is an interesting result because FCBF has fewer computational cost than SVM-RFE.

6 Conclusions

When combining feature selection and classification algorithms for microarray gene expression, the common criterion to decide the best number of selected attributes is to choose the number of genes that maximizes the classifier precision.

This paper shows that changing the criterion of maximum classifier precision for choosing a configuration that do not significantly worsen the best classifier precision, the number of selected genes reduce to the range [10-50] for all tested data sets. Moreover, for 7 out of 10 data sets, 20 or less attributes are selected.

Regarding which combinations perform best for a given data set, only very general conclusion can be drawn. Differences on average rankings only indicates that random attribute selection is to be avoided. SVM obtains consistently good rankings combined with ReliefF or SVM-RFE for 40 or more number of selected attributes. Between 50 and 90 genes SVM-RFE+3-NN also obtains good rankings. For 40 or less genes, SVM performs consistently good with FCBF and SVM-RFE, with a small advantage for FCBF. For twenty or less genes, Naïve Bayes with SVM-RFE obtains the best rankings. If we focus on 40 or less genes, SVM-RFE+NB and FCBF+SVM are the configurations to try by default.

Acknowledgments. This work has been partially funded by Junta de Castilla y León through grant VA100A08. Authors want to thank F. Díez, E. Manso and J. Rodríguez for useful discussions on this work.

References

1. Chai, H., Domeniconi, C.: An evaluation of gene selection methods for multi-class microarray data classification. In: Proceedings of the Workshop W9 on Data Mining and Text Minig for Bioinformatics, pp. 3–10 (2004)
2. Demšar, J.: Statistical comparisons of classifiers over multiple data sets. Journal of Machine Learning Research 7, 1–30 (2006)
3. Ding, C., Peng, H.: Minimum redundancy feature selection from microarray gene expression data. Journal of Bioinformatics and Computational Biology 3(2), 185–205 (2005)
4. Ferri, C., Hernández-Orallo, J., Modroiu, R.: An experimental comparison of performance measures for classification. Pattern Recognition Letters (September 2008)
5. Garcia, S., Herrera, F.: An Extension on "Statistical Comparisons of Classifiers over Multiple Data Sets" for all Pairwise Comparisons. Journal of Machine Learning Research 9, 2677–2694 (2008)

6. Golub, T.R., Stomin, D.K., Tamayo, P.: Molecular classification of cancer: Class discovery and class prediction by gene expression monitoring. Science 286, 531 (1999)
7. Guyon, I., Weston, J., Barnhill, S., Vapnik, V.: Gene selection for cancer classification using support vector machines. Machine Learning 46, 389–422 (2002)
8. Kira, K., Rendell, L.A.: A practical approach to feature selection. In: Sleeman, D., Edwards, P. (eds.) Machine Learning: Proceedings of International Conference (ICML-92), pp. 249–256 (1992)
9. Kononenko, I.: Estimating attributes: analysis and extension of relief. In: Proc European Conference on Machine Learning, pp. 171–182 (1994)
10. Li, T., Zhang, C., Oghara, M.: A comparative study of feature selection and multiclass classification methods for tissue classification based on gene expression. Bioinformatics 20(15), 2429–2437 (2004)
11. Li, W., Yang, Y.: How many genes are needed for a discriminant microarray data analysis? In: Critical Assessment of Techniques for Microarray Data Mining Workshop, pp. 137–150 (2000)
12. Li, Z., Zhang, L., Chen, H.: Are filter methods very effective in gene selection of microarray data? In: IEEE International Conference on Bioinformatics and Biomedicine Workshops, BIBMW2007, pp. 97–100 (2007)
13. Nadeau, C., Bengio, Y.: Inference for the generalization error. Machine Learning 52(3), 239–281 (2003)
14. Ridge, K.: Kent ridge bio-medical dataset (2009), http://datam.i2r.a-star.edu.sg/datasets/krbd/
15. Saeys, Y., Inza, I., Larrañaga, P.: A review of feature selection techniques. Bioinformatics 23, 2507–2517 (2007)
16. Robnik Sikonja, M., Kononenko, I.: An adaptation of relief for attribute estimation in regression. In: Fisher, D.H. (ed.) Machine Learning: Proceedings of the Fourteenth International Conference (ICML-97), pp. 296–304 (1997)
17. Stiglic, G., Rodríguez, J.-J., Kokol, P.: Feature selection and classification for small gene sets. In: Chetty, M., Ngom, A., Ahmad, S. (eds.) PRIB 2008. LNCS (LNBI), vol. 5265, pp. 121–131. Springer, Heidelberg (2008)
18. Symons, S., Nieselt, K.: Data mining microarray data - Comprehensive benchmarking of feature selection and classification methods (Pre-print), http://www.zbit.uni-tuebingen.de/pas/preprints/GCB2006/SymonsNieselt.pdf
19. Tang, Y., Zhang, Y., Huang, Z.: FCM-SVM-RFE gene feature selection algorithm for leukemia classification from microarray gene expression data. In: FUZZ'05, The 14th IEEE International Conference on Fuzzy Systems, pp. 97–101 (2005)
20. Witten, I., Frank, E.: Data Mining: Practical Machine Learning Tools and Techniques, 2nd edn. Morgan Kaufmann, San Francisco (2005)
21. Xiong, M., Fang, Z., Zhao, J.: Biomarker identification by feature wrappers. Genome Research 11, 1878–1887 (2001)
22. Yu, L., Liu, H.: Feature selection for high-dimensional data: A fast correlation-based filter solution. In: Proceedings of the Twentieth International Conference on Machine Learning (ICML-2003), Washington DC (2003)

Sequential Pattern Mining in Multi-relational Datasets

Carlos Abreu Ferreira[1,2,3], João Gama[1], and Vítor Santos Costa[2]

[1] LIAAD-INESC LA
[2] CRACS-INESC LA, University of Porto
[3] ISEP-Institute of Engineering of Porto

Abstract. We present a framework designed to mine sequential temporal patterns from multi-relational databases. In order to exploit logic-relational information without using aggregation methodologies, we convert the multi-relational dataset into what we name a *multi-sequence database*. Each example in a multi-relational target table is coded into a sequence that combines intra-table and inter-table relational temporal information. This allows us to find heterogeneous temporal patterns through standard sequence miners. Our framework is grounded in the excellent results achieved by previous propositionalization strategies. We follow a pipelined approach, where we first use a sequence miner to find frequent sequences in the multi-sequence database. Next, we select the most interesting findings to augment the representational space of the examples. The most interesting sequence patterns are discriminative and class correlated. In the final step we build a classifier model by taking an enlarged target table as input to a classifier algorithm. We evaluate the performance of this work through a motivating application, the hepatitis multi-relational dataset. We prove the effectiveness of our methodology by addressing two problems of the hepatitis dataset.

1 Introduction

Multi-relational databases are widely used to represent and store data. Quite often, data accumulates over time. In multidimensional databases, we have a number of *fact* tables referencing *dimension* tables. Dimension tables are expected to grow slowly over time. In contrast, fact tables can grow quickly over time. In this work we assume that data stored in fact tables are sequences that reflect the evolution of a phenomenon of interest. As an example, consider a multi-relational dataset in a medical domain. A patient is subject to sequences of examinations, where a set of measurements, corresponding to results of different analysis, are taken. For each patient, we have a sequence of measurements over time. Our hypothesis is that the evolution of these measurements might encode relevant information for the diagnosis. The problem we address here is therefore *how can we explore that information?* In more general terms, can we obtain *implicit* multi-relational information that can be used to learn predictive and accurate decision models? We believe that intra-table and inter-table temporal patterns can be used

P. Meseguer, L. Mandow, and R.M. Gasca (Eds.): CAEPIA 2009, LNAI 5988, pp. 121–130, 2010.

for this purpose. In order to do so, we propose a framework whose architecture is grounded in the propositionalization methodology [1,2].

We propose *MuSeR*, an algorithm to discover Multi-Sequential patterns in Relational data. The algorithm is organized as a pipeline where we start by converting the multi-relational data into what we call a *multi-sequence database*. In this new database each example is a heterogeneous sequence built from inter-relational information. In a second phase, we use a sequence miner to learn the frequent sequences. Next, in a third phase, we select interesting frequent sequences. We extract discriminative frequent ones, e.g. those that appear in only one class, and using a chi-square filter we remove class unrelated sequences. The fourth phase maps the discriminative sequences to binary attributes, that indicate the presence or absence of the learned sequence for a particular example. Last, we induce a classifier model using a propositional algorithm.

We believe that this methodology is suitable to explore time related data stored in multi-relational datasets. To evaluate our methodology, we analyze the multi-relational hepatitis dataset used in the PKDD '04 competition. This is a challenging and complex dataset that has several open problems. In our experiments we address two classification problems. Furthermore, when addressing the two problems we find sequence patterns that are expect to be useful to uncover relations among short term change and long term change examination parameters. We evaluate the effectiveness of our methodology by measuring the accuracy and the usefulness of the generated classifiers models. A comparison against a reference algorithm, RUSE-WARMR [1] algorithm, is also presented.

In section two we present some methodologies and related work. In section three we discuss our framework in detail. Next, at section four, we describe the motivation dataset and present and discuss the obtained results. At the end of the document we conclude and present future research directions.

2   Methods and Related Work

A wide range of algorithms have been developed to mine sequential data in an efficient way. To the best of our knowledge, the first proposal to perform sequential data mining was the GSP [3] algorithm. This algorithm search procedure is inspired in the well known transactional APRIORI algorithm. The algorithm uses candidate-generation strategy to find all frequent sequences. This strategy requires multiple database pass/consult, and can be ineffective on large datasets. PrefixSpan [4] applies pattern-growth strategy to efficiently find the complete set of frequent sequences. The algorithm explores prefix projection databases. In each iteration only the databases having a given frequent prefix (the projection databases) are consulted. Other algorithms such as SPIRIT [5], that constrain the search space, and like CloSpan [6], that return a set of closed sequential patterns, exist. A different approach is to use post-processing methodologies, filters, to select interesting patterns. Among this strategies some use sequential ad-hoc selection, that are model unrelated, whereas others use wrapper filters, an algorithm-based selection technique.

The problem of finding sequence patterns can be even harder to solve if we consider an heterogeneous multi-sequence database. Even if we can use valuable logic-relational information to constrain and direct sequence search. Algorithms like FOIL [7] and GOLEM [8] that use ILP approaches were the first ones to explore successfully the richness of multi-relational data.

Recently some algorithms were presented that combine ILP algorithms with other techniques. Two main strategies are used. One is known as propositional-ization [2,1] methodology, which can be seen as a sequential approach. Usually an ILP algorithm augments the descriptive power of the target table by project-ing clauses, new attributes, on the target table. Alternatively, one can tightly integrate feature selection and model induction [9,10]. Some ILP algorithms, like WARMR [11] algorithm, are able to explore time information by using ag-gregation methodologies, losing relevant, mainly, short-time changing data.

Non-ILP approaches have also been used to find frequent patterns in multi-relational data. In [12] the authors combined a decision tree classifier with the Graph Based Induction algorithm (DT-GBI) to study three problems in the Hepatitis dataset. To apply DT-GBI a pre-processing step converts, using an aggregation strategy, all data to a graph space where each graph is an aggre-gated time sequence of the patient inspections. The algorithm works by simul-taneous growing the tree and discover frequent patterns (subgraphs) using GBI. Yamada [13] developed a decision tree algorithm suitable to deal with the time-series of the hepatitis dataset. The attribute tested at the inner nodes are data time-series examples. To test and measure the similarity among time-series, the authors used Dynamic Time Warping method.

3 Algorithm Description

In this section we present MuSeR framework. This new methodology explores logic-relational, mainly, heterogeneous sequential data presented across a multi-relational dataset, to build descriptive and high accurate classifier models. In the first phase we convert the multi-relational data into a multi-sequence database. Then, in a second phase, we run a sequence miner to find all sequential patterns in each class partition. Next, considering the huge number of these findings, we introduce two filters to select the discriminative and class related patterns. In a fourth phase, the most interesting frequent sequences are projected into the target table obtaining an enlarged target table. In the last phase, we learn a classifier model by taking the enlarged target table as input to a propositional classifier.

To best explain our framework we follow the Algorithm pseudo-code 1 and explain each one of the major components.

1- Pre-Processing Coding. To illustrate the conversion procedure that we explain in this subsection, we follow the simple example presented at table 1. This table contains some relations and ground facts of one example registered in the hepatitis dataset. In this table we have three database relations: *patientinfo*,

---

input : a multi-relational dataset **r**; two thresholds λ and δ;
output: a classifier model

1 **Pre-Processing Coding**
  s ← conversion (**r**)
2 **Frequent Patterns**
  $s_1,\dots,s_k$ ← partition (**s**)
  for $i = 1$ *to* k **do**
  $\quad\lfloor\ sf_i$ ← SequenceMiner(s_i,λ)
3 **Filtering**
  S_{disc} ← discriminate($sf_1,\dots,sf_k$)
  S_{inter} ← chi-square(S_{disc},δ)
4 **Mapping**
  $r_{EnlargedTarget}$ ← Mapping(S_{inter}, r_{target})
5 **Classifier Induction**
  ClassifierIndution($r_{EnlargedTarget}$)

Algorithm 1. Framework pseudo-code

that contains patient information and the label of each patient; *hematexam*, the table that register periodic hematologic examinations; and table *inhospexam* that register in hospital blood and urinalysis examinations. Also we present some ground facts. We can see, among other information, that the patient 50 is a female having hepatitis C subtype. Also we can see that in the hematological examination, at 1981-05-09, the patient get normal values in all but the PLT parameter, where a high value was registered. Then, two months later the patient repeated the examination obtaining some low values, parameters WBC, RGB and HGB, and no high value. Also, the patient made in-hospital examinations. We present the result of a ALB measurement.

The algorithm that we presented here takes a multi-relational dataset as input, usually represented as a database of Prolog facts. To explore the richness of this representation, mainly temporal patterns, we introduce a strategy that converts the multi-relational data into an amenable multi-sequence database. Though, all data conversion strategy is grounded in logical-relational knowledge base and time ordering. Thus, for each example in the multi-relational target table we find all linked relations that have temporal records. Then, among all this relations we sort all records regarding the time order (see table 1B). This way we obtain a chronological sequence of multiple events for each example. Using this ordering we build an attribute-value sequence for each example(table 1D). In this new sequence each subsequence corresponds to all records registered in given date/time. Then, using a knowledge base (table 1C) we codify the attribute-value sequences into an integer number sequence (table 1E). The construction of this knowledge base is done accordingly to the type of attributes in each database relation. For each discrete attribute we find the range of attribute values and for each attribute-value we build a unique Prolog ground fact. This ground fact is a three element tuple having the attribute name, the attribute value and a unique integer number that identifies the attribute-value. When dealing with

Table 1. Illustrative conversion data

A. Database relations	
$patientinfo(mid, hepatitisType, ExamDate, fibroDegree, fibroActivity, ptSex, ptBirth)$ $hematexam(mid, Date, SeqNum, WBC, RBC, HGB, HCT, MCV, MCH, MCHC, PLT)$ $inhospexam(mid, examDate, ExamN, ExamName, Result)$	
B. Database of ordered prolog ground facts	C. Knowledge base
$patientinfor(50, C, 19920702, 1, 2.0, f, 19441201)$ $hematexam(50, 19810509, 1, normal, normal, normal, normal, normal, normal, normal, high)$ $inhospexam(50, 19810519, 1, alb, normal)$ $hematexam(50, 19810703, 1, normal, low, low, low, normal, normal, normal, normal)$	$hematKB(wbc, normal, 2)$ $hematKB(hgb, low, 9)$ $hematKB(hgb, high, 11)$ $hematKB(plt, normal, 30)$ $resinKB(alb, normal, 36)$
D. Patient 50 attribute-value sequence	
(wbc=normal hgb=high plt=normal) (alb=normal) (wbc=normal hgb=low plt=normal alb=normal)	
E. Patient 50, sequence coding	
(2 11 30) (36) (2 9 30 36)	

continuous attributes, first we apply a discretization strategy and then proceed as explained in the procedure used to code discrete attributes. The discretization is problem and domain specific and depends either on the available information or is accomplished by using a discretization algorithm.

In the resulting sequence database, each sequence corresponds to an example in the target table and each subsequence corresponds to all one time events. Using the example in table 1, the patient examinations are coded in table 1E. After this pre-processing stage we get a multi-sequential database suitable to be explored by a flat sequential miner.

2- Frequent Patterns. When mining the multi-sequence database we aim to find interesting patterns that augment the descriptive power of raw data and are useful to build high accurate models. We run a sequence miner, using λ a user-defined support threshold, in each class-partition of the multi-sequence database. Getting all class frequent patterns, sf_i. Regarding the nature of the sequence miner, the type and dimension of problem being addressed we usually get an overall huge number of findings. Among these there are high discriminative patterns and class correlated patterns that must be retained and uninteresting and redundant patterns that must be eliminated.

3- Filtering. Though, we also define a pruning strategy to select discriminative and class correlated frequent patterns. To select discriminative sequences we introduce the *Discriminative Filter*. Using this filter we select intra-class discriminative sequences, S_{disc}. Those that were found only in one of the partitions. This is accomplished by using a simple matching.

After eliminating non-discriminative patterns some class uncorrelated patterns remain. To eliminate some of these we use the *Chi-square filter*. This filter uses chi-square statistical test and the δ significance value.

By applying sequentially these two filters we get a set of interesting patterns. To incorporate the descriptive power in the final classifier model we first project each of the new sequences/features in the multi-relational target table.

4- Mapping. The mapping of each of the above selected sequences/features in the target table is done by using Boolean attributes. For each feature we add a new Boolean attribute to the target table. The value of each new attribute, for each example, is computed according to the following rule. If the sequence associated with the new attribute is a sub-sequence of the example sequence, the new attribute takes value one. Otherwise the attribute takes value zero. This way we get an enlarged target table that includes the primitive attributes and the new Boolean attributes.

5- Classifier Induction. In this last step we learn our classifier model. Taking the enlarged target table as input to a classifier algorithm we induce a classification model. This classifier can use either primitive attributes or new ones, the sequential patterns.

4   Experimental Evaluation

In this section we evaluate experimentally our methodology using the hepatitis multi-relational dataset. First we describe experiments setup. Then we introduce the problem and present the pre-processing of the data. Next, we introduce both hepatitis problems that we address and, for each problem, we present the obtained results. At the end of the section we will discuss the obtained results.

4.1   Experimental Configuration

All the results that we present bellow were obtained using an AMD Athlon machine having 2GB of ram. To evaluate our framework we use PrefixSpan algorithm as the sequence miner and WEKA [14] J48 algorithm, a C4.5 clone algorithm, as the classifier induction algorithm. Also we use YAP[1] prolog compiler. We use this tool to convert the multi-relational data into a multi-sequence database, to eliminate non-discriminative patterns and to project the PrefixSpan findings on the target table.

We evaluate our work using the PKDD '04 challenge hepatitis multi-relational dataset. The dataset consists of seven tables registering a long term, between 1982 and 1990, monitoring of 771 patients who have hepatitis B or C.

To best evaluate our contribution we compare our algorithm against RUSE-WARMR, a three step ILP relational algorithm. This reference algorithm combines sequentially WARMR ILP algorithm and C4.5 algorithm. We run our algorithm by setting PrefixSpan support values equal to 90% and 80%. Also we evaluate the algorithm using different values of the chi-square filter, the δ value. Also we present results, *No-Chi*, using only the discriminative filter. For comparison purposes we also present the results of running RUSE-WARMR without using any filter, *Standard*. The quality of the results is validated on a stratified ten-fold cross validation and some statistical measures. We compute the mean generalization error, the standard deviation and compute Wilcoxon hypothesis test p-value. This last test is used to measure how significantly our algorithm differs form the reference algorithm.

---

[1] http://www.dcc.fc.up.pt/ vsc/Yap/

Table 2. MuSeR in B vs. C subtype problem

δ	Mean Error	Std. Deviation
5	23.05	6.86
10	22.75	6.74
25	22.82	5.63
No-Chi	22.76	5.63

Table 3. WARMR+C4.5 results

δ	Mean Error	Std. Deviation
5	34.87	8.48
25	37.39	7.19
No-Chi	37.76	5.85
Standard	41.63	9.2

4.2 Pre-processing

The hepatitis dataset is a huge and complex dataset. There are too many patient records and too many attributes that describe patient examinations. Besides that, when we address some problems like the fibrosis degree we are faced with an unbalanced dataset. Different from the majority, in this work we use all the examples, whether we are solving the subtype or fibrosis degree problems. We only eliminate the records that are registered after a ground biopsy. This ground biopsy is a biopsy where each patient is classified into one of subtypes and fibrosis degrees. We use the biopsy results to label the patients and build a labeled tuple. Regarding the search space complexity and available computer resources, we use only *patientinfo*, *inhospital* and *hematological* examinations and select 15 features. We select GOT, GPT, TTT, ZTT, T-CHO, CHE, ALB, TP, T-BIL, D-BIL, I-BIL, ICG-15, PLT, WBC and HGB features. Considering that each one of these features is a numerical one, having a wide range of values, we discretize each one accordingly to reference values available at *inlab* table or by using medical knowledge. We discretize every feature into three bins: low, normal and high. We do not use any technique to estimate the values of the examinations parameters.

After this pre-processing, we obtain a dataset suitable to be used as input to the MuSeR algorithm and amenable to tackle both of the problems that we propose to solve.

4.3 Hepatitis Problems

The hepatitis dataset is a challenging one that has many open problems. In this work we address the hepatitis subtype problem and the hepatitis fibrosis degree problem. The first problem is a binary problem, whereas we want to classify a patient into B or C subtype. The fibrosis degree problem is a multi-class classification problem. Like [12], we define a binary problem, fibrosis degrees 2 and 3 against fibrosis degree 4.

Hepatitis Subtype. After pre-processing we get 206 patients labeled hepatitis B and 297 labeled hepatitis C. In table 2 we present the obtained results. The presented results were obtained by setting MuSeR λ's parameter to 80% and using different δ values. We also run MuSeR by setting $\lambda = 90\%$, this time the obtained results do not differ significantly from the ones obtained by the best configuration of the reference algorithm.

In figure 1 we present the tree model generated at the best run. In this run we obtained the best overall accuracy, 91%. This result was obtained by setting the chi-square threshold to 5%.

In this particular example the nodes of the tree use both sequence patterns and primitive attributes. The obtained tree model contains split tests using both primitive attributes and sequence patterns. For lack of space we present none of the sequence patterns.

Hepatitis Fibrosis. As said above we do not address the five class fibrosis degree problem. We address a binary classification problem aiming to discriminate among patients having fibrosis degree 2, 3 and 4. As we have 122 and 87 patients having fibrosis degree 2 and 3, respectively, and 67 patients having the last stage of fibrosis, stage four, we define an unbalanced binary problem. We get 209 patients of $\{2, 3\}$-class and 67 of the $\{4\}$-class.

Different from the above presented results, in the fibrosis problem we do not observe the contribution of the λ parameter. The results obtained using different values of both parameters were almost the same. By setting $\lambda = 80\%$ and $\delta = 5\%$ we obtained 24.17% mean accuracy and 2.64% standard deviation. Using the same support value and other δ values we obtained no significant changes. Even if we use only the discriminative filter we get no significance improvements, we obtained 24.52% mean accuracy and 3.13% standard deviation. Again, if we do not use any of the filters and set $\lambda = 80\%$ we are unable to run the MuSeR algorithm.

The best result that we obtained using WARMR+C4.5 algorithm was 24.17% mean error and the worst result was 42.06%. This last result was obtained without using any filter.

In Figure 2 we present the most accurate model tree that we obtained in the MuSeR 10-cv experiments. This tree was obtained in the fourth fold and using $\lambda = 80\%$ and $\delta = 5\%$. In this run we obtained a generalization error of 21.3%.

4.4   Analysis of Results

The hepatitis dataset is a complex dataset having a large amount of data and whereas each table has a wide number of attributes. Though, the majority of works that address any of the problems underlying this dataset use pre-processing and sample strategies to reduce the amount of data and to balance class distributions, e.g. [12]. In almost all existing works there exist some details, regarding dataset balancing strategies, that are impossible to repeat.

Regarding these constrains the results obtained in both problems, mainly the subtype problem, are quite impressive. The obtained results were approximately equal or better than the best results presented by previous works. The works that obtained comparable results use sampling strategies to reduce and balance the number of examples. When evaluating MuSeR methodology on the subtype problem, using 10-cv, in two iterations that we run, setting chi-square parameter equal to 10%, we obtained generalization errors of 11%, and 9%. In all works

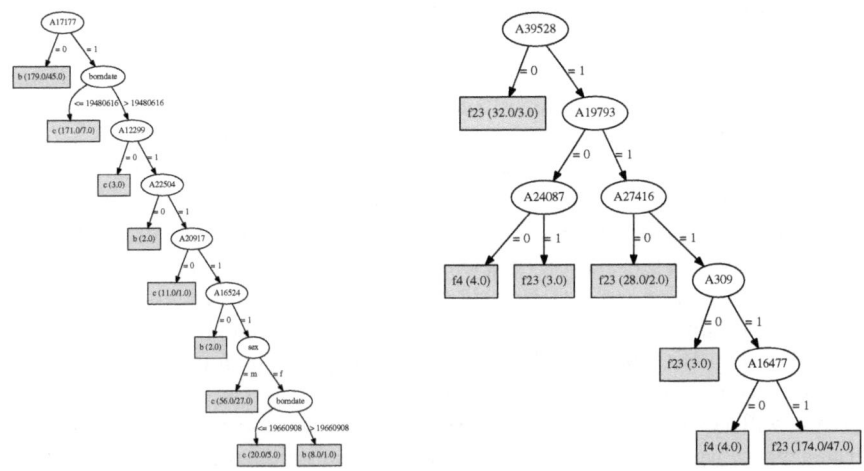

Fig. 1. Best decision tree: subtype problem **Fig. 2.** Best decision tree: fibrosis problem

that address this problem the best result obtained in a single iteration was higher than 21%. Some works, the ones that do not explore temporal patterns, obtained generalization errors values higher than 40%. The results are even more impressive if we compared MuSeR against the RUSE-WARMR reference algorithm, also using all the available examples and the time records. In the subtype problem we obtained, for all chi-square values, approximately 10% reduction in the mean generalization error. Also, using the Wilcoxon hypothesis test, the performance of our algorithm is, with statistical significance, better than the reference algorithm.

The effectiveness of the filters is not clear when analyzing the presented results, yet it is fundamental the use of both filters. Without the use of both filters we could not obtain the presented results. The number of patterns found by the sequence miner makes impossible to run any classifier on the augmented target table. We think that both filters will proof their usefulness when running MuSeR with a lower sequence miner support value.

The results obtained when addressing the Fibrosis were almost equal to the ones obtained by the reference algorithm, but the obtained patterns are much more interesting and have a higher clinical value. Regarding the above mentioned issues and that we do not used the antigen or antibody examinations, the comparison against other works, rather than RUSE-WARMR, is even hard to analyze.

Also, we think that the obtained patterns require the analysis of a clinical technician. We are not specialists in hepatitis but regarding the knowledge we obtained when studying the disease we can say that some of the obtained patterns are coherent with current knowledge. Others, we expect, will be useful to unveil the mechanisms of disease progression.

5   Conclusions and Future Work

In this work we presented *MuSeR*, a multi-sequential framework that explores relational and sequential information stored in multi-relational datasets. The main contribution of the proposed system is a method that explores temporal patterns presented in relational data without losing valuable logic-relational information. In the experimental evaluation the algorithm produces accurate and readable models. In comparison to the reference algorithm, a composition WARMR + C4.5, that does not explore sequential information, we have significant better results. Also in some runs of our algorithm we have the best results among the ones that we can find in current bibliography. The algorithm has some limitations related to the huge number of sequential patterns found. In the future, we will try to reduce the search space by imposing constrains in the search space. Also we will try other filters. In particular, we want use lower support values. Furthermore, we wish to evaluate our algorithm using other datasets.

References

1. Ferreira, C.A., Gama, J., Costa, V.S.: RUSE-WARMR: Rule Selection for Classifier Induction in Multi-relational Data-Sets. In: ICTAI, pp. 379–386 (2008)
2. Zelezny, F., Lavrac, N.: Propositionalization-Based Relational Subgroup Discovery with RSD. Machine Learning, 33–63 (2006)
3. Agrawal, R., Srikant, R.: Mining Sequential Patterns. In: ICDE, pp. 3–14 (1995)
4. Pei, J., Han, J., Mortazavi-asl, B., Pinto, H., Chen, Q., Dayal, U., Hsu, M.: PrefixSpan: Mining Sequential Patterns Efficiently by Prefix-Projected Pattern Growth. In: ICDE, pp. 215–224 (2001)
5. Garofalakis, M., Rastogi, R., Shim, K.: Mining Sequential Patterns with Regular Expression Constraints. IEEE Trans. on Know. and Data Eng., 223–234 (2002)
6. Yan, X., Han, J., Afshar, R.: CloSpan: Mining Closed Sequential Patterns in Large Datasets. In: SDM, pp. 166–177 (2003)
7. Quinlan, J.R., Cameron-Jones, R.M.: Induction of Logic Programs: FOIL and Related Systems. New Generation Computing, 287–312 (1995)
8. Muggleton, S., Feng, C.: Efficient Induction Of Logic Programs. Academic Press, London (1990)
9. Landwehr, N., Kersting, K., De Raedt, L.: nFOIL: Integrating Naïve Bayes and FOIL. In: AAAI, pp. 795–800 (2005)
10. Davis, J., Burnside, E., Page, D., Dutra, I., Costa, V.S.: Learning Bayesian networks of rules with SAYU. In: MRDM, p.13 (2005)
11. Dehaspe, L., Toivonen, H.: Discovery of frequent DATALOG patterns. Data Min. Knowl. Discov. (1999)
12. Ohara, K., Yoshida, T., Geamsakul, W., Motoda, H., Washio, T., Yokoi, H., Takabayashi, K.: Analysis of Hepatitis Dataset by Decision Tree Graph-Based Induction. Proceedings of Discovery Challenge, 173–184 (2004)
13. Yamada, Y., Suzuki, E., Yokoi, H., Takabayashi, K.: Decision-tree Induction from Time-series Data Based on a Standard-example Split Test. In: ICML, pp. 840–847 (2003)
14. Witten, I., Frank, E.: Data mining: practical machine learning tools with Java Implementations. Morgan Kaufmann, San Francisco (1999)

CBR Outcome Evaluation for High Similar Cases: A Preliminary Approach*

José M. Juarez[1], Manuel Campos[2], Antonio Gomariz[1],
José T. Palma[1], and Roque Marín[1]

[1] Information and Communication Engineering Department, University of Murcia, Spain
{jmjuarez,agomariz,jtpalma,roquemm}@um.es
[2] Computer Science and Systems Department, University of Murcia, Spain
manuelcampos@um.es

Abstract. Case-based reasoning has demonstrated to be a suitable similarity-based approach to develop decision-support system in different domains. However, in certain scenarios CBR finds difficulties to obtain a reliable solution when retrieved cases are highly similar. For example, patients from an Intensive Care Unit are critical patients in which slight variations of monitored parameters have a deep impact on the patient severity evaluation. In this scenario, it seems necessary to extend the system outcome in order to indicate the reliance of the solution obtained. Main efforts in the literature for CBR evaluation focus on case retrieval (i.e. similarity) or a retrospective analysis. However, these approaches do not seem to suffice when cases are very close. To this end, we propose three techniques to obtain a reliance solution degree, one based on case retrieval and two based on case adaptation. We also show the capacities of this proposal in a medical problem.

1 Introduction

The key idea of Case Based Reasoning (CBR) is to tackle a current problem by referring to similar problems that have already been solved in the past (retrieval step) [5] and to adapting these old solutions to the current problem (adapt step). Once the current case has its adapted solution, the CBR system provides end user with the outcome. Therefore, the correctness of the outcome depends on the reliance of the retrieval and adaptation steps. In practise, it is well-know that one advantage of CBR methodology is that it produces easy-comprehensive systems, however a CBR system behaves as a black box, since the user receives a new solution (a value) that lacks of any explanatory element. This is particularly evident in the medical domain, for example, severe burned patients are critical monitored patients in an Intensive Care Unit (ICU). In this medical domain, the physicians require in real time to know patient's state and to estimate a severity score. A CBR system that provides a patient's survival indicator for supporting therapy decisions in a ICU could be useful for medical purposes. For a particular incoming case, the outcome could be *survive*. The physician could interpret that similar cases in

---

* This study was partially financed by the Spanish MEC through projects TIN2006-15460-C04-01, PET2007_0033, the SENECA 08853/PI/08, and the Excellence Project P07-SEJ-03214.

P. Meseguer, L. Mandow, and R.M. Gasca (Eds.): CAEPIA 2009, LNAI 5988, pp. 131–140, 2010.

the knowledge base also survive. However, in this scenario this is useless, since most of the cases are very similar and only slight differences of their characteristics allows the system to predict whether the patient survives or not. Therefore, additional information must be included to explain the accuracy of this outcome in order to be considered.

Main efforts in the literature for CBR evaluation focus on the retrieval step or a retrospective analysis. The work done by [2] proposed evaluating the CBR systems based on the precision and the efficiency. The retrieval accuracy measure of Gupta et al. [4] measures the average rank of the applicable case, while in [8] the frequency of successful retrievals is measured. In [3], the authors present evaluation criteria by considering a confidence rank based on similarity functions.

However, for critical domains (e.g. medical decision-making scenarios) we identify two major problems in these approaches. Firstly, they are mainly focused on evaluating the reliance of the retrieval step, forgetting the adaptation process. Secondly, in these domains, retrieved cases are highly close, in other words, the outcome is not significative or does not represent of the current scenario.

Therefore, new mechanisms for the solution evaluation are required in these scenarios. We believe that this evaluation must also consider the adaptation step. Due to the fact that the adaptation depends on the retrieve step, both are evaluated with a single reliance degree. In particular, this evaluation could be based on the estimation of a reliance degree on the adapted solution to solve the current case.

In this paper we present a methodological approach to describe how to obtain a reliance degree based on the adapted solution. Therefore, the outcome of our CBR system will consist of the adapted solution and the reliance degree on this solution to solve the problem. We also illustrate the suitability of our approach by presenting its implementation and experiments in a real problem of an ICU.

2   CBR and Adaptation Step

CBR can be considered a methodology for the development of knowledge-based systems. CBR is typically described by a cyclical process (see Figure 1), comprising the following four steps [1]: the Retrieve step searches in the Case Library (CL), the knowledge base, for the most similar cases; in the Adaptation step, the cases attempt to solve the current problem; the Revise step checks the adapted solution; and the Retain step stores the adapted solution in the Case Library.

CBR systems store in the CL the set of solved problems (cases) and receive, as input, a new problem to be solved (current case). Thus, CBR systems attempt to solve the new problem by searching in the CL for the most similar cases (retrieved cases). Once the matching cases are retrieved, a CBR system will attempt to reuse the solutions suggested by the retrieved cases. However, in many circumstances the solution might not be close enough. The CBR system must then adapt the solution stored in the retrieved cases to the needs of the current case [13].

CBR community considers three types of adaptation: direct adaptation (just applies the solution of the most similar retrieved case), structural adaptation (implies rules or formulae directly to the solutions to obtain a new one) and derivational adaptation (reuses the original rules or formulae using in the original solutions to produce a new solution) [11].

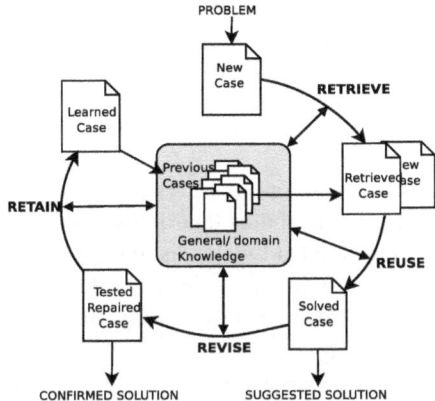

Fig. 1. CBR cycle proposed by Aadmodt and Plaza in 1994

On the one hand, knowledge-intensive CBR systems find difficulties to perform adaptation and they require of complex models to drive the adaptation process. On the other hand, most common CBR applications imply simple solutions consisting of a single component such as a dichotomy, discrete/continuous quantitative or qualitative values. In these scenarios, there is a wide range of simple rules and formulae available for performing a successful adaptation for these solutions: boolean values logic operators for dichotomic values; average, maximum, minimum and many others for quantitative values; and statistical or semantic operators for qualitative values.

2.1   CBR System

In this work, we motivate the different proposals by describing a CBR system in a real-life medical scenario. In particular, we present our CBR system to assist ICU physicians concerning the survival of infected burned patients. To this end, in this section we provide a detailed description of the key aspects of this system: case description, case similarity, solution adaptation and the CL.

Case Description. The generalized idea that a case is essentially composed of two components (problem and solution) already persists [9,10]. In this work, we formalize a case as a match between elements of the space of possible problems (set P) and the space of possible solutions (set S), that is:

$$C \in P \times S \tag{1}$$

Where each problem ($p \in P$) is composed of a finite number of parameter values. Note that these values could be qualitative (e.g. $temperature = 37.5$) or dichotomic (e.g. $presence - of - pneumonia = yes$). Finally, the solution ($s \in S$) is composed by a single component (e.g. $survive = yes$).

Similarity functions. In order to obtain solution accuracy in a CBR system, it is essential to establish how similarity can be measured. In this work, we adopt the normalized similarity function (σ), that is:

$$\sigma : C \times C \rightarrow [0..1] \tag{2}$$

In our proposal, the similarity function measures the similarity between cases, quantifying the similarity between the attributes that define their problems. Therefore, similarity measures could be considered at two levels: global similarity and local similarity. The local similarity function (σ_i) quantifies how similar two attributes are. whilst the global similarity function(σ^{global}) states how similar two cases are by the use of local similarities.

Note that the attributes of our cases are dichotomic or quantitative values and thereby two different local similarity functions must be defined. In particular we propose:

$$\sigma_{dic}(a_i, a_j) = \begin{cases} 1 \text{ if } a_i = a_j \\ 0 \text{ if } a_i \neq a_j \end{cases} \tag{3}$$

$$\sigma_{cua}(a_i, a_j) = 1 - \frac{\mid a_i - a_j \mid}{max} \tag{4}$$

Where max is the maximum value of the attribute. The computation of global similarity is defined by the following expression:

$$\sigma^{global}(case, case') = \frac{\sum_{i=1}^{n} w_i * \sigma_i(a_i, a_i')}{\sum_{i=1}^{n} w_i} \tag{5}$$

Where a_i and a_i' are attributes of $case$ and $case'$, $w_i \in [0, 1]$ is the weight associated to the ith attribute, and σ_i is the corresponding local similarity function depending on the numerical or non-numerical attributes.

Adaptation functions. After retrieving the most similar case(s), the second step in solving a current problem using a CBR system is the derivation of the retrieved solution(s) to solve the new problem.

We formally describe the adaptation as follows:

$$\alpha : C \times C_{CL}^{n} \rightarrow Solution \tag{6}$$

Where C_{CL} is the space of cases in the CL and C_{CL}^{n} is its power set. In this work, we have considered three alternative strategies of case adaptation. The simplest form is the *Direct adaptation*, the intuitive idea of copying the solution of the most similar case. Secondly, the *Transformation* method obtains, from the solutions of the retrieved cases and a given set of operations, the adapted solution (s_α).

Note that, in our cases, the solution states if the patient survives or not (dichotomic value). Therefore, in this work the *Transformation* operations consist of considering an optimistic, pessimistic or frequentest approach of the survival of the retrieved cases of patients.

Formally, we describe the *Direct adaptation* by the formula α_{direct} as follows:

$$\alpha_{direct}(c_{cu}, \{(p_1, s_1), \ldots, (p_n, s_n)\}) = \{s_i, i \in [1, n]$$
$$| \sigma^{global}(c_{cu}, (p_i, s_i)) \geq \sigma^{global}(c_{cu}, (p_j, s_j)) \forall j \in [1, n]\}. \tag{7}$$

Where (p_i, s_i) are the retrieved cases and c_{cu} is the current case.

In the same way, for the *Transformation* operators can be represented by α_{or} (optimistic), α_{and} (pesimistic), and α_{mode} (frequentist). That is,

$$\alpha_{or}^k(c_{cu}, \{(p_1, s_1), \ldots, (p_n, s_n)\}) = \bigvee_{i=1}^{k} s_i. \tag{8}$$

Where k $(k \leq n)$ is the number of retrieved solutions to be considered for adaptation. Analogy,

$$\alpha_{and}^k(c_{cu}, \{(p_1, s_1), \ldots, (p_n, s_n)\}) = \bigwedge_{i=1}^{k} s_i. \tag{9}$$

$$\alpha_{mode}^k(c_{cu}, \{(p_1, s_1), \ldots, (p_n, s_n)\}) = mode(\{s_1, \ldots, s_k\})) \tag{10}$$

For instance, let us suppose the most similar cases have the following solutions, ordered by decreasing similarity: $s_1 = survive$, $s_2 = survive$ and $s_3 = \neg survive$. Using α_{direct}, the CBR system predicts that the patient survives (s_1). According to the pessimistic adaptation ($s_1 \wedge s_2 \wedge s_3$) the patient prognosis is $\neg survive$, however using the optimistic approach ($s_1 \vee s_2 \vee s_3$) the prediction is $survive$. Finally the frequentist approach ($mode(\{survive, survive, \neg survive\}) = survive$) also predicts that the patient will survive.

3 Reliance Solution Degree

For CBR systems, we define the reliance solution degree concept (ρ) and we propose it as an indicator on the CBR system to obtain an effective solution. In other words, ρ is an estimation of the accuracy of the adapted solution (s_α). This is an open concept that could be interpreted in different ways, depending on the features and domain of the CBR system. From a methodological perspective, two main aspects to define ρ must be considered. One is the nature of the reliance degree (dichotomic, linguistic label, quantitative value). In this work we will consider a normalised quantitative version of the reliance solution degree, that is, $\rho \in [0, 1]$. Another aspect is the different methods that could be used to measure the reliance of the adapted solution. According to this, we identify two main approaches. Firstly, a reliance degree based on the retrieve step, such as those inspired in the CBR system reliance evaluation proposed in [3]. For instance, it is possible to compare the s_α to those solutions of the most similar cases, that is, considering the retrieved cases that reach a similarity threshold. Secondly, one step forward is to check if it is possible to obtain the solution of s_α using the retrieved cases

Table 1. Retrieval-step based rules

ID	ANTECEDENT	PARTIAL ρ_{re}
R1	$Sol_{1st_{case}} = Sol_{2nd_{case}}$	0.3846
R2	$Sol_{1st_{case}} = Sol_{3rd_{case}}$	0.2885
R3	$Sol_{1st_{case}} = Sol_{4th_{case}}$	0.1923
R4	$Sol_{1st_{case}} = Sol_{5th_{case}}$	0.0962
R5	$Sol_{1st_{case}} = Sol_{6th_{case}}$	0.0385

with alternative adaptation methods. Therefore, the more matches of the same s_α we obtain with different adaptation methods, the higher the reliance solution degree is. One advantage of this approach is that, apart from evaluating the solution, it evaluates in an implicit manner the reliance of both the retrieval and adaptation step.

In order to illustrate this proposal, we present three rule-based methods to obtain the reliance solution degree, one based on the retrieval step and two based on adaptation.

Regarding the retrieval step approach, the antecedent of the rule analyses the retrieved solutions and their relative position, ordered by similarity. That is, the first case is the most similar to the current case, the second case is the second most similar and so on. The consequent part of the rule indicates the partial reliance degree if this condition occurs. Since different rules could be fired, the overall reliance solution degree (ρ_{re}) is the sum of the partial calculus. For instance, if the most similar case (Sol_{1st}) has the same solution as the solution of the third most similar case (Sol_{3rd}), then the partial reliance degree (ρ_{re}) is 0.2885. Table 1 depicts a complete example of these rules, described and weighted by the experts.

In this work, we propose a second type of reliance solution degree. This novel degree type is based on the Adapt step and can be described, from a methodological perspective, as follows:

1. To select the adaptation method (called objective adaptation) used in the CBR system to obtain the adapted solution (s_α).
2. To select a catalogue of (alternative) adaptation methods, different from the objective adaptation method.
3. To define the mechanisms to compare the solutions obtained from this methods catalogue and the s_α, that is, how ρ is calculated.

For example, lets suppose a medical CBR system to classify patients in the survival or non-survival sets (dichotomic value) that uses the α_{direct} as the *objective adaptation method* (step 1). Following the aforementioned steps, we must select a catalogue of adaptation methods (step 2), for instance: α_{and}^2, α_{and}^3, α_{and}^4, α_{or}^2, α_{or}^3, α_{or}^4, α_{mode}^3, and α_{mode}^5. Finally, it is needed to describe the mechanisms to compare the solution obtained by *objective adaptation method* and those obtained by those methods of the catalogue (step 3).

For instance, one simple approach to model this mechanism is to use a rule-based technique where the rules gather the knowledge required to establish the reliance solution degree. The antecedent part of each rule covers the matching between the *objective adaptation method* (α_{direct}) and each of the methods used in the catalogue (α_{and}^2, α_{and}^3,

Table 2. Adaptation-based rules

A) ADDITIVE RULES		B) MUTUALLY EXCLUSIVE RULES	
ANTECEDENT	Part.ρ_{add}	ANTECEDENT	ρ_{ex}
$\alpha_{direct} = \alpha_{and}^2$	0.0541	$\alpha_{direct} = \alpha_{and}^4 = \alpha_{and}^3 = \alpha_{and}^2 = \alpha_{or}^4 = \alpha_{or}^3 = \alpha_{or}^2 = \alpha_{mode}^3 = \alpha_{mode}^5 =$	1
$\alpha_{direct} = \alpha_{and}^3$	0.1081		
$\alpha_{direct} = \alpha_{and}^4$	0.2162	$\alpha_{direct} = \alpha_{mode}^3 = \alpha_{mode}^5 \wedge \alpha_{and}^2 = \alpha_{and}^3 = \alpha_{and}^4 \wedge \alpha_{or}^2 = \alpha_{or}^3 =$	0.7
$\alpha_{direct} = \alpha_{or}^2$	0.0541	$\alpha_{or}^4 \wedge \alpha_{and}^2 \neq \alpha_{or}^2 \wedge \alpha_{and}^3 \neq \alpha_{or}^3 \wedge \alpha_{and}^4 \neq \alpha_{or}^4$	
$\alpha_{direct} = \alpha_{or}^3$	0.1081	$\alpha_{mode}^3 \neq \alpha_{mode}^5 \wedge \alpha_{and}^4 \neq \alpha_{or}^4 \wedge \alpha_{and}^3 \neq \alpha_{or}^3 \wedge \alpha_{and}^2 \neq \alpha_{or}^2$	0.4
$\alpha_{direct} = \alpha_{or}^4$	0.2162	$\alpha_{direct} = \alpha_{mode}^3 = \alpha_{mode}^5 \wedge (\alpha_{and}^2 \neq \alpha_{and}^3 \vee \alpha_{or}^2 \neq \alpha_{or}^3)$	0.3
$\alpha_{direct} = \alpha_{mode}^3$	0.0811	$\alpha_{mode}^3 \neq \alpha_{mode}^5 \wedge (\alpha_{and}^2 \neq \alpha_{and}^3 \vee \alpha_{or}^2 \neq \alpha_{or}^3)$	0.1
$\alpha_{direct} = \alpha_{mode}^5$	0.1622	$\alpha_{direct} = \alpha_{mode}^3 = \alpha_{mode}^5 \wedge (\alpha_{and}^3 \neq \alpha_{and}^4 \vee \alpha_{or}^3 \neq \alpha_{or}^4)$	0.3
$\alpha_{direct} = \alpha_{mode}^7$	0.2162	$\alpha_{mode}^3 \neq \alpha_{mode}^5 \wedge (\alpha_{and}^3 \neq \alpha_{and}^4 \vee \alpha_{or}^3 \neq \alpha_{or}^4)$	0.1

α_{and}^4, α_{or}^2, etc.), whilst the consequent states a degree (value) of reliance. In order to define these rules, having in mind the knowledge acquisition problem, two different scenarios can be considered.

On the one hand, an initial approach is to define simple matching situations, such as $IF\ \alpha_{direct} = \alpha_{or}^3\ THEN\ \rho = 0.082$ or $IF\ \alpha_{direct} = \alpha_{mode}^3\ THEN\ \rho = 0.134$. Here, different rules could be fired, and the the overall reliance solution degree (ρ_{add}) is the sum of the partial reliance degrees of the rules fired. Therefore, the partial degrees must be normalised (see Table 2-A) in order to be additive.

On the other hand, for more specific situations, rules could be more complex. In other words, the antecedent of each rule describes a complete matching scenario and states the final value. Therefore, in this case the rules are mutually exclusive (see Table 2-B) and the consequent of the rule is the reliance solution degree (ρ_{ex}).

Therefore the outcome of our CBR system consist of the solution of the problem its reliance degree, that is $S = <S_\alpha, \rho>$.

3.1 Experiments

Under medical supervision, a total of 89 patients admitted at the ICU with major burns and complications by infections were selected from the Health Information System. Each patient record consists of medical parameters such as: sex (male/female), weight, age, hepatic comorbidity (y/n), cardiac comorbidity (y/n), arterial hypertension (y/n), or diabetes (y/n). Due to the reduced volume of this database, statistical approaches will not always provide accurate results for survival assessment. Furthermore, previous work in this domain [6,12] based on intensive knowedge acquisition cannot be included since clinical problems do not always make for etiological consensus. Therefore, the use of CBR seems a suitable approach to develop decision support systems to help physicians to quantify the severity of the patient. However, classical CBR approaches provide a simple outcome that indicates if the patient survives or not. In this scenario, the use of the reliance solution degree seems useful since it extends the outcome information to help physicians to improve the comprehension of the system outcome.

Once the CL is defined, our CBR system requires the calibration of the similarity measure. To this end, the attribute weights of the global similarity measure must be assigned (Expression 5), stating the relevance of each parameter with respect to the patient survival. In particular, we selected the Mutual Information measure (MI), based on Shannon Entropy (H) [7]. The outcome of the system consists of the adapted solution (the patient survival) and the reliance solution degree of the given outcome $S = <S_\alpha, \rho>$. The adaptation step of the system uses the *Direct adaptation method* described in Expression 7. In order to evaluate the proposals described in this paper, the experiments will consider the following approaches: the reliance degree based on the retrieval step (described in Table 1) and the reliance degree approaches based on the additive adaptation and mutually exclusive adaptation (described in Table 2 A and B).

System Evaluation. The evaluation of the CBR system is carried out by a survival test $(S_\alpha = \{survive, \neg survive\})$ using a leave-one-out approach. The reliance solution degree gives support to the outcome, indicating the reliance of the solution obtained. If the degree is considered low, the physician must discard the system outcome to make their decisions. Therefore, this study focuses on the impact of the reliance solution degree to the system accuracy and the final decision made by the physician. The evaluation of the CBR system consists of the evaluation of: (1) the solution given S_α (i.e. the survival of the patient) and (2) the evaluation of the utility of its reliance degree ρ.

The evaluation of the solution S_α is carried out by the study of the classification capacity of the system. In this case, we have obtained the following results: classification accuracy (0.753), specificity (0.694) and sensitivity (0.792). In order to evaluate the reliance degree (ρ), we define two concepts: *reliance threshold* and the *correction score*.

The *reliance threshold* is a value that indicates the minimum value of the reliance solution degree to consider acceptable the outcome of the system. In other words, if the ρ is greater than the *reliance threshold*, the system outcome should be considered acceptable by the physicians, if not, the system outcome should be discarded.

The *correction score* (CS) is calculated as follows:

$$CS = \sum_{i=1}^{|CL|} cs_i \tag{11}$$

$$cs_i = \begin{cases} 1 & \text{if } s_\rho \neq s_\alpha \wedge s_\rho = patientSurvival \\ -1 & \text{if } s_\rho \neq s_\alpha \wedge s_\alpha = patientSurvival \\ 0 & \text{in other case} \end{cases} \tag{12}$$

Where s_ρ is the solution suggested by considering the result of the reliance solution degree, the s_α is the solution of the system (survives or not) and the *patientSurvival* is the real solution of the problem. That is, CS indicates if the reliance solution degree correctly supports the physician in the final solution. If the CS is positive, we can conclude that, in most of the cases, the reliance solution degree warns the physician to do not consider those system outcomes that in training set were incorrect.

In Figure 2 is depicted the evolution of the CS for different values of the *reliance threshold* considering the reliance solution degree proposed (similarity based, the additive adaptation based and the mutually exclusive adaptation based).

According to the experiments (Figure 2) the *reliance threshold* is valid between 0.05 and 0.4, that is, while the CS is positive. In particular, the CS is maximized when the *reliance threshold* is between 0.05 and 0.2. For instance, when the reliance solution

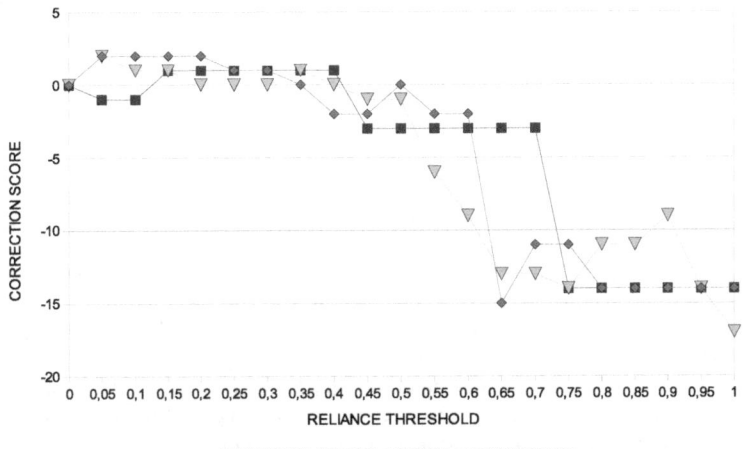

Fig. 2. Experiments

degree is over 0.2, the outcome solution should be considered supported by the reliance solution. In other case, the expert could consider other medical factors not included in the database. Since CS is positive for certain values of the *reliance threshold*, the information provided by the reliance solution degree helps the expert to obtain a better decision than using only the solution adapted by a traditional CBR approach. Moreover, the information provided by the adaptation-based approaches obtains better results than the similarity-based technique between 0.05 and 0.3.

4   Conclusion

In critical decision support systems based on CBR where retrieved cases are highly similar, it seems necessary to extend the system outcome in order to indicate the reliance of the solution obtained. In this work we propose different techniques to obtain a reliance solution degree and we demonstrate its suitability by incorporating these proposals in a CBR system applied in a real-life medical problem.

First, we propose the application of the same CBR principles to quantify this reliance degree of the solution, in particular, considering the retrieval and adaptation step. This approach is based on a catalogue of current adaptation functions to support the correctness of the adapted solution. Related works in the field [3,4,8] suggest the use of the similarity criteria for the evaluation of CBR systems. Unlike these proposals, in our work we also include alternative proposals based on the adaptation step. The use of the adaptation step is a novel approach in the field.

The experiments carried out with data of major burn patients of a ICU suggest the need of a correct tuning of the parameters, and proof the suitability of the proposed techniques in concrete medical problems. On the one hand, despite the technique is initially domain independent, one main disadvantage of the implemented version is the use of rules that requires the validation of medical staff. On the other hand, the results obtained demonstrates the suitability of our proposal since they indicate a clear improvement of the decision made. In particular, the adaptation-based techniques proposed in this paper seem to obtain the best results.

Future works will focus on the application similar techniques taking into account the temporal dimension.

References

1. Aamodt, A., Plaza, E.: Case-based reasoning: Foundational issues, methodological variations, and system approaches. AI Communications 7(1), 39–59 (1994)
2. Aha, D.W., Breslow, L.A.: Refining conversational case libraries. In: Leake, D.B., Plaza, E. (eds.) ICCBR 1997. LNCS, vol. 1266, pp. 267–278. Springer, Heidelberg (1997)
3. Bogaerts, S., Leake, D.B.: What evaluation criteria are right for CCBR? considering rank quality. In: Roth-Berghofer, T.R., Göker, M.H., Güvenir, H.A. (eds.) ECCBR 2006. LNCS (LNAI), vol. 4106, pp. 385–399. Springer, Heidelberg (2006)
4. Gupta, K.M., Aha, D.W., Sandhu, N.: Exploiting taxonomic and causal relations in conversational case retrieval. In: Craw, S., Preece, A.D. (eds.) ECCBR 2002. LNCS (LNAI), vol. 2416, pp. 133–147. Springer, Heidelberg (2002)
5. Huellermeier, E.: Case-Based Approximate Reasoning. Springer, New York (2007)
6. Juárez, J.M., Campos, M., Palma, J., Marín, R.: Computing context-dependent temporal diagnosis in complex domains. Expert Systems with Applications 35(3), 991–1010 (2007)
7. Klir, G.J., Folger, T.A.: Fuzzy Sets, Uncertainty, and Information. Prentice-Hall, N.J. (1992)
8. Kohlmaier, A., Schmitt, S., Bergmann, R.: Evaluation of a similarity-based approach to customer-adaptive electronic sales dialogs. In: Empirical Evaluation of Adaptive Systems. Proceedings of the workshop held at the 8th International Conference on User Modelling, pp. 40–50 (2001)
9. Kolodner, J.L., Leake, D.B.: A Tutorial Introduction to Case-Based Reasoning, ch. 2, pp. 31–65. American Association for Artificial Intelligence (1996)
10. Koton, P.: Using experience in learning and problem solving. Technical Report, MIT/LCS/TR-441 (1989)
11. Leake, D.B.: CBR in Context: The Present and The Future, ch. 1, pp. 31–65. American Association for Artificial Intelligence (1996)
12. Palma, J., Juárez, J.M., Campos, M., Marín, R.: A fuzzy theory approach for temporal model-based diagnosis. Artificial Intelligence in Medicine 38, 197–218 (2006)
13. Watson, I.: Case-based reasoning is a methodology not a technology. Knowledge-Based Systems 12, 303–308 (1999)

On the Suitability of Combining Feature Selection and Resampling to Manage Data Complexity*

Raúl Martín-Félez and Ramón A. Mollineda

DLSI and Institute of New Imaging Technologies
Universitat Jaume I, Castellón, Spain
{martinr,mollined}@uji.es

Abstract. The effectiveness of a learning task depends on data complexity (class overlap, class imbalance, irrelevant features, etc.). When more than one complexity factor appears, two or more preprocessing techniques should be applied. Nevertheless, no much effort has been devoted to investigate the importance of the order in which they can be used. This paper focuses on the joint use of feature reduction and balancing techniques, and studies which could be the application order that leads to the best classification results. This analysis was made on a specific problem whose aim was to identify the melodic track given a MIDI file. Several experiments were performed from different imbalanced 38-dimensional training sets with many more accompaniment tracks than melodic tracks, and where features were aggregated without any correlation study. Results showed that the most effective combination was the ordered use of resampling and feature reduction techniques.

Keywords: Data complexity, feature reduction, class imbalance problem, melody finding, music information retrieval.

1 Introduction

Supervised classification methods are based on the inference of a decision boundary from a set of training samples. The quality of the classifier performance should be affected by the merits and shortcomings of the algorithm, and by the intrinsic difficulty of learning from those samples (*data complexity*) [1]. Some sources of data complexity are class overlap, irrelevant and redundant features, noisy samples, class imbalance, low ratios of the sample size to dimensionality, among others. These challenges are often managed before learning by means of preprocessing techniques in order to improve the generalization power of the

---

* This research was partially supported by the Spanish Ministry of Innovation and Science under projects Consolider Ingenio 2010 CSD2007-00018 and DPI2006-15542, and by the FPI grant PREDOC/2008/04 from the Universitat Jaume I. We would also like to thank the *PRAI-UA Group* at the University of Alicante for providing us with the datasets used in this paper.

P. Meseguer, L. Mandow, and R.M. Gasca (Eds.): CAEPIA 2009, LNAI 5988, pp. 141–150, 2010.

training data. When two or more of these problems coincide, the original training set needs to be many times preprocessed, but in which order should the preprocessing techniques be applied?

Little effort has been made to analize the relevance of the application order of several preprocessing techniques. A related paper is [2] where the combined effect of class imbalance and overlapping on classifier performance is analysed. Other studies focus on solutions to the co-occurrence of class imbalance and irrelevant features. A preliminary work [3], within the Web categorization domain, suggests that feature selection techniques are not very appropriate for imbalanced data sets. As a result, a feature selection framework which selects features for positive and negative classes separately is proposed, and the resulting features are explicitly combined. Another work [4] goes a step beyond and applies feature subset selection before balancing the original dataset to predict the protein function from amino acid sequence features. The modified training set feeds a Support Vector Machine (SVM), which gives more accurate results than those provided by the same classifier trained from the original data. Nevertheless, the contrary combination of techniques was not considered, so no conclusions can be drawn about their most suitable application order.

This paper focuses on the joint use of feature reduction and balancing techniques, and studies which is the application order that leads to the best classification results. Experiments are based on the problem of identifying the melodic track of a given MIDI file. This structure is a kind of digital score composed of a set of tracks where usually only one of them is the melody while the remaining tracks contain the accompaniment. This leads to a two-class imbalance problem which has many more accompaniment tracks (majority class) than melodic tracks (minority class). As in the previous work [5], several corpora of MIDI files of different music genres generate a collection of imbalanced training sets with 38 features that were aggregated without any previous study. This configures a suitable scenario to evaluate the goal of this paper.

2   Methodology

An overview of the solution scheme is shown in Figs. 1 and 2 where the five main steps are remarked. The following subsections explain these steps.

2.1   Track Feature Extraction

This step builds vector representations for all tracks of the MIDI files included in both the training and test corpora. As a result, as can be seen in Fig. 1, two related sets of track vectors are obtained for training (TRA) and testing purposes ($TEST$). Tracks are described using 38 features [5] and the class label (melody or accompaniment). These features summarize the musical content of each track by measuring some aspects such as the pitch, duration and syncopation of notes, intervals between notes, duration and importance of the rests, and so on.

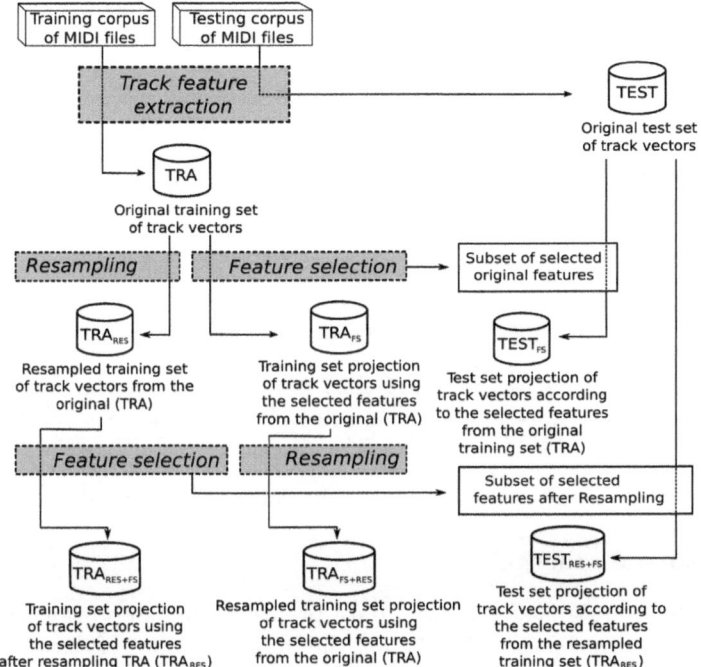

Fig. 1. Generation of datasets used in this work

2.2 Resampling

The original training set (TRA) leads to a two-class imbalance problem because it contains many less melodic tracks than accompaniment tracks. One way to deal with imbalance is to resample the original TRA either by over-sampling the minority class (melody track) or by under-sampling the majority class (accompaniment track) until the class sizes are similar. Considering that the complexity of the original TRA will be managed by joint preprocessing both imbalance and feature space, Fig. 1 shows the application of resampling methods before (TRA_{RES}) and after (TRA_{FS+RES}) using feature reduction techniques.

In this work two resampling methods have been used: *Synthetic Minority Over-sampling TEchnique (SMOTE)* [6] for over-sampling and *Random Under-Sampling (RUS)* [7] for under-sampling the training set. *SMOTE* is a method that generates new synthetic samples in the minority class. For each sample of this class, this algorithm computes the k intra-class nearest neighbours, in this paper $k = 5$, and several new instances are created by interpolating the focused sample and some of its neighbours randomly selected. Its major drawback is an increase in the computational cost. In contrast, RUS is a non-heuristic method that aims to balance class distributions by randomly discarding samples of the majority class. Its major drawback is that it can ignore potentially useful data.

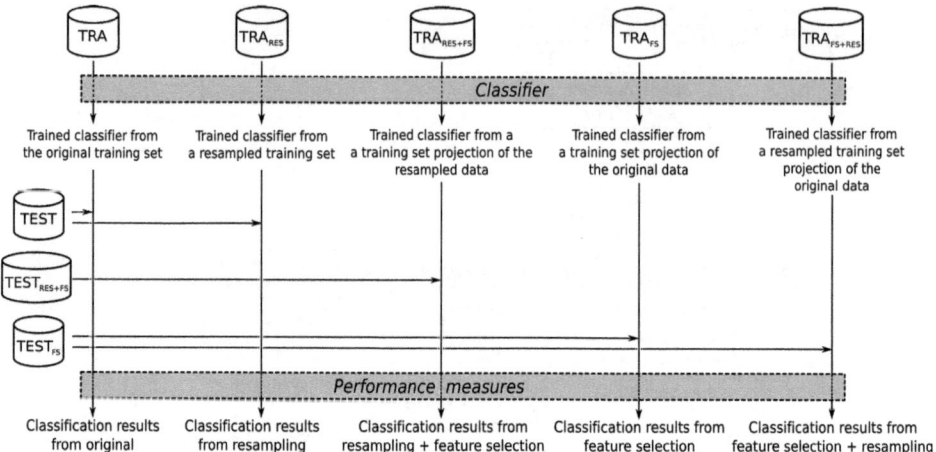

Fig. 2. Experimental design using the datasets introduced in Fig. 1

2.3 Feature Reduction

Feature reduction [8] is an essential data preprocessing step prior to use a classifier. This process consists of reducing the dimensionality of data with the aim of allowing classifiers to operate faster and, in general, more effectively. Feature reduction methods can be separated according to many criteria, for example: i) selection versus extraction of discriminant features and ii) supervised versus unsupervised. In this work, a supervised selection technique and an unsupervised extraction method have been used. The former is *Correlation-based Feature Selection (CFS)* [8], and the latter is *Principal Components Analysis (PCA)* [9].

CFS ranks feature subsets according to the degree of redundancy among the features. It searches subsets of features that are individually well correlated with the class but have low inter-correlation. *PCA* consists of a transformation of the original features into a smaller number of uncorrelated new features called principal components. PCA can be used for dimensionality reduction by retaining those principal components, from most to least importance, that accounts for a given proportion of the variance (in this work, the 95%).

As the complexity of the original TRA will be managed by joint preprocessing both feature space and imbalance, Fig. 1 shows the application of feature reduction techniques before (TRA_{FS}) and after (TRA_{RES+FS}) using resampling methods. Unlike the resampling methods which only involve training sets, the use of new feature spaces produces the projection of test sets on them giving rise to two new derived test sets: $TEST_{FS}$ and $TEST_{RES+FS}$.

2.4 Classifiers

The aim of the classification stage is to identify the melodic track in each MIDI file. This process is made up of two decision levels: i) *track level*, where individual tracks are classified into either melodic or accompaniment classes and ii) *MIDI file level*, in which identification of the melodic track of a MIDI file is carried out based on results at track level. As regards the sets used for training and testing (see Fig. 2), the effectiveness of the detection of the melodic track at MIDI file level is evaluated. A detailed description of this process is as follows:

Track level

1. Given a track, a classifier assigns probabilities of membership of both classes (melody and accompaniment)
2. Tracks are discarded when one of the following two conditions is satisfied:
   - the difference between both probabilities is lower than 0.1
   - the probability of being melody is higher than the non-melody probability, but lower than 0.6

MIDI file level

1. Given all non-discarded tracks from the same MIDI file, the one with the highest positive difference between the two probabilities of being melody and accompaniment respectively, is selected as the melodic track
2. The decision is considered a *hit* if
   - *True Positive*: the selected track is originally labelled as melody, or
   - *True Negative*: in a file with no melodic track, no track is classified as melody. However, all MIDI files used in the experiments have a well-defined melodic track, thus no True Negative cases occur
3. The decision is considered a *miss* if
   - *False Positive*: the selected melody track is originally labelled as accompaniment, or
   - *False Negative*: in a file with a melodic track, all its tracks have been discarded or classified as accompaniment

The base classifiers used at track level are 1-NN and SVM because of their diversity in terms of the geometry of their decision boundaries.

2.5   Performance Measures in Class Imbalance Problems

A typical metric for measuring the performance of learning systems is classification accuracy rate, which for a two-class problem can be easily derived from a 2×2 confusion matrix defined by i) TP (True positive) and ii) TN (True Negative), which are the numbers of positive and negative samples correctly classified, respectively, and iii) FP (False positive) and iv) FN (False Negative), which are the numbers of misclassified negative and positive samples, respectively. This measure can be computed as $Acc = (TP + TN)/(TP + FN + TN + FP)$.

However, empirical evidence shows that this measure is biased with respect to the data imbalance and proportions of correct and incorrect classifications [10]. These shortcomings have motivated a search for new measures, for example: (i) *True positive rate* (or *recall*) is the percentage of positive examples which are correctly classified, $TPr = TP/(TP + FN)$; (ii) *Precision* (or *purity*) is defined as the percentage of samples which are correctly labelled as positive, $Precision = TP/(TP + FP)$; and (iii) *F-measure* which combines TPr and

Table 1. Corpora used in the experiments

CorpusID	Music Genre	Midi Files	Tracks non-melody	melody
CL200	Classical	198	489	198
JZ200	Jazz	197	561	197
KR200	Popular	159	1171	159
CLA	Classical	84	284	84
JAZ	Jazz	1006	3131	1006
KAR	Popular	1247	9416	1247

Precision giving a global vision focused on the positive class, $F\text{-}measure = (2 * TPr * Precision)/(TPr + Precision)$. Other well-known measures like AUC and $Gmean$ can not be used due to their strong dependence on the $True\ negative\ rate$ which is zero in our experiments (see Sect. 2.4).

3 Experimental Results

3.1 Datasets

Experiments involve six datasets of track vectors obtained from the same number of corpora of MIDI files created in [11] (see Table 1 for details). These corpora contain MIDI files of three different music genres: classical music (CL200 and CLA), jazz music (JZ200 and JAZ) and popular music in karaoke format (KR200 and KAR). From each corpus, a corresponding dataset of 38-dimensional track vectors is available (see Sect. 2.1) where each vector has been manually labelled as melody or non-melody by a trained musicologist.

These corpora can be divided into two groups with regard to their data complexity and also due to their sizes. A first group includes CL200, JZ200 and KR200 because they have in common a similar number of MIDI files (close to 200). Moreover, most of them have well-defined melodic tracks which make them suitable for training purposes. In contrast, CLA, JAZ and KAR are more heterogeneous corpora and, consequently, lead to more challenging tasks [11].

3.2 Experimental Design

In the following experiment, each classifier is trained with samples from two music genres taken from CL200, JZ200 and KR200, and is tested with samples of the remaining style taken from CLA, JAZ and KAR. In particular, the following three pairs of training and test sets were considered: i) (JZ200+KR200, CLA), ii) (CL200+KR200, JAZ) and iii) (CL200+JZ200, KAR). The rationale behind these data partitions is to maximize the independence between the training and the test sets, and to find out whether the effectiveness of music track identification depends on the music genres using for training and testing.

The main aim of the experiments is to study the importance of the order of applying two preprocessing techniques, resampling and feature reduction, to jointly reduce the complexity of training datasets. As it was seen in Sect. 2.2

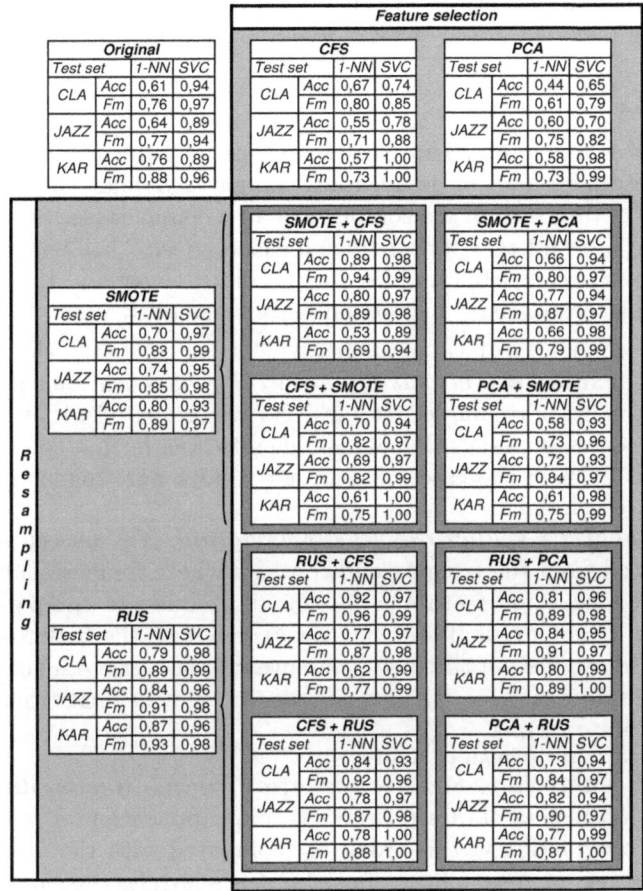

Fig. 3. Averaged results of experiments

and Sect. 2.3, two different algorithms of each preprocessing technique have been used: SMOTE and RUS for resampling, and CFS and PCA for feature reduction. The experimental design is based on the 2 × 2 crossing of these four methods considering the two possible sequences of each specific pair, producing eight different combinations. Fig. 3 shows all the results. Apart from comparisons among classification performances obtained from these ordered combinations of methods, these results are also compared with those provided by the only use of each particular technique and from the original imbalanced training set.

Due to the random behaviour of SMOTE and RUS, each experiment that involves these techniques was performed 10 times and their results were averaged. The classification results are given in terms of Accuracy (Acc) and Fmeasure (Fm), that were computed taking into account only MIDI files with at least one melody track in contrast with previous related works [5,11] where Accuracy was computed including also MIDI files without any melody track.

The implementations of the classifiers and the feature reduction tecniques used are those included in the WEKA toolkit[1] with their default parameters.

3.3 Analysis of Results

The results presented in Fig. 3 are analysed in the following three ways organized from a low to a high level of detail. Each comparative analysis involves all the possible cases obtained from the combination of a classifier (see Sect.2.4), a data partition (see 3.2) and two performance measures (see 2.5). The percentage of favourable cases is computed and used as an index to explain the usefulness of a preprocessing technique or a combination of some of them.

- **Level A** (the highest level of analysis)
  - **A.1 Resampling versus Original.** The classification results obtained from the use of resampled training sets are compared with those provided by the corresponding original training sets (see the first column in Fig. 3). In the 100% of the cases, the former results were higher than those of the latter ones.
  - **A.2 Feature reduction versus Original.** The classification results obtained from the training and test sets whose dimensionality has been reduced by some feature reduction technique are compared with the results of the original 38-dimensional task (see the first row in Fig. 3). Only in the 25% of the cases, the former results were higher than those of the latter ones, so the fact of reducing dimensionality alone tends to deteriorate results.
- **Level B** (a middle level of analysis)
  - **B.1 Resampling+Feature reduction versus Resampling.** The classification results obtained from the joint application of resampling and feature reduction in this order, are compared with the results provided by the use of resampling alone. In this analysis, the boxes with titles in the forms *SMOTE+** and *RUS+** are compared with the boxes titled *SMOTE* and *RUS* respectively. In the 52% of cases, the joint use of resampling and features reduction produced performance measures equal to or greater than those obtained from the only application of resampling. Therefore, the ordered use of both techniques does not seem to guarantee better results with respect to resampling, which already produced a massive improvement on the original results (see level A.1).
  - **B.2 Feature reduction+Resampling versus Feature reduction.** The classification results obtained from the joint application of feature reduction and resampling in this order, are compared with the results provided by the use of feature reduction alone. In this study, the boxes with titles in the forms *CFS+** and *PCA+** are compared with the boxes titled *CFS* and *PCA* respectively. In the 97% of cases, the joint use of features reduction and resampling produced performance measures equal to or greater than those obtained from the only application of feature reduction. However, this result should be carefully considered because,

---

[1] http://www.cs.waikato.ac.nz/ml/weka/

as can be seen in the level A.2, the plain selection of features does not seem effective with respect to the original results.

- **Level C** (the lowest level of analysis)

  - • *C.1 Resampling+Feature reduction versus Feature reduction + Resampling.* The results of the two ways of combining resampling and feature reduction analysed in level B are compared to find out which order is more effective. It involves the 8 central boxes with titles made of two acronyms. Each box is contrasted with the one that has its reverse title, for example, *SMOTE+CFS* versus *CFS+SMOTE*. Considering the four comparable pairs of boxes, in the 79% of cases, Resampling+Feature reduction gave better results than the contrary combination.

  - • *C.2 SMOTE versus RUS.* The two resampling techniques used in the experiments are compared (SMOTE and RUS). Each box that involves a particular resampling technique is compared with the corresponding one, i.e., that with the same title pattern as a function of the other resampling method. Considering the five comparable pairs of boxes, in the 90% of cases, results of RUS are equal to or outperform the results of SMOTE. From this analysis, RUS seems to be more appropriate than SMOTE to manage the task complexity. In addition, RUS reduce the size of the training set and hence the time to build a classifier.

  - • *C.3 CFS versus PCA.* The two feature reduction methods used in the experiments are compared (CFS and PCA). Each box that involves a particular feature reduction technique is compared with the corresponding one, i.e., that with the same title pattern as a function of the other feature reduction method. Considering the five comparable pairs of boxes, in the 70% of cases, results of CFS are equal to or outperform results of PCA. From this analysis, CFS seems to be more appropriate than PCA to deal with the problem. Besides, CFS reduces significantly the data dimensionality by choosing specific features, while PCA requires the 38 original features before to transform them into principal components.

  - • *C.4 1-NN versus SVC.* The two classifiers used in the experiments are compared (1-NN and SVC). This analysis involves all the boxes where each 1-NN result is compared with the corresponding internal SVC result. In the 100% of cases SVC outperforms 1-NN results. SVC appears to be more robust than 1-NN regarding to the genres used for training and testing, and also, considering both imbalanced and balanced contexts.

Taking into account all the previous analysis, the best solution is that where training data are preprocessed by RUS and CFS in this order, and test data are filtered by CFS and classified with SVM. In general, the ordered use of resampling and feature reduction leads to better results than the reverse combination. The posterior use of CFS produced a drastic reduction of the number of features, from 38 to an average of 11, while keeping or improving the performance results provided by the plain application of RUS. Besides, this combination of techniques obtained high and similar results for the three music genres tested, so it seems to be independent of the music style of the training samples.

4   Conclusions

This paper studies the effectiveness of the joint application of two preprocessing techniques, resampling and feature reduction, considering their order of use. They were validated over the problem of identifying the melodic track of MIDI files belonging to three music genres: classical, jazz and popular. The higher number of accompaniment tracks compared to the number of melody tracks defines a two-class imbalance problem what, along with the wide set of primary features, explains the combined use of resampling and feature reduction methods.

As in [4], our experiments show that benefits associated to resample training data are greater than those related to the use of feature reduction. However, unlike [4], we consider all the possible ways in which they can be applied, either individually or jointly in both directions. It supports the thesis suggested by [3], that the application of feature reduction methods on imbalanced data has a low efectiveness. The most effective solution was the joint use of resampling and feature selection methods in this order because, apart from sharing the best classification results with the application of resampling alone, this approach significantly reduced the data dimensionality. Besides, these good results are similar for the three music genres tested which could indicate the independence of the solution from the music style used for training.

References

1. Basu, M., Ho, T.: Data Complexity in Pattern Recognition. Springer, New York (2006)
2. García, V., Alejo, R., Sánchez, J.S., Sotoca, J.M., Mollineda, R.A.: Combined effects of class imbalance and class overlap on instance-based classification. In: Corchado, E., Yin, H., Botti, V., Fyfe, C. (eds.) IDEAL 2006. LNCS, vol. 4224, pp. 371–378. Springer, Heidelberg (2006)
3. Zheng, Z., Wu, X., Srihari, R.: Feature selection for text categorization on imbalanced data. SIGKDD Explor. Newsl. 6(1), 80–89 (2004)
4. Al-shahib, A., Breitling, R., Gilbert, D.: Feature selection and the class imbalance problem in predicting protein function from sequence. Applied Bioinf. 4 (2005)
5. Martín, R., Mollineda, R., García, V.: Melodic track identification in midi files considering the imbalanced context. In: 4th IbPRIA, Póvoa de Varzim (2009)
6. Chawla, N.V., Bowyer, K.W., Hall, L.O., Kegelmeyer, W.P.: Smote: Synthetic minority over-sampling technique. J. Artif. Intell. Res (JAIR) 16, 321–357 (2002)
7. Kotsiantis, S.: Mixture of expert agents for handling imbalanced data sets. Annals of Mathematics, Computing & TeleInformatics 1, 46–55 (2003)
8. Hall, M.: Correlation-based feature subset selection for machine learning (1999)
9. Jolliffe, I.T.: Principal Component Analysis, 2nd edn. Springer, Heidelberg (2002)
10. Provost, F., Fawcett, T.: Analysis and visualization of classifier performance: Comparison under imprecise class and cost distributions. In: Proc. of the 3rd ACM SIGKDD, pp. 43–48 (1997)
11. Rizo, D., Ponce de León, P., Pérez-Sancho, C., Pertusa, A., Iñesta, J.: A pattern recognition approach for melody track selection in midi files. In: Proc. of the 7th ISMIR, Victoria, Canada, pp. 61–66 (2006)

Automated Constraint Selection for Semi-supervised Clustering Algorithm*

Carlos Ruiz[1], Carlos G. Vallejo[2],
Myra Spiliopoulou[3], and Ernestina Menasalvas[1]

[1] Facultad de Informatica, Universidad Politecnica de Madrid, Spain
cruiz@cettico.fi.upm.es, emenasalvas@fi.upm.es
[2] Department of Computer Languages and Systems, Universidad de Sevilla, Spain
vallejo@us.es
[3] Faculty of Computer Science, Magdeburg University, Germany
myra@iti.cs.uni-magdeburg.de

Abstract. The incorporation of background knowledge in unsupervised algorithms has been shown to yield performance improvements in terms of model quality and execution speed. However, performance is dependent on the quantity and quality of the background knowledge being exploited. In this work, we study the issue of selecting Must-Link and Cannot-Link constraints for semi-supervised clustering. We propose *"ConstraintSelector"*, an algorithm that takes as input a set of labeled data instances, from which constraints can be derived, ranks these instances on their usability and then derives constraints from the top-ranked instances only. Our experiments show that *ConstraintSelector* chooses, respectively reduces, the set of candidate constraints without compromising the quality of the derived model.

1 Introduction

The use of background knowledge in clustering enjoys increasing interest, because it has the potential to improve the quality of the extracted model and reduce the speed of convergence. In semi-supervised clustering, Must-Link and Cannot-Link constraints on data instances have been successfully used to guide the clustering process towards a high-quality result [14,1,5], or to partition the dataset in a way that reflects the user's perception of the data [9].

Constraints can be derived from a set of already labelled data or from existing domain information. It has been empirically shown that the achieved improvement depends strongly on the set of selected constraints [14,4,5,9]. In the studies of [7,8] it is even shown that an inappropriate selection of constraints can even lead to performance deterioration for the clustering algorithm. A mechanism is therefore necessary that can select the most appropriate set of constraints to build an optimal model. In this study, we propose *"ConstraintSelector"*, a

---

* Part of this work is partially finance under project TIN2008-05924 of Ministry of Science and Innovation.

P. Meseguer, L. Mandow, and R.M. Gasca (Eds.): CAEPIA 2009, LNAI 5988, pp. 151–160, 2010.

mechanism that processes a set of labeled data instances and selects the most appropriate ones for the generation of Must-Link and Cannot-Link constraints. The *ConstraintSelector* uses underpinnings of instance-based learning [10,13] to rank the labeled instances and select the most informative ones. Constraints are then derived for them and enforced during semi-supervised clustering. We show that this approach leads to a high-quality model for a small set of selected labeled instances.

The rest of the paper is organized as follows: In Section 2 we discuss automatic and interactive methods that have been proposed for constraint selection in semi-supervised clustering. Section 3 contains the underpinnings of the instance-based learning methods WITS [10] and WIRS [13], on which the *ConstraintSelector* is built; the *ConstraintSelector* is described thereafter. In Section 4, we describe the experimental settings for the evaluation of the *ConstraintSelector*, and elaborate on our experimental results. The last Section concludes the study with a summary and outlook for further open research issues.

2   Related Work

Semi-supervised clustering methods exploit background knowledge to guide the clustering process. Instance-level constraints are a specific and popular form of background knowledge: They refer to instances that must belong to the same cluster (Must-Link constraints) or assigned to different clusters (Cannot-Link constraints) [14]. Research has shown that the selection of the constraint set has a substantial influence on the quality of the output clustering model [14,7,8].

The conventional approach towards the constraint selection problem lays in generating random sets of constraints from the given set of labeled data and then compute the quality achieved by the semi-supervised algorithm as the *average quality* achieved when using those random constraint-sets [9,5,12]. However, constraints may be incoherent or may not be representative of the whole population. Also, the *constraint-set* may be limited for some applications due to memory-size considerations (as in stream mining). Therefore, only the best constraints should be selected for semi-supervised clustering, whereupon the notion "best" should be properly defined as well.

Some authors propose an interactive solution to the constraint-selection problem [4,6]: the appropriateness of a constraint is deduced through user feedback. Another thread of research defines measures on the utility of constraints, calculating how beneficial is the use of a constraint in a dataset [7,8].

On the first group, Cohn et al. [4] propose an interactive method, with which a user establishes relationships among documents in a database as well as their membership to certain groups. This knowledge is then used to obtain the most appropriate clustering *from the user perspective*. Similarly, Davidson et al. [6] propose an incremental interactive algorithm with constraint selection. They show that constraint-selection is an NP-hard problem in their setting, but they identify several conditions that are sufficient to devise efficient solutions. They derive rules on the types of constraints that can be added and constraint-set properties that must be satisfied when the constraint-set is updated. The main advantage of both approaches is that user knowledge is exploited to the user's satisfaction, resulting in constraints that are intuitive. However, the dependency on the user's perception and the need for constant interaction with the user limit the generalizability of the approach.

On the second group, Davidson et al. [7] propose two quantitative measures to explain how constraints influence the quality of the output clustering model: The *information measure* refers to the amount of information which is provided by a set of constraints and cannot be determined by the algorithm's objective function, and the *coherence measure* counts the number of agreements between the constraint and the metrics of the algorithm. The authors show that performance is high for sets of constraints with high values for both measures and that the performance is poor if the set is incoherent. Also, in a further recent work, Green and Cunningham [8] define a method that derives constraints without human supervision based on a co-association matrix between pairs of elements from a set of instances that belong to an *ensemble clustering*. After that, most representative elements are used to build initial clusters and adding instances with difficult assigment based on the incertitude level.

3 Our Approach: Semi-supervised Clustering with a Constraint Selector

Our method performs semi-supervised clustering on a *reduced* set of initial constraints, but instead of using a random heuristic for constraints generation from the labeled dataset, we use a constraint selection heuristic inspired by the algorithms WITS [10] and WIRS [13]. WITS and WIRS have been originally designed for instance reduction in nearest-neighbour classification: They take as input a set of labeled instances and select those most appropriate for learning the classifier. In our problem specification, we rather use WITS/WIRS to select those labeled instances from which constraints are generated.

We first describe WITS [10] and then its variation WIRS [13]. We then explain how we use the ranked instances to derive a set of constraints, which we exploit for semi-supervised clustering.

3.1 Instance Selection with WITS and WIRS

The methods WITS and WIRS for instance selection have been inspired by nearest-neighbour classification algorithms: A kNN classifier assigns each newly arriving instance to the class to which the instance's k closest neighbours belong. The main drawback of this method is the high overhead in time (to compare each arriving instance with all instances used to build the classifier) and in space (to store all instances). This overhead is reduced by so-called *instance reduction* techniques, which aim to reduce the number of labeled instances considered, without reducing the classification quality. In this paper, we consider two such techniques, WITS [10] and WIRS [13], but our task is not to eliminate instances from the dataset but rather rank them and derive constraints only from a selection of highly ranked instances.

WITS for Typicality-Based Instance Selection. The *Weighted Instance Typicality Search* algorithm (WITS) proposed by Morring and Martinez [10] builds upon the concept of instance *typicality* proposed by Zhang [16]. *Typicality* measures how representative is an instance for a class. It is defined as the ratio of the *intra-class similarity* to the *extra-class similarity*, both of which are averages of similarities between objects belonging to the same, resp. different classes. As usual, instance similarity $sim(x, y) := 1 - dist(x, y)$ for some distance metric.

Data points close to the central point of a class (the mean) exhibit higher intra-class similarity and thus higher typicality than points at the its border. Therefore, WITS smooths away class borders and thus covers classification problems in which the classification decision at border regions is very complex.

WITS takes as input a set of labeled instances T and returns them as a set S of weighted instances, built as follows. First, T is split into *buckets* – one per class. Then, the algorithm performs multiple iterations. In each iteration, it computes the misclassification error upon the subset S of T and then takes as *candidate* the instance x with the highest typicality, choosing it from the bucket with the highest misclassification rate thus far. WITS assigns a weight to x, computed so as to minimize the misclassification error in $S \cup x$. If the inclusion of x to S reduces the misclassification error substantially (i.e. $S \cup x$ yields a lower error than S), then S is extended. WITS stops when all instances in T have been included in S or if the misclassification error cannot be reduced further.

For the calculation of the misclassification error, WITS considers only the one nearest neighbour. For the identification of neighbours, WITS uses the *Heterogeneous Value Difference Metric* (HVDM) proposed in [15]: HVDM is mapped to the Euclidean distance for continuous attributes and to the *Value Difference Metric* (VDM) for nominal attributes. The idea of this metric is that two symbols $w = x_{aj}$ and $z = x_{bj}$ of a nominal input x_j are closer to each other, if the conditional probabilities $P(y = s|x_j = w)$ and $P(y = s|x_j = z)$ are similar for each possible class s. A simple VDM metric $d()$ can be defined as:

$$d(x_j, y_j) = \sum_{s=1}^{S_y} |P(y = s|x_j = w) - P(y = s|x_j = z)| = \sum_{s=1}^{S_y} \left| \frac{N_{w,s}}{N_w} - \frac{N_{z,s}}{N_z} \right|.$$

(1)

Once a VDM is defined for nominal values, the distance between two instances is a possibly weighted combination of distances between pairs of continuous values and pairs of nominal values.

WIRS for Instance Ranking. The *Weighted Instance Ranking Search* algorithm WIRS proposed by Vallejo et al. [13] is a variation of WITS, in which instance weights are computed by an algorithm *InstanceRank* that is inspired by the PageRank method [3]. In particular, WIRS models the labeled instances in T as nodes of a graph, connecting two nodes with an edge that is weighted with the similarity between them. By this, the graph is undirected and fully connected. Then, the *InstanceRank* of a node reflects the number of nodes to which it is similar [13].

As in WITS, WIRS partitions the input set T into one *bucket* per class. However, it also ranks the buckets in descending order, taking the number of errors and the rank of the instances in the bucket as basis. Similarly to WITS, an instance is only selected for inclusion in the output set if its inclusion highly improves the results.

3.2   Constraint Selection upon a Ranked List of Instances

We apply WIRS upon the small set of labeled instances, from which Must-Link and Cannot-Link constraints are to be generated. We anticipate different options, which depend on how many ranked lists of instances are generated and how the instances are selected from this list.

Constraints on a single ranked list of instances. We use WIRS to rank all labeled instances into a global list, i.e. independently of class membership. Then, we can take the top-N instances and generate all constraints involving them. Alternatively, we can generate constraints for all instances, use the rank of the instances to derive ranks for the constraints and then select the top-M constraints.

A constraint involves two instances, hence its rank can be computed as (a) the maximum of the ranks of the instances in it, (b) the sum of the instance ranks or (c) the average of the instance ranks.

Constraints on multiple ranked lists. We apply WIRS to rank the labeled instances of each class separately. Then, we can select for the ith-class the top-n_i instances, where n_i may be the same for all classes or may vary with the prior probability of the class. The latter option allows us to select more instances for strongly represented classes or, contrary to it, to oversample among the weakly represented classes.

Alternatively, we can generate constraints for all instances and then rank the constraints as before. To take the class distribution into account, we can weight the rank of each instance with the prior probability of the class to which it belongs.

Constraints on multiple reduced ranked lists.   In our current implementation, we use the ability of WIRS/WITS to rank the instances of each class separately and select those most appropriate and representative for learning the classifier in order to generate the constraints. As pointed out in [13], this option yields better results for the nearest-neighbour classification problem. This is intuitive, since the separately ranked lists allow to take into account the particularities of each class. The number of instances for each class is given by WIRS/WITS depending on each dataset.

The resulting set of constraints is input to the semi-supervised clustering algorithm. The approach is independent of the clustering algorithm in use. We have coupled the constraint selection process with our own density-based semi-supervised algorithm C-DBSCAN [12] and with the MPCKMeans algorithm proposed in [2].

4   Experimentation and Results

We have studied the behaviour of our *ConstraintSelector* on the quality of a constraint-based clustering algorithm. We have coupled our method with two semi-supervised clustering algorithms, MPCKMeans [2] and C-DBSCAN [12]. As baseline we use the traditional approach of incorporating a set of randomly selected constraints to the semi-supervised clustering algorithm.

4.1   Sets of Data and Constraints

To study the impact of the *ConstraintSelector* on clustering quality, we need to simulate the real scenario of constraint exploitation. We have run two experiments. In the first one, we study how the *ConstraintSelector* affects the performance of constraint-based clustering algorithms for various datasets. In the second experiment, we vary the number of labeled instances that are input to the constraint selection mechanism.

Experiment A: We study the datasets (Glass, Ionosphere, Iris, Zoo, and Sonar) from de the UCI repository[1]. For the *ConstraintSelector*, we consider the following instance ranking and constraint selection options:

- *Random-5% and Random-10%:* This algorithm selects randomly the 5% and 10% of instances from the original datasets to generate constraints.
- WITS-R: *ConstraintSelector* with WITS for instances reduction.
- WIRS-R: *ConstraintSelector* with WIRS for instances reduction.

Experiment B: We consider one dataset from the the UCI repository, the Pima Indians (or Diabetes) dataset. We split the dataset D into one partition A for constraint generation and one partition B for semi-supervised clustering. We apply the *ConstraintSelector* to rank the instances of partition A and to generate constraints from the top-ranked instances.

The number of data instances, for which constraints are available, is usually much smaller than the whole dataset. Therefore, when partitioning D into A and B, we set that A is $\frac{1}{m}$ of D, with $m = 2, 3, 4, \ldots$. Moreover, we require that A contains at least 50 instances; this prevents the generation of partitions that are too small to be informative. Then, we set $B = D \setminus A$. We denote the A-partitions as A_m, i.e. $A_2, A_3, \ldots$ and generate them so that $A_{m1} \subset A_{m2}$ for each $m1 > m2$ ($\frac{1}{m1} < \frac{1}{m2}$). We compared the following variants of the *ConstraintSelector*:

- *Baseline:* This algorithm uses all constraints generated from A_m.
- *Random-5% and Randon-10%:* This algorithm selects randomly the 5% of instances from A_m to generate contraints.
- WITS-R: *ConstraintSelector* with WITS upon A_m for instance reduction.
- WIRS-R: *ConstraintSelector* with WIRS upon A_m for instance reduction.

---

[1] http://www.ics.uci.edu/~mlearn/MLRepository.html

4.2   Evaluation Measurements

We use the Rand Index [11] to compare results against the initial labelled data. The Rand Index computes the similarity of partitions based on agreements and disagreements for two clusterings, acquiring the highest value 1 when the clusters are exactly the same.

Next to the RandIndex value for each experiment, we compute the *Reduction* achieved by WITS-R, WIRS-R, i.e. the absolute number and relative percentage of labeled instances retained for constraint generation.

4.3   Results for Experiment A

The results for this experimentation setting is shown in the Table 1. We have used the MPCKMeans semi-supervised clustering algorithm proposed in [2]. For the constraints reduction with WIRS-R, the results are always better than Rand-5 and Rand-10 and the number of labeled instances needed is close to 10% on average. The performance of WITS-R is superior to Rand-5, Rand-10 with respect to the number of instances used to compute the constraints, but the RandIndex values are inferior to those of WIRS-R and comparable or inferior to the values of Rand-5, Rand-10 for all but one datasets.

Table 1. MPCKMeans with Constraint Selection for Experiment A

	Glass (214 ins.)	Ionosphere (351 ins.)	Iris (150 ins.)	Sonar (208 ins.)	Zoo (101 ins.)
Rand-5 (Min-Max)	0.61 (0.57-0.65)	0.57 (0.55-0.58)	0.90 (0.83-0.90)	0.50 (0.49-0.51)	0.87 (0.86-0.91)
Rand-10 (Min-Max)	0.62 (0.44-0.67)	0.58 (0.57-0.59)	0.91 (0.85-0.92)	0.50 (0.50-0.51)	0.89 (0.86-0.91)
WITS-R (Reduction)	0.64 6(2.80%)	0.58 9(2.56%)	0.86 10(6.67%)	0.5 4(1.92%)	0.84 10(9.9%)
WIRS-R (Reduction)	0.66 24(11.2%)	0.60 12(3.42%)	0.96 12(8.00%)	0.51 24(11.54%)	0.92 11(10.89%)

Table 2. C-DBSCAN with Constraint Selection for Experiment A

	Glass (214 ins.)	Ionosphere (351 ins.)	Iris (150 ins.)	Sonar (208 ins.)	Zoo (101 ins.)
Rand-5 (Min-Max)	0.47 (0.47-0.49)	0.73 (0.71-0.74)	0.89 (0.82-0.94)	0.56 (0.53-0.62)	0.91 (0.90-0.95)
Rand-10 (Min-Max)	0.48 (0.46-0.54)	0.75 (0.71-0.76)	0.92 (0.86-0.93)	0.65 (0.55-0.69)	0.92 (0.90-0.98)
WITS-R (Reduction)	0.47 6(2.80%)	0.74 9(2.56%)	0.63 10(6.67%)	0.53 4(1.92%)	0.90 10(9.9%)
WIRS-R (Reduction)	0.47 24(11.2%)	0.75 12(3.42%)	0.72 12(8.00%)	0.55 24(11.54%)	0.91 11(10.89%)

In Table 2, we depict the same experiment for a density-based semi-supervised clustering algorithm, C-DBSCAN [12]. WITS-R and WIRS-R show comparable performance to each other and to Rand-5, while Rand-10 is superior to the other methods for the Sonar dataset. We suspect that the inferior performance of WITS-R and WIRS-R when combined to C-DBSCAN is caused by different assumptions on the shape of clusters: WITS and WIRS assume that clusters are spherical when selecting neighbours, while C-DBSCAN does not assume spherical clusters.

4.4   Results for Experiment B

We have varied the number of labeled instances considered for ranking and subsequently constraint selection with the *ConstraintSelector* and passed the derived constraints to MPCKMeans [2] and to C-DBSCAN [12] as for Experiment A. The results are depicted in Table 3 and Table 4, respectively.

By juxtaposing the two tables, we see that C-DBSCAN performs better to MPCKMeans for this dataset, independently of constraint exploitation. This can indicate two points: 1) MPCKMeans is more affected by wrong or bad constraints than C-DBSCAN, so its performance is worse; 2) the clusters in the Pima dataset

Table 3. MPCKMeans with *ConstraintSelector* in Experiment B

Pima dataset	$A = \frac{1}{2}$ (ins. 384) $B = \frac{1}{2}$ (ins. 384)	$A = \frac{1}{3}$ (ins. 256) $B = \frac{2}{3}$ (ins. 512)	$A = \frac{1}{4}$ (ins. 192) $B = \frac{3}{4}$ (ins. 576)	$A = \frac{1}{5}$ (ins. 154) $B = \frac{4}{5}$ (ins. 614)
Baseline	0.50	0.51	0.52	0.51
Rand-5 (Min-Max)	0.51 0.50-0.51	0.51 0.50-0.51	0.51 0.50-0.51	0.51 0.50-0.52
Rand-10 (Min-Max)	0.52 0.50-0.52	0.51 0.50-0.52	0.51 0.50-0.52	0.51 0.50-0.51
WITS-R (Reduction)	0.51 12(3.1%)	0.52 6(2.3%)	0.52 16(8.3%)	0.51 2(1.2%)
WIRS-R (Reduction)	0.52 14(3.6%)	0.53 16(6.2%)	0.53 23(11.9%)	0.53 13(8.4%)

Table 4. C-DBSCAN with *ConstraintSelector* in Experiment B

Pima dataset	$A = \frac{1}{2}$ (ins. 384) $B = \frac{1}{2}$ (ins. 384)	$A = \frac{1}{3}$ (ins. 256) $B = \frac{2}{3}$ (ins. 512)	$A = \frac{1}{4}$ (ins. 192) $B = \frac{3}{4}$ (ins. 576)	$A = \frac{1}{5}$ (ins. 154) $B = \frac{4}{5}$ (ins. 614)
Baseline	0.61	0.65	0.65	0.65
Rand-5 (Min-Max)	0.48 0.46-0.50	0.46 0.42-0.50	0.51 0.47-0.52	0.51 0.47-0.52
Rand-10 (Min-Max)	0.57 0.51-0.61	0.57 0.52-0.61	0.55 0.51-0.62	0.56 0.54-0.63
WITS-R (Reduction)	0.56 12(3.1%)	0.54 6(2.3%)	0.56 16(8.3%)	0.52 2(1.2%)
WIRS-R (Reduction)	0.59 14(3.6%)	0.57 16(6.2%)	0.60 23(11.9%)	0.60 13(8.4%)

are not spherical so that MPCKMeans is at a disadvantage. In fact, the performance of MPCKMeans varies only marginally with constraint selection and is not affected as the number of instances input to the *ConstraintSelector* is reduced.

For C-DBSCAN, the results in Table 4 are more informative. The performance of the Baseline is superior to semi-supervised clustering with constraint selection, indicating that the exploitation of *all* labeled instances leads to better results. However, the RandIndex for the Baseline increases as the number of labeled instances considered is reduced from 384 to 256. This is in lieu with the observation of [7] that non-useful constraints may affectthe performance of the constraint-based clustering algorithm, althought due to its grid nature C-DBSCAN is less sensitive.

Among the alternative methods for instance ranking and constraint selection, WIRS-R shows superior and rather stable performance. It is remarkable that the performance of Rand-10 varies considerably. When studying the number of instances retained by WITS-R vs WIRS-R, we see that WITS-R tends to select less instances, but this leads to a performance degradation in comparison to WIRS-R.

5   Conclusion

Selecting a proper set of constraints in semi-supervised clustering is an important issue, because different available constraints may influence clustering performance positively or negatively. In this study, we propose *ConstraintSelector*, a heuristic method that invokes an instance-ranking algorithm to order the labeled instances available for semi-supervised clustering, and then generates constraints from the top-ranked instances only.

We have combined the *ConstraintSelector* with different constraint-based clustering algorithms, notably with two algorithms based on K-Means (i.e. a spherical clustering algorithm) and on a density-based algorithm. Our results show that instance-based ranking and selective generation of constraints improves clustering performance with smaller set of contraints.

For the *ConstraintSelector*, we have used two instance-ranking algorithms, WITS [10] and WIRS [13]. Both algorithms assume that the underlying data classes have spherical form. They use this assumption to define and exploit neighbourhoods among instances. In our experiments, we observed that this assumption may lead to less satisfactory results if the model contains non-spherical clusters. In such a case, the use of all constraints leads to better performance. We intend to study this observation deeper and consider algorithms for instance ranking and constraint selection that do not assume particular cluster shapes.

References

1. Basu, S., Banerjee, A., Mooney, R.J.: Semi-supervised Clustering by Seeding. In: ICML'02: Proc. Int. Conf. on Machine Learning, pp. 19–26 (2002)
2. Bilenko, M., Basu, S., Mooney, R.J.: Integrating Constraints and Metric Learning in Semisupervised Clustering. In: ICML'04: Proc. of the 21th Int. Conf. on Machine Learning, pp. 11–19 (2004)

160   C. Ruiz et al.

3. Brin, S., Page, L.: The anatomy of a large-scale hypertextual web search engine. Computer Networks and ISDN Systems 30(1-7), 107–117 (1999)
4. Cohn, D., Caruana, R., McCallum, A.: Semi-supervised clustering with user feedback. Technical Report TR2003-1892, Cornell University (2003)
5. Davidson, I., Ravi, S.S.: Clustering with Constraints: Feasibility Issues and the k-Means Algorithm. In: SIAM 2005: Society for Industrial and Applied Mathematics Int. Conf. on Data Mining Int. Conf. in Data Mining (2005)
6. Davidson, I., Ravi, S.S., Ester, M.: Efficient Incremental Constrained Clustering. In: KDD'07: Proc. of the 13th ACM SIGKDD Int. Conf. on Knowledge Discovery and Data Mining, pp. 240–249 (2007)
7. Davidson, I., Wagstaff, K., Basu, S.: Measuring Constraint-Set Utility for Partitional Clustering Algorithms. In: Fürnkranz, J., Scheffer, T., Spiliopoulou, M. (eds.) PKDD 2006. LNCS (LNAI), vol. 4213, pp. 115–126. Springer, Heidelberg (2006)
8. Greene, D., Cunningham, P.: Constraint selection by committee: An ensemble approach to identifying informative constraints for semi-supervised clustering. In: Kok, J.N., Koronacki, J., Lopez de Mantaras, R., Matwin, S., Mladenič, D., Skowron, A. (eds.) ECML 2007. LNCS (LNAI), vol. 4701, pp. 140–151. Springer, Heidelberg (2007)
9. Halkidi, M., Gunopulos, D., Kumar, N., Vazirgiannis, M., Domeniconi, C.: A Framework for Semi-Supervised Learning Based on Subjective and Objective Clustering Criteria. In: ICDM 2005: Proc. of the 5th IEEE Int. Conf. on Data Mining, pp. 637–640 (2005)
10. Morring, B.D., Martinez, T.R.: Weighted Instance Typicality Search (WITS): A Nearest Neighbor Data Reduction Algorithm. Intelligent Data Analysis 8(1), 61–78 (2004)
11. Rand, W.M.: Objective Criteria for the Evalluation of Clustering Methods. Journal of the American Statistical Association 66, 846–850 (1971)
12. Ruiz, C., Spiliopoulou, M., Menasalvas, E.: C-DBSCAN: Density-Based Clustering with Constraints. In: An, A., Stefanowski, J., Ramanna, S., Butz, C.J., Pedrycz, W., Wang, G. (eds.) RSFDGrC 2007. LNCS (LNAI), vol. 4482, pp. 216–223. Springer, Heidelberg (2007)
13. Vallejo, C.G., Troyano, J.A., Ortega, F.J.: WIRS: Un algoritmo de reducción de instancias basado en ranking. In: Borrajo, D., Castillo, L., Corchado, J.M. (eds.) CAEPIA 2007. LNCS (LNAI), vol. 4788, pp. 327–336. Springer, Heidelberg (2007)
14. Wagstaff, K., Cardie, C.: Clustering with Instance-level Constraints. In: ICML 2000: Proc. of 17th Int. Conf. on Machine Learning, pp. 1103–1110 (2000)
15. Wilson, D.R., Martinez, T.R.: Improved heterogeneous distance functions. Journal of Artificial Intelligence Research (JAIR) 1, 1–34 (1997)
16. Zhang, J.: Selecting typical instances in instance-based learning. In: ML'92: Proc. of the 9th Int. Workshop on Machine Learning, pp. 470–479 (1992)

Empirical Hardness for Mixed Auctions*

Pablo Almajano[1], Jesús Cerquides[2], and Juan A. Rodriguez-Aguilar[1]

[1] IIIA, Artificial Intelligence Research Institute
CSIC, Spanish National Research Council
{palmajano,jar}@iiia.csic.es
[2] UB, WAI, Dep. Matemàtica Aplicada i Anàlisi
Universitat de Barcelona
cerquide@maia.ub.es

Abstract. Mixed Multi-Unit Combinatorial Auctions (MMUCAs) offer a high potential to be employed for the automated assembly of supply chains of agents. However, little is known about the factors making a winner determination problem (WDP) instance hard to solve. In this paper we empirically study the hardness of MMUCAs: (i) to build a model that predicts the time required to solve a WDP instance (because time can be an important constraint during an auction-based negotiation); and (ii) to assess the factors that make a WDP instance hard to solve.

Keywords: mixed multi-unit combinatorial auction, machine learning.

1 Introduction

In [1] we introduced the so-called *mixed multi-unit combinatorial auctions* (henceforth *MMUCA* for short) and discussed the issues of bidding and winner determination. Mixed auctions are a generalisation of the standard model of combinatorial auctions (CAs) [2]. Thus, rather than negotiating over goods, in mixed auctions the auctioneer and the bidders can negotiate over *supply chain operations* (henceforth *transformations* for short), each one characterised by a set of input goods and a set of output goods. A bidder offering a transformation is willing to produce its output goods after having received its input goods along with the payment specified in the bid. While in standard CAs, a solution to the winner determination problem (WDP) is a set of atomic bids to accept that maximises the auctioneer's revenue, in mixed auctions, the *order* in which the auctioneer "uses" the accepted transformations matters. Thus, a *solution* to the WDP is a *sequence of operations*. For instance, if bidder *Joe* offers to make dough if provided with butter and eggs, and bidder *Lou* offers to bake a cake if provided with enough dough, the auctioneer can accept both bids whenever he uses Joe's operation before Lou's to obtain baked cakes from butter and eggs. Since the existence of a solution is not guaranteed in the case of MMUCAs (unlike classical CAs), attention is focused not only on the winner determination

---

* Funded by projects IEA (TIN2006-15662-C02-01), AT (CSD2007-0022), EVE (TIN2009-14702-C02-01, TIN2009-14702-C02-02).

P. Meseguer, L. Mandow, and R.M. Gasca (Eds.): CAEPIA 2009, LNAI 5988, pp. 161–170, 2010.
© Springer-Verlag Berlin Heidelberg 2010

problem, but also on the feasibility problem of deciding whether a given instance admits a solution at all. In fact, an important and peculiar source of complexity for MMUCAs lays hidden in this latter problem as noticed in [3].

The WDP for MMUCAs is a complex computational problem. In fact, one of the fundamental issues limiting the applicability of MMUCAs to real-world scenarios is the computational complexity associated to the WDP. In particular, it is proved in [1] that the WDP for MMUCAs is $\mathcal{NP}$-complete. And yet little is known about its hardness, namely about what makes a WDP instance hard to solve. Hence, on the one hand some WDP instances may unexpectedly take longer to solve than required (time is important in auction-based negotiations). On the other hand, lack of knowledge about the hardness of MMUCA prevents the development of specialised winner determination algorithms. Unlike classical CAs, little is known about whether polynomial-time solvable classes of MMU-CAs can be singled out based on the structural and topological properties of the instances at hand. Thus, in this paper we try to make headway in the understanding of the hardness of MMUCAs by applying the methodology described in [4] that Lleyton-Brown et al successfully apply to CAs. The results in this paper must be regarded as the counterpart of the results about empirical hardness obtained in [4] for CAs.

The paper is organised as follows. In section 2 we outline an integer program introduced in [5] to efficiently solve the WDP for MMUCAs. In section 3 we outline the methodology introduced in [4] to subsequently employ it to build a model that predicts the time required by the integer program to solve a WDP instance. Next section 5 further exploits the methodology to assess the factors that make a WDP instance hard to solve. Finally, section 6 draws some conclusions and sets paths to future research.

2   CCIP: A Topology-Based Solver

In this section we summarise CCIP, a mapping of the MMUCA WDP into an integer program (IP) that drastically reduces the number of decision variables required by the original IP described in [1] by exploiting the topological features of the WDP. CCIP will be employed in forthcoming sections to analyse the empirical hardness of the MMUCA WDP. Notice that hereafter we limit to outlining the intuitions underlying CCIP. We refer the reader to [5] for a detailed IP formulation.

Consider that after receiving a bunch of bids, we draw the relationships among goods and transformations, as shown in Figure 1 (a). There, we represent goods at trade as circles, transformations as squares, a transformation input goods as incoming arrows and its output goods as outgoing arrows. Thus, for instance, transformation t_0 offers one unit of good g_2 and transformation t_2 transforms one unit of g_2 into one unit of g_4. Say that the auctioneer requires a multiset of goods $U_{out} = \{g_2, g_3\}$. Row 1 in table 1 stands for a valid solution sequence. Indeed, it stands for a valid solution sequence because at each position, enough input goods are available to perform the following transformation. Notice too

Table 1. Partial sequences of transformations

Position	1	2	3	4	5	6	7	8	9	10	11
Sequence 1	t_0	t_2			t_1		t_4				
Sequence 2	t_0	t_1	t_2	t_4							
Sequence 3	t_2	t_1	t_0	t_4							
Solution template	t_0	t_1	t_2 t_3 t_4	t_2 t_3 t_4	t_2 t_3 t_4	t_5	t_9	t_{10}	t_6 t_7	t_6 t_7	t_8

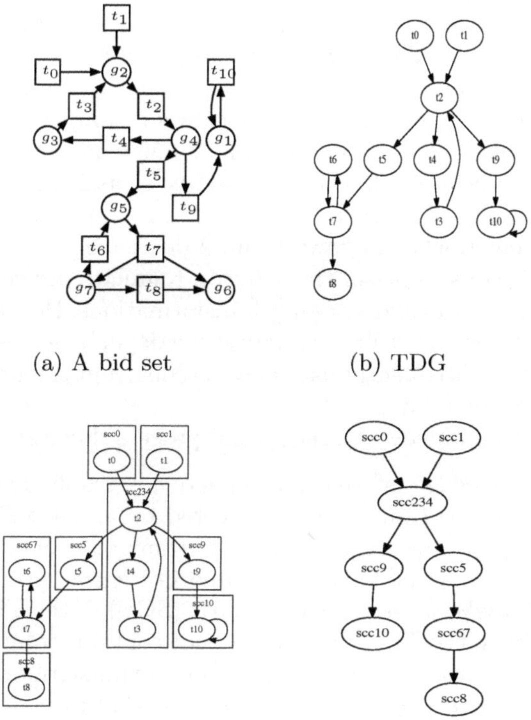

(a) A bid set

(b) TDG

(c) SCCs of the TDG

(d) The strict order

Fig. 1. An MMUCA bid set, the corresponding TDG, SCC, and Order Relation

that likewise row 1, row 2 also stands for a valid solution sequence because even though they differ in the ordering among transformations, both use exactly the same transformations, and both have enough goods available at each position. However, row 3 in table 1 is not a valid sequence, although it contains the same transformations, because t_2 lacks enough input goods (g_2) to be used.

In Figure 1 (a), it is clear that transformations that have no input goods can be used prior to any other transformation. Thus, transformations t_0 and t_1 can come first in the solution sequence. Moreover, we can *impose* that t_0 comes before t_1 because swapping the two would yield an equivalent solution. If we now consider transformations t_2, t_3, t_4, we observe that: (i) they *depend* on the output goods of t_0 and t_1; and (ii) we cannot impose an arbitrary order among them because they form a cycle and then they can feed with input goods one another (they depend on one another). However, no permutation of the three can be discarded for the valid solution sequence. Furthermore, whatever their order, we can always use them before transformations t_5 and t_9 (since these depend on g_4) without losing solutions.

Assuming that the auctioneer does not care about the ordering of a solution sequence as long as enough goods are available for every transformation in the sequence, we can impose "a priori" constraints on the ordering of transformations without losing solutions. The way of imposing such constraints is via a *solution template*, a pattern that any candidate sequence must fulfill to be considered as a solution. For instance, row 4 in table 1 shows a sample of solution template. A solution sequence *fulfilling* that template must have transformations t_0 in position 1 and t_1 in position 2, whereas it is free to assign positions 3, 4, or 5, to the transformations in $\{t_2, t_3, t_4\}$. For instance, row 3 of table 1 does not fulfill the template in row 4, whereas rows 1 and 2 do.

Notice that the constraints in the solution template derive from our analysis of the dependence relationships among transformations. Hence, in order to build a solution template, we must firstly analyse the dependence relationships among transformations to subsequently use them to constrain the positions at which a transformation can be used.

At this aim, we can follow the sequential process illustrated in Figure 1:

1. Define the so-called transformation dependency graph (TDG), a graph where two transformations t and t' are connected by an edge if they have a good that is both output of t and input to t' (direct dependence). Figure 1 (b) depicts the TDG for the bids represented in Figure 1(a).

2. Assess the *strongly connected components* (SCC) of the TDG. Depending on the received bids, the TDG may or may not contain strongly connected components. In order to constrain the position of transformations, we transform the TDG in an acyclic graph where the nodes that form a strongly connected component are collapsed into a single node. The main idea is that the positions of transformations in a strongly connected component are drawn from the same set of positions, but we cannot impose any order regarding the position each transformation takes on. In Figure 1(c) we identify strongly connected components or SCCs in the graph. In figure 1(d) we can see the graph resulting from transforming (collapsing) each SCC into a node.

If there is a strict order among transformations (e.g. like the one depicted in Figure 1(d)), then we can always construct a solution template that restricts the positions that can be assigned to those transformations in a way that, if a solution sequence fulfills the solution template, the strict order is also fulfilled [6]. For instance, consider the solution template in row 4 in table 1 that we construct considering the strict order in Figure 1(d). Since the solution sequences in rows 1 and 2 of table 1 fulfill the solution template in row 4, they both fulfill the strict order.

Now we are ready to characterise valid solutions to the MMUCA WDP. Looking back at the solution sequences in rows 1 and 2 of table 1, we realise that both are *partial sequences*. A partial sequence is a sequence with "holes", meaning that there can be some positions in the sequence that are *empty*. Therefore, a valid solution to the MMUCA WDP can be encoded as a partial sequence of transformations that *fulfills* some solution template.

3   Empirical Hardness Models

In [4], Leyton-Brown et al. propose a general methodology to analyze the empirical hardness of $\mathcal{NP}$-hard problems. The purpose of the methodology is twofold. On the one hand, given an algorithm to solve some hard problem, it provides the guidelines to build (learn) a model that predicts the running time required by the algorithm to solve an instance of the problem. On the other hand, the methodology also discusses techniques to analyse the factors that determine how hard some distributions or individual instances are to solve (by the algorithm under study). Moreover, since the methodology is successfully applied to the particular case of CAs, it appears as an appropriate tool for analysing the empirical hardness of the WDP for MMUCAs. Our purpose will be to employ to: (i) build a model to predict the running time of the solver outlined in section 2; and (ii) to analyse the factors that make the WDP for MMUCAs hard. Before we apply the methodology (in forthcoming sections) to MMUCA, next we summarise its main steps[1]:

1. *Select an algorithm* as the objective of the empirical hardness analysis.
2. *Select an instance distribution.* To generate instances of the problem, it is eventually convenient to employ some artificial instance generator.
3. *Select features* of the problem instances. The values these features take on will be mapped to a predicted run-time. The features have to be good ones, avoiding uninformative features.
4. *Collect data.* Generate a good number of instances with the instance distribution selected at step 2. Then, solve the instances using the algorithm selected at step 1 and extract the features selected at step 3. Finally, divide the instances in three separate sets, namely one for training, one for validation, and one for testing.
5. *Build a model.* Choose a machine learning algorithm to learn to predict the running time required by the algorithm selected at step 1 to solve some problem instance characterised by the values of the features selected at step 3. Statistical regression techniques are the most convenient tool for this goal.

4   A Empirical Hardness Model for MMUCA

In this section we apply the methodology outlined in section 3 to build a model that predicts the running time of the solver outlined in section 2.

---

[1] We refer the interested reader to [4] for full details.

Step 1: Selecting an algorithm. As discussed in section 2, MMUCA WDPs can be solved via integer linear programming (ILP). We select an ILOG CPLEX implementation of the integer program outlined in section 2 (fully described in [5]), because it is the fastest algorithm reported in the literature, largely outperforming the solver in [1].

Step 2: Selecting an instance distribution. In order to generate instance distributions we resort to the artificial data set generator for MMUCA WDPs introduced in [7]. The algorithm takes inspiration on the structure of supply chains, whose formation has been identified as a very promising application domain for MMUCA [5,1]. A supply chain is composed of levels (or *tiers*). Each tier contains goods that are subsequently transformed into other goods within another tier in the supply chain. Within this setting, their generator allows to flexibly generate:

- *Supply chain structures with a varying number of levels.* Modelling from complex supply chains involving multiple levels (for example the making of a car) to simple supply chains involving a few parties.
- *Transformations of varying complexity.* Varying complexity on the goods involved in the input and output sides of the transformations in a supply chain.
- *Transformations representing different production structures.* The input and output goods from a transformation may come from different levels.
- *Bids per level.* Different bid distributions may appear at different levels, to control the degree of *competition* in the market.

Step 3: Selecting Features. In order to generate a list of features we start from the features described in [4] regarding the study of CAs. However, there are major differences between CAs and MMUCAs that lead to the list of features in table 2.

First of all, as formerly argued in [5] and [7], the *topological features* of the search space handled by the WDP matter. Indeed, while in [5] Giovannucci et al. observed that the order of the number of variables required by CCIP, the IP, is directly related to the size of the largest strongly connected component

Table 2. Groups of features

#Feature	Topological features
1-8	Node size statistics: average, maximum, minimum and standard deviation.
9-12	Node degree statistics: average, maximum, minimum and standard deviation.
13	Edge density: sum of all node degrees divided by the sum of the degrees in a complete graph.
14	Depth: The largest path in the SCC graph.
#Feature	Problem size features
15	Number of transformations.
16	Number of goods.
#Feature	Price-based features
17-20	Price statistics: average, max, min and standard deviation of prices.

(SCC), in [7] Vinyals et al. empirically observed that large SCCs (cycles) lead to high solving times. Therefore, we must consider the structural properties of the SCC graph (like the one in figure 1). Hence, we shall consider: inner features of SCCs (node size statistics), external features of SCCs (node degree statistics), general properties of the SCC graph (edge density and depth). Importantly, notice that these features were not considered when studying CAs in [4] because the topology of the search space for CAs is different.

Secondly, regarding problem size features, MMUCAs are again different from CAs because the former consider the notion of transformation. Therefore, we shall consider both the number of goods and transformations.

Finally, although Leyton-Brown et al. found in [4] that price-based features are not among the main factors driving the hardness of a WDP, we still consider them because although two WDPs may have similar SCC graphs, their optimal solutions might be different when considering different bid prices.

Step 4: Collecting Data. To collect data, we generated 2250 WDP instances with the generator in [7] after setting the probability of generating cycles ($p_b = 0.1$), the number of goods ($n_g = 20$), and the number of transformations ($n_t = 200$). Such parameters allow us to generate WDP instances whose solving times are acceptable. Moreover, the fact that we employ a probability distribution to generate cycles (parameterised by p_b) leads to WDP instances of varying complexity. This is because we observed in [7] that the solving time is sensitive to cycles in WDP instances. In other words, solving the WDP is costly when there are cycles. Such WDP instances may be output by the generator when the probability of generating cycles (p_b) is positive, as we set above[2].

Thereafter, once solved the WDP instances we solve them using CCIP, the integer program we have selected as a solver at step 1 above. Since eventually some WDP instances may take too long, we defined a maximum solving time (4500 seconds). If CCIP does not find any valid solution before the deadline, the instance is rejected and a new instance is generated and solved. In this way we avoid to deal with outliers in the empirical analysis. Once solved the problems, we extracted the values for the selected features described at the step 3 above. For each problems instance, the values of the features along with the solving time compose the data that will be subsequently employed to learn the model. Finally, we divided the data (features' values along with solving times) in three sets following the step 4 in the methodology described above: one for training, one for validation, and one for testing.

Step 5: Building Models. We decided to use linear regression (following the guidelines in [4]) to build a model that predicts the solving time of CCIP because: (i) it reduces the learning time; and (ii) it makes more intuitive to analyse and interpret the resulting models. We use as response variable an exponential model, applying the (base-10) logarithm to the CPLEX running times. As for error metrics, we do not apply the inverse transformation. In this way, we manage to

---

[2] Notice that some WDP instances may have no cycles, others may have several cycles, and cycles may encompass a varying number of transformations.

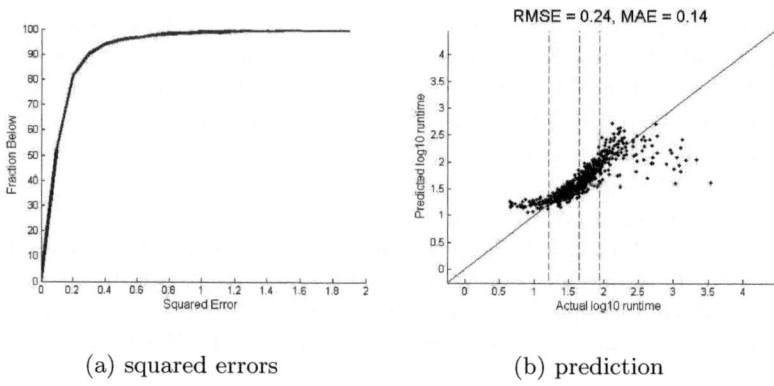

(a) squared errors   (b) prediction

Fig. 2. Prediction scatter plot

uniformly penalize all the responses. We consider two error metrics: the squared-error metric (RMSE), because it is the most used in linear regression, and the mean absolute error (MAE), because it is more intuitive.

Figure 2(a) shows the cumulative distribution of squared errors on the test set. The horizontal axis represents the squared error, whereas the vertical axis corresponds to the cumulative distribution of squared errors on the test sets, namely the fraction of instances that were predicted with an error not exceeding the squared error in the x-value. Notice that the absolute error is greater than 1 (10 seconds) for only for 1% of the predictions.

Figure 2(b) shows a scatter plot of the predicted running time versus the actual running time in (base 10) logarithmic scales. In this case study, the RMSE is 0.24, whereas the MAE is 0.14. Because they indicate an average error of less than 1.8 seconds whenever the solving time ranges between 4.4 seconds and 4487 seconds, we conclude that the prediction model is acceptable. We also observe that most WDPs (actual run-times between 10 seconds and 100 seconds) are predicted with high accuracy, whereas predictions for WDPs with low solving times (easy WDPs) are pessimistic and predictions for WDPs with high solving times (hard WDPs) are optimistic. This occurs because the instance distribution generated at step 2 did not contain enough examples of easy and hard WDPs.

5   Analysing MMUCA Problem Hardness

In this section we analyse the MMUCA WDP hardness using the model produced in section 4 to assess the features that make the problem hard to solve.

As a first step, we assess the relationship between the *best* subset of features of a given size (ranging from 1 to 17) and the RMSE. In other words, a relationship between the features that minimise the RMSE (out of all the features in table 2) for each number of features. Figure 3(a) plots how the RMSE varies as the size of the subset of features increases. In order to obtain the best subset of features

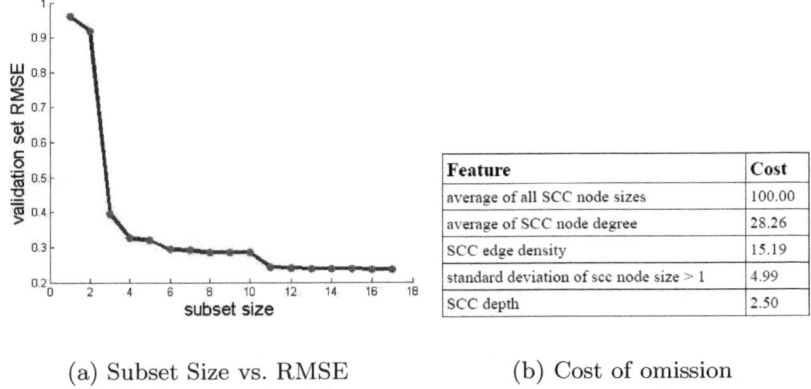

Feature	Cost
average of all SCC node sizes	100.00
average of SCC node degree	28.26
SCC edge density	15.19
standard deviation of scc node size > 1	4.99
SCC depth	2.50

(a) Subset Size vs. RMSE   (b) Cost of omission

Fig. 3. Linear Regression

for each subset size we employ a heuristic algorithm, the so-called forward-select, which begins with an empty set of features to progressively add one feature at each time. Forward-select adds as a new feature the one with the lowest RMSE when testing with the validation set. Based on the results in figure 3(a), we decided to analyse the model selecting five features because the RMSE slightly varies for more than five features.

We analyzed this five features' *cost of omission* in our model to evaluate the *importance* of each particular feature. The *cost of omission* for a particular feature is computed by analysing how its omission impacts on the RMSE: we train a model that omits the feature to subsequently compute the resulting increase on the RMSE. Figure 3(b) ranks the cost of omission, namely the impact of the hardness of the WDP, of the best five features. Several comments apply:

(1) The average of all SCC node sizes appears as the most important feature. Hence, the largest the SCCs, the harder the WDP. This result is in line with the theoretical results in [5].

(2) The second and the third places are the average of SCC node degrees and the SCC edge densities. Both features refer to an SCC node degree, namely to an SCC's number of children. Since the higher the number of children, the larger the number of potential solution sequences of the WDP, it is not surprising that features referring to SCC nodes' degrees have a high impact on the hardness of the WDP.

(3) The fourth position refers to SCCs whose size is greater than one, namely to SCCs containing cycles. In some sense, though less important than the top feature in the ranking, this feature is complementary to that one because it refers to the sizes of SCCs.

(4) The feature with the lowest cost of omission, the SCC graph depth, also influences the hardness of the problem because it indicates the maximum number of transformations that can compose a solution sequence, namely the maximum length of the solution sequence.

To summarise, complementary features 1 and 4 refer to the inner features of SCCs and refer to the impact of cycles on the hardness of the WDP. This is in line with the results in [7]. Furthermore, features 2 and 3 indicate that they are also important because they have a strong impact on the number of potential solution sequences to evaluate to solve the WDP. Finally, feature 5 is also relevant because it influences the lengths of those potential sequences. Therefore, unlike the analysis in [4] for CAs, our study shows that the features that most impact the hardness of the WDP for MMUCAs are all topological.

6   Conclusions and Future Work

In this paper we employed the methodology described in [4] to analyse the empirical hardness of CAs. With this methodology we obtained a model that successfully predicts the time to solve MMUCA winner determination problems. Therefore, we can effectively assess whether the WDP can be solved in time when there are constraints regarding the time to solve the WDP. Furthermore, we analyzed the hardness of the MMUCA WDP to learn that the topological features (of the SCC graph) are the ones that most impact the hardness of the problem. These results complement the theoretical results in [3]. We argue that specialised algorithms to solve the MMUCA WDP can benefit from this analysis. Regarding future work, we plan to complete our empirical study by analysing supply chains of varying sizes (in terms of number of goods and transformations).

References

1. Cerquides, J., Endriss, U., Giovannucci, A., Rodríguez-Aguilar, J.A.: Bidding languages and winner determination for mixed multi-unit combinatorial auctions. In: IJCAI, pp. 1221–1226 (2007)
2. Cramton, P., Shoham, Y., Steinberg, R. (eds.): Combinatorial Auctions. MIT Press, Cambridge (2006)
3. Valeria Fionda, G.G.: Charting the tractability frontier of mixed multi-unit combinatorial auctions. In: Proceedings of IJCAI 2009, pp. 134–139 (2009)
4. Leyton-Brown, K., Nudelman, E., Shoham, Y.: Empirical hardness models for combinatorial auctions. In: Cramton, et al. (eds.) [2], ch. 19, pp. 479–504
5. Giovannucci, A., Vinyals, M., Rodríguez-Aguilar, J.A., Cerquides, J.: Computationally-efficient winner determination for mixed multi-unit combinatorial auctions. In: Proceedings of the Seventh International Joint Conference on Autonomous Agents and Multi-agent Systems, pp. 1071–1078 (2008)
6. Giovannucci, A., Cerquides, J., Rodriguez-Aguilar, J.A.: Proving the correctness of the CCIP solver for MMUCA, Tech. rep., IIIA-CSIC (2007)
7. Vinyals, M., Giovannucci, A., Cerquides, J., Meseguer, P., Rodriguez-Aguilar, J.A.: A test suite for the evaluation of mixed multi-unit combinatorial auctions. Journal of Algorithms 63, 130–150 (2008)

Developing Strategies for the ART Domain

Javier Murillo, Víctor Muñoz, Beatriz López, and Dídac Busquets

Institut d'Informàtica i Aplicacions
Campus Montilivi, edifice P4, 17071 Girona
{jmurillo,vmunozs,blopez,busquets}@eia.udg.edu

Abstract. In this paper we propose the design of an agent for the ART Testbed, a tool created with the goal of objectively evaluate different trust strategies. The agent design includes a trust model and a strategy for decision making. The trust model is based on the three components of trust considered in ART, namely direct, indirect (reputation) and self trust (certainty). It also incorporates a variable time window size based on the available information that allows the agent to easily adapt to possible changes in the environment. The decision-making strategy uses the information provided by the trust model to take the best decisions to achieve the most benefits for the agent. This decision making tackles the exploration versus exploitation problem since the agent has to decide when to interact with the known agents and when to look for new ones. The agent, called Uno2008, competed in and won the Third International ART Testbed Competition held at AAMAS in March 2008.

Keywords: Competitive multi-agent systems, Trust, Reputation, ART Testbed.

1 Introduction

Competitive multi-agent systems where a set of self-interested agents interact with others, offering and requesting services, to achieve their goals, pose challenges in relation to the trust modeling of an agent aimed at ensuring the right decisions are taken. It is very important to choose correctly the agents to interact with. To this end, agents usually incorporate a trust model of the other agents that tells information about which agents to trust and which to avoid [10].

The Agent Reputation and Trust Testbed was created in order to simulate these conditions and to provide a standard problem scenario in which different approaches to modeling and applying trust and strategies in multi-agent systems can be compared [5]. It simulates an environment in which the participant agents act as art *appraisers* that compete to obtain the most clients. Appraisers receive more clients, and thus more profit, for giving more accurate appraisals. The simulator generates a fixed total number of clients that request appraisals for paintings that belong to different artistic eras. The appraiser agents have varying levels of *expertise* in the different eras, making them experts in some but ignorant about others. These expertises can vary through time. For the agents to perform the appraisals, they can ask other agents for their opinions and set a weight for

P. Meseguer, L. Mandow, and R.M. Gasca (Eds.): CAEPIA 2009, LNAI 5988, pp. 171–180, 2010.
© Springer-Verlag Berlin Heidelberg 2010

each of them in the simulator. The final appraisal is then computed as the mean of the agents' weighted appraisals.

An important feature of the ART Testbed is that it is not necessary for the agents to provide good information. For each agent's request they can decide whether to cooperate or to act maliciously. Thus, trust and reputation become important factors for an agent in deciding when and from whom to request opinions. A perfect trust model is difficult to obtain, because the agents can change their behavior through time. Therefore, the design of a strategy to take correct decisions based on an incomplete trust model (which may contain mistakes) is also an important factor if the aim of the agent is to obtain maximum benefits.

In order to decide which agents to interact with, the agent has to deal with the exploration versus exploitation problem [11], because it must decide whether to interact with a known opinion provider agent or to explore some unknown ones and possibly discover better provider agents. If the agent is only focused on exploitation it might obtain good short-term results but bad ones in the long term, since exploration allows the agent to discover better provider agents than its normal providers, or to have substitute providers in case the quality of a provider diminishes for some reason, a circumstance that is quite likely to happen in the ART Testbed. Therefore, as an agent is usually limited in the number of interactions it can perform (due to interaction costs), it is necessary to decide which interactions to dedicate to exploration, and which to exploitation.

Trust has been defined in different ways for different domains, but for the ART Testbed domain the most accurate is: "Trust is the confidence or belief in the competence, utility or satisfaction expected from other agents concerning a particular context" [6]. Under this definition, the trust in an agent to provide a specific service can be understood as an estimator of the expected quality that will be obtained from that service. In the literature we find a large number of papers [3,7] in which trust models and strategies have been designed for the ART domain. A remarkable work is the agent that won the 2006 and 2007 international competitions. This agent, known as IAM [12], consists of three main parts: a lie detector to detect malicious agents, a variance estimator to estimate the quality of the other agents, and an optimal weight calculator to measure its own behavior against others. We must also cite the agents for the ART domain that have preceded this work; agents with specific trust models that, despite their simplicity, were successful in national competitions [8]. The contribution of this article is the complete design of an agent for the ART Testbed domain using the trust model that we present and some specific domain strategies. A more detailed description of the decision making strategy for generic competitive environments is given in [9].

This paper is organized as follows. First, we describe the different components of an agent inside the ART framework, in order to perform the decision making process. Then, we provide in section 3 the trust model, and show how this model is used to develop several decision making strategies for service requesting (section 4) and service providing (section 5). In section 6 we show the results obtained in the 2008 ART competition. Finally, we end with some conclusions.

2   Agent Architecture

In the ART framework, the architecture of an agent can be designed on the basis of two main components: the trust model and the decision making (strategy), as shown in Figure 1. First, the trust model contains the available information about other agents that feeds the decision-making process. The trust model is continuously updated with the new information coming from the interactions performed with other agents. From this model the old information is removed (forgotten) in order to keep the data up to date. Second, in the decision-making component two main blocks can be distinguished. The first block of the decision making weights the other agents according to the trust model, and selects which agents will be requested. The agent uses the second block of decision making to determine the quality of the answers to the incoming requests. The first block is activated by the agent itself each time it has to perform an appraisal. The second block is activated only if a request is received (reaction).

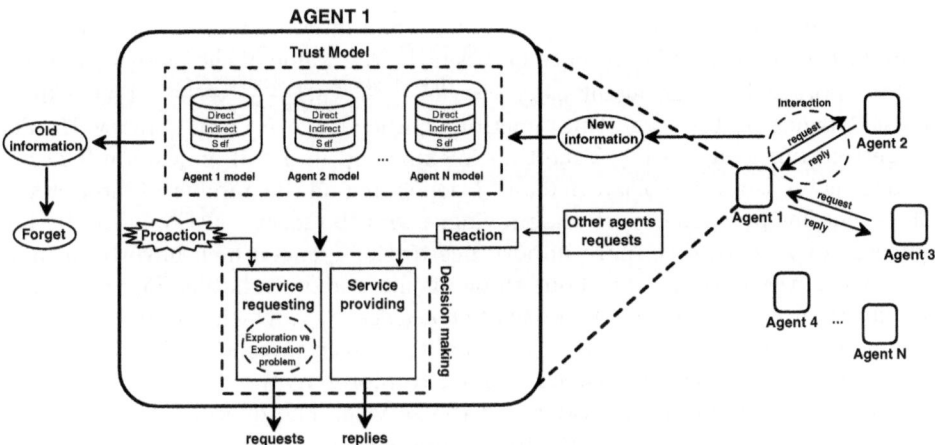

Fig. 1. Agent diagram

3   Trust Model

Agents can conduct opinion transactions, appraisers can exchange reputations, or information about the trustworthiness of other appraisers, and certainties or information about its own expertise. Each kind of interaction implies a payment from the requesting agent to the requested agent of a given amount of money. The payment costs are more expensive for direct interactions than for other kinds of interactions. Thus, the trust model can be designed based on three different components: direct (opinion transactions), indirect (reputations), and self (certainties) trust.

3.1 Model Components

Direct trust $(DT_{p,s})$ is based on the agent's own experiences gained directly from the providers, and is therefore the most reliable source of information. If past experiences with a given provider have been successful with a service, then the agent expects that the results of future interactions will be good as well.

Equation 1 shows the way the $DT_{p,s}$ is computed using a forgetting function (ω), knowledge (K) and honesty (H). Each of these components are described below. I_p represents the interactions with respect to the provider p, for all its services and time steps. $I_{p,s}$ is the subset of I_p corresponding to service s. $Q_{p,t,s}$ is a value (between 0 and 1) that represents the average of the individual qualities $(q_{p,t,s,j})$ of all the interactions in time step t with provider p about service s, that is weighted according to their age. T is the current time step.

$$DT_{p,s} = \frac{\sum_{t=0}^{T} \omega(t,T) \cdot Q_{p,t,s}}{\sum_{t=0}^{T} \omega(t,T)} \cdot K(I_{p,s}) \cdot H(I_p) \tag{1}$$

The measurement of the quality of an individual interaction $q_{p,t,s,j}$ can be computed as the percentual difference between the real value of the painting and the value appraised by the agent $q_{p,t,s,j} = \frac{|realValue - appraisedValue|}{realValue}$. Thus, direct trust depends on the forgetting function ω, knowledge K, and honesty H. The forgetting function is a key issue that is explained in detail on section 3.2. The knowledge K is a value between 0 and 1 depending on the number of interactions the agent has performed with the provider p and the service s (Equation 2). The purpose of K is to give more importance to the agents which have been more interacted, the information about these agents is more reliable. The maximum weight is only set when the *quantity of knowledge*, $\gamma_{p,s}$, which the provider p has about the service s is higher than or equal to a given threshold NK. Otherwise, the weight is set linearly between 0 and 1 to represent the degree of knowledge the agent has about the provider and the service. The quantity of knowledge, $\gamma_{p,s}$, is defined by counting up the total number of interactions $(|I_{p,t,s}|)$ the agent had with the provider and the service in question, appropriately weighted with the forgetting function $\gamma_{p,s} = \sum_{t=0}^{T} \omega(t,T) \cdot |I_{p,t,s}|$, where $I_{p,t,s}$ is the subset of $I_{p,s}$ corresponding to timestep t.

$$K_{p,s}(I_{p,s}) = \begin{cases} 1 & \gamma_{p,s} \geq NK \\ \frac{\gamma_{p,s}}{NK} & \gamma_{p,s} < NK \end{cases} \tag{2}$$

In order to avoid malicious agents another factor that can be taken into account is the honesty H. It counts the number of lies made by an agent in a way analogous to the knowledge, so that if an agent has lied more than a given number of times NH, it will be discarded as opinion provider. We consider that an agent has lied intentionally when the error committed in a single appraisal is higher than a certain threshold. This threshold has been calculated with reference to the formula used by the simulator to compute the standard deviation of the error committed by an agent in an appraisal [4,8]. For example if the error is greater than

3 standard deviations the probability of an unintentional mistake is almost zero. Note that the liar detection should be ad-hoc for each domain where our approach is used.

Indirect trust $(IT_{p,s})$ is also known as *reputation*[1] or *recommendation*[6]. This component is not based on experiences lived directly by the agent. These experiences are lived by a third party and then communicated to the agent. It is computed in a way analogous to direct trust, where Q is the average of the received reputations.

Self trust $(ST_{p,s})$, which some authors call *advertisement trust* [6] or certainty in the ART Testbed, is based on information coming from the provider itself. This is usually the least reliable information source because as the agents are self-interested they will probably report higher values than the real ones.

3.2 Forgetting Function

Choosing the correct time window size is a key factor in properly detecting changes in the environment. Large window sizes give more robust results but do not react as well to changes. Conversely, small window sizes adapt better to changes although with less accuracy, as they are based on smaller amounts of information. A compromise has to be made between having sufficient information in order to achieve a high level of information accuracy (big window size), and adaptation to changes (small window size). To that end, we propose a dynamic window size, as an attempt to unite the advantages of both. The mechanism decides on a small size when the information contained in a given space is sufficient to obtain a reliable result, and a larger size when it does not have sufficient information. The forgetting function $\omega(t, T)$ is shown in Equation 3.

$$\omega(t,T) = \begin{cases} 0 & T - t \geq \phi_t \\ f_\omega(T,t) & 0 < T - t < \phi_t \end{cases} \qquad \phi_t = min(\beta, \alpha) \qquad (3)$$

$$\beta = T - arg\max_i \sum_{i=t}^{T} |I_{p,i,s}^x| \geq \xi$$

where $f_\omega(T,t)$ is the function that defines the weights of the interactions considered inside the time window (this function could be for example an exponential or a cosine function between $\frac{3\pi}{2}$ and 2π [6], both giving more weight to recent interactions and low weights to old interactions), and ϕ_t is the value representing the variable size of the agent's time window. These equations define a dynamic time window, with a maximum size given by the parameter α, which is reduced whenever the number of interactions with the provider p regarding service s ($\sum_{i=t}^{T} |I_{p,i,s}|$) has been high; in this case we search for the minimum size β of the time window, so that the number of interactions inside it is higher than or equal to a given constant number (ξ).

4 Strategies for Service Requesting

An agent inside the ART framework has to deal with two kinds of decision making processes: how to request services to other agents, and how to provide services. Regarding service requesting, an agent can perform two kind of requests: appraisals and reputations. Regarding the former, the agent should interact with the other agents in order to obtain a good appraisal for a given client paint. Regarding the later, the agent should interact with the other agents in order to know which are good appraisers.

4.1 Strategies for Appraisal Requesting

The decision-making process involves the resolution of the exploration versus exploitation problem, given that the number of interactions to perform in ART is limited. The key point here is the need to decide at every moment how much effort to spend on exploring for new unknown providers, and how much on exploiting the known ones. In order to make this possible, the agents are grouped in the following categories, according to the information stored about them in the trust model regarding a given service:

- **Group TK (Totally Known agents):** These are the agents which have been interacted with more than (or equal to) NK times (the knowledge threshold of Equation 2), inside the time window.
- **Group PK (Partially Known agents):** Agents with a number of interactions greater than zero but still under the knowledge threshold. These providers would probably become future providers in the event any of the existing ones failed.
- **Group AU (Almost Unknown gents):** Agents without any direct interaction, but for which there is indirect or self information.
- **Group TU (Totally Unknown agents):** These are the agents without any information about, either direct, indirect or self.

Note that the membership of agents in the different groups changes through time, with all the agents belonging to the last group (TU) at the beginning. As the forgetting function gradually forgets interactions it is possible that agents from higher groups move to lower groups. These categories are used to define our exploration versus exploitation strategy. Let the total number of interactions be limited to L, due to cost restrictions. Then, given a new set of services to be fulfilled, the agent exploits a set of M providers and explores a set of N agents, so that at the end the set of interacted agents is $L = M + N$.

Exploitation. Exploiting the trust model in the ART domain means using the opinion received from an agent (asking for it and setting a weight greater than 0 for it in the simulator). On the other hand, exploration consists of requesting and then putting a weight of 0 in the simulator. In both cases, the agent pays the same price (the price of an opinion) and the agent will know in the following time step (when the real values of the previous paintings are received) whether the agent was a good appraiser, a bad appraiser or a liar. In order to select the agents for exploitation, it is preferable to select from the providers belonging to the first group (TK), the ones that the agent thinks will provide good quality (or higher than a given threshold QT) in supplying the requested service, since the information about these agents is more reliable. They can be good or bad, then the threshold QT is used to select only the best agents and avoid the bad ones. The expected quality is obtained with the direct trust component, $DT_{p,s}$. In the case that there are not sufficient agents conforming to the above restrictions, the agent can use as providers the remaining agents from the first group, or the best agents from the second group (at a higher level of risk). The amount of effort dedicated to exploitation is given by the quality threshold QT, so that agents with a trust value higher than this threshold will be used as appraisers, with an upper limit of $L = \frac{clientFee \cdot questionPercentage}{opinionCost}$, in order to spend a given percentage ($questionPercentage$) of the earnings of an opinion ($\frac{clientFee}{opinionCost}$). If there are still interactions left ($M < L$), the remaining ($N = L - M$) will be used in the exploration process.

Exploration. The idea of the exploration process is to gradually raise agents from lower to higher groups until they conform to the first group's constraints. Choosing correctly the agents for exploration will move more agents to the known category, thus allowing the agent to have candidates for future exploitation, in the event that any regular providers are lost. The agents to explore are taken from groups PK, AU and TU, with the available interactions (N) being distributed according to the three following phases:

1. Select agents from the PK group. Agents are sorted in descending order according to their direct trust regarding the service to be covered s ($DT_{p,s}$), and only the N best (if available) are selected. The objective of this phase is to know about these agents, in order to move them to the TK group.
2. If there are still interactions left, the agents are taken from the AU group. These agents are arranged and selected in descending order according to their indirect trust ($IT_{p,s}$). These agents will belong to the PK group in the next time step.
3. Finally, the agents are selected from the TU group randomly (we don't have information about these agents), in order to obtain some direct information in the next timestep (the agent will belong to the AU group).

The different phases of the mechanism are subsequently executed until the available exploration interactions (N) are exhausted.

4.2   Strategies for Reputation Tests

A "reputation test" is performed to determine which agents are suitable to be asked for indirect trust (i.e., they are good reputators). This test is done to eliminate agents that are not able to send good reputations or simply that do not use reputation. The test consists of asking each agent about our reputation for different eras. With the results obtained, we can determine if the answers are *coherent*. Coherency is achieved using different features. First, the agent must have given at least one reputation a value lower than 0.5 and another one with a value higher than 0.5 (i.e. the agent has to have detected that we are good at some eras and bad at others). Secondly, the error produced, has to be under a given threshold in at least a given number of eras. All the agents passing this test will be marked as good reputators. The three best reputators are asked about the unknown agents. After that, the average of the three received references, if they are all similar, are used to select the agent to find out about first. In the initial time steps no trust model has yet been built, and indirect trust is not useful either, because initially nobody knows anybody, so any received reputations would not be right. Therefore, we use here the self trust values obtained from the agents to decide which agents to rely on when asking for appraisals. The agent starts requesting reputations at a pre-fixed timestep.

5   Strategies for Service Providing

The second decision making mandatory of is how to deal with the requests applied by other agents. Lying is not beneficial since in the long term the other agents (to which we lied) either stop trusting, stop asking, or even start lying to us [2]. Thus, we lose possible information sources if we lie. Moreover, in a dynamic environment, an agent that at a given time is not a source of information can become one in the future. However, most of the agents in the ART domain use the "tit for tat" strategy which consists of *lying to untruthful agents and telling the truth to truthful agents*. This strategy is generally good because it is very rare that an untruthful agent will become an information source in the future. This strategy means that truthful agents usually have more benefits than untruthful agents, because they have more information sources. Instead we consider that telling the truth *even* to untruthful agents may make the agent become one of the few opinion providers for untruthful agents. Consequently, the former will benefit from the latter's revenues. With regard to reputation requests, we also answer them truthfully. In doing so, the agents with good trust models (that make use of indirect trust) are favored over the rest, and we expect them to answer back in the same way, thereby achieving mutual collaboration [2].

6   Results

For the experimentation, we have designed an agent, named Uno2008, with the following characteristics. The knowledge and honesty thresholds KN and HN have been set at 10. Regarding the time window, we have used a maximum size of 10 ($\alpha = 10$), which is reduced when the number of interactions is greater than 20 in less than 10 time steps ($\xi = 20$); these values have been found empirically. The function f_ω, used to weight the region of the window considered, has been set to a constant function equal to 1. In other words, we give the same importance to all the interactions inside the window. The agent participated in the 2008 International ART Testbed Competition held in Estoril, Portugal at AAMAS.

In this competition 11 agents were registered from 7 different countries. Five dummy agents (seimmud) were also added to the games. The agents could not use self opinions. The competition consisted of three different kinds of games, the first with low dynamics (# eras to change $(ETC) = 1$, amount of expertise change $(AEC) = 0.05$), the second with medium dynamics (# $ETC = 3$, $AEC = 0.1$) and the third with high dynamics (# $ETC = 3$, $AEC = 0.3$). Each of the games was repeated three times, and the average of earnings of the agents in the three games was computed to determine the final scores.

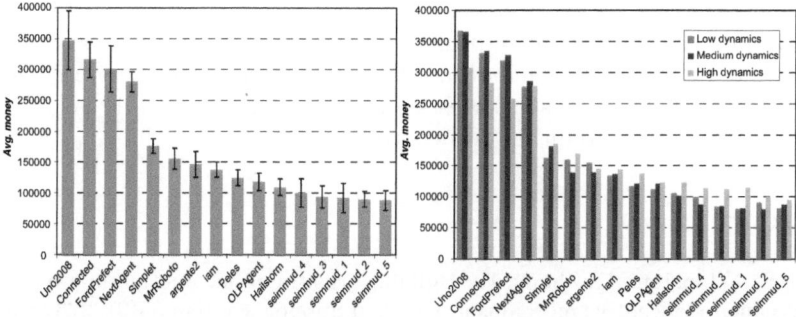

Fig. 2. Left: Average and standard deviation of the earnings. Right: total earnings divided in low, medium and high dynamics.

The overall results are shown in Figure 2 (left), where the y axis represents the average earnings obtained for each agent in all the games, with its standard deviation. Our agent, Uno2008, managed to win the competition by obtaining the highest score. Figure 2 (right) shows the results separated for the three kinds of dynamics. Here we can observe how the effect of dynamics affects the best agents by decreasing their benefits and increasing the benefits of the worst agents. In any case, Uno2008 obtained the best results in all three categories.

7   Conclusions

In this article, a trust model has been presented together with strategies for using it in a decision-making process. The model is based on three trust components: direct, indirect and self. Direct trust is based on the agent's own experiences, indirect trust is based on other agent's experiences, and self trust is the publicity that an agent transmits about itself. Another issue to take into account is that the environment changes. For this reason, the trust model incorporates a forgetting function based on a variable time window that allows fast and correct adaptation to changes using the minimum amount of information available.

The data of an agent's trust model has to be processed in order for the best decisions to be taken and leading to its benefits being maximized or its objectives being obtained. Three main strategies have been developed for this purpose: 1) an strategy for requesting appraisals; 2) a second strategy for deciding upon good reputators; and 3) and strategy for providing services. Regarding the former, the process of making the decisions involves the exploitation versus exploration problem, using the trust model. To solve this problem, we classify the agents in four categories (totally known, partially known, almost unknown and totally unknown). We use a method for exploration that combines the random factor with the probability of finding good information in partially known agents.

The design of the agent was tested in the ART Testbed domain. It participated in the 2008 international competition held in Estoril (in AAMAS), which it won. For the future, we are thinking about the possible application of the agent in other domains, such as Internet electronic service providers.

The approach is applicable to other domains where competitive and self interested agents interact with each other offering and requesting services. However, the trust parameters and strategies should be adapted. This is an interesting matter to take into account for future work.

References

1. Ba, S., Whinston, A., Zhang, H.: Building trust in online auction markets through an economic incentive mechanism. Decision Support System 35(3), 273–286 (2003)
2. Conte, R., Paolucci, M.: Reputation in Artificial Societies: Social Beliefs for Social Order. Kluwer Academic Publishers, Dordrecht (2002)
3. Costa, A.D., Lucena, C.J.P.: Computing Reputation in the Art Context: Agent Design to Handle Negotiation Challenges. In: Trust in Agent Societies, AAMAS (2008)
4. Fullam, K., Klos, T., Muller, G., Sabater, J., Schlosser, A., Topol, Z., Barber, S., Rosenschein, J., Vercouter, L., Voss, M.: A Specification of the Agent Reputation and Trust (ART) Testbed: Experimentation and Competition for Trust in Agent Societies. In: Proc. of the 4th AAMAS, pp. 512–518 (2005)
5. Fullam, K., Sabater, J., Barber, S.: Toward a testbed for trust and reputation models. Trusting Agents for Trusting Electronic Societies, 95–109 (2005)
6. Gómez, M., Carbó, J., Benac, C.: Honesty and trust revisited: the advantages of being neutral about other's cognitive models. JAAMAS 15, 313–335 (2007)
7. Kafali, O., Yolum, P.: Trust Strategies for the ART Testbed. In: The Workshop on Trust in Agent Societies at AAMAS 2006, pp. 43–49 (2006)
8. Muñoz, V., Murillo, J.: Agent UNO: Winner in the 2nd Spanish ART competition. Revista Iberoamericana de Inteligencia Artificial 39, 19–27 (2008)
9. Muñoz, V., Murillo, J., López, B., Busquets, D.: Strategies for Exploiting Trust Models in Competitive Multiagent Systems. In: Braubach, L., van der Hoek, W., Petta, P., Pokahr, A. (eds.) MATES 2009. LNCS, vol. 5774, pp. 79–90. Springer, Heidelberg (2009)
10. Sabater, J.: Trust and Reputation for Agent Societies, Monografies de l'institut d'investigació en intel.ligència artificial, 20, PhD Thesis (2003)
11. Sutton, R., Barto, A.G.: Introduction to Reinforcement Learning. MIT Press, Cambridge (1998)
12. Teacy, L., Huynh, T.D., Dash, R.K., Jennings, N.R., Luck, M., Patel, J.: The ART of IAM: The Winning Strategy for the 2006 Competition. In: Proceedings of the 10th International Workshop on Trust in Agent Societies, pp. 102–111 (2007)

A Multiagent Solution to Adaptively Classify SOAP Message and Protect against DoS Attack

Cristian I. Pinzón, Juan F. De Paz, Javier Bajo, and Juan M. Corchado

Universidad de Salamanca, Plaza de la Merced s/n, 37008, Salamanca, Spain
{cristian_ivanp,fcofds,jbajope,corchado}@usal.es

Abstract. SOAP messages use XML code, which makes them vulnerable to denial of service (DoS) attacks and puts the availability of web services at risk. This article presents an adaptive solution for dealing with DoS attacks in web service environments. The solution proposes a distributed hierarchical multi-agent architecture that implements a robust mechanism of classification based on an advanced CBR-BDI agent. The agent incorporates a case-based reasoning engine that integrate a Perceptron Multilayer neural network during the re-use phase to classify incoming SOAP messages and reject those that are considered malicious. A prototype of the architecture was developed and the results obtained are presented in this study.

Keywords: SOAP message, XML Security, multiagent systems, CBR, ANN.

1 Introduction

In order to obtain interoperability between web service platforms, communication between web servers is carried out via an exchange of messages. These messages, referred to as SOAP messages, are based on standard XML and are primarily exchanged using HTTP (Hyper Text Transfer Protocol) [1]. XML messages must be parsed in the server, which opens the possibility of an attack if the messages themselves are not well structured or if they include some type of malicious code. Resources available in the server (memory and CPU cycles) can be drastically reduced or exhausted while a malicious SOAP message is being parsed. This type of attack is known as a denial of service (DoS) attack and is perpetrated at the web service level because of the intrinsic relationship it has with the XML standard for coding SOAP messages.

A number of standards for guaranteeing the security of messages have been proposed to date, including WS-Security [2], WS-Policy [3], WS-Trust [4], WS-SecureConversation [5], etc. However, the proposed solutions focus exclusively on the aspects of message integrity and confidentiality, and user authentication and authorization [5].

This article presents a distributed hierarchical multiagent architecture for dealing with DoS attacks in web service environments. The architecture incorporates a CBR-BDI [7] agent with reasoning, learning and adaptation capabilities. The idea of a CBR mechanism is to exploit the experience gained from similar problems in the past and

P. Meseguer, L. Mandow, and R.M. Gasca (Eds.): CAEPIA 2009, LNAI 5988, pp. 181–190, 2010.

then adapt successful solutions to the current problem. The CBR engine initiates what is known as the CBR cycle, which is comprised of 4 phases. The classifier agent uses a Multilayer Perceptron neural network (MLP), which is incorporated into the re-use phase of the CBR cycle. By combining the CBR mechanism and the MLP, the system acquires learning capabilities and is able to adapt to changes in attack patterns for SOAP messages, thus facilitating the classification task when a SOAP message contains a DoS attack.

The rest of the paper is structured as follows: section 2 presents the problem that has prompted most of this research work. Section 3 focuses on the details of the multiagent architecture; section 4 explains in detail the classification model integrated within the classifier agent. Finally, section 5 describes how the classifier agent has been tested and presents the results obtained.

2   Web Service Security Problem Description

Attacks usually occur when the SOAP messages either come from a malicious user or are intercepted during the transmission by a malicious node that introduces different kinds of attacks.

The following list contains descriptions of some known types of attacks that can result in a DoS attack, as noted in [8] [9] [10].

- Oversize Payload: It reduces or eliminates the availability of a web service when a message with a large payload is parsed within the server.
- Coercive Parsing: An XML parser can analyze a complex format and lead to an attack because the memory and processing resources are being used up.
- Injection XML: The structure of a XML document is modified with a malicious code.
- SOAP header attack: Some SOAP message headers are overwritten while they are passing through different nodes before arriving at their destination.
- Replay Attack: Sent messages are completely valid, but they are sent en masse over short periods of time in order to overload the web service.

All web service security standards focus on strategies independent from DoS attacks [5]. In the following, we will revise those works that focus on denial of web service attacks and will compare to our approach as shown in Table 1.

A "XML Firewall" is proposed by [8]. Messages that are sent to a web service are intercepted and parsed to check the validity and the authenticity of the contents. If the contents of the messages do not conform to the policies that have been set, the messages will be dropped by the firewall. Gruschka and Luttenberger [6] propose an application level gateway system "Checkway". They focus on a full grammatical validation of messages by Checkway before forwarding them to the server. Checkway generates an XML Schema from a web service description and validates all web service messages against this schema. An adaptive framework for the prevention and detection of intrusions was presented in [9]. Based on a hybrid focus that combines agents, data mining and diffused logic, it is supposed to filter attacks that are either already known or new. Agents that act as sensors are used to detect violations to the normal profile using the data mining technique such as clustering, association rules and sequential association rules. The anomalies are then further analyzed using fuzzy logic to determine genuine attacks so as to reduce false alarms. An approach to countering DDoS and XDoS attacks against web services is presented by [11]. The system carries out request message authentication and validation before the requests are processed by the web services providers. The scheme has two modes: the normal mode and the under-attack mode. In the under-attack mode, the service requests need to be authenticated and validated before being processed. Finally, a recent solution proposed by [12] presents a Service Oriented Traceback Architecture (SOTA) to cooperate with a filter defense system, called XDetector. XDetector, is a Back Propagation Neural Network, trained to detect and filter XDoS attack message. Once an attack has been discovered by SOTA and the attacker's identity known, XDetector can filter out these attack messages.

Table 1 presents a comparison of our approach with the current approaches aimed at detecting DoS attacks in web services environments. Those parameters that couldn't be evaluated are marked with a hyphen.

Table 1. Comparison of selected models approaches vs. our approach

	XML Firewall	CheckWay Gateway	ID/IP framework	DDoS and XDoS	SOTA & XDetector	Our Approach
Distributed Approach	No	No	No	No	Yes	Yes
Learning ability	No	No	Yes	No	Yes	Yes
Adaptive ability	No	No	Yes	No	No	Yes
Balances the Workload	No	No	-	No	Yes	Yes
Tolerance to Failure	No	Yes	-	-	-	Yes
Scalability	Yes	-	Yes	Yes	Yes	Yes
Ubiquity	No	No	No	No	No	Yes

According to the results shown in Table 1, our approach outperforms the existing models with respect to:

a.) Distributed Approach: our approach is based on a multiagent architecture that can execute tasks derived from the classification process in a distributed way. b) Adaptive ability: our approach includes one type of intelligent agents that was designed to learn and adapt to changes in attack patterns and new attacks c.) Balances the Workload: our approach was designed to distribute the classification task load throughout the various layers of the hierarchical architecture. d.) Tolerance to Failure: our approach has a hierarchical design that can facilitate error recovery through the instantiation of new agents. e.) Scalability: our approach is capable of growing (by means of the instantiation of new agents) according to the needs of its environment. f.) Ubiquity: our approach provides a ubiquitous alert mechanism to notify security personnel in the event of an attack.

Our approach presents novel characteristics that have not heretofore been considered in previous approaches. The next section presents the architecture in greater detail.

3   Multiagent Architecture

Agents are characterized by their autonomy; which gives them the ability to work independently in real-time environments [13]. Furthermore, when they are integrated within a multiagent system they can also offer collaborative and distributed assistance in carrying out tasks [14].

One of the main characteristics of the multiagent architecture proposed in this paper is the incorporation of CBR-BDI [7] deliberative agents. The CBR-BDI classifier agents implemented here use an intrusion detection technique known as anomaly detection. In order to carry out this type of detection, it is necessary to extract information from the structure and content of the SOAP messages and the messages processing tasks.

Our proposal is a distributed hierarchical multiagent architecture integrated for 3 levels with distinct BDI agents. The hierarchical structure makes it possible to distribute tasks on the different levels of the architectures and to define specific responsibilities. The architecture presented in figure 1 shows the three levels with BDI agents organized according to their roles.

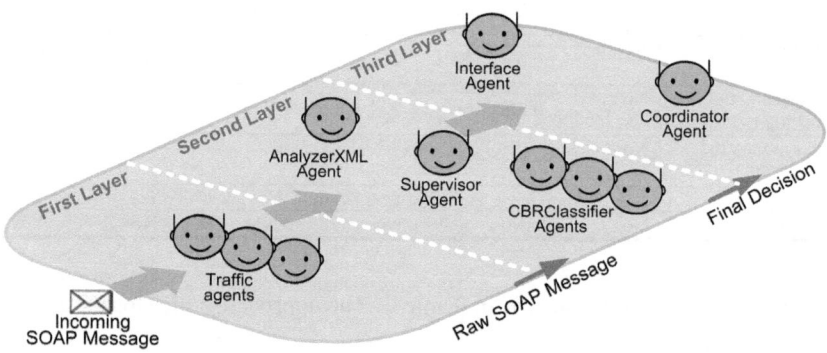

Fig. 1. Design of the multiagent architecture proposed

The following section describes the functionality of the agents located in each layer of the proposed hierarchical structure.

- Traffic agents (layer 1): Capture any traffic directed towards the server. JPCAP [15] is the API used to identify and capture any traffic that contains SOAP message packets. The captured SOAP messages are sent to the next layer in order to carry out the classification process. In addition to these tasks, Traffic agents use an IP register to monitor user activities. This type of monitoring makes it possible to identify suspicious activities similar to message replication attacks.

- CBRClassifier agents (layer 2): These CBR-BDI agents carry out the classification process. In order to initiate this phase, it is necessary to have previously started a syntactic analysis on the SOAP message to extract the required data. Once the data have been extracted from the message, a CBR mechanism is initiated by using a Multilayer Perceptron (MLP) neural network in the re-use phase.
- Supervisor Agent (layer 2): This agent supervises the AnalyzerXML agent since there still exists the possibility of an attack during the syntactic processing of the SOAP message.
- AnalyzerXML Agent (layer 2): This agent executes the syntactic analysis of the SOAP message. The analysis is performed using SAX as parser. Because SAX is an event driven API, it is most efficient primarily with regards to memory usage, and strong enough to deal with attack techniques. The data extracted from the syntactic analysis are sent to the CBRClassifier agents.
- Coordinator Agent (layer 3): This agent is in charge of supervising the correct overall functioning of the architecture. Additionally, it oversees the classification process. Each time a classification is tagged as suspicious, the agent interacts with the Interface Agent to request an expert review. Finally, this agent controls the alert mechanism and manages the actions required for responding to the attack.
- Interface Agent (layer 3): This agent was designed to function in different devices (PDA, Laptop, and Workstation). It facilitates ubiquitous communication with the security personnel when an alert has been sent by the Coordinator Agent. Additionally, it facilitates the process of adjusting the global configuration of the architecture.

4 Mechanism for the Classification of Malicious SOAP Messages

The application of agents and multiagent systems facilitates taking advantage of the inherent capabilities of the agents. Nevertheless, it is possible to increase the reasoning and learning capabilities by incorporating a case-based reasoning (CBR) mechanism into the agents. In the case at hand, a CBR classifier agent (CBR-BDI) is responsible for classifying the incoming SOAP messages. In the BDI (Beliefs Desires Intentions) model, the internal structure of an agent and its capacity to choose is based on mental aptitudes: agent behaviour is composed of beliefs, desires, and intentions [7]. A BDI architecture has the advantage of being intuitive and capable of rather simply identifying the process of decision-making and how to perform it.

Case-based Reasoning is a type of reasoning based on the use of past experiences [16]. The purpose of case-based reasoning systems is to solve new problems by adapting solutions that have been used to solve similar problems in the past. The fundamental concept when working with case-based reasoning is the concept of case. A case can be defined as a past experience, and is composed of three elements: A problem description which describes the initial problem, a solution which provides the sequence of actions carried out in order to solve the problem, and the final state which describes the state achieved once the solution was applied. The way in which cases are managed is known as the case-based reasoning cycle. This CBR cycle consists of four sequential steps: retrieve, reuse, revise and retain [16]. A CBR engine requires the use of a database with which it can generate models such as the solution of a new problem based on past experience.

In the specific case of SOAP messages, it manages a case memory for each service offered by the web service environment, which permits it to handle each incoming message based on the particular characteristics of each web service available. Each new SOAP message sent to the architecture is classified as a new case study object. Based on the structure and content of the SOAP messages and the message processing tasks, we can obtain a series of descriptive fields. These fields are extracted from the SOAP message and provide the case description for the CBRClassifier agent. Table 2 presents the fields used in describing the case for the CBR in this layer.

Table 2. Case Description - CBR

Fields	Type	variable
IDService	Int	i
MaskSubnet	String	m
SizeMessage	Int	s
NTimeRouting	Int	n
LengthSOAPAction	Int	l
MustUnderstandTrue	Boolean	u
NumberHeaderBlock	Int	h
NElementsBody	Int	b
NestingDepthElements	Int	d
NXMLTagRepeated	Int	t
NLeafNodesBody	Int	f
NAttributesDeclared	Int	a
CPUTimeParsing	Int	c
SizeKbMemoryParser	Int	k

Applying the nomenclature shown in the table above, each case description is given by the following tuple:

$$c = \left(i,m,s,n,l,u,h,b,d,t,f,a,c,k,P/c_{\cdot im},x^p,x^r\right) \tag{1}$$

For each incoming message received by the agent and requiring classification, we will consider both the class that the agent predicts and the class to which the message actually belongs. x^p represents the class predicted by the CBRClassifier agent belonging to the group. $x^p \in X = \{a,g,u\}$; a, g, u represent the values attack, good and undefined respectively; and x^r is the class to which the attack actually belongs $x^r \in X = \{a,g,u\}$, $P/c_{\cdot im}$ is the solution provided by the neural network MLP associated to service i and subnet mask m.

The reasoning memory used by the agent is defined by the following expression: $P = \{p_1,...,p_n\}$ and is implemented by means of a MLP neural network. Each P_i is a reasoning memory related to a group of cases dependent of the service and subnet mask of the client. The Multilayer Perceptron (MLP) is the most widely applied and researched artificial neural network (ANN) model. MLP networks implement mappings from input space to output space and are normally applied to supervised learning tasks [17]. The Sigmoidal function was selected as the MLP activation function, with a range of values in the interval [0, 1]. It is used to detect if the SOAP message is classified as an attack or not. The value *0* represents a legal message (non attack) and *1* a malicious message (attack). The sigmoidal activation function is given by

$$f(x) = \frac{1}{1 + e^{-ax}} \qquad (2)$$

The CBR mechanism executes the following phases:

Retrieve: Retrieves the cases that are most similar to the current problem, considering both the type of web service to which the message belongs and the network mask that contains the message.

- Expression 3 is used to select cases from the case memory based on the type of web service and the network mask.

$$c_{.im} = f_s(C) = \{c_j \in C / c_{j.i} = c_{n+1 \cdot i}, c_{j \cdot m} = c_{n+1 \cdot m}\} \qquad (3)$$

- Once the similar cases have been recovered, the neural network MLP $P / c_{.im}$ associated to service i and mask m is then recovered.

Reuse: The classification of the message is begun in this phase, based on the network and the recovered cases. It is only necessary to retrain the neural network when it does not have previous training. The entries for the neural network correspond to the case elements $s, n, l, u, h, b, d, t, f, a, c, k$. Because the neurons exiting from the hidden layer of the neural network contain sigmoidal neurons with values between [0, 1], the incoming variables are redefined so that their range falls between [0.2-0.8]. This transformation is necessary because the network does not deal with values that fall outside of this range. The outgoing values are similarly limited to the range of [0.2, 0.8] with the value 0.2 corresponding to a non-attack and the value 0.8 corresponding to an attack. The training for the network is carried out by the error Backpropagation Algorithm [18]. The weights and biases for the neurons at the exit layer are updated by following equations:

$$w_{kj}^p(t+1) = w_{kj}^p(t) + \eta(d_k^p - y_k^p)(1 - y_k^p)y_k^p y_j^p + \mu(w_{kj}^p(t) - w_{kj}^p(t-1)) \qquad (4)$$

$$\theta_k^p(t+1) = \theta_k^p(t) + \eta(d_k^p - y_k^p)(1 - y_k^p)y_k^p + \mu(\theta_k^p(t) - \theta_k^p(t-1)) \qquad (5)$$

The neurons at the intermediate layer are updated by following a procedure similar to the previous case using the following equations:

$$w_{ji}^p(t+1) = w_{ji}^p(t) + \eta(1 - y_j^p)y_j^p(\sum_{k=1}^{M}(d_k^p - y_k^p)(1 - y_k^p)y_k^p w_{kj})x_i^p + \mu(w_{ji}^p(t) - w_{ji}^p(t-1)) \qquad (6)$$

$$\theta_j^p(t+1)=\theta_j^p(t)+\eta(1-y_j^p)y_j^p(\sum_{k=1}^{M}(d_k^p-y_k^p)(1-y_k^p)y_k^p w_{kj})+\mu(\theta_j^p(t)-\theta_j^p(t-1)) \qquad (7)$$

where w_{kj}^p represents the weight that joins neuron j from the intermediate layer with neuron k from the exit layer, t the moment of time and p the pattern in question. d_k^p represents the desired value, y_k^p the value obtained for neuron k from the exit layer, y_j^p the value obtained for neuron j from the intermediate layer, η the learning rate and μ the momentum. θ_k^p represents the bia value k from the exit layer. The variables for the intermediate layer are defined analogously, keeping in mind that i represents the neuron from the entrance level, j is the neuron from the intermediate level, M is the number of neurons from the exit layer.

When a previously trained network is already available, the message classification process is carried out in the revise phase. If a previously trained network is not available, the training is carried out following the entire procedure beginning with the cases related to the service and mask, as shown in equation (8).

$$p_r = MLP^t(c_{.im}) \qquad (8)$$

Revise: This phase reviews the classification performed in the previous phase. The value obtained by exiting the network $y = P_r^e(c_{n+1})$ may yield the following situations:

- If $y > \mu_1$ then it is considered an attack

- Otherwise, if $y < \mu_2$, then the message is considered a non-attack or legal

- Otherwise, the message is marked as suspicious and is filtered for subsequent revision by a human expert. To facilitate the revision, an analysis of the neural network sensibility is shown so that the relevance of the entrances can be determined with respect to the predicted value.

Retain: If the result of the classification is suspicious or if the administrator identifies the classification as erroneous, then the network $P/c_{.im}$ repeats the training by incorporating a new case and following the BackPropagation training algorithm.

$$p_r = MLP^t(c_{.im} \cup c_{n+1}) \qquad (9)$$

5   Conclusions and Results

Traditional security mechanisms for guaranteeing the integrity and confidentiality of SOAP messages do not offer protection against DoS attacks in web service environments.

This article has presented a distributed hierarchical multiagent architecture for classifying SOAP messages. The architecture was designed to exploit the distributed capacity of the agents. Additionally, an advanced classification mechanism was

designed to filter incoming SOAP messages. The proposed mechanism of classification is based on a multiagent architecture whose core is a CBR-BDI agent that incorporates a case-based reasoning engine in conjunction with a neural network of the
type Multilayer Perceptron. It is a novel mechanism that had never been used in this
type of problems. While the capability of CBR systems is limited to adapting and
learning, neural networks can offer predictions, thus turning the solution into a robust
classification mechanism with capabilities spanning from automatic learning to adaptation, and the ability to approach new changes that appear in DoS attacks patterns
contained in SOAP messages. A prototype of our proposed solution was based on a
classification mechanism and developed in order to evaluate its effectiveness. The
tests of the simulation were carried out within a small web application developed with
Java Server Page and hosted in a Apache Tomcat 6.0.18 Server by using as web
service engine, Apache Axis2 1.4.1. The tests were organized within 6 blocks with a
specific number of requests (50, 100, 150, 200, 250 and 300) that allowed evaluating
the effectiveness of the classifier agent in accordance with the gained experience.
Within the blocks were included legal and illegal requests. Figure 3 shows the results
obtained.

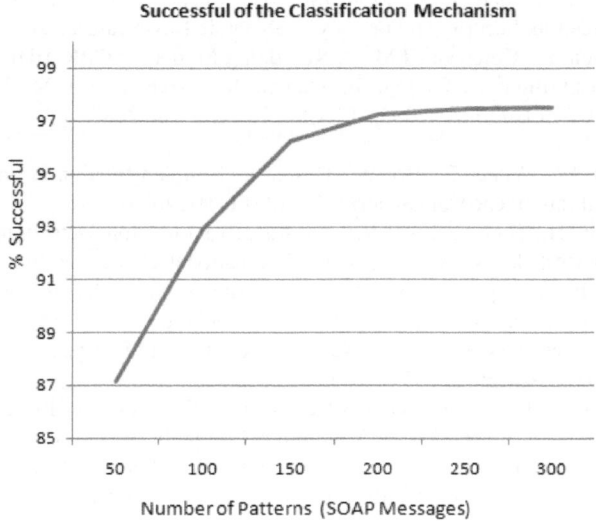

Fig. 3. Effectiveness of the classification mechanism integrated within the CBRClassifier agent
according to the number of patterns

Figure 3 shows the percentage of prediction with regards to the number of patterns
(SOAP messages) for the classification mechanism. It is clear that as the number of
patterns increases, the success rate of prediction also increases in terms of percentage.
This is influenced by the fact that we are working with CBR systems, which depend
on a larger amount of data stored in the memory of cases.

Future works are expected to develop the tools for obtaining a complete solution.
With the advantage of a distributed process for classification tasks, it would be possible to evaluate both the effectiveness of the classification mechanism, and the response time.

Acknowledgments. This development has been partially supported by the Spanish Ministry of Science project TIN2006-14630-C03-03 and The Professional Excellence Program 2006-2010 IFARHU-SENACYT-Panama.

References

1. Weerawarana, S., Curbera, F., Leymann, F., Storey, T., Ferguson, D.F.: Web Services Platform Architecture: SOAP, WSDL, WS-Policy, WS-Addressing, WS-BPEL, WS-Reliable Messaging, and More. Prentice Hall PTR, Englewood Cliffs (2005)
2. Nadalin, A., Kaler, C., Monzillo, R., Hallam-Baker, P.: Web Services Security: SOAP Message Security 1.1, WS-Security 2004 (2006)
3. Bajaj, S., Box, D., Chappell, D., Curbera, F., Daniels, G., Hallam-Baker, P., Hondo, M.: Web Services Policy Framework (WS-Policy) version 1.2 (2006)
4. Anderson, S., Bohren, J., Boubez, T., Chanliau, M., Della, G., Dixon, B.: Web Services Trust Language, WS-Trust (2004)
5. Anderson, S., Bohren, J., Boubez, T., Chanliau, M., Della-Libera, G., Dixon, B.: Web Services Secure Conversation Language (WS-SecureConversation) Version 1.1 (2004)
6. Gruschka, N., Luttenberger, N.: Protecting Web Services from DoS Attacks by SOAP Message Validation. Security and Privacy in Dynamic Environments 201, 171–182 (2006)
7. Laza, R., Pavon, R., Corchado, J.M.: A Reasoning Model for CBR_BDI Agents Using an Adaptable Fuzzy Inference System. In: Conejo, R., Urretavizcaya, M., Pérez-de-la-Cruz, J.-L. (eds.) CAEPIA/TTIA 2003. LNCS (LNAI), vol. 3040, pp. 96–106. Springer, Heidelberg (2004)
8. Loh, Y., Yau, W., Wong, C., Ho, W.: Design and Implementation of an XML Firewall. Computational Intelligence and Security 2, 1147–1150 (2006)
9. Yee, G., Shin, H., Rao, G.S.V.R.K.: An Adaptive Intrusion Detection and Prevention (ID/IP) Framework for Web Services. In: International Conference on Convergence Information Technology, pp. 528–534. IEEE Computer Society, Washington (2007)
10. Jensen, M., Gruschka, N., Herkenhoner, R., Luttenberger, N.: SOA and Web Services: New Technologies, New Standards - New Attacks. In: Fifth European Conference on Web Services-ECOWS '07, pp. 35–44 (2007)
11. Ye, X.: Countering DDoS and XDoS Attacks against Web Services. In: IEEE/IFIP International Conference on Embedded and Ubiquitous Computing, pp. 346–352 (2008)
12. Chonka, A., Zhou, W., Xiang, Y.: Defending Grid Web Services from XDoS Attacks by SOTA. In: IEEE International Conference on Pervasive Computing and Communications, pp. 1–6 (2009)
13. Carrascosa, C., Bajo, J., Julian, V., Corchado, J.M., Botti, V.: Hybrid multi-agent architecture as a real-time problem-solving model. Expert Syst. Appl. 34, 2–17 (2008)
14. Corchado, J.M., Bajo, J., Abraham, A.: GerAmi: Improving Healthcare Delivery in Geriatric Residences. IEEE Intelligent Systems 23, 19–25 (2008)
15. Fujii, K.: Jpcap - A network packet capture library for applications written in Java (2000), http://netresearch.ics.uci.edu/kfujii/jpcap/doc/index.html
16. Aamodt, A., Plaza, E.: Case-based reasoning: foundational issues, methodological variations, and system approaches. AI Commun. 7, 39–59 (1994)
17. Gallagher, M., Downs, T.: Visualization of learning in multilayer perceptron networks using principal component analysis. IEEE Transactions on Systems, Man, and Cybernetics, Part B: Cybernetics 33(1), 28–34 (2003)
18. LeCun, Y., Bottou, L., Orr, G.B., Müller, K.R.: Efficient BackProp. In: Neural Networks - Tricks of the Trade, p. 546. Springer, Heidelberg (1998)

Adding Morphological Information to a Connectionist Part-Of-Speech Tagger

Francisco Zamora-Martínez[1], María José Castro-Bleda[2],
Salvador España-Boquera[2], and Salvador Tortajada-Velert[3]

[1] Departamento de Ciencias Físicas, Matemáticas y de la Computación
Universidad CEU-Cardenal Herrera
46115 Alfara del Patriarca (Valencia), Spain
[2] Departamento de Sistemas Informáticos y Computación
[3] IBIME, Instituto de Aplicaciones de Tecnologías de la Información y de las
Comunicaciones Avanzadas (ITACA)
Universidad Politécnica de Valencia
Camino de Vera s/n, 46022 Valencia, Spain
{fzamora,mcastro,sespana,stortajada}@dsic.upv.es

Abstract. In this paper, we describe our recent advances on a novel approach to Part-Of-Speech tagging based on neural networks. Multilayer perceptrons are used following corpus-based learning from contextual, lexical and morphological information. The Penn Treebank corpus has been used for the training and evaluation of the tagging system. The results show that the connectionist approach is feasible and comparable with other approaches.

1 Motivation

The major purpose on Natural Language Processing (NLP) research is to parse and understand language. Before achieving this goal several techniques have to be developed focussing on intermediate tasks such as Part-Of-Speech (POS) tagging. POS tagging attempts to label each word in a sentence with its appropriate part of speech tag from a previously defined set of tags or categories. Thus, POS tagging helps in parsing the sentence, which is in turn useful in other NLP tasks such as information retrieval, question answering or machine translation.

POS tagging can be seen as a disambiguation task because the mapping between words and the tag-space is usually one-to-many. There are words that have more than one syntactic category. This POS tagging process tries to determine which of the tags from a finite set of categories is the most likely for a particular use of a word in a sentence. In order to decide the correct POS tag of a word there are basically two possible sources of information. The first one is the contextual information. This information is based on the observation of the different sequences of tags, where some POS sequences are common, while others are unlikely or impossible. For instance, a personal pronoun is likely to be followed by a verb rather than by a noun. The second source of information is called the lexical information and is based on the word itself since it can give

P. Meseguer, L. Mandow, and R.M. Gasca (Eds.): CAEPIA 2009, LNAI 5988, pp. 191–200, 2010.
© Springer-Verlag Berlin Heidelberg 2010

a crucial information about the correct tag. For instance, the word "*object*" can be a noun or a verb, thus the set of possible tags for this word is significantly reduced. Currently, nearly all modern taggers make use of a combination of contextual and lexical information.

Different approaches have been proposed for solving POS tagging disambiguation. The most relevant ones are ruled-based tagging [1], probabilistic models [2] or based on Hidden Markov Models [3, 4], on memory-based learning [5] and on the maximum entropy principle [6]. Hybrid approaches which combine the power of ruled-based and statistical POS taggers have been developed, like transformation-based learning [7]. Recently, support vector machines have also been developed for POS tagging with very good results [8, 9].

In the last few years, connectionist approaches to POS tagging have been increasingly investigated due to the ability of neural networks to learn the associations between words and tags and to generalize to unseen examples from a representative training data set. A connectionist approach called *Net-Tagger* performed considerably well as compared to statistical approaches in [10]; neural networks were used for syntactic disambiguation in [11]; a Kohonen network was trained using the LVQ algorithm to increase accuracy in POS tagging in [12]; feed-forward neural networks were used to generate tags for unknown languages in [13]; recurrent neural networks were used for this task in [14]; other examples are [15–17].

In the next section, the classical probabilistic model for POS tagging is presented. Then, the connectionist model is introduced in Section 2. The corpus used for training and testing the POS tagger was the well-known Penn Treebank Corpus [18], presented in Section 3. How to add morphological information is described in Section 4. The morphological features are quite straightforward: they capture suffix/prefix information of words, as well as features indicating capitalization and presence of punctuation signs in a word. The training procedure of the multilayer perceptrons is explained in Section 5. Final results are shown in Section 6 and comparisons with other methods and some conclusions are remarked in Section 7.

1.1   Probabilistic Model for POS Tagging

One of the main approaches for POS tagging tasks is based on stochastic models [19]. From this point of view, POS tagging can be defined as a maximization problem. Let $T = \{t_1, t_2, \ldots, t_{|T|}\}$ be a set of POS tags and let $\Omega = \{w_1, w_2, \ldots, w_{|\Omega|}\}$ be the vocabulary of the application. The goal is to find the sequence of POS tags that maximizes the probability associated to a sentence $w_1^n = w_1 w_2 \ldots w_n$, i.e.:

$$\hat{t}_1^n = \underset{t_1^n}{\operatorname{argmax}} P(t_1^n | w_1^n). \tag{1}$$

Using Bayes' theorem the problem is reduced to:

$$\hat{t}_1^n = \underset{t_1^n}{\operatorname{argmax}} P(w_1^n | t_1^n) P(t_1^n). \tag{2}$$

The estimation of these parameters is time consuming and some assumptions are needed in order to simplify the computation of the expression (2). For these models, it is assumed that words are independent of each other and a word's identity only depends on its tag, thus we obtain the *lexical* probabilities,

$$P(w_1^n|t_1^n) \approx \prod_{i=1}^{n} P(w_i|t_i). \tag{3}$$

Another assumption establishes that the probability of one tag to appear only depends on its predecessor tags,

$$P(t_1^n) \approx \prod_{i=1}^{n} P(t_i|t_{i-1}, t_{i-2}, \ldots, t_{i-k+1}), \tag{4}$$

if a k-gram class is considered to get the *contextual* probabilities.

With these assumptions, a typical probabilistic model following equations (2), (3) and (4) is expressed as:

$$\hat{t}_1^n \approx \operatorname*{argmax}_{t_1^n} \prod_{i=1}^{n} P(w_i|t_i)P(t_i|t_{i-1}, t_{i-2}, \ldots, t_{i-k+1}), \tag{5}$$

where $\hat{t}_1^n$ is the best estimation of POS tags for the given sentence w_1^n. The probabilistic model has some limitations: it does not model long-distance relationships and the contextual information takes into account the context on the left while the context on the right is not considered. Both limitations can be overwhelmed using artificial neural networks models, although in this paper we just considered to exploit the contextual information on the right side of the ambiguous word.

2   Connectionist Model for POS Tagging

A connectionist model for POS tagging based on a multilayer perceptron network trained with the error backpropagation algorithm was presented in a previous work [16]. In that model, both the ambiguous input word and its label-level contextual information were used to predict its POS tag. The main difference between that model and the classical probabilistic models was that future context, i.e. the context on the right, was taken into account. Thus, the input to the multilayer perceptron consisted in the tags of the words surrounding the ambiguous word to be tagged (past and future context) and the word itself. The output of the network was the probability of each tag given the input; therefore, the network learnt the following mapping:

$$F(w_i, c_i, t_i, \Theta) = \Pr(t_i|w_i, c_i, \Theta), \tag{6}$$

where Θ represents the network weights, c_i refers to the group of tags t_{i-p}, $t_{i-(p-1)}$, $\ldots$, t_{i-1}, t_{i+1}, $\ldots$, $t_{i+(f-1)}$, t_{i+f}, being p the size of the past (left)

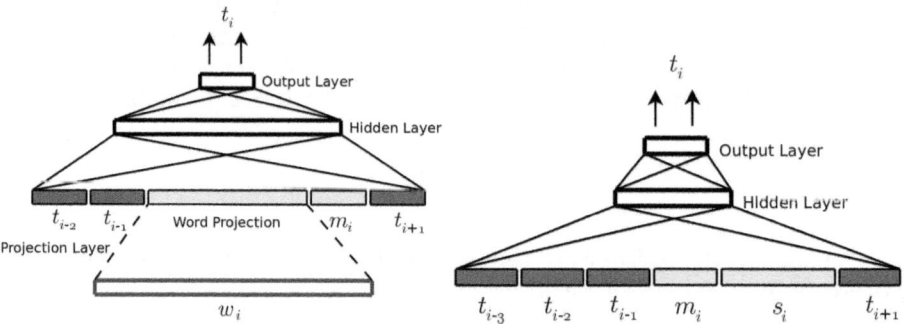

Fig. 1. MLP_{Known} and MLP_{Unk}: A multilayer perceptron for POS tagging known ambiguous words (left) and unknown words (right). The known ambiguous input word w_i is locally codified at the input of the projection layer. Morphological information is encoded as m_i and s_i. Different contexts t_j are represented.

context, and f the size of the future (right) context. The ambiguous input word w_i and each tag t_j associated to the context of w_i are locally codified, i.e. the unit representing the word (or the tag) is activated while the others are not.

In that first approach to connectionist POS tagging [16], a typical multilayer perceptron with one hidden layer was used. In following works, we added to the net a new hidden layer that performs a projection of the locally codified word to a more compact distributed codified word [17, 20]. This projection layer was required because the size of the vocabulary of ambiguous words in the Penn Treebank Corpus labeling task [17] was larger than in our previous experiments [16].

When the model is evaluated, there are words that have been never seen during training and, thus, they do not belong neither to the vocabulary of known ambiguous words nor to the vocabulary of known non-ambiguous words. These words will be called "unknown words". We experienced in our previous work [17] that unknown words present the hardest problem for the network to tag correctly. In that work, we compared two different connectionist POS tagging systems and concluded that it was better to combine two multilayer perceptrons in a single system, where one is dedicated to the known ambiguous words and the other one is specialized in unknown words (see Fig. 1). We will refer to this system as connectionist POS tagging system, the multilayer perceptron specialized in unknown words will be MLP_{Unk} and the one for known ambiguous words, MLP_{Known}.

Besides, as pointed out at the introduction, another useful source of information has been used in this work: morphological information corresponding to the input word and to the context. Thus, equation (6) is better expressed for the MLP_{Known} which is dedicated to known words as:

$$F_{Known}(w_i, m_i, c'_i, t_i, \Theta_K) = \Pr(t_i | w_i, m_i, c'_i, \Theta_K), \qquad (7)$$

m_i corresponds to morphological information related to the known ambiguous input word w_i. The context c'_i is c_i enriched to have some morphological information into account.

Table 1. Partitions from the Penn Treebank corpus for training, tuning and testing

Dataset	Directory	Num. of sentences	Num. of words	Vocabulary size
Training	00-18	38 219	912 344	34 064
Tuning	19-21	5 527	131 768	12 389
Test	22-24	5 462	129 654	11 548
Total	00-24	49 208	1 173 766	38 452

When dealing with unknown words, we can add even more relevant morphological information, and the function can be expressed as:

$$F_{Unk}(m_i, s_i, c'_i, t_i, \Theta_U) = \Pr(t_i|m_i, s_i, c'_i, \Theta_U), \tag{8}$$

where s_i corresponds to additional morphological information related to the unknown input i-th word and the context is also enriched to have some morphological information into account.

3 The Penn Treebank Corpus

The corpus used in the experiments was the well-known part of the Wall Street Journal that had been processed in the Penn Treebank Project [18]. This corpus consists of a set of English texts from the Wall Street Journal distributed in 25 directories containing 100 files with several sentences each one. The total number of running words is about one million. The whole corpus was automatically labeled with a POS tag and a syntactic labeling. The POS tag labeling consists of a set of 45 different categories. Two more tags were added as beginning and ending sentence markers, thus resulting in a total amount of 47 different POS tags. The POS tagging system was trained to deal with sentences extracted from the Penn Treebank corpus. In order to achieve this, original lines in the corpus were segmented into sentences taking the symbols ".", ";", "!", "?" as sentence boundaries. The corpus was divided in three sets: training, tuning and test. The main characteristics of these partitions are described in Table 1.

4 Morphological Information

4.1 Preprocessing

In order to reduce the dimensions of the vocabulary and to have samples of unknown words for training, we randomly partitioned the training corpus in ten parts of equal size, and words that appeared just in one partition were considered as unknown words. In this way, 1 520 unknown running words were obtained.

To eliminate erroneous tags, a POS label cut-off was set to a relative frequency of one per cent. That is, POS tags appearing in a word less than 1% of its possible tags, were eliminated. For example, the word "*are*" is ambiguous in the corpus because it appears 3 639 times like VBP and one time like NN, NNP and IN. After this preprocessing, "*are*" is not ambiguous anymore.

4.2   Adding Morphological Information

Morphological information from the input word was used to preprocess it or
was added to the input of the corresponding multilayer perceptron as expressed
previously in equations (7) and (8). Morphological information is also used in
other similar works [3, 8–10, 21]. The POS tagging system used the morphological
information as follows:

- Input words were preprocessed using two morphological filters:

  - Deleting the prefixes from the composed words (using a set of the 125
    more common English prefixes). In this way, some unknown words were
    converted to known words.
  - All the cardinal and ordinal numbers (except "one" and "second" that
    are polysemic) were replaced with the special token *CD*.

- Adding new features to the input of the neural models to obtain relevant
  morphological information to be considered in the POS tagging:

  - Three input units were added to indicate if the input word has the first
    capital letter, all caps or a subset. More than one of these input units
    can be activated, and none if the word is in lowercase letters. This is
    an important morphological characteristic and it was also added to the
    POS tags of the context in MLP_{Known} and MLP_{Unk}.
  - Another feature of the networks input is a unit indicating if the word
    has any *dash* "-".
  - Another feature of the networks input is a unit indicating if the word
    has any *point* ".".
  - Finally, a suffix analysis was done to deal with unknown words. From
    all words in the training set that share the same suffix (not necessarily a
    linguistically meaningful suffix) of some predefined maximum length (set
    to 10, according to [3]), the probability distribution of their POS tags
    was computed. This process found 709 suffixes. To reduce this number,
    an agglomerative hierarchical clustering process [22–24] was followed,
    and an empirical set of 188 clusters was chosen. Finally, a set of the 21
    most common grammatical suffixes plus a the set of the 188 automat-
    ically obtained suffixes, were added to the MLP_{Unk} input, in order to
    indicate whether or not that suffix is present in the unknown word (0 or
    1 activation for the corresponding input unit).[1]

After doing this morphological preprocessing, the vocabulary from the training
partition of the Penn Treebank corpus was fixed to 6 239 ambiguous words and
25 798 unambiguous words. Table 2 shows the number of running words of each
type in the used partitions of the Penn Treebank.

---

[1] Notice that more than one suffix can be activated for an input word. For example,
the word "*sizes*" activates two suffixes: "-es" and "-s".

Table 2. Number of ambiguous, unambiguous and unknown words in each partition after preprocessing. The vocabulary of known ambiguous words is 6 239.

Dataset	Num. of words	Unambiguous	Ambiguous	Unknown
Training	912 344	549 272	361 704	1 368
Tuning	131 768	77 347	51 292	3 129
Test	129 654	75 758	51 315	2 581
Total	1 173 766	702 377	464 311	7 078

5   Training the Connectionist POS Taggers

The MLPs used as POS classifiers were trained with the error backpropagation algorithm [25]. In order to select a good configuration for each network, a scanning of the network topology and other parameters has been performed using the tuning set. The following combinations were tested for the MLP_{Known}: a projection layer of 0, 25, 50, and 75 units, and a combination of one or two hidden layers. For the MLP_{Unk} we tested different number of training patterns and number of suffixes, along with combinations of one or two hidden layers.

The best topology and parameters of the multilayer perceptrons are shown in Table 3. Then the next step is to evaluate the impact of the amount of contextual information in the accuracy of the model. In these experiments the networks were trained like a classifier. Under this assumption, when the model is tagging a word, the past and future context are extracted from the correct tags. The results of the different combination of contextual information are shown in Table 4. The classification error rate is calculated for the tuning set of the corpus.

Table 3. Parameters of the MLP_{Known} and MLP_{Unk}, where p is the size of the left (past) context, and f is the size of the right (future) context. The size of the vocabulary of known ambiguous words is $|\Omega'| = 6\,239$ and there are $|T| = 47$ POS tags, and $|S| = 209$ suffixes. $|M| = 5$ is the morphological information associated to the input word, whereas $|M'| = 3$ is the morphological information added to the context (only capitalization information).

Parameter	MLP_{Known}	MLP_{Unk}
Input layer size	$|T + M'|(p + f) + 50 + |M|$	$|T + M'|(p + f) + |M| + |S|$
Output layer size	$|T|$	$|T|$
Projection layer size	$|\Omega'| \to 50$	–
Hidden layer(s) size	100-75	175-100
Hidden layer act. func.	Hyperbolic Tangent	
Output layer act. func.	Softmax	
Learning rate	5×10^{-3}	
Momentum	1×10^{-3}	
Weight decay	1×10^{-7}	

Table 4. POS tagging error rate (in %) for the tuning set. MLP_{Known} **error** refers to the classification error for known ambiguous words. MLP_{Unk} **error** refers to the classification error for unknown words.

<table>
<tr><td colspan="5" align="center">MLP_{Known} error</td></tr>
<tr><td></td><td colspan="4" align="center">Future</td></tr>
<tr><td>Past</td><td>2</td><td>3</td><td>4</td><td>5</td></tr>
<tr><td>2</td><td>6.30</td><td>6.26</td><td>6.25</td><td>6.31</td></tr>
<tr><td>3</td><td>6.28</td><td>6.22</td><td>6.20</td><td>6.31</td></tr>
<tr><td>4</td><td>6.28</td><td>6.27</td><td>6.28</td><td>6.31</td></tr>
</table>

<table>
<tr><td colspan="4" align="center">MLP_{Unk} error</td></tr>
<tr><td></td><td colspan="3" align="center">Future</td></tr>
<tr><td>Past</td><td>1</td><td>2</td><td>3</td></tr>
<tr><td>1</td><td>12.56</td><td>12.46</td><td>12.40</td></tr>
<tr><td>2</td><td>12.27</td><td>12.08</td><td>12.37</td></tr>
<tr><td>3</td><td>12.59</td><td>11.95</td><td>12.24</td></tr>
<tr><td>4</td><td>12.72</td><td>12.34</td><td>12.46</td></tr>
</table>

For the experiments we have used a toolkit for pattern recognition tasks developed by our research group [26]. The best configuration found for experiments with known ambiguous words was a past context of 3 labels and a future context of 4 labels, and for the experiments with unknown words, the best configuration was achieved with a context of 3 past labels and 2 future labels.

6   Connectionist POS Tagger Performance

The connectionist POS tagging system is composed of two multilayer perceptrons, which are combined: MLP_{Known} is dedicated to known ambiguous words, i.e., ambiguous words included in the training vocabulary, and MLP_{Unk}, which is specialized in unknown words. The latter is trained with the words selected as unknown during the preprocessing of the corpus (see Section 4) plus the words that appeared less than 4 times. Finally, the whole connectionist POS tagging system can be expressed as:

$$F(w_i, m_i, s_i, c'_i, t_i, \Theta_K, \Theta_U) = \begin{cases} 0, & \text{if } t_i \notin T_{w_i}, \\ 1, & \text{if } T_{w_i} = \{t_i\}, \\ F_{know}(w_i, m_i, c'_i, t_i, \Theta_K), & \text{if } w_i \in \Omega', \\ F_{Unk}(m_i, s_i, c'_i, t_i, \Theta_U), & \text{in other case.} \end{cases} \quad (9)$$

where Ω' is the vocabulary of known ambiguous words, T_{w_i} is the set of possible POS labels of the input word w_i (information from the training partition). Observe that T_{w_i} is the set of open labels (nouns, verbs, adverbs and adjectives) when the input word is unknown.

The POS tagging performance for the whole system for the tuning set and test sets is 3.2% and 3.3%, respectively. It is important to observe that non-ambiguous words (words with $T_{w_i} = \{t_i\}$) implies a POS tagging error of 0.5% in the system, due to label errors in the test and that words that appear to be non-ambiguous words in training can be, in fact, ambiguous words. It is possible to compare these results with [17], where our system without morphological features obtains a 4.3% of total POS tagging test error, worse than the 3.3% test result presented here.

Table 5. POS tagging performance (in %) for the test set. Other approximations: SVMs (Support Vector Machines), MT (Machine Translation techniques), TnT (Statistic Models), RANN (Recurrent Neural Networks). **KnownAmb** refers to the disambiguation error for known ambiguous words. **Unknown** refers to the disambiguation error for unknown words. **Total** is the total disambiguation error, with ambiguous, non-ambiguous, and unknown words.

Model	KnownAmb	Unknown	Total
SVMs [9]	6.1	11.0	2.8
MT [21]	-	23.5	3.5
TnT [3]	7.8	14.1	3.5
NetTagger [10]	-	-	3.8
HMM Tagger [27]	-	-	5.8
RANN [14]	-	-	8.0
Our approach	6.7	10.3	3.3

7   Discussion

To evaluate the system, a comparison with other approaches is necessary. A lot of works have used the same corpus and the same partitions. A selection of the best systems is shown in Table 5, compared with the performance of our approach. The results are shown in terms of disambiguation error.

Our best result is a 3.3% of total disambiguation error. This result is very close to the best, achieved with SVMs [9]. Our immediate goal is to build a POS labels graph as the result of classifying the ambiguous words into POS labels with the connectionist POS tagger. A language model of POS tags can be used in order to help a Viterbi search to find the best tag's path in the graph.

Acknowledgements

This work has been partially supported by the Spanish Ministerio de Educación y Ciencia (TIN2006-12767, TIN2008-06856-C05-02, PTQ-08-01-06802).

References

1. Voutilainen, A.: Handcrafted rules. In: Syntactic Wordclass Tagging, pp. 217–246. H. van Halteren (1999)
2. Merialdo, B.: Tagging English Text with a Probabilistic Model. Comp. Linguistics 20(2), 155–171 (1994)
3. Brants, T.: TnT: a statistical part-of-speech tagger. In: Proc. of the 6th Conf. on Applied Natural Language Processing, pp. 224–231 (2000)
4. Pla, F., Molina, A.: Improving Part-of-Speech Tagging using Lexicalized HMMs. Natural Language Engineering 10(2), 167–190 (2004)
5. Daelemans, W., et al.: MBT: A Memory-Based Part-of-Speech Tagger Generator. In: Proc. of the 4th Workshop on Very Large Corpora, pp. 14–27 (1996)
6. Ratnaparkhi, A.: A Maximum Entropy Part-Of-Speech Tagger. In: 1st Conf. on Empirical Methods in Natural Language Processing, pp. 133–142 (1996)

7. Brill, E.: Transformation-Based Error-Driven Learning and Natural Language Processing: A Case Study in Part-of-Speech Tagging. Comp. Linguistics 21(4) (1995)
8. Giménez, J., Márquez, L.: Fast and accurate Part-of-Speech tagging: the SVM approach revisited. In: Proc. of the 4th RANLP, pp. 153–163 (2003)
9. Giménez, J., Márquez, L.: SVMTool: A general POS tagger generator based on Support Vector Machines. In: Proc. of the Fourth Conf. on Language Resources and Evaluation, pp. 43–46 (2004)
10. Schmid, H.: Part-of-Speech tagging with neural networks. In: Proc. of COLING 1994, pp. 172–176 (1994)
11. Benello, J., Mackie, A., Anderson, J.: Syntactic category disambiguation with neural networks. Computer Speech and Language 3, 203–217 (1989)
12. Martín Valdivia, M.: Algoritmo LVQ aplicado a tareas de Procesamiento del Lenguaje Natural. PhD thesis, Universidad de Málaga (2004)
13. Marques, N., Pereira, G.: A POS-Tagger generator for Unknown Languages. Procesamiento del Lenguaje Natural 27, 199–207 (2001)
14. Pérez-Ortiz, J., Forcada, M.: Part-of-speech tagging with recurrent neural networks. In: Proc. of the Int. Joint Conf. on Neural Networks, pp. 1588–1592 (2001)
15. Ahmed Raju, S., Chandrasekhar, P., Prasad, M.: Application of multilayer perceptron network for tagging parts-of-speech. In: Language Engineering Conf. (2002)
16. Tortajada, S., Castro, M.J., Pla, F.: Part-of-Speech tagging based on artificial neural networks. In: 2nd Language & Technology Conf. Proc., pp. 414–418 (2005)
17. Zamora-Martínez, F., et al.: A connectionist approach to Part-Of-Speech Tagging. In: Int. Conf. on Neural Computation (2009)
18. Marcus, M.P., Santorini, B., Marcinkiewicz, M.A.: Building a large annotated corpus of English: The Penn Treebank. Comp. Linguistics 19(2), 313–330 (1993)
19. Jurafsky, D., Martin, J.H.: Speech and Language Processing. Prentice Hall, Englewood Cliffs (2000)
20. Zamora, F., Castro, M., España, S.: Fast evaluation of connectionist language models. In: Cabestany, J., Sandoval, F., Prieto, A., Corchado, J.M. (eds.) IWANN 2009. LNCS, vol. 5517, pp. 144–151. Springer, Heidelberg (2009)
21. Gascó, G., Sánchez, J.A.: Part-of-Speech Tagging Based on Machine Translation Techniques. In: Martí, J., Benedí, J.M., Mendonça, A.M., Serrat, J. (eds.) IbPRIA 2007. LNCS, vol. 4477, pp. 257–264. Springer, Heidelberg (2007)
22. Jain, A.K., Murty, M.N., Flynn, P.J.: Data clustering: a review. ACM Comput. Surv. 31(3), 264–323 (1999)
23. Mollineda, R.A., Vidal, E.: A relative approach to hierarchical clustering. In: Pattern Recognition and Applications, vol. 56, pp. 19–28. IOS Press, Amsterdam (2000)
24. Zamora-Martínez, F., España-Boquera, S., Castro-Bleda, M.: Behaviour-based Clustering of Neural Networks applied to Document Enhancement. In: Sandoval, F., Prieto, A.G., Cabestany, J., Graña, M. (eds.) IWANN 2007. LNCS, vol. 4507, pp. 144–151. Springer, Heidelberg (2007)
25. Rumelhart, D., Hinton, G., Williams, R.: Learning internal representations by error propagation. In: Rumelhart, D.E., McClelland, J.L. (eds.) PDP: Computational models of cognition and perception, I, pp. 319–362. MIT Press, Cambridge (1986)
26. España, S., et al.: Efficient BP Algorithms for General Feedforward Neural Networks. In: Mira, J., Álvarez, J.R. (eds.) IWINAC 2007. LNCS, vol. 4527, pp. 327–336. Springer, Heidelberg (2007)
27. Cutting, D., Kupiec, J., Pedersen, J., Sibun, P.: A practical part-of-speech tagger. In: Proc. of the 3th Conf. on Applied Natural Language Processing, pp. 133–140 (1992)

A Look-Ahead B&B Search for Cost-Based Planning

Raquel Fuentetaja, Daniel Borrajo, and Carlos Linares López

Departamento de Informática, Universidad Carlos III de Madrid
{rfuentet,clinares}@inf.uc3m.es, dborrajo@ia.uc3m.es

Abstract. This paper focuses on heuristic cost-based planning. We propose a combination of a heuristic designed to deal with this planning model together with the usage of look-ahead states based on relaxed plans to speed-up the search. The search algorithm is a modified Best-First Search (*BFS*) performing Branch and Bound (B&B) to improve the last solution found. The objective of the work is to obtain a good balance between the quality of the plans and the search time. The experiments show that the combination is effective in most of the evaluated domains.

1 Introduction

Planning has achieved significant progress in the last years. This progress is mainly due to powerful heuristic search planners. However, the main efforts have focused on obtaining the solutions faster. In comparison to their predecessors, current planners can solve much more complex problems in considerably less time. These advances have motivated the planning research community to move towards obtaining quality plans maintaining a good balance between quality and speed. In fact, in the last International Planning Competition (IPC-2008) there was a track for STRIPS planning with action costs, in which the evaluation criterion was the quality obtained in a fixed time bound.

Usually, in cost-based planning the quality of plans is inversely proportional to their cost. Most of planners able to deal with cost-based planning have been developed from 2003 until now, as METRIC-FF [6], SIMPLANNER [10], SAPA [4], SGPlan5 [3], and LPG-td(quality) [5]; or the new planners participating in the last competition where LAMA [9] was the winner. Most of these planners use a combination of heuristics together with a search mechanism. One of the problems of applying heuristic search in cost-based planning is that existing heuristics are in general more imprecise than heuristics for classical planning. It is more difficult to estimate costs than estimating number of actions, because the magnitude of the errors the heuristic commits can be much larger, given that costs of actions can be very different. For this reason, the simple combination of a cost-based heuristic with a search algorithm is not enough. Depending on the search algorithm either we can solve few problems or obtain bad quality plans. Some additional technique is needed to help the search algorithm. For example, in the LAMA planner, this technique involves the use of *landmarks* and a combination of heuristics. In this paper, we apply the idea of look-ahead states [11]. The use of look-ahead states reduces significantly the search time in classical planning but has been very little explored in cost-based planning [1]. However, there are multiple ways to implement the idea of look-ahead states: different methods can be defined to compute relaxed

P. Meseguer, L. Mandow, and R.M. Gasca (Eds.): CAEPIA 2009, LNAI 5988, pp. 201–211, 2010.

plans and to compute look-ahead states from relaxed plans. Also different search algorithms can be used. In this paper we test one such combinations which provides good results.

This paper is organized as follows: first we define formally the cost-based planning model. Then, we explain the method to boost the search using look-ahead states. This involves to define how look-ahead states are obtained and how they are used in a search algorithm that takes into account cost information. Finally, we include our experimental results and some conclusions.

2   The Cost-Based Planning Model

We consider a cost-based planning problem as a STRIPS planning problem with action costs. A cost-based planning problem is a tuple $(\mathcal{P}, \mathcal{A}, \mathcal{I}, \mathcal{G})$, where $\mathcal{P}$ is a set of propositions, $\mathcal{A}$ is a set of grounded actions (throughout the paper, we will refer to grounded actions simply as actions), and $\mathcal{I} \subseteq \mathcal{P}$ and $\mathcal{G} \subseteq \mathcal{P}$ are the initial state and the set of goals respectively. As in STRIPS planning, each action $a \in \mathcal{A}$ is represented as three sets: $pre(a) \subseteq \mathcal{P}$, $add(a) \subseteq \mathcal{P}$ and $del(a) \subseteq \mathcal{P}$ (preconditions, adds and deletes). Each action also has a fixed cost, $cost(a)$.[1] A plan $\alpha = \{a_1, a_2, \ldots, a_n\}$ is an ordered set of grounded actions $a_i \in \mathcal{A}$, that achieves a goal state from the initial state $\mathcal{I}$ ($\mathcal{G} \subseteq apply(a_n, apply(a_{n-1}, \ldots apply(a_1, \mathcal{I}) \ldots)))$[2] and whose cost is $cost(\alpha) = \sum_{a_i \in \alpha} cost(a_i)$.

An optimal plan for solving a cost-based planning problem is a plan α^* with the minimum cost. Obtaining optimal plans, as in STRIPS planning, is usually far from being computationally feasible in most medium-size problems. Though there are also optimal planners, usually, cost-based planners combine a non-admissible heuristic with a heuristic search algorithm and obtain suboptimal solutions. In this paper we also propose a suboptimal planner.

3   Using Look-Ahead States in Cost-Based Planning

The work reported in [11], applied in the YAHSP planner, shows that the use of look-ahead states based on Relaxed Plans (*RPs*) in classical planning reduces significantly the number of evaluated states (and therefore the search time) of a forward heuristic planner. However, this reduction usually implies an increase in plan length, even using a complete *BFS* algorithm. The success of the approach for reducing the search time, strongly depends on the quality of the relaxed plans (i.e the similarity between the relaxed plan and the real plan). At the same time, the quality of the *RPs* strongly depends on the planning domain. As it was shown by the experiments in [11], *RPs* have less quality in domains where there are many subgoals interactions or with limited resources, though usually these domains are also difficult for the rest of planners. [11]

---

[1] The conceptual planning model defined does not need numerical state variables, though in the standard language for planning (PDDL), action costs are usually expressed using them.

[2] The function $apply(a_i, S_j)$ returns the state after applying action a_i in state S_j.

proposes some heuristic considerations in order to improve the quality of the *RPs* and to compute the look-ahead state, considering *RPs* similar to the ones computed by the FF planner [7].

In this paper we wanted to test whether the idea of look-ahead states works in cost-based planning, where the objective is to find *good* quality solutions. An important issue is to obtain relaxed plans sensitive to cost information. Given that relaxed plans are the basis to generate look-ahead states, and we pretend to obtain good quality plans, the relaxed plan should be a good guidance not only to obtain a solution but to obtain a *good* solution. We initially discarded the method of METRIC-FF because the relaxed plan is the same built for the problem without costs. Instead, we have chosen the heuristic explained below, though any other heuristic whose computation produces a relaxed plan sensitive to costs can be applied.

3.1   A Cost-Based Heuristic

To compute the heuristic, we build the relaxed planning graph in increasing levels of cost. The algorithm (detailed in Figure 1) receives the state to be evaluated, s, the goal set, $\mathcal{G}$, and the relaxed domain actions, $\mathcal{A}^+$. Then, it follows the philosophy of the Dijkstra algorithm: from all actions whose preconditions have become true in any Relaxed Planning Graph (*RPG*) level before, generate the next action level by applying those actions whose cumulative cost is minimum. The minimum cumulative cost of actions in an action layer i, is associated with the next propositional layer (that contains the effects of those actions). This cost is denoted as $cost\_limit_{i+1}$ (initially $cost\_limit_0 = 0$). The algorithm maintains an open list of applicable actions (*OpenApp*) not previously applied. At each level i, all new applicable actions are included in *OpenApp*. Each new action in this list includes its cumulative cost, defined as the cost of executing the action, $cost(a)$, plus the cost of supporting the action, i.e. the cost to achieve the preconditions. Here the support cost of an action is defined as the cost limit of the previous propositional layer, $cost\_limit_i$, that represents the cost of the most costly precondition (i.e it is a *max* cost propagation process). Actions with minimum cumulative cost at each iteration are extracted from *OpenApp* and included in the corresponding action level, A_i, i.e. only actions with minimum cumulative cost are executed. The next proposition layer P_{i+1} is defined as usual, including the add effects of actions in A_i. The process finishes with success, returning a Relaxed Planning Graph (*RPG*), when all goals are true in a proposition layer. Otherwise, when *OpenApp* is the empty set, it finishes with failure. In such a case, the heuristic value of the evaluated state is ∞.

Once we have a *RPG* we extract a *RP* using an algorithm similar to the one applied in METRIC-FF [6]. Applying the same tie breaking policy in the extraction procedure, and unifying some details, the *RPs* we obtain could be obtained with the basic cost-propagation process of SAPA with *max* propagation and ∞-look-ahead, as described in [2]. However, the algorithm to build the *RPG* in SAPA follows the idea of a breadth-first search with cost propagation instead of Dijkstra. The main difference is that our algorithm guarantees the minimum cost for each proposition at the first propositional level containing the proposition.

Finally, the heuristic value of the evaluated state is computed as the sum of action costs for the actions in the *RP*. Since we generate a relaxed plan, we can use the *helpful*

$$
\begin{aligned}
&\textbf{function } \text{compute\_RPG\_hlevel } (s, \mathcal{G}, \mathcal{A}^+)\\
&\textbf{let } i = 0;\ P_0 = s;\ OpenApp = \emptyset;\ cost\_limit_0 = 0;\\
&\textbf{while } G \not\subseteq P_i \textbf{ do}\\
&\qquad OpenApp = OpenApp \cup \left\{ a \in \mathcal{A}^+ \setminus \underset{j<i}{\cup} A_j \mid pre(a) \subseteq P_i \right\}\\
&\qquad \textbf{forall } \text{new action in } OpenApp \textbf{ do } cum\_cost(a) = cost(a) + cost\_limit_i\\
&\qquad A_i = \left\{ a \mid a \in \underset{a \in OpenApp}{\arg\min}\ cum\_cost(a) \right\}\\
&\qquad cost\_limit_{i+1} = \underset{a \in OpenApp}{\min}\ cum\_cost(a)\\
&\qquad P_{i+1} = P_i \underset{a \in A_i}{\cup}\ add(a)\\
&\qquad \textbf{if } OpenApp = \emptyset \textbf{ then return } \text{fail}\\
&\qquad OpenApp = OpenApp \setminus A_i\\
&\qquad i = i + 1\\
&\textbf{return } P_0, A_0, P_1, ..., P_{i-1}, A_{i-1}, P_i
\end{aligned}
$$

Fig. 1. Algorithm for building the *RPG*

actions applied in [6] to select the most promising successors in the search. Helpful actions are the applicable actions in the evaluated state that add at least one proposition required by an action of the relaxed plan and generated by an applicable action in it.

3.2   Considerations for Computing the Look-Ahead State

Look-ahead states are obtained by successively applying the actions in the *RP*. There are several heuristic criteria we apply to obtain a good look-ahead state. Some of these considerations have been adopted from Vidal's work in the classical planning case [11], as: (1) we first build the *RP* ignoring all actions deleting top level goals. Relaxed actions have no deletes. So, when an action in the *RP* deletes a top-level goal, probably there will not be another posterior action in the *RP* for generating it. In this case, the heuristic value will be probably a bad estimate; and (2) we generate the look-ahead state using as many actions as possible from the *RP*. This allows to boost the search as much as possible. We do not use other techniques applied in classical planning as the method to replace one *RP* action with another domain action, when no more *RP* actions can be applied [11]. Initially, we wanted to test whether the search algorithm itself is able to repair *RPs* through search.

Determining the *best* order to execute the actions in the *RP* is not an easy task. One can apply the actions in the same order they appear in the *RP*. However, the *RP* comes from a graph built considering that actions are applicable in parallel and they have no deletes. So, following the order in the *RP* can generate plans with bad quality. The reason is that they may have many *useless* actions: actions applied to achieve facts other actions delete. We have the intuition that delaying the application of actions as much as possible (until the moment their effects are required) can alleviate this problem. So, we perform a process of value propagation for actions in the *RP*, their preconditions and effects. The value associated to a proposition represents the level in the *RPG* the proposition is required (we have higher values for propositions required later). The value v_g for each top level goal g is the index of the first level in the *RPG* containing the goal. Then, values are propagated backwards from effects to actions and from actions to preconditions as Figure 2 shows.

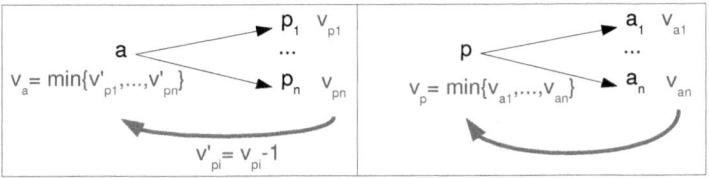

Fig. 2. Value propagation process

Values of actions (v_a) represent the level where their preconditions are required, that is the level where their effects are required minus one. Thus, every effect propagates to the action its level minus one, and then the value for the action is computed as the minimum. Values of propositions (v_p) are the minimum value of the actions where they are preconditions. We use the values v_a of each action in the *RP* in the generation of the look-ahead state for giving priority to actions with lower v_a values, as explained below.

The Figure 3 shows a high-level algorithm describing the whole process for computing the look-ahead state. In the outer *while* the *current_order* is initialized to the minimum v_a value for the *RP* actions. Then, the algorithm execute an applicable

---

function compute_lookahead (*node*)
let *parent* = *node*; *new_state* = **true**
if (*length*(*node.RP*) < 2 OR *length*(*node.RP*) = ∞) **return** *fail*
while *new_state* **do**
    new_state = **false**
    current_order = *min_v$_a$*(*node.RP*);
    while *current_order* ≤ *max_v$_a$*(*node.RP*) **do**
        forall *action* = next_not_applied (*node.RP, current_order*)
            if applicable(*parent, action*) **then**
                if *not*(expensive_repeated_state(*parent, action*)) **then**
                    parent = apply(*parent, action*)
                    new_state = **true**
            else
                nrep_states = *nrep_states* + 1
                if *nrep_states* < 10 **then**
                    deactivate(*action*)
                    compute_RP_hlevel(*parent*)
                    return compute_lookahead(*parent*)
                else return *fail*
        if not *new_state* **then** *current_order*++
if *parent* ≠ *node* **return** *parent*
else return *fail*

Fig. 3. High-level algorithm for computing the look-ahead state

action in the current state (*parent*) with v_a=*current_order*, updating the current state. This is done for each action with v_a=*current_order*. If no action with this v_a value can be applied (i.e. no *new_state* is generated), *current_order* is incremented by one. Otherwise, the algorithm continues in the outer *while* and resets newly *current_order* to the minimum v_a value.

In some cases the execution of the actions in the *RP* can lead to a repeated state, s. We prune s if it has a higher *g-value* than the existing one. Then, instead of taking as current state the parent of the pruned one, we prefer to generate a new relaxed plan from this previous state, but ignoring the last action in the planning graph (i.e. the action that generates the repeated state). However, we do not want to spend much time doing this, so we limit to 10 the number of times a new relaxed plan is built to avoid a repeated state (variable $nrep\_states$ is initialized to 0 each time the algorithm is called from the search algorithm). This number has been chosen empirically.

3.3   The Search Algorithm

Usually Best-First Search (BFS) algorithms are more adequate for finding near-optimal solutions than local search algorithms as for example Enforced Hill Climbing [7]. Also, as they have memory, they can be easily extended to obtain better solutions systematically, just by continue searching. For this reasons the search algorithm we employ is a *weighted-BFS* with evaluation function $f(n) = g(n) + \omega \cdot h(n)$, modified in the following aspects: first, the algorithm performs a Branch and Bound search. Instead of stopping when the first solution is found, it attempts to improve this solution: the cost of the last solution plan found is used as a bound such that all states whose *g-value* is higher than this cost bound are pruned. As the heuristic is non-admissible we prune by *g-values* to preserve completeness; second, the algorithm uses three lists: the *open* list, and two secondary lists (the *sec-ha* list, and the *sec-non-ha* list). Nodes are evaluated when included in *open*, and each node saves its relaxed plan. As aforementioned, relaxed plans are first built ignoring all actions deleting top-level goals (when this produces an ∞ heuristic value, the node is re-evaluated considering all actions). When a node is extracted from *open*, its look-ahead state is included in the *open* list, its helpful successors are included in the *sec-ha* list, and its non-helpful successors in the *sec-non-ha* list. Each time a new (non repeated) look-ahead state is found the algorithm continues extracting the next node from *open*. Otherwise, if there are nodes in *sec-ha*, they are inserted into *open*. However, if *sec-ha* is empty, all nodes in *sec-non-ha* are included in *open*. This algorithm delays the inclusion in *open* of other successors of the same node distinct of the look-ahead state. Usually, the look-ahead state has a *g-value* higher than the other direct successors, causing a worse *f-value*. However we want to give the opportunity to the search algorithm to expand first the look-ahead state as it can facilitate to find a fast solution, saving heuristic evaluations. Finally, repeated states with higher *g-values* are pruned. The algorithm finishes when *open* is empty. Figure 4 shows a high-level description of the search algorithm (for the sake of simplicity the algorithm does not include the repeated states prune and the *cost_bound* prune for the Branch and Bound).

```
function BB-LBFS ()
let cost_bound = ∞; plans = ∅; open = I; sec_ha = ∅; sec_non_ha = ∅
while open ≠ ∅ do
    node ← pop_best_node(open)
    if goal_state(node) then /* solution found */
        plans ← plans ∪ {node.plan}
        cost_bound = cost(node.plan)
    else
        lookahead = compute_lookahead(node)
        sec_ha ← sec_ha ∪ helpful_successors(node)
        sec_non_ha ← sec_non_ha ∪ non_helpful_successors(node)
        if lookahead then
            open ← open ∪ {lookahead}
        else if sec_ha then
            open ← open ∪ sec_ha
            sec_ha = ∅
        else
            open ← open ∪ sec_non_ha
            sec_non_ha = ∅
```

Fig. 4. High-level BB-LBFS algorithm

4   Experimental Results

We have implemented the ideas in this paper in a planner based on the code of METRIC-FF, which we call CBP *(Cost-Based Planner)*. This planner allows cost-based planning using different heuristics and search algorithms. We have used some numeric domains from IPC3 and IPC5, excluding all numerical burden not related to the action costs. For uniformity, we modified the problems of the same domain so that all have the same metric expression. The considered domains are: *Zenotravel, Satellite, Driverlog, Depots* and *Pipesworld*. We also use three of the domains developed by E. Keyder and H. Geffner for planning with action costs [8]: the *Travelling, Assignment* and *Minimum Spanning Tree* domains. We contrast the quality of the obtained plans in several time stamps: 5, 25, 125, 625 and 1800 seconds. We use the following configurations in order to determine the adequacy of the application of look-ahead states in cost-based planning: (1) *bbl-bfs* is the configuration explained in the paper with B&B search and look-ahead states, with $\omega = 3$; [3] and (2) *bb-bfs* is the same configuration but without using look-ahead states. Besides, in order to know how competitive the approach is, we compare also with other cost-based planners. We use the planners LPG-td(quality), that is known to perform quite well; and METRIC-FF since it is the base of our code. In four domains we also compare with LAMA. In the other domains, LAMA is not included because the computation of action costs uses arithmetic expressions in the increase effects that LAMA does not support. Since LPG-td(quality) is stochastic we ran the planner five times, plotting the median, as its authors usually do.

---

[3] This is the ω used in Vidal's work [11].

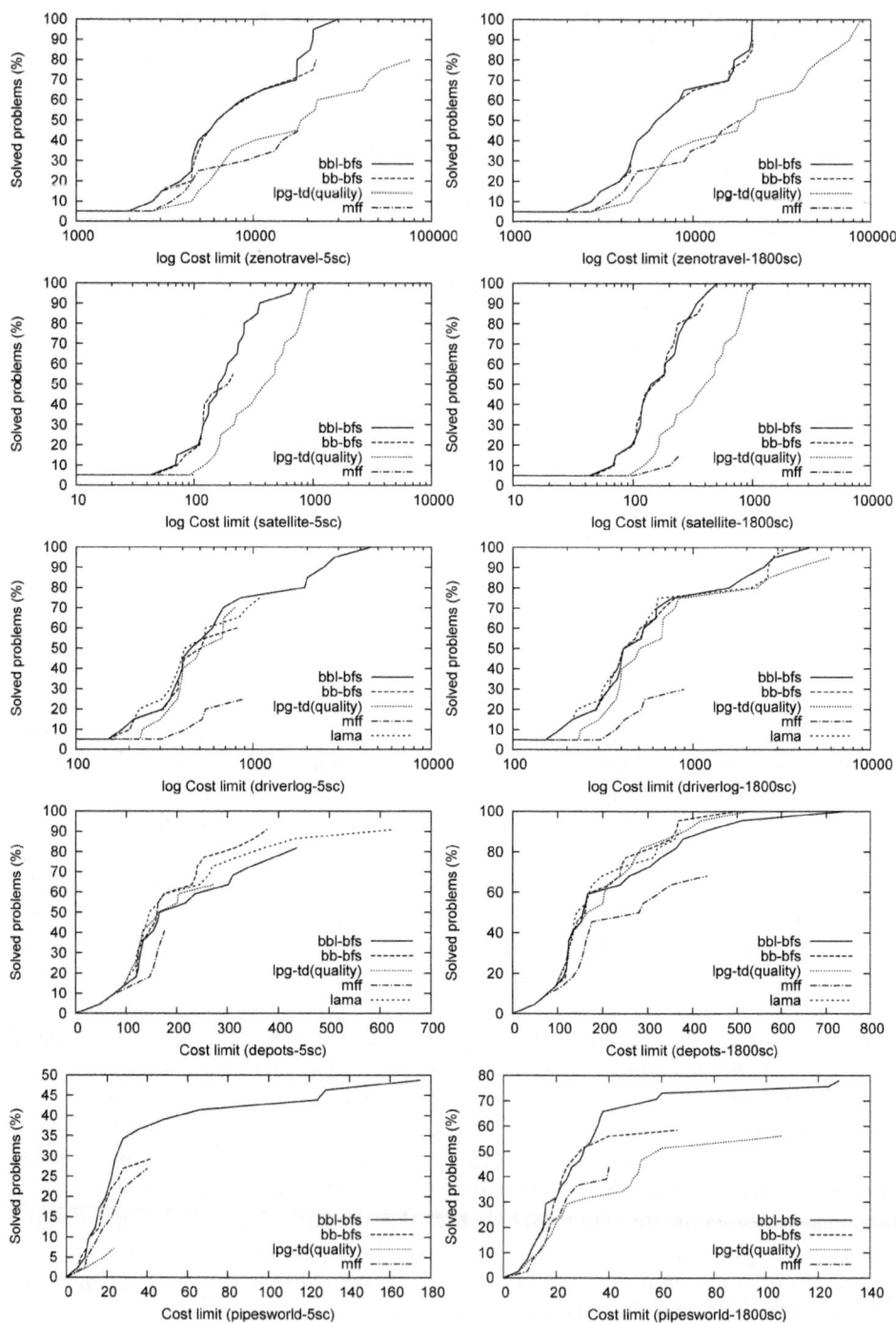

Fig. 5. Some of the experimental results (I)

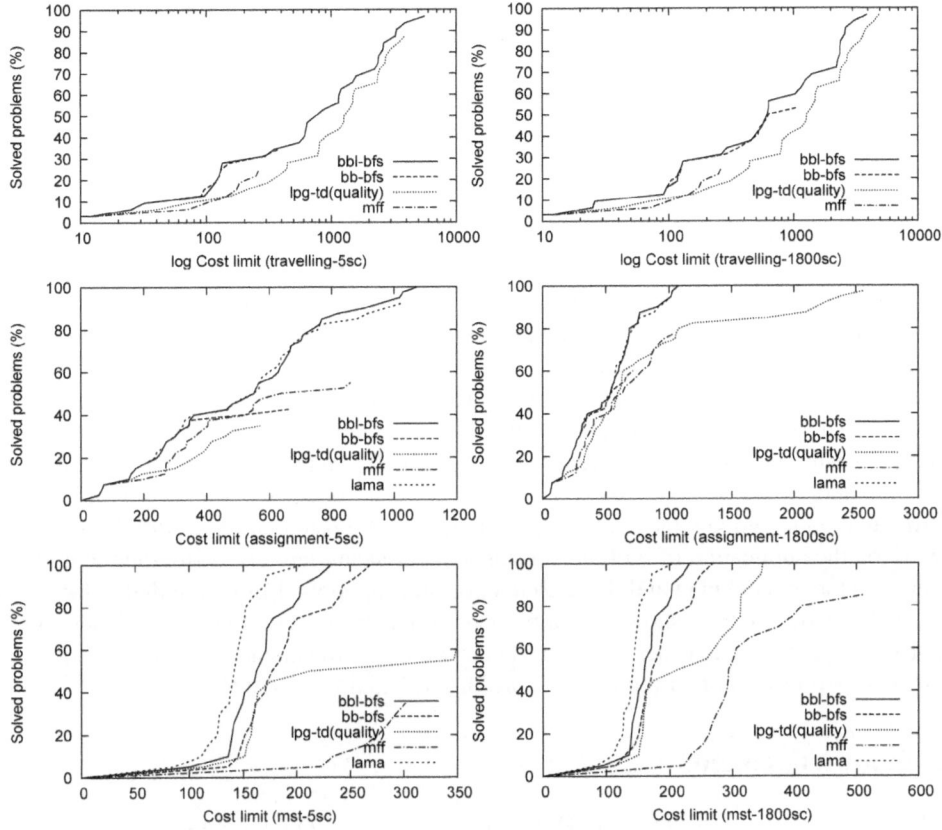

Fig. 6. Some of the experimental results (II)

Results in the first and last time stamps are shown in Figures 5 and 6. Due to lack of space, other time stamps cannot be shown. The graphics show the percentage of solved problems with plan cost lower than the one indicated by the x-axis.[4] Only configurations achieving the 100% solve all the problems. From the results, the following general conclusions can be extracted: in very small time bounds, the use of look-ahead states (*bbl-bfs*) allows to solve many more problems than the same search without using look-aheads (*bb-bfs*), maintaining the quality or even improving it. The exception is the *Depots* domain, in which *bbl-bfs* performs worse than *bb-bfs* in quality in all time stamps, while the number of solved problems is very similar. As the time progresses, both algorithms solve more problems. In easy domains as *Zenotravel* and *Satellite* good solutions are found quickly, so the available time does not improve them very much. At the last time stamp, in some domains, as in *Zenotravel*, *Satellite* and *Driverlog*, qualities tend to be similar. However *bbl-bfs* solves more problems (in *Driverlog* a 25% more). In the other domains, *bbl-bfs* clearly outperforms *bb-bfs*. The only exception is *Depots*. This domain is characterised by a high level of interacting subgoals. In such types of

---

[4] For the sake of clarity some results are presented in logarithmic scale.

domains *RPs* have poor quality, and the use a look-ahead strategy based on *RPs* is less adequate. Regarding the performance of the other planners, *bbl-bfs* outperforms LPG in all domains but in *Depots*. In small time bounds it outperforms also LAMA in *Driverlog* and *Assingment*, but at the last time stamps results in *Driverlog* and *Assingment* are very similar, while in *Depots* LAMA behaves better. In *Mst*, LAMA is the best planner in all time stamps. On the other hand, METRIC-FF is clearly outperformed in all time stamps.

5   Conclusions

This paper introduces an approach for dealing with cost-based planning that involves the use of look-ahead states to boost the search, based on a relaxed plan graph heuristic that reasons about costs; and a search algorithm that tries to improve each solution found. The experiments show that the approach is effective for cost-based planning, offering a good trade-off between quality and time in most of the evaluated domains. In domains where the are many interacting subgoals, *RPs* have not good enough quality and the approach is less adequate. The paper also introduces several considerations in order to obtain a good look-ahead state from a given relaxed plan that extends previous work on the application of look-ahead states in classical planning. Also, the method to generate the relaxed plan and the search algorithm we apply differ from that work.

In this paper we have shown the approach is competitive. Future work includes comparing the technique to order the relaxed plan with a vanilla method to test its adequacy, and comparing with other planning algorithms as Vidal's or LAMA.

Acknowledgements

The authors thank E. Keyder and H. Geffner for some of the domains used in this paper. This work has been partially supported by the Spanish MICINN project TIN2008-06701-C03-03 and the UC3M-CAM project CCG08-UC3M/TIC-4141.

References

1. Benton, J., van den Briel, M., Kambhampati, S.: A hibrid linear programming and relaxed plan heuristic for partial satisfaction planning problems. In: Proc. of the 17th ICAPS, pp. 34–41 (2007)
2. Bryce, D., Kambhampati, S.: How to skin a planning graph for fun and profit: A tutorial on planning graph based reachability heuristics. AI Magazine 28(1), 47–83 (2007)
3. Chen, Y., Hsu, C., Wah, B.: Temporal planning using subgoal partitioning and resolution in SGPlan. JAIR 26, 323–369 (2006)
4. Do, M.B., Kambhampati, S.: Sapa: A scalable multi-objective heuristic metric temporal planner. JAIR 20, 155–194 (2003)
5. Gerevini, A., Saetti, A., Serina, I.: Planning with numerical expressions in LPG. In: Proc. of the 16th ECAI, pp. 667–671 (2004)
6. Hoffmann, J.: The Metric-FF planning system: Translating "ignoring delete lists" to numeric state variables. JAIR 20, 291–341 (2003)
7. Hoffmann, J., Nebel, B.: The FF planning system: Fast plan generation through heuristic search. JAIR 14, 253–302 (2001)

 8. Keyder, E., Geffner, H.: Heuristics for planning with action costs revisited. In: Proc. of the 18th ECAI (2008)
 9. Richter, S., Helmert, M., Westphal, M.: Landmarks revisited. In: Proc. of the 23rd AAAI, pp. 975–982 (2008)
10. Sapena, O., Onaindía, E.: Handling numeric criteria in relaxed planning graphs. In: Lemaître, C., Reyes, C.A., González, J.A. (eds.) IBERAMIA 2004. LNCS (LNAI), vol. 3315, pp. 114–123. Springer, Heidelberg (2004)
11. Vidal, V.: A lookahead strategy for heuristic search planning. In: Proc. of the 14th ICAPS, pp. 150–159 (2004)

A Tabu Search Algorithm to Minimize Lateness in Scheduling Problems with Setup Times

Miguel A. González, Camino R. Vela, and Ramiro Varela

A.I. Centre and Department of Computer Science,
University of Oviedo, (Spain) Campus de Viesques s/n, Gijón, 33271, Spain
raist@telecable.es, {crvela,ramiro}@uniovi.es
http://www.aic.uniovi.es/Tc

Abstract. We face the Job Shop Scheduling Problem with Sequence Dependent Setup Times and maximum lateness minimization as objective function. We propose a disjunctive graph representation for this problem that allows to define the concept of critical path properly. From this representation, we have defined a neighborhood structure suitable to cope with lateness minimization. This neighborhood structure is exploited in combination with a Tabu Search algorithm. We report results from an experimental study across conventional benchmark instances showing that this approach outperforms some of the current state-of-the-art methods.

1   Introduction

The Job Shop Scheduling Problem with Sequence Dependent Setup Times (SDST-JSP) is a generalization of the classical Job Shop Scheduling Problem (JSP) in which a setup operation on a machine is required when the machine switches between two jobs. In this way the SDST-JSP models many real situations better than the JSP, as it happens for example in some situations arising in semiconductor industry [Balas et al., 2008]. At the same time, the presence of setup times changes significatively the nature of this problem so as the well-known results and methods for the JSP are not directly applicable to the SDST-JSP.

In the last decades, scheduling problems with setup considerations have been subject to intensive research. Consequently, in the literature several approaches can be found that, in general, try to extend solutions that were successful for the classical JSP. For example, the branch and bound algorithm proposed in [Brucker and Thiele, 1996] is an extension of well-known algorithms proposed in [Brucker et al., 1994] and [Carlier and Pinson, 1994]. Also, in [Balas et al., 2008] the authors extend the shifting bottleneck heuristic proposed in [Adams et al., 1988] for the JSP. In [Vela et al., 2010] and [González et al., 2008] two hybrid approaches are proposed that combine a genetic algorithm with local search procedures. In all these cases, makespan minimization is considered as objective. However, other objective functions are also of great interest, such as for example lateness minimization.

P. Meseguer, L. Mandow, and R.M. Gasca (Eds.): CAEPIA 2009, LNAI 5988, pp. 212–221, 2010.

In this paper we consider the SDST-JSP with maximum lateness minimization. To solve this problem we propose a Tabu Search (TS) algorithm. TS has not a theoretical performance guarantee but it has a solid track record of empirical performance in solving several scheduling problems [Nowicki and Smutnicki, 2005], [Zhang et al., 2008]; sometimes combined with other meta-heuristics such as Genetic Algorithms [González et al., 2008], [Vela et al., 2010], [González Rodríguez et al., 2007].

In the next section we formulate the SDST-JSP and introduce the notation used across the paper. In section 3, we describe the main components of the TS algorithm. Section 4 reports results from the experimental study. Finally, in section 5 we summarize the main conclusions and propose some ideas for the future.

2   Description of the Problem

The SDST-JSP requires scheduling a set of N jobs $\{J_1, \ldots, J_N\}$ on a set of M physical resources or machines $\{R_1, \ldots, R_M\}$. Each job J_i consists of a set of tasks or operations $\{\theta_{i1}, \ldots, \theta_{iM}\}$ to be sequentially scheduled and a due date d_j. Each task θ_{ij} has a single resource requirement, a fixed duration $p_{\theta_{ij}}$ and a start time $st_{\theta_{ij}}$ whose value should be determined.

After an operation θ_{ij} leaves the machine and before an operation θ_{kl} enters the same machine, a setup operation is required with duration $S_{\theta_{ij}\theta_{kl}}$. $S_{0\theta_{ij}}$ is the setup time required before θ_{ij} if this operation is the first one scheduled on the machine.

The SDST-JSP has two binary constraints: precedence constraints and capacity constraints. Precedence constraints, defined by the sequential routings of the tasks within a job, translate into linear inequalities of the type: $st_{\theta_{ij}} + p_{\theta_{ij}} \leq st_{\theta_{i(j+1)}}$ (i.e. θ_{ij} before $\theta_{i(j+1)}$). Capacity constraints that restrict the use of each resource to only one task at a time translate into disjunctive constraints of the form: $st_{\theta_{ij}} + p_{\theta_{ij}} + S_{\theta_{ij}\theta_{kl}} \leq st_{\theta_{kl}} \lor st_{\theta_{kl}} + p_{\theta_{kl}} + S_{\theta_{kl}\theta_{ij}} \leq st_{\theta_{ij}}$, where θ_{ij} and θ_{kl} are operations requiring the same machine. The objective is to obtain a feasible schedule such that the maximum lateness, defined as

$$L_{max} = \max_{1 \leq i \leq N}\{C_i - d_i\} \qquad (1)$$

is minimized, where C_i is the completion time of job i. This problem is denoted by $J|s_{ij}|L_{max}$ according to the $\alpha|\beta|\gamma$ notation used in the literature.

2.1   The Disjunctive Graph Model Representation

The disjunctive graph is a common representation model for scheduling problems. The definition of such graph depends on the particular problem. We propose here the following definition for the $J|s_{ij}|L_{max}$ problem. A problem instance may be represented by a directed graph $G = (V, A \cup E \cup I_1 \cup I_2 \cup I_3)$. Each node in the set V represents a task of the problem, with the exception of the dummy nodes *start*, *end$_j$* $1 \leq j \leq M$ and *end*. All these nodes represents operations with processing time 0 and are used for the purpose of giving G a particular structure. The arcs of A are called *conjunctive arcs* and represent precedence constraints and the arcs of E are called *disjunctive arcs* and represent capacity constraints. The set E is partitioned into subsets E_i, with $E = \cup_{i=1,\dots,M} E_i$. E_i corresponds to resource R_i and includes an arc (v, w) for each pair of operations requiring that resource. Each arc (v, w) of A is weighted with the processing time of the operation at the source node, p_v, and each arc (v, w) of E is weighted with $p_v + S_{vw}$. The set I_1 includes arcs of the form $(start, v)$ for each operation v of the problem. These arcs are weighted with S_{0v}. The set I_2 includes arcs (θ_{iM}, end_i), $1 \leq i \leq N$, weighted with $p_{\theta_{iM}}$. Finally, the arcs of I_3 are of the form (end_i, end) and are weighted with $-d_i$.

A feasible schedule is represented by an acyclic subgraph G_s of G, $G_s = (V, A \cup H \cup J_1 \cup I_2 \cup I_3)$, where $H = \cup_{i=1\dots M} H_i$, H_i being a hamiltonian selection of E_i. J_1 includes arcs $(start, v_i)$ for all $i = 1 \dots M$, v_i being the first operation of H_i. Therefore, finding a solution can be reduced to discovering compatible Hamiltonian selections, i.e. processing orderings for the operations requiring the same resource, or partial schedules, that translate into a solution graph G_s without cycles. The maximum lateness of the schedule is the cost of a *critical path*. A *critical path* is a directed path in G_s from node *start* to node *end* having the largest cost. Nodes and arcs in a critical path are termed *critical*. The critical path is naturally decomposed into subsequences $B_1, \dots, B_r$ called *critical blocks*. A *critical block* is a maximal subsequence of at least two operations in a critical path requiring the same machine. The concepts of critical path and critical block are of major importance for scheduling problems due to the fact that most of the formal properties and solution methods rely on them. For example, most of the neighborhood structures used in local search algorithms, such as that described in section 3, consist in reversing arcs in a critical path.

Figure 1 shows a solution to a problem with 3 jobs and 3 machines. Dotted arcs represent the elements H and J, while arcs of A are represented by continuous arrows.

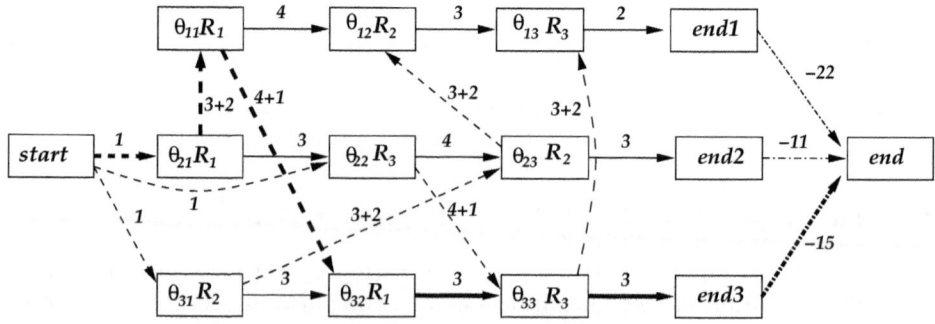

Fig. 1. A feasible schedule to a problem with 3 jobs and 3 machines. Bold face arcs show a critical path whose length, i.e. the maximum lateness, is 2.

The proposed graph representation allows reducing the problem of minimizing maximum lateness to the standard problem of makespan minimization. In this way, the results and algorithms developed for makespan minimization may be in principle adapted to cope with maximum lateness minimization. In this process, we have to be aware of the differences in the problem formulation: now we have M dummy operations, $end_1 \ldots end_M$, having negative durations, $-d_1 \cdots -d_m$, and requiring no resources.

3   Tabu Search for the SDST-JSP

Tabu search is an advanced local search technique that can escape from local optima by selecting non improving neighbors temporarily. In order to avoid revisiting recently visited solutions and also to search new promising regions of the search space, a tabu search algorithm maintains a tabu list with a set of moves which are not allowed when generating the new neighborhood. In [Dell' Amico and Trubian, 1993], [Nowicki and Smutnicki, 2005] or [Zhang et al., 2008] we can find examples of successful tabu search algorithms for the JSP with makespan minimization. In particular, in [Zhang et al., 2008] the best solutions known for a number of the largest JSP instances taken from conventional repositories are reported.

Algorithm 1 shows the tabu search algorithm we have considered here. This algorithm is quite similar to other tabu search algorithms described in the literature [Glover, 1989], [Glover and Laguna, 1997]. In the first step the initial solution is generated and evaluated. Then, it iterates over a number of steps. In each iteration, the neighborhood of the current solution is built and one of the neighbors is selected for the next iteration. After a number of iterations without improvement, the search is restarted from a previous solution taken from the elite solution stack. The tabu search finishes after a number of iterations *maxGlobalIter*, or when the elite solution stack gets empty and returns the best solution reached so far.

Initial solution. We have chosen to start the search from a randomized semiactive schedule. To generate schedules we use the Serial Schedule Generation Scheme (SSGS), proposed in [Artigues et al., 2005]. This schedule builder chooses one of the available operations at random and assigns it the earliest starting time that satisfies all constraints with respect to the previous scheduled operations. An operation is available when its predecessor in the job sequence has already been scheduled. It continues until all operations get scheduled. This algorithm always produces active schedules, provided that the triangular inequality for the setup times holds. Otherwise, it might produce even no semiactive schedules. So, we use the following rescheduling algorithm after SSGS: the operations in the chromosome are visited from left to right and each one is scheduled at the earliest time accordingly to previous operations.

The neighborhood structure. The neighborhood structure N_L^S proposed in this paper is adapted from that termed N^S in [González et al., 2008] and

---

Require: A scheduling problem instance P
Ensure: A schedule H for instance P
  Generate an initial solution s_0;
  Set the current solution $s = s_0$, the best solution $s_B = s$, and the best $L_{max} = f(s_B)$;
  $globalIter = 0$, $improveIter = 0$;
  Empty the tabu list, and push s onto the elite solution stack L (LIFO list);
  while $globalIter < maxGlobalIter$ **do**
    if $improveIter = maxImproveIter$ **then**
      if The solution stack L is empty **then**
        return T he solution s_B and L_{max},
      else
        Pop the solution s_L on top of the solution stack L;
        Set the current solution $s = s_L$;
        Set $improveIter = 0$;
        Clear the tabu list and the cycle detection structure;
    Set $globalIter = globalIter+1$, set $improveIter = improveIter+1$;
    Generate neighbors of the current solution s by means of the neighborhood structure;
    Let s^* be the best neighbor not being tabu or satisfying the aspiration criterion and not leading to a cycle. Update the tabu list and the cycle detection structure accordingly;
    if $f(s^*) < L_{max}$ **then**
      Set $s_B = s^*$, $L_{max} = f(s^*)$, $improveIter = 0$, and push s^* onto the elite solution stack L;
  return T he solution s_B and L_{max};

Algorithm 1. The Tabu Search Algorithm

[González et al., 2009]. N^S was defined to cope with makespan minimization and it is based on previous structures given in [Matsuo et al., 1988] and [Van Laarhoven et al., 1992] to cope with the standard JSP. These structures have given rise to some of the most outstanding algorithms for the JSP such as, for example, the algorithms proposed in [Dell' Amico and Trubian, 1993], [Nowicki and Smutnicki, 2005], [Balas and Vazacopoulos, 1998], [Zhang et al., 2008]. N_L^S is based on the following two results. Their proofs are very similar to that of analogous theorems given in [González et al., 2008] for N^S. The head of an operation u, denoted r_u, is the largest cost of a path from $start$ to u in the solution graph, and PJ_u and SJ_u denote the predecessor and successor of u respectively in the job sequence

Theorem 1. *Given a critical block of the form $(b' \ v \ b \ w \ b'')$, where b, b' and b'' are sequences of operations, a sufficient condition for an alternative path from v to w not existing is that*

$$r_{PJ_w} < r_{SJ_u} + p_{SJ_u} + \min\{S_{kl}/(k,l) \in E, J_k = J_u\}, \forall u \in \{v\} \cup b \quad (2)$$

Theorem 2. *Let H be a schedule and $(b' \ v \ b \ w \ b'')$ a critical block, where b, b' and b'' are sequences of operations of the form $b = (u_1 \ldots u_n)$, $b' = (u'_1 \ldots u'_{n'})$*

and $b'' = (u_1'' \ldots u_{n''}'')$. Even if the schedule H' obtained from H by moving w just before v is feasible, H' does not improve H if the following condition holds

$$S_{u_n',v} + S_{u_n w} + S_{wu_1''} \le S_{u_n',w} + S_{wv} + S_{u_n u_1''}. \tag{3}$$

If $n = 0$, u_n should be substituted by v in (3).

Therefore, the neighborhood structure N_L^S is defined as follows.

Definition 1 (N_L^S). Let operation v be a member of a critical block B. In a neighboring solution v is moved to another position in B, provided that condition (3) doesn't hold and that the sufficient condition of feasibility (2) is preserved.

Maximum Lateness estimation. As it is usual, for the sake of efficiency the selection rule is based on maximum lateness estimations instead of computing the actual maximum lateness of all neighbors. For this purpose, we extend here the procedure *lpathS* given in [Vela et al., 2010] for makespan estimation, which in its turn extends the *lpath* rule given for the JSP in [Taillard, 1993]. This procedure takes an input sequence of operations of the form $(Q_1 \ldots Q_q)$ after a move, all of them requiring the same machine. Being $(Q_1 \ldots Q_q)$ a permutation of the sequence $(O_1 \ldots O_q)$ before the move. For each $i = 1 \ldots q$, *lpathS* estimates the cost of the longest path from node *start* to node *end* through Q_i. The maximum of these values is taken as the maximum lateness estimation for the neighboring schedule. For N_L^S, if w is moved before v in a block of the form $(b'\ v\ b\ w\ b'')$, the input sequence is $(w\ v\ b)$.

The tabu list. The basic role of tabu list is to prevent the search process from turning back to solutions visited in previous steps. In order to reduce computational cost, we have chosen to store in the tabu list the attributes of moves rather than the attributes of solutions. So, the tabu list stores the arcs that have recently been reversed. These arcs can not be reversed, with the exception of those satisfying the aspiration criterion. When a neighbor is chosen for the next iteration, the tabu list is updated with all the arcs that have been reversed to generate this neighbor. Then, a new neighbor is marked as tabu if it requires reversing at least one arc of the tabu list. The length of the tabu list is usually of critical importance. In this paper we have used a dynamic length for the tabu list, as it is proposed in [Dell' Amico and Trubian, 1993].

Cycle checking. The cycle prevention procedure is based on that proposed in [Dell' Amico and Trubian, 1993] for the JSP. In a cyclic solution, a solution $s(i)$ after i iterations is equal to a solution $s(i + k)$ after $i + k$ iterations, for some positive k, and the arc selected to move from $s(i + k)$ to $s(i + k + 1)$ is the same as the arc selected previously to move from $s(i)$ to $s(i + 1)$. In order to detect this situation, a witness arc is chosen for each move and the value of the estimated maximum lateness of the resulting neighbor is associated with it. Then, the maximum lateness of each neighbor is compared with that associated to the witness arc of the corresponding move. If these values coincide for more than $Tcycle$ consecutive iterations, the search is supposed to be in a cycle and so the neighbor is discarded, unless it satisfies the aspiration criterion given in the next section.

Move selection and aspiration criterion. The selection rule chooses the neighbor with the lowest estimated maximum lateness, discarding suspect-of-cycle and tabu neighbors (unless they satisfy the aspiration criterion). A side effect of implementing a *partial attribute* tabu list is that it may lead to giving a tabu status to an unvisited solution or even an interesting solution. So the algorithm uses an aspiration criterion which allows to accept any move provided that its estimated maximum lateness is lower than that of the current best solution found so far. If all possible moves are tabu or lead to a cycle, and none of them satisfy the aspiration criterion, a feasible neighbor is chosen at random.

Recovery of elite solutions. Each time a new solution improves the current best so far, it is stored in a stack L. Then every $maxImproveIter$ iterations without improvement, the current solution is replaced with one extracted from L (in the experiments we have chosen $maxImproveIter = maxGlobalIter/Size(L)$). This is a technique commonly used to avoid the algorithm getting trapped in local optima. The size of L is restricted to a small value (10 in our experiments) in order to avoid bookkeeping bad solutions from the beginning of the search. When L is full, every new solution replaces the oldest one. When recovery to a previous solution from L, the state of the algorithm must be reconsidered. We have tried a number of possibilities with very similar results, so we have chosen to reset the tabu list, the cycle detection structure and the number of iterations without improvement to their initial values.

4   Experimental Study

Our purpose is to compare the TS algorithm with the Shifting Bottleneck algorithm with Guided Local Search (SB+GLS) proposed in [Balas et al., 2008]. To do that we consider the benchmark instances they have used, the data set i305 proposed in [Ovacik and Uzsoy, 1994]. The TS algorithm is given an equivalent amount of time, being aware of the differences between the target machines. SB+GLS was implemented in C language and run on a Sun Ultra 60 with UltraSPARC-II processor at 360MHz., while TS was coded in C++ and run in a Intel Core 2 Duo at 2.6GHz. So, we leave TS running for a time about 6,6% of the time reported in [Balas et al., 2008]. We have considered this equivalence from the comparisons given in www.spec.org.

Table 1 summarizes the results from SB-GLS reported in [Balas et al., 2008] and the results from TS across the same instances. In all cases the results are averaged for groups of 20 instances. In the later case, we report the best and average values of maximum lateness, the time taken in a single run and the maximum number of iterations of TS. As we can observe, TS gets much better maximum lateness than SG-GLS. Not only the best value of all 30 runs is better, but also the average value is better as well, when the time taken in both algorithms is equivalent. In the next series of experiments, we consider the five first instances of the four groups with 20 jobs, as done in [Balas et al., 2008], and leave TS running for a much larger number of iterations. The objective is to assess the ability of TS to improve if it is given a larger run time. The results are

Table 1. Results from SB-GLS and TS across all 160 instances. The values are averaged for groups of 20 instances.

Problems	Size	SB-GLS	TS Results				
			Best	Avg.	Std D	Time	N.Iter
1-20	10 × 5	361.65	305.40	313.02	8.62	0.13	5000
21-40	20 × 5	93.85	-122.15	-90.92	15.03	3.91	60000
41-60	10 × 10	1087.10	1010.85	1032.43	18.79	0.39	12000
61-80	20 × 10	815.20	526.60	572.59	21.95	6.64	100000
81-100	10 × 15	1650.65	1577.45	1597.51	13.04	1.01	25000
101-120	20 × 15	1521.00	1205.30	1281.19	36.54	6.78	75000
121-140	10 × 20	2158.85	2076.95	2097.92	14.34	1.52	30000
141-160	20 × 20	2097.00	1815.35	1906.07	49.12	6.66	65000

Table 2. Illustrating the benefit of a longer Tabu Search

Problem	Size	SB-GLS	Avg-TS(s)	Avg-TS(l)	Best-TS
21		493	295.6	266.5	246
22		-158	-310.9	-335	-367
23	20 × 5	156	-64.4	-87.1	-106
24		-81	-164.5	-184.8	-226
25		-64	-335.1	-362.1	-368
61		548	404.9	385.3	344
62		707	479.6	441.4	403
63	20 × 10	1035	770.3	750.3	728
64		988	677.9	651	630
65		553	344.1	316.8	293
101		1511	1368.6	1315.6	1284
102		1459	1337.6	1269.9	1237
103	20 × 15	1487	1285.1	1225.7	1186
104		1934	1609.3	1535.6	1505
105		1756	1470.7	1393.8	1331
141		1871	1665.9	1604	1575
142		1902	1754.5	1666.4	1618
143	20 × 20	2223	2022.8	1930.3	1885
144		2092	1861.1	1778.1	1738
145		1987	1776.1	1691.1	1633

summarized in Table 2. For each one of the 20 instances considered, we show the best solutions reported in [Balas et al., 2008], the average maximum lateness in the same conditions as it Table 1 (**Avg-TS(s)**) and with the new conditions, i.e. 10^6 iterations for TS (**Avg-TS(l)**), and the best solution reached by TS. As it could be expected, the maximum lateness obtained by TS improves when it is given a larger number of iterations. The best solutions reported in Table 2 can be downloaded from the web site http://www.aic.uniovi.es/tc/ (section Almacen + Test Problems).

5   Conclusions

We have considered the job shop problem with sequence dependent setup times, where the objective is to minimize the maximum lateness. We have used a Tabu Search algorithm and designed a new neighborhood to cope with lateness. We have reported results from an experimental study across the benchmarks proposed in [Ovacik and Uzsoy, 1994] and compared our algorithm with one of the most representative state-of-the-art methods: the shifting bottleneck heuristic combined with guided local search proposed in [Balas et al., 2008]. The results of this study show that our approach outperforms this state-of-the-art-method.

As future work we will combine TS with a Genetic Algorithm and leave the combined approach run for a larger time. We expect that the combined approach will reach much better solutions than the TS alone, as it has happened in [González et al., 2009] where a similar combination has obtained very good solutions for the same problem with makespan minimization. Also, we plan to adapt other results and algorithms from makespan minimization to maximum lateness minimization.

Acknowledgements

This work has been supported by the Spanish Ministry of Science and Education under research project MEC-FEDER TIN2007-67466-C02-01 and by Principality of Asturias under grant FICYT-BP07-109.

References

[Adams et al., 1988] Adams, J., Balas, E., Zawack, D.: The shifting bottleneck procedure for job shop scheduling. Managament Science 34, 391–401 (1988)

[Artigues et al., 2005] Artigues, C., Lopez, P., Ayache, P.: Schedule generation schemes for the job shop problem with sequence-dependent setup times: Dominance properties and computational analysis. Annals of Operations Research 138, 21–52 (2005)

[Balas et al., 2008] Balas, E., Simonetti, N., Vazacopoulos, A.: Job shop scheduling with setup times, deadlines and precedence constraints. Journal of Scheduling 11, 253–262 (2008)

[Balas and Vazacopoulos, 1998] Balas, E., Vazacopoulos, A.: Guided local search with shifting bottleneck fo job shop scheduling. Management Science 44(2), 262–275 (1998)

[Brucker et al., 1994] Brucker, P., Jurisch, B., Sievers, B.: A branch and bound algorithm for the job-shop scheduling problem. Discrete Applied Mathematics 49, 107–127 (1994)

[Brucker and Thiele, 1996] Brucker, P., Thiele, O.: A branch and bound method for the general-job shop problem with sequence-dependent setup times. Operations Research Spektrum 18, 145–161 (1996)

[Carlier and Pinson, 1994] Carlier, J., Pinson, E.: Adjustment of heads and tails for the job-shop problem. European Journal of Operational Research 78, 146–161 (1994)

[Dell' Amico and Trubian, 1993] Dell' Amico, M., Trubian, M.: Applying tabu search to the job-shop scheduling problem. Annals of Operational Research 41, 231–252 (1993)

[Glover, 1989] Glover, F.: Tabu search–part I. ORSA Journal on Computing 1(3), 190–206 (1989)

[Glover and Laguna, 1997] Glover, F., Laguna, M.: Tabu Search. Kluwer Academic Publishers, Dordrecht (1997)

[González et al., 2008] González, M.A., Vela, C.R., Varela, R.: A new hybrid genetic algorithm for the job shop scheduling problem with setup times. In: Proceedings of the Eighteenth International Conference on Automated Planning and Scheduling (ICAPS 2008), Sidney, AAAI Press, Menlo Park (2008)

[González et al., 2009] González, M.A., Vela, C.R., Varela, R.: Genetic algorithm combined with tabu search for the job shop scheduling problem with setup times. In: Mira, J., Ferrández, J.M., Álvarez, J.R., de la Paz, F., Toledo, F.J. (eds.) IWINAC 2009. LNCS, vol. 5601, pp. 265–274. Springer, Heidelberg (2009)

[González Rodríguez et al., 2007] González Rodríguez, I., Vela, C.R., Puente, J.: A memetic approach to fuzzy job shop based on expectation model. In: Proceedings of IEEE Int. Conf. on Fuzzy Systems, FUZZ-IEEE 2007, pp. 692–697 (2007)

[Matsuo et al., 1988] Matsuo, H., Suh, C., Sullivan, R.: A controlled search simulated annealing method for the general jobshop scheduling problem. Working paper 03-44-88, Graduate School of Business, University of Texas (1988)

[Nowicki and Smutnicki, 2005] Nowicki, E., Smutnicki, C.: An advanced tabu search algorithm for the job shop problem. Journal of Scheduling 8, 145–159 (2005)

[Ovacik and Uzsoy, 1994] Ovacik, I., Uzsoy, R.: Exploiting shop floor status information to schedule complex job shops. Journal of Manufacturing Systems 13(2), 73–84 (1994)

[Taillard, 1993] Taillard, E.: Benchmarks for basic scheduling problems. European Journal of Operational Research 64, 278–285 (1993)

[Van Laarhoven et al., 1992] Van Laarhoven, P., Aarts, E., Lenstra, K.: Job shop scheduling by simulated annealing. Operations Research 40, 113–125 (1992)

[Vela et al., 2010] Vela, C.R., Varela, R., González, M.A.: Local search and genetic algorithm for the job shop scheduling problem with sequence dependent setup times. Journal of Heuristics 16(2), 139–165 (2010), doi:10.1007/s10732-008-9094-y

[Zhang et al., 2008] Zhang, C.Y., Li, P., Rao, Y., Guan, Z.: A very fast TS/SA algorithm for the job shop scheduling problem. Computers and Operations Research 35, 282–294 (2008)

Improving Local Search for the Fuzzy Job Shop Using a Lower Bound

Jorge Puente[1], Camino R. Vela[1],
Alejandro Hernández-Arauzo[1], and Inés González-Rodríguez[2]

[1] A.I. Centre and Department of Computer Science,
University of Oviedo, Spain
{puente,alex,crvela}@uniovi.es
http://www.aic.uniovi.es/Tc
[2] Department of Mathematics, Statistics and Computing,
University of Cantabria, Spain
ines.gonzalez@unican.es

Abstract. We consider the fuzzy job shop problem, where uncertain durations are modelled as fuzzy numbers and the objective is to minimise the expected makespan. A recent local search method from the literature has proved to be very competitive when used in combination with a genetic algorithm, but at the expense of a high computational cost. Our aim is to improve its efficiency with an alternative rescheduling algorithm and a makespan lower bound to prune non-improving neighbours. The experimental results illustrate the success of our proposals in reducing both CPU time and number of evaluated neighbours.

1 Introduction

Scheduling forms an important body of research since the late fifties, with multiple applications in industry, finance and science [1]. Traditionally, it has been treated as a deterministic problem that assumes precise knowledge of all data. However, modelling real-world problems often involves processing uncertainty, for instance in activity durations. In the literature we find different proposals for dealing with ill-known durations [2]. Perhaps the best-known approach is to treat them as stochastic variables. An alternative is to use fuzzy numbers or, more generally, fuzzy intervals in the setting of possibility theory, which is said to provide a natural framework, simpler and less data-demanding than probability theory, for handling incomplete knowledge about scheduling data (c.f. [3],[4]).

The complexity of scheduling problems such as job shop means that practical approaches to solving them usually involve heuristic strategies [5]. Extending these strategies to problems with fuzzy durations in general requires a significant reformulation of both the problem and solving methods. Proposals from the literature include a neural approach [6], genetic algorithms [7],[8],[9], simulated annealing [10] and genetic algorithms hybridised with local search [11],[12].

In the following, we consider a job shop problem with task durations given as triangular fuzzy numbers. Based on a definition of criticality and neighbourhood

P. Meseguer, L. Mandow, and R.M. Gasca (Eds.): CAEPIA 2009, LNAI 5988, pp. 222–232, 2010.

structure from [12], a new rescheduling algorithm is given and a lower bound for the makespan is defined and used to increase the efficiency of the local search. The potential of the proposals is illustrated by the experimental results.

2   Job Shop Scheduling with Uncertain Durations

The *job shop scheduling problem*, also denoted *JSP*, consists in scheduling a set of jobs $\{J_1, \ldots, J_n\}$ on a set of physical resources or machines $\{M_1, \ldots, M_m\}$, subject to a set of constraints. There are *precedence constraints*, so each job J_i, $i = 1, \ldots, n$, consists of m tasks $\{\theta_{i1}, \ldots, \theta_{im}\}$ to be sequentially scheduled. Also, there are *capacity constraints*, whereby each task θ_{ij} requires the uninterrupted and exclusive use of one of the machines for its whole processing time. A feasible schedule is an allocation of starting times for each task such that all constraints hold. The objective is to find a schedule which is *optimal* according to some criterion, most commonly that the *makespan* is minimal.

2.1   Uncertain Durations

In real-life applications, it is often the case that the exact time it takes to process a task is not known in advance, and only some uncertain knowledge is available. Such knowledge can be modelled using a *triangular fuzzy number* or TFN, given by an interval $[n^1, n^3]$ of possible values and a modal value n^2 in it. For a TFN N, denoted $N = (n^1, n^2, n^3)$, the membership function takes the following triangular shape:

$$\mu_N(x) = \begin{cases} \frac{x - n^1}{n^2 - n^1} & : n^1 \leq x \leq n^2 \\ \frac{x - n^3}{n^2 - n^3} & : n^2 < x \leq n^3 \\ 0 & : x < n^1 \text{ or } n^3 < x \end{cases} \tag{1}$$

In the job shop, we essentially need two operations on fuzzy numbers, the sum and the maximum. These are obtained by extending the corresponding operations on real numbers using the *Extension Principle*. However, computing the resulting expression is cumbersome, if not intractable. For the sake of simplicity and tractability of numerical calculations, we follow [10] and approximate the results of these operations, evaluating the operation only on the three defining points of each TFN. It turns out that for any pair of TFNs M and N, the approximated sum $M + N \approx (m^1 + n^1, m^2 + n^2, m^3 + n^3)$ coincides with the actual sum of TFNs; this may not be the case for the maximum $\max(M, N) \approx (\max(m^1, n^1), \max(m^2, n^2), \max(m^3, n^3))$, although they have identical support and modal value.

The membership function of a fuzzy number can be interpreted as a possibility distribution on the real numbers. This allows to define its expected value [13], given for a TFN N by $E[N] = \frac{1}{4}(n^1 + 2n^2 + n^3)$. It coincides with the neutral scalar substitute of a fuzzy interval and the centre of gravity of its mean value [3]. It induces a total ordering $\leq_E$ in the set of fuzzy numbers [10], where for any two fuzzy numbers M, N $M \leq_E N$ if and only if $E[M] \leq E[N]$.

2.2   Fuzzy Job Shop Scheduling

A job shop problem instance may be represented by a directed graph $G = (V, A \cup D)$. V contains one node $x = m(i-1) + j$ per task θ_{ij}, $1 \leq i \leq n$, $1 \leq j \leq m$, plus two additional nodes 0 (or *start*) and $nm + 1$ (or *end*), representing dummy tasks with null processing times. Arcs in A, called *conjunctive arcs*, represent precedence constraints (including arcs from node *start* to the first task of each job and arcs form the last task of each job to node *end*). Arcs in D, called *disjunctive arcs*, represent capacity constraints; $D = \cup_{j=1}^{m} D_j$, where D_i corresponds to machine M_i and includes two arcs (x, y) and (y, x) for each pair x, y of tasks requiring that machine. Each arc (x, y) is weighted with the processing time p_x of the task at the source node (a TFN in our case). A feasible task processing order σ is represented by a *solution graph*, an acyclic subgraph of G, $G(\sigma) = (V, A \cup R(\sigma))$, where $R(\sigma) = \cup_{i=1...m} R_i(\sigma)$, $R_i(\sigma)$ being a hamiltonian selection of D_i. Using forward propagation in $G(\sigma)$, it is possible to obtain the starting and completion times for all tasks and, therefore, the schedule and the makespan $C_{max}(\sigma)$.

The schedule will be fuzzy in the sense that the starting and completion times of all tasks and the makespan are TFNs, interpreted as possibility distributions on the values that the times may take. However, the task processing ordering σ that determines the schedule is crisp; there is no uncertainty regarding the order in which tasks are to be processed.

Given that the makespan is a TFN and neither the maximum nor its approximation define a total ordering in the set of TFNs, it is necessary to reformulate what is understood by "minimising the makespan". In a similar approach to stochastic scheduling, it is possible to use the concept of expected value for a fuzzy quantity and the total ordering it provides, so the *objective* is to minimise the expected makespan $E[C_{max}(\sigma)]$, a crisp objective function. Durations are kept fuzzy, which contributes to the resulting schedule's robustness [14].

Another concept that needs some reformulation in the fuzzy case is that of criticality, an issue far from being trivial. In [10], an arc (x, y) in the solution graph is taken to be critical if and only if the completion time of x and the starting time of y coincide in any of their components. In [12], it is argued that this definition yields some counterintuitive examples and a more restrictive notion is proposed. From the solution graph $G(\sigma)$, three *parallel solution graphs* $G^i(\sigma)$, $i = 1, 2, 3$, are derived with identical structure to $G(\sigma)$, but where the cost of arc $(x, y) \in A \cup R(\sigma)$ in $G^i(\sigma)$ is p_x^i, the i-th component of p_x. Each parallel solution graph $G^i(\sigma)$ is a disjunctive graph with crisp arc weights, so in each of them a critical path is the longest path from node *start* to node *end*. For the fuzzy solution graph $G(\sigma)$, a path will be considered to be *critical* if and only if it is critical in some $G^i(\sigma)$. Nodes and arcs in a critical path are termed critical and a critical path is naturally decomposed into critical blocks, these being maximal subsequences of tasks requiring the same machine.

3   Improved Local Search

Part of the interest of critical paths stems from the fact that they may be used to define neighbourhood structures for local search. Roughly speaking, a typical local search schema starts from a given processing order, calculates its neighbourhood and then neighbours are evaluated in the search of an improving solution. In *simple hill-climbing*, evaluation stops as soon as a first improving neighbour is found, which will then replace the original solution. Local search starts again from that improving neighbour, so the procedure finishes when no neighbour satisfies the acceptance criterion.

3.1   Previous Approaches

Clearly, a central element in any local search procedure is the definition of neighbourhood. For the crisp job shop, a well-known neighbourhood, which relies on the concepts of critical path and critical block, is that proposed in [15], extended to the fuzzy case in [12] using the given definition of criticality:

Definition 1. *Given a task processing order π and an arc $v = (x, y) \in R(\pi)$, let $\pi_{(v)}$ denote the processing order obtained from π after an exchange in the order of tasks in arc v. Then, the* neighbourhood structure *obtained from π is given by $H(\pi) = \{\pi_{(v)} : v \in R(\pi) \text{ is critical}\}$.*

It can be proved that if π is a feasible task processing order, then all elements in its neighbourhood $H(\pi)$ are feasible. This feasibility property limits the search to the subspace of feasible task orders and avoids feasibility checks for the neighbours, hence reducing computational load and avoiding the loss of feasible solutions usually encountered for feasibility checking procedures.

The proposal to extend the neighbourhood structure proposed in Van Laarhoven et al. [15] to the fuzzy case originally stems from [10], but using the earlier definition of critical arc for fuzzy durations. Let this neighbourhood be denoted by H'. The set of critical arcs, according to the definition based on parallel graphs, is a strict subset of the critical arcs according to [10]. Thus the neighbourhood H is strictly included in H'. It can be shown that those neighbours from $H' - H$ can never improve the makespan. Indeed, this is a consequence of the fact that, for a feasible processing order π, if $\sigma = \pi_{(v)}$ where v is not critical (in the sense of H) in $G(\pi)$, then $\forall i, \quad C_{max}^i(\pi) \leq C_{max}^i(\sigma)$ and hence $E[C_{max}(\pi)] \leq E[C_{max}(\sigma)]$.

Neighbourhood structures have been used in different metaheuristics to solve the fuzzy job shop. In [10], neighbourhood H' is used in a simulated annealing algorithm. The same neighbourhood is used in [11] for a memetic algorithm (MA) hybridising a local search procedure (LS) with a genetic algorithm (GA) using permutations with repetition as chromosomes. Combining LS and GAs was an approach already successful for fuzzy flow shop [16]; the results in [11] show a clear synergy between the GA and the LS, with the hybrid method also comparing favourably with the simulated annealing from [10] and a GA from [7].

The same memetic algorithm is used in [12], but here the local search procedure uses the neighbourhood based on parallel graphs, H. The experimental results reported in [12] show that this new memetic algorithm performs better than state-of-the-art algorithms. Despite satisfactory, the results also suggest that the algorithm has reached its full potential and, importantly, most of the computational time it requires corresponds to the local search. In order to obtain better metaheuristics for the fuzzy job shop, it is necessary to improve the neighbourhood structure and reduce the computational cost of the local search. Additionally, the parallel graph framework causes neighbourhood structures in the fuzzy case to usually contain considerably more individuals than in the classical setting, with the consequent increase in computational cost. This further justifies the need of a greater effort to improve efficiency.

In the following, we propose improve the local search efficiency in two ways. A first idea is to change the scheduling method in the local search algorithm, evaluating neighbours in a more efficient manner. A second idea is to actually avoid the evaluation of certain neighbours by means of makespan lower bounds.

3.2   Scheduling Neighbours

The well-known concepts of head and tail of a task are easily extended to the fuzzy framework. For a solution graph $G(\pi)$ and a task x, let $P\nu_x$ and $S\nu_x$ denote the predecessor and successor nodes of x on the machine sequence (in $R(\pi)$) and let PJ_x and SJ_x denote the predecessor and successor nodes of x on the job sequence (in A). The *head* of task x is the starting time of x, a TFN given by $r_x = \max\{r_{PJ_x} + p_{PJ_x}, r_{P\nu_x} + p_{P\nu_x}\}$, and the *tail* of task x is the time lag between the moment when x is finished until the completion time of all tasks, a TFN given by $q_x = \max\{q_{SJ_x} + p_{SJ_x}, q_{S\nu_x} + p_{S\nu_x}\}$.

Clearly, the makespan coincides with the head of the last task and the tail of the first task: $C_{max} = r_{nm+1} = q_0$. Other basic properties that hold for each parallel graph $G^i(\pi)$ are the following: r_x^i is the length of the longest path from node 0 to node x; $q_x^i + p_x^i$ is the length of the longest path from node x to node $nm + 1$; and $r_x^i + p_x^i + q_x^i$ is the length of the longest path from node 0 to node $nm + 1$ through node x: it is a lower bound for $C_{max}^i(\pi)$, being equal if node x belongs to a critical path in $G^i(\pi)$.

As explained above, for a task processing order π and a critical arc (x, y) in $G(\pi)$, the reversal of that arc produces a new feasible processing order $\sigma = \pi_{(x,y)}$ with solution graph $G(\sigma)$. This situation is illustrated in Figure 1. The schedule after the move may be calculated as for any solution, using forward propagation from 0 onwards in the graph $G(\sigma)$. This has been the method used in [12]. Alternatively, the evaluation of neighbouring solutions may be done very quickly (in time $O(N)$), as shown in [17] for the classical JSP.

Let r and q denote the heads and tails in $G(\pi)$ (before the move) and let r' and q' denote the heads and tails in $G(\sigma)$ (after the move). For every task a previous to x in π, $r_a' = r_a$ and for every task b posterior to y in π, $q_b' = q_b$.

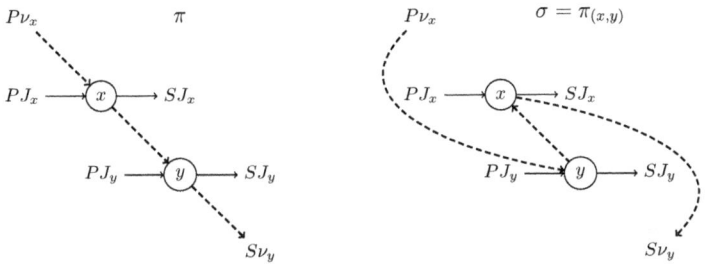

Fig. 1. Situation before (π) and after (σ) the reversal of a critical arc (x, y)

The heads and tails for x and y after the move (see Figure 1) are given by the following:

$$r'_y = \max\{r_{PJ_y} + p_{PJ_y}, r_{P\nu_x} + p_{P\nu_x}\}, \quad r'_x = \max\{r_{PJ_x} + p_{PJ_x}, r'_y + p_y\}$$
$$q'_x = \max\{q_{SJ_x} + p_{SJ_x}, q_{S\nu_y} + p_{S\nu_y}\} \quad q'_y = \max\{q_{SJ_y} + p_{SJ_y}, q'_x + p_x\}$$

Therefore, we need only re-calculate the heads of tasks from x onwards and the tails of tasks previous to y in the graph $G(\sigma)$. We propose to incorporate this quick way of evaluating neighbours in H to the local search algorithm, an idea which, albeit simple, may prove a considerable reduction in computational load.

3.3   Makespan Lower Bound

At each iteration of the local search, only those neighbours with improving makespan are of interest. Hence, another way of reducing computational cost is to foresee, by means of a makespan lower bound, that certain neighbours are certainly not improving, thus avoiding unnecessary calculations. A well-known and inexpensive lower bound for the makespan in the crisp case was proposed by Taillard in [17]. In the following, we generalise this bound to the fuzzy case.

For a processing order π and tasks x and y, let $P_\pi(x \vee y)$ denote the set of all paths in the solution graph $G(\pi)$ containing x or y, $P_\pi(x \wedge y)$ denote the set of all paths in $G(\pi)$ containing both x and y and let $P_\pi(\neg x)$ denote de set of all paths in $G(\pi)$ not containing x. Also, for a given set of paths P, let $D[P]$ denote the TFN such that $D^i[P]$ is the length of the longest path from P in the parallel graph G^i, $i = 1, 2, 3$.

Proposition 1. *Let $\sigma = \pi_{(v)}$, where $v = (x, y)$ is an arc in $G(\pi)$. Then, the makespan for the new solution is given by:*

$$C_{max}(\sigma) = \max\{D[P_\sigma(x \vee y)], D[P_\pi(\neg x)]\} \qquad (2)$$

Proof. For every $i = 1, 2, 3$, $C^i_{max}(\sigma) = \max\{D^i[P_\sigma(x \vee y)], D^i[P_\sigma(\neg x \wedge \neg y)]\}$. Since the only arcs that change between $G(\pi)$ and $G(\sigma)$ are $(P\nu_x(\pi), x)$, (x, y), $(y, S\nu_y(\pi))$, those paths not containing x nor y are the same in both graphs $G(\pi)$ and $G(\sigma)$, so $C^i_{max}(\sigma) = \max\{D^i[P_\sigma(x \vee y)], D^i[P_\pi(\neg x \wedge \neg y)]\}$.

228 J. Puente et al.

Now, for every path in $G(\pi)$ containing y but not containing x, either it starts in y or it contains the arc (PJ_y, y). In both cases, the subpath to y is identical in both $G(\pi)$ and $G(\sigma)$. If the path does not contain $S\nu_y$, it is still a path in $G(\sigma)$ and if it does contain the arc $(y, S\nu_y)$, then substituting $(y, S\nu_y)$ by $(y, x), (x, S\nu_y)$ we obtain a longer path in $G(\sigma)$. Therefore, $D^i[P_\pi(\neg x \wedge y)] \leq D^i[P_\sigma(x \vee y)]$ and we may write:

$$C^i_{max}(\sigma) = \max\{D^i[P_\sigma(x \vee y)], D^i[P_\pi(\neg x \wedge \neg y)], D^i[P_\pi(\neg x \wedge y)]\}$$
$$= \max\{D^i[P_\sigma(x \vee y)], D^i[P_\pi(\neg x)]\} \qquad \square$$

The previous proposition shows that $C_{max}(\sigma)$ can be calculated as the maximum of two elements and suggests an easy-to-compute lower bound:

Corollary 1. *Let $c(\pi, x, y)$ and LB_F be two TFNs defined by:*

$$c(\pi, x, y)^i = \begin{cases} 0 & \text{if } (x, y) \text{ is critical in } G^i(\pi), \\ C^i_{max}(\pi) & \text{otherwise.} \end{cases}, i = 1, 2, 3 \qquad (3)$$

$$LB_F = \max\{c(\pi, x, y), r'_x + p_x + q'_x, r'_y + p_y + q'_y\} \qquad (4)$$

Then, $LB_F^i \leq C^i_{max}(\sigma)$ for all i and hence $LB_F \leq_E C_{max}(\sigma)$, thus providing a lower bound for the makespan $C_{max}(\sigma)$.

Proof. Using heads and tails, by the propoposition above, $C^i_{max}(\sigma) \leq D^i[P_\sigma(x \vee y)] = (\max\{r'_x + p_x + q'_x, r'_y + p_y + q'_y\})^i$. Suppose now that the reversed arc (x, y) is critical in $G^i(\pi)$ but is not critical in $G^j(\sigma)$. If none of the arcs that change after a move is contained in a critical path of $G^j(\pi)$, then that path, with length $C^j_{max}(\pi)$, remains unchanged in $G^j(\sigma)$. If it contains arc $(P\nu_x(\pi), x)$ then the resulting path in $G(\sigma)$ is longer. Analogously, if the critical arc in $G^j(\pi)$ contains $(y, S\nu_y(\pi))$, then the resulting path in $G(\sigma)$ is longer. Therefore, in every component j where (x, y) is not critical there is always a path in $G^j(\sigma)$ with length greater or equal than $C^j_{max}(\pi)$. $\square$

The lower bound LB_F may be used in the acceptance criterion of the LS to decide whether a neighbour σ is chosen or not without any loss in makespan quality: if $E[C_{max}(\pi)] \leq E[LB_F]$, we may discard σ as a non-improving neighbour without evaluating it, since $E[LB_F] \leq E[C_{max}(\sigma)]$.

4 Experimental Results

We now consider 12 benchmark problems for job shop: the well-known FT10 and FT20, and the set of 10 problems identified in [18] as hard to solve for classical JSP: La21, La24, La25, La27, La29, La38, La40, ABZ7, ABZ8, and ABZ9. Ten fuzzy versions of each benchmark are generated following [10] and [12], so task durations become symmetric TFNs where the modal value is the original

Table 1. Rescheduling algorithm: CPU time of MA vs. GVPV08

Problem	Size	GVPV08	MA	red%
FT10	10 × 10	801.2	588.2	26.59%
FT20	20 × 5	1693.9	682.1	59.73%
La21		1769.4	1072.8	39.37%
La24	15 × 10	1562.4	950.1	39.19%
La25		1722.8	993.7	42.32%
La27		4137.8	2242.8	45.80%
La29	20 × 10	3936.0	2071.7	47.37%
La38		3037,6	2556.7	15.83%
La40	15 × 15	3220.4	2652.2	17.64%
ABZ7		7396.1	5294.7	28.41%
ABZ8	20 × 15	8098.5	5780.9	28.62%
ABZ9		7308.0	5652.1	22.66%

duration, ensuring that the optimal solution to the crisp problem provides a lower bound for the fuzzified version. In total, we consider 120 fuzzy job shop instances, 10 for each of the 12 crisp benchmark problems.

The goal of this section is to evaluate empirically the contribution of our proposals to improving local search efficiency. We consider the memetic algorithm presented in [12], denoted GVPV08 in the following, which improved previous approaches from the literature in terms of makespan optimisation. GVPV08 combines a genetic algorithm with a simple hill-climbing local search procedure based on the neighbourhood structure H, with high computational load for the local search. We shall use GVPV08 as a baseline algorithm and introduce the different improvements proposed herein in the local search module, to evaluate their contribution towards improving efficiency.

The first experiment consists in incorporating the new rescheduling algorithm to GVPV08, obtaining a new hybrid algorithm denoted MA, which is run with the same parameters as GVPV08 (population size 100 and 200 generations). Notice that the schedules will be the same with both methods (it is only the way of calculating them that changes), so the final solution is identical in terms of makespan. Table 1 shows the average across each family of ten fuzzy instances of the total CPU time (in seconds) taken by 30 runs of GVPV08 and MA. It shows a clear reduction in time for MA, ranging from a minimum (15.83%–17.64%) for the square problems of size 15 × 15 and a maximum (59.73%) obtained for FT20 of size 20 × 5; for identical number of jobs, the greater the number of resources, the greater the reduction. In any case, the rescheduling based on heads and tails is always more efficient than the original one, with an average reduction in CPU time of 34.5%.

Having ascertained the net increase in efficiency with the new rescheduling algorithm, we proceed to analyse the contribution of the lower bound. We consider a variation of the most efficient algorithm MA, denoted MA(LBF), which

Table 2. Comparison of number of evaluated neighbours and CPU time (in seconds)

Problem	No. Neighbours			CPU time		
	MA	MA(LBF)	red.%	MA	MA(LBF)	red.%
FT10	2.83E+07	3.49E+06	87.67	588.2	183.1	68.87
FT20	6.78E+07	5.11E+06	92.47	682.1	257.2	62.29
La21	4.46E+07	5.61E+06	87.41	1072.8	331.4	69.11
La24	3.87E+07	5.37E+06	86.13	950.1	315.1	66.84
La25	4.28E+07	5.68E+06	86.73	993.7	328.9	66.90
La27	8.37E+07	9.55E+06	88.59	2242.8	593.2	73.55
La29	7.85E+07	8.74E+06	88.87	2071.7	562.5	72.85
La38	5.16E+07	7.74E+06	84.98	2556.7	570.9	77.67
La40	5.42E+07	8.22E+06	84.81	2652.2	595.7	77.54
ABZ7	9.74E+07	1.36E+07	85.99	5294.7	1053.9	80.10
ABZ8	1.08E+08	1.53E+07	85.91	5780.9	1138.5	80.31
ABZ9	9.65E+07	1.40E+07	85.50	5652.1	1081.9	80.86

incorporates the lower bound LB_F to avoid unnecessary evaluations. Again, changes w.r.t. GVPV08 do not concern makespan values and the parameters used for GVPV08 guaranteed convergence, so there is no point in comparisons based on makespan values nor in prolonging computation time in an attempt to improve the makespan of the final solution. The interest is instead in evaluating the contribution of the proposals to reducing the number of evaluated neighbours and the CPU time required by local search.

Table 2 shows the average across the ten fuzzy instances of each family of problems of the total number of evaluated neighbours and CPU time (in seconds) for 30 runs of both MA(LBF) and MA (notice that the latter evaluates the same neighbours than GVPV08). The average reduction for MA(LBF) w.r.t. MA and GVPV8 is 87.09%, with a standard deviation of 6.25%; the minimum (84.81%, 84.98%) is obtained for square problems of size 15×15 and the maximum (92.47%) is obtained for FT20 of size 20×5. As above, for identical number of jobs, the greater the number of resources, the greater the reduction. It is remarkable that the number of evaluated neighbours using the lower bound is practically reduced in an order of magnitude. CPU time is also considerably reduced, 73.07% in average, although this rate is not linear in neighbour reduction. The reason is the extra cost in MA(LBF) of marking those components where the arc is critical. For small-size problems in the first rows, the cost of labelling arcs means a CPU time reduction which is in average 15% smaller than the reduction in number of neighbours (with the exception of FT20, where the labelling proves most expensive). As the problem size increases (and we descend in Table 2) the computational cost becomes less significant, with a loss in CPU time reduction w.r.t. the neighbours reduction of less than 7.5% in average. This suggests that the advantage of using the lower bound is greater as the problem size and difficulty increase. Notice that the labelling process could also be used in order to incorporate neighbour-ordering heuristics to the local search.

5   Conclusions

We have considered a job shop problem with uncertain durations modelled as TFNs and have proposed two changes in a local search method from the literature to improve its efficiency. We have first proposed a different algorithm to reschedule neighbours and then a lower bound for neighbours' makespan which allows to prune the local search and avoids unnecessary calculations of makespan. The results show that the proposals greatly increase the efficiency of the local search, with considerable reductions in the number of evaluated neighbours and CPU times, without affecting the makespan of the final solution. This allows for future extensions of the criticality model and therein-based search methods to more general and expressive fuzzy representations.

Acknowledgements. This work supported by MEC-FEDER Grants TIN2007-67466-C02-01 and MTM2007-62799.

References

1. Pinedo, M.L.: Scheduling. Theory, Algorithms, and Systems, 3rd edn. Springer, Heidelberg (2008)
2. Herroelen, W., Leus, R.: Project scheduling under uncertainty: Survey and research potentials. European Journal of Operational Research 165, 289–306 (2005)
3. Dubois, D., Fargier, H., Fortemps, P.: Fuzzy scheduling: Modelling flexible constraints vs. coping with incomplete knowledge. European Journal of Operational Research 147, 231–252 (2003)
4. Słowiński, R., Hapke, M. (eds.): Scheduling Under Fuzziness. Studies in Fuzziness and Soft Computing, vol. 37. Physica-Verlag, Heidelberg (2000)
5. Brucker, P., Knust, S.: Complex Scheduling. Springer, Heidelberg (2006)
6. Tavakkoli-Moghaddam, R., Safei, N., Kah, M.: Accessing feasible space in a generalized job shop scheduling problem with the fuzzy processing times: a fuzzy-neural approach. Journal of the Operational Research Society 59, 431–442 (2008)
7. Sakawa, M., Kubota, R.: Fuzzy programming for multiobjective job shop scheduling with fuzzy processing time and fuzzy duedate through genetic algorithms. European Journal of Operational Research 120, 393–407 (2000)
8. Petrovic, S., Fayad, S., Petrovic, D.: Sensitivity analysis of a fuzzy multiobjective scheduling problem. International Journal of Production Research 46(12), 3327–3344 (2007)
9. González Rodríguez, I., Puente, J., Vela, C.R., Varela, R.: Semantics of schedules for the fuzzy job shop problem. IEEE Transactions on Systems, Man and Cybernetics, Part A 38(3), 655–666 (2008)
10. Fortemps, P.: Jobshop scheduling with imprecise durations: a fuzzy approach. IEEE Transactions of Fuzzy Systems 7, 557–569 (1997)
11. González Rodríguez, I., Vela, C.R., Puente, J.: A memetic approach to fuzzy job shop based on expectation model. In: Proc. of IEEE International Conference on Fuzzy Systems, FUZZ-IEEE 2007, London, pp. 692–697. IEEE, Los Alamitos (2007)

12. González Rodríguez, I., Vela, C.R., Puente, J., Varela, R.: A new local search for the job shop problem with uncertain durations. In: Proc. of the Eighteenth International Conference on Automated Planning and Scheduling (ICAPS-2008), Sidney, pp. 124–131. AAAI Press, Menlo Park (2008)
13. Liu, B., Liu, Y.K.: Expected value of fuzzy variable and fuzzy expected value models. IEEE Transactions on Fuzzy Systems 10, 445–450 (2002)
14. González Rodríguez, I., Puente, J., Varela, R., Vela, C.R.: A study of schedule robustness for job shop with uncertainty. In: Geffner, H., Prada, R., Machado Alexandre, I., David, N. (eds.) IBERAMIA 2008. LNCS (LNAI), vol. 5290, pp. 31–41. Springer, Heidelberg (2008)
15. Van Laarhoven, P., Aarts, E., Lenstra, K.: Job shop scheduling by simulated annealing. Operations Research 40, 113–125 (1992)
16. Ishibuchi, H., Murata, T.: A multi-objective genetic local search algorithm and its application to flowshop scheduling. IEEE Transactions on Systems, Man, and Cybernetics–Part C: Applications and Reviews 67(3), 392–403 (1998)
17. Taillard, E.D.: Parallel taboo search techniques for the job shop scheduling problem. ORSA Journal on Computing 6(2), 108–117 (1994)
18. Applegate, D., Cook, W.: A computational study of the job-shop scheduling problem. ORSA Journal of Computing 3, 149–156 (1991)

Data-Driven Student Knowledge Assessment through Ill-Defined Procedural Tasks

Jaime Gálvez, Eduardo Guzmán, and Ricardo Conejo

Dpto. de Lenguajes y Ciencias de la Computación, Universidad de Málaga,
Bulevar Louis Pasteur, 35, Campus de Teatinos,
29071 Málaga, Spain
{jgalvez,guzman,conejo}@lcc.uma.es

Abstract. The Item Response Theory (IRT) is a statistical mechanism success-fully used since the beginning of the 20th century to infer student knowledge through tests. Nevertheless, existing well-founded techniques to assess procedural tasks are generally complex and applied to well-defined tasks. In this paper, we describe how, using a set of techniques we have developed based on IRT, it is possible to infer declarative student knowledge through procedural tasks. We describe how these techniques have been used with undergraduate students, in the object oriented programming domain, through ill-defined procedural exercises.

Keywords: Student modeling, student assessment.

1 Introduction

Since the birth of the first teaching systems, Artificial Intelligence (AI) techniques have been used in order to try to provide those systems with the required capabilities to emulate human tutors [1]. Knowledge representation, student modeling and cognitive diagnosis (or student knowledge inference) are only some of the capabilities involved in the development of education systems. AI is used in this context to offer students a personalized learning process according to their needs, adapting to them in order to influence them in as positive a way as possible.

From the student modeling perspective, several techniques for representing (and diagnosing) student characteristics, such as his/her knowledge level, his/her conceptual errors, etc., can be found in the literature (cf. [2]). Nowadays, there exist well-founded assessment mechanisms, based on statistical theories such as *the Item Response Theory* (IRT) [3]. This theory is used successfully to infer the student knowledge using tests. Nevertheless, the use of existing well-founded techniques to assess the knowledge using procedural activities such as problems, are generally complex. In this context, proposals such as *Model Tracing* [4] or others based on Bayesian networks [5], involve a great effort to model the procedural activities, since the set of steps the student could carry out should be defined a priori [6]; and therefore, the modeling of those domains becomes an arduous task.

In preliminary studies [7] we used well-founded techniques to evaluate how we can perform an assessment of the student knowledge in a domain with well-defined tasks:

P. Meseguer, L. Mandow, and R.M. Gasca (Eds.): CAEPIA 2009, LNAI 5988, pp. 233–241, 2010.
© Springer-Verlag Berlin Heidelberg 2010

this assessment is the result of the application of the Simplex optimization algorithm. In the paper cited, techniques based on the IRT were described, and its suitability was evaluated. In this paper we focus on a domain where the solution space makes tasks be ill-defined. The hypothesis from which we start is that, using the proposed techniques, the student's declarative knowledge inferences are equivalent to those that would be provided using an IRT-based test. The strength of our proposal is that much less problems are required to achieve an accurate assessment diagnosis.

The article is structured as follows: In the next section, the domain modeling technique that we use in our approach, called Constraint-Based Modeling (CBM), is described. Next, we will explain the fundamentals of the IRT. In section 4, the key ideas of this work are presented. Section 5 focuses on explaining the more relevant features of the educational tool we have developed. Subsequently, in section 6, the experiment performed with the educational tool to verify our hypothesis is described, together with the results obtained. Finally, conclusions and future work are presented.

2   Constraint-Based Modeling

The use of CBM in the learning environment contributes to improve the student learning process, making students learn from their own mistakes when solving a problem from a particular domain. The CBM is based on Ohlsson's theory [8] of learning from performance errors. According to it, learning is a two-step process: In the first, an error is detected while an activity is being performed; and afterwards, it is corrected. Errors may take place when the students try to solve a problem but either they do not have the required declarative knowledge or they are unable to apply the procedure appropriately.

To detect errors, CBM-based tutor systems generate a representation of the solution the student is building, which is updated according to the actions performed by the student in the system interface. In CBM, the domain is represented by a set of principles, which will be compared with the student solution representation and in this way it will be inferred which domain principles are being violated by that solution. The principles that form the domain are considered to be the basic unit of knowledge in the CBM and they are represented by constraints about the state that must be satisfied by all possible correct solutions of all problems. In other words, a correct solution to a problem will never generate a representation that violates some of the constraints of the domain.

According to CBM, each constraint is defined by an ordered pair of conditions: C_r, C_s; where C_r is the relevant condition, which is employed to determine the sort of problems and states for which the constraint is relevant, thus, where it could be applied. C_s is the satisfaction condition and contains the error condition associated to a certain principle that a solution for a given problem could infringe. When the C_r of a constraint is true, for a certain state of a problem solution, it is said that the constraint is significant, from the pedagogical point of view, and therefore, C_s should also be true. Otherwise, the constraint has been violated, which implies that one or more errors have occurred. After detecting those errors, the student model is updated and the system should provide the student with some feedback and apply some corrective action that helps the student to correct his/her conceptual mistake.

The results obtained by several tutors based on the CBM prove the effectiveness of this approach in learning tasks [9] and its suitability as compared with other similar proposals. Nevertheless, Ohlsson and Mitrovic [10] have remarked that, to allow the systems that use the CBM be able to help when taking pedagogical decisions, it is necessary to have a long term student model. In that sense, most of the existing proposals based on CBM (with the exception of some that include Bayesian networks [11]), infer the student knowledge as a proportion of the constraints the student knows. However, this heuristic does not have characteristics that are mandatory in a knowledge diagnosis system (and in general for every system of this type), such as the invariance. For this reason, estimations based on heuristics are strongly conditioned by the particular problems the student has made.

3   Item Response Theory

The IRT, developed by Thurstone [3], is the most popular discipline, based on statistical techniques, for quantitatively measuring certain traits such as the intelligence, skills and/or, knowledge level in a given concept, personality, etc. This theory is based on two principles [12]: According to the first, the knowledge that a student has in a test question (or *item*) can be quantified through a factor called *knowledge level*. The second principle establishes that the relationship between the probability of answering an item correctly and the student knowledge level can be described by means of a monotonically increasing function named *Item Characteristic Curve* (ICC). The higher the student knowledge level, the higher the probability of answering correctly. This function is the central element of the IRT. One of the most frequently used functions (and perhaps, the most popular) to model the ICC is the three-parameter logistic function (3PL):

$$P(u = 1|\theta) = c_i + (1 - c_i)\frac{1}{1 + e^{-1.7a_i(\theta - b_i)}} \tag{1}$$

where $P(u_i = 1/\theta)$ is the probability of answering correctly the item i given the student knowledge level θ, which is normally measured using a continuous scale between $[-3.0, .., 3.0]$. The three parameters that characterize this curve depend on the item and they are:

- The *discrimination* (a_i), which is a value proportional to the slope of the curve and the higher it is, the more the item discerns between the inferior and superior knowledge levels.
- The *difficulty* (b_i), which corresponds to the value of the knowledge level for which the probability of answering correctly is the same as that of answering incorrectly (without taking into account randomly selected responses).
- The *guessing* (c_i), which measures precisely the probability that a student will answer correctly even though he/she may not possess the knowledge required to do so, modeling thus, those situations where the student answers randomly.

The popularity of the IRT is a direct consequence of the consistence of its results. In other proposals such as the *Classic Test Theory*, the results of estimating the student knowledge depend on the sample of students used to perform the test and, thus, the results in the test are not comparable to those obtained in other different tests. The results obtained by applying the IRT however posses several properties such as the invariance. In other words, the knowledge level inferred using this approach does not depend on the test. Therefore, if two tests which assess the same concept, are administered to the same student, the results obtained would be very similar.

In order to apply the IRT it is necessary to have available the ICC values corresponding to each item in the domain. To achieve this, a data driven procedure called *calibration* is required. Calibration is a statistical process for which data must be available on a student population sample previously evaluated / tested. Through this procedure, the parameters that characterize each ICC are inferred. The input to this procedure is based on the results from those students who did tests using the questions whose curves we wish to infer.

4   Assessment Combining the IRT and CBM through Procedural Tasks

Through the IRT, student knowledge inferences can be made with desirable characteristics such as the invariance. Nevertheless, in theory, the IRT is difficult to apply when the goal is to assess activities of procedural type. Indeed, to carry out an assessment similar to that made by a teacher for a problem solved by a student, but using the IRT, it would be necessary to build a very large number of items that were focused on all the issues that could be evaluated with only one problem.

Our proposal aims to solve the inconveniences that present both the IRT and the CBM, by means of a set of assessment techniques combining the two approaches. The goal is to improve the heuristics that are normally used in the CBM for updating the long term student model. This improvement consists of introducing inference techniques of the student knowledge inspired by IRT fundamentals. Therefore, the evidence that the student provides about his/her knowledge will be the actions that he/she performs while resolving a problem. Those actions will be translated into violations (or satisfactions) of constraints from a set of constraints used to represent the domain matter.

In the IRT the elements used to determine the student knowledge are the items, however in our proposal the constraints are used. Thus, every constraint will have associated a characteristic curve that we have named *Constraint Characteristic Curve* (CCC). This curve has the opposite shape to an ICC since, while this last represents the probability of answering correctly (knowledge), the CCC represents the probability of violating a constraint in a given problem (detection of incorrect knowledge). When a constraint is violated, this implies a lack of knowledge and, therefore, the necessary curve to represent it must monotonically decrease. The higher the student knowledge level, the lower the probability of that constraint being violated. In the IRT, it would be equivalent to a wrong response to an item.

The student knowledge distribution $P(\theta \mid \Phi, \tau)$ would be calculated as the product of the CCCs of those constraints that have been violated, joined with the opposite curves for those that, being relevant for the problem, have not been violated. This form of calculating the student knowledge is based on the inference mechanisms used in the IRT:

$$P(u = 1|\theta) = c_i + (1 - c_i)\frac{1}{1 + e^{-1.7a_i(\theta - b_i)}} \tag{2}$$

where $\Phi = p_1, p_2, ..., p_m$ represents the set of problems solved by the student and $\tau = c_1, c_2, ..., c_n$ the collection of constraints pertaining to the domain. $P(c_j / \theta)$ is the characteristic curve of the constraint c_j; r_{ij} is a binary variable that indicates whether or not the constraint is relevant to the problem p_i; and f_{ij} is another binary variable that indicates whether the student action in the problem p_i has produced the violation of the constraint c_j.

In our previous work [13] we used discrete curves whose values are the pairs knowledge level / probability, simplifying noticeably the necessity of data required by the IRT to infer the characteristic curves. In this proposal, the CCCs are also discrete and every value indicates the probability of a student with certain knowledge level violating a constraint.

The result of applying equation 2 is a distribution of probabilities where, for each level of knowledge, the probability of the student knowledge level corresponding to that level is expressed. In order to calculate the denominated knowledge level two strategies can be applied: taking the distribution's expected value (or mean) (*Expectation a Posteriori*), or also, choosing the mode (*Maximum a Posteriori*).

5 OOPS

To put into practice the model proposed in the previous section, we have used a new version of OOPS (Object Oriented Programming System) [14]. This new version incorporates fundamentals elements of CBM. OOPS focuses on the Object-Oriented programming domain and allows emulating the behavior of a human tutor during the student learning process, detecting the gaps in their knowledge and acting to rectify the situation. This tool permits the students to construct object-oriented programs in the pseudo-language used in the School of Telecommunication Engineering at the University of Málaga (Spain) as a result of doing exercises. These exercises are based on defining and implementing classes (attributes and methods), according to a stem provided by the system. The construction is done visually using the drag and drop technique. The student has to select from a toolbar the elements needed to construct an object-oriented program, and drop them into the workspace.

Once the student decides to correct his/her solution, the system will initialize its inference engine, which uses the domain model constraints for detecting the student's errors. With these errors, the student model is updated and, unless the system is working in evaluation mode, the students will be shown feedback to help them to correct their conceptual error.

The current architecture of OOPS is based on a generic framework [15] defined for the construction of Web-based Intelligent Learning Environments, based on problem solving tasks. For this reason, OOPS is structured in the following modules:

1. The most external component, the *interface* (see Figure 1), through which teachers and students can insert or solve problems, respectively. Teachers can configure the system to show information such as the hint/feedback messages.

2.   The main part of OOPS is the *pedagogical module*, which has the components required for estimating the student knowledge, such as the estimation algorithms, a JESS inference engine [16] for identifying the violated constraints, or those elements needed to control the pedagogical actions used to instruct the student in the most suitable way, such as the adaptive problem selection module.
3.   The *domain model*, formed by the set of constraints and problems.
4.   The *student model*, which contains the violated and the satisfied constraints, the knowledge estimation distributions and the logs with the actions performed by the student in each problem.

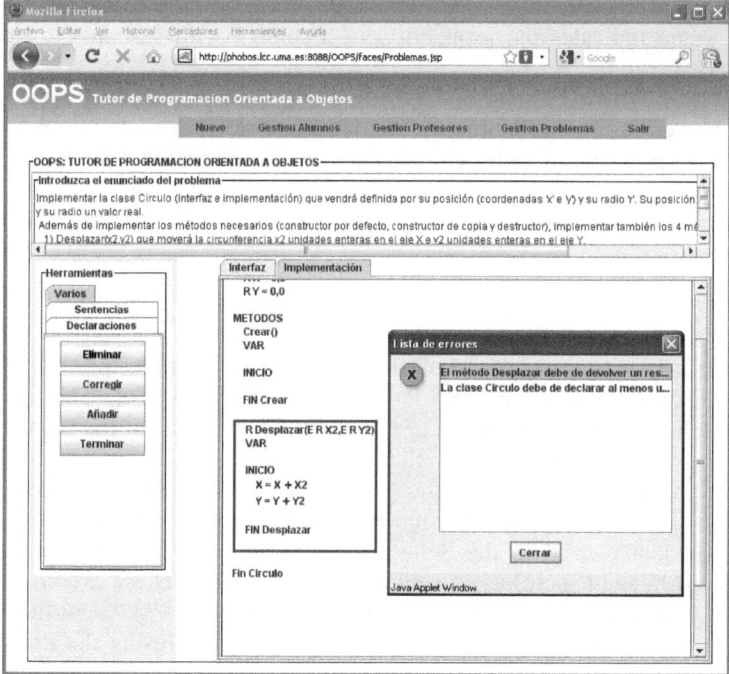

Fig. 1. OOPS interface

6   Experiments

To check the validity of our diagnostic technique through ill-defined procedural tasks, we carried out an experiment with undergraduate students. Our goal was to allow the students to put into practice their knowledge of object-oriented programming in a session which took place in a controlled environment (in a teaching laboratory). The session was structured as follows: First, a test was administered using the Siette web-based system [17], which provides IRT-based assessments. Next, students used OOPS to solve two problems.

We stated the following hypothesis: if we infer the student knowledge level through IRT tests (in this experiment through Siette) and with our model (implemented in OOPS), the results obtained should be similar.

6.1 Experiment Design

The experiment was design in such a way that in both parts (the test and the problems) the same kind of knowledge was measured. Accordingly, the test questions were elaborated carefully to assess the same concepts used in the practical problems proposed in OOPS. For this purpose, in OOPS two problems were selected involving basic concepts of object-oriented programming. That is, the most relevant domain constraints were checked in those problems. We used a subset of 15 significant constraints, according to some domain experts. The set of questions were developed taking into account the subset of constraints. Two test questions were created for each constraint. As a result, these questions assessed the same concept the constraint gauged and this led to a total of 30 test questions.

The experiment was carried out in May of 2009 with undergraduate students studying Technical Engineering in Telecommunications from the University of Málaga (Spain). These students had previously received face-to-face lessons on object-oriented programming. A total of 20 students participated in the experiment. After being administered the test (where the solutions were never shown), the students started using OOPS. Initially, all of them took a problem (whose results were not considered in the posterior analysis) simply for training on the system. Next, they took two programming problems in OOPS.

6.2 Data Analysis

Once the data from both systems were obtained, we processed this information using a tool called MULTILOG [18], which is one of the most popular for IRT-based analysis. First, we calibrated the ICCs according to the 3PL IRT-based model. To this end, we used the test results represented in a matrix of boolean values. This matrix, needed by MULTILOG, contained, for each student and item (question), a value indicating whether or not the concept evaluated was known by the student. Subsequentyly, the obtained calibration was used in conjunction with the test results to infer the student knowledge estimation.

Analogously, data obtained through OOPS were used to calibrate the CCCs. In this case, the matrix used by MULTILOG represented whether or not the constraint was violated (that is, whether or not the concept is known) during the problem resolution. The curves computed after this step, were used again with the student data collected by OOPS, to generate the student knowledge estimations.

Our main aim was to obtain homogeneous results in relation to the knowledge source assessed and the nature of the data used to estimate this knowledge. Regarding the knowledge source, we used the previously mentioned correspondence between constraints and items; and for the nature of the data used to make the estimations, we use a MULTILOG input matrix with the same meaning and format. That is, a true value, indicating the knowledge of certain concept; and a false value, in those cases in which this concept is erroneously known.

240   J. Gálvez, E. Guzmán, and R. Conejo

Finally, we should mention that MULTILOG was used in both cases, in order to ensure that calibration and inference techniques were the same.

6.3 Results

To carry out the comparison of both estimations, a paired t-Student was used with 95% confidence factor. This statistic is commonly used to compare the difference between two small-sized populations. The null hypothesis was that the difference between the population means was zero. The analysis gave a p-value of 0.7972 which clearly suggests that we cannot reject the previous null hypothesis and, therefore, there was no significant difference between the evaluations obtained with OOPS, using our model which combines IRT and CBM, and those given by Siette where the 3PL model was applied.

7 Conclusions and Future Work

The techniques described in this paper provide several advantages to the procedural activities assessment. The student knowledge estimations are invariant, i.e. they do not depend on the set of problems solved by the student, and the estimation accuracy degree can be controlled. Furthermore, it is a statistical inference mechanism where CCCs are estimated using historical information about a sample of the student performance while they took these problems.

Our initial hypothesis was that the most popular statistical techniques used for determining the student knowledge in testing, can also be used in procedural activities. Therefore, through these procedural activities, we can obtain similar results to those obtained with an IRT-based test. The conclusions of our experiment with ill-defined tasks, suggest that our hypothesis is correct. As a consequence, we can carry out well-founded assessments, using only a few procedural activities. To obtain a similar assessment result through tests, a high number of questions would be needed.

IRT-based tests can be administered adaptively, through *adaptive testing*, where each question is selected dynamically, in terms of the student estimated knowledge level. Moreover, the test size is also decided dynamically in terms of the required estimation accuracy. In this sense, our future work will focus on the development of a mechanism for the adaptive administration of procedural activities.

In this work, we have estimated the student declarative knowledge through procedural activities. Currently, we are working on extending the model to also evaluate procedural knowledge. Likewise, since the model presented in this paper has been applied to two different domains, it is also necessary to extend the study of another evaluation system which confirms the hypothesis stated in these experiments.

Acknowledgments. This work has been co-financed by the Spanish Ministry of Science and Innovation (TIN2007-67515) and by the Andalusian Regional Ministry of Science, Innovation and Enterprise (TIC-03243). The authors wish to thank prof. David Bueno and his students for their willingness to participate in the experiments described in this paper.

References

1. Brooks, R.A.: Intelligence without representation. Artificial Intelligence 47, 139–159 (1991)
2. Greer, J., McCalla, G.: Student Modeling: The Key to Individualized Knowledge-based Instruction. Springer, Heidelberg (1994)
3. Thurstone, L.L.: A method of scaling psychological and educational tests. Journal of Educational Psychology 16, 433–451 (1925)
4. Anderson, J.R., Boyle, C.F., Corbett, A.T., Lewis, M.W.: Cognitive modeling and intelligent tutoring. Artificial Intelligence 42, 7–49 (1990)
5. Conati, C., Gertner, A., VanLehn, K.: Using Bayesian networks to manage uncertainly in student modeling. User Modeling & User-Adapted Interaction 12(4), 371–417 (2002)
6. Hayes, J.R.: Cognitive psychology: Thinking and creating. Dorsey Press, Homewood (1978)
7. Gálvez, J., Guzmán, E., Conejo, R., Millán, E.: Student Knowledge Diagnosis Using Item Response Theory and Constraint-Based Modeling. In: The 14th International Conference on Artificial Intelligence in Education (AIED 2009), vol. 200, pp. 291–298 (2009)
8. Ohlsson, S.: Constraint-based Student Modeling. In: Student Modeling: The Key to Individualized Knowledge-based Instruction, pp. 167–189. Springer, Heidelberg (1994)
9. Mitrovic, A., Martin, B., Suraweera, P.: Intelligent Tutors for All: The Constraint-Based Approach. IEEE Intelligent Systems, IEEE Educational Activities Department 22, 38–45 (2007)
10. Ohlsson, S., Mitrovic, A.: Constraint-based knowledge representation for individualized instruction. Computer Science and Information Systems 3, 1–22 (2006)
11. Mayo, M., Mitrovic, A.: Optimising ITS behaviour with Bayesian networks and decision theory. International Journal of Artificial Intelligence in Education 12, 124–153 (2001)
12. Hambleton, R.K., Swaminathan, H., Rogers, J.H.: Fundamentals of Item Response Theory (Measurement Methods for the Social Science). Sage Publications, Inc., Thousand Oaks (1991)
13. Guzmán, E., Conejo, R., Pérez-de-la-Cruz, J.L.: Adaptive Testing for Hierarchical Student Models. User Modeling and User-Adapted Interaction 17, 119–157 (2007)
14. Gálvez, J., Guzmán, E., Conejo, R.: HA blended E-learning experience in a course of object oriented programming fundamentals. Knowledge-Based Systems 22(4), 279–286 (2009)
15. Gálvez, J., Guzmán, E., Conejo, R.: A SOA-Based Framework for Constructing Problem Solving Environments. In: The 8th IEEE International Conference on Advanced Learning Technologies, pp. 126–128 (2008)
16. Friedman-Hill, E.J.: JESS, The Java Expert System Shell. SAND–98-8206 (1997)
17. Guzmán, E., Conejo, R., Pérez-de-la-Cruz, J.L.: Improving Student Performance using Self-Assessment Tests. IEEE Intelligent Systems 22, 46–52 (2007)
18. Thissen, D.: Multilog: Multiple, categorical item analysis and test scoring using item response theory (version 5.1). Mooresville, In Scientific Software (1988)

Recursive Probability Trees for Bayesian Networks

Andrés Cano, Manuel Gómez-Olmedo, Serafín Moral, and Cora B. Pérez-Ariza

Dept. Computer Science and Artificial Intelligence
University of Granada, Granada, 18071, Spain
{acu,mgomez,smc,cora}@decsai.ugr.es

Abstract. This paper proposes a new data structure for representing potentials. Recursive probability trees are a generalization of probability trees. Both structures are able to represent context-specific independencies, but the new one is also able to hold a potential in a factorized way. This new structure can represent some kinds of potentials in a more efficient way than probability trees, and it can be the case that only recursive trees are able to represent certain factorizations. Basic operations for inference in Bayesian networks can be directly performed upon recursive probability trees.

Keywords: Bayesian networks inference, approximate computation, deterministic algorithms, probability trees.

1 Introduction

Bayesian networks [1] are graphical models that have become a prominent modeling tool for problems involving uncertainty. They enable efficient representation of joint probability distributions by exploiting independencies among the variables. The independencies are encoded in the graphical structure by means of the d-separation criterion. Bayesian networks decompose the joint probability distribution into a set of local probability distributions, one for each variable in the network. Each local distribution specifies a conditional probability distribution for a variable given its parents. Traditionally, these distributions are codified using conditional probability tables, that require a size that grows exponentially in the number of parents. In the last years, some alternative representations for probability distributions have been introduced. Among them, can be found *probability trees* [2,3,4] that try to capture *context-specific independencies* within distributions, making possible smaller representations than tables in case those independencies are detected. The basic operations in potentials can be performed directly in probability trees, and so they can be used directly in any propagation algorithm for Bayesian networks. Martínez et al. [5,6,7] have defined algorithms that even decompose probability trees in smaller ones. They use this decomposition in different propagation algorithms.

This paper introduces a new data structure for representing potentials: *recursive probability trees*. These are a generalization of probability trees. They are

P. Meseguer, L. Mandow, and R.M. Gasca (Eds.): CAEPIA 2009, LNAI 5988, pp. 242–251, 2010.

also tree structures that allow to represent context-specific independencies, but now they can maintain a potential in a factorized way. The recursivity comes by the fact that each factor can be again represented by a recursive subtree, and so on. So the capacity to represent context-specific independencies and decomposition of potentials at the same time, usually produce more compact representations than standard probability trees. As in the case of probability trees, the basic operations in potentials can be performed directly upon this new structure, which could lead to substantial advantages in inference with Bayesian networks.

The remainder of this paper is structured as follows. The next section describes the problem of probabilities propagation in Bayesian networks and the use of probability trees to represent potentials compactly. Section 3 introduces recursive probability trees. Section 4 shows the algorithms for making the basic operations with potentials using recursive probability trees. Section 5 presents several examples where recursive trees take advantage over other data structures. And finally, Section 6 gives the conclusions and future work.

2 Inference in Bayesian Networks and Probability Trees

Let $\mathbf{X} = \{X_1, \ldots, X_n\}$ be a set of variables. Make the assumption that each variable X_i takes values on a finite set of states Ω_{X_i} (the domain of X_i). Denote by x_i one of the values of X_i, $x_i \in \Omega_{X_i}$. If I is a set of indices, we shall write $\mathbf{X}_I$ for the set $\{X_i | i \in I\}$. $N = \{1, \ldots, n\}$ will denote the set of indices of all the variables in the network; thus $\mathbf{X} = \mathbf{X}_N$. The Cartesian product $\times_{i \in I} \Omega_{X_i}$ will be denoted by $\Omega_{\mathbf{X}_I}$. The elements of $\Omega_{\mathbf{X}_I}$ are called configurations of $\mathbf{X}_I$ and will be written with $\mathbf{x}$ or $\mathbf{x}_I$. We denote $\mathbf{x}_I^{\downarrow \mathbf{X}_J}$ to the *projection* of the configuration $\mathbf{x}_I$ to the set of variables $\mathbf{X}_J$, $\mathbf{X}_J \subseteq \mathbf{X}_I$.

A mapping from a set $\Omega_{\mathbf{X}_I}$ into $\mathbb{R}_0^+$ will be called a *potential* p for $\mathbf{X}_I$. Given a potential p, let $s(p)$ be the set of variables for which p is defined. The process of inference in probabilistic graphical models requires the definition of two operations on potentials: *combination* $p_1 \otimes p_2$ (multiplication) and *marginalization* $p^{\downarrow J}$ (by summing out all the variables not in X_J).

A *Bayesian network* is a directed acyclic graph, where each node represents a random event X_i, and the topology of the graph shows the independence relations between variables according to the d-separation criterion [1]. Each node X_i also has a conditional probability distribution $p_i(X_i | \Pi(X_i))$ for that variable, given its parents $\Pi(X_i)$. A conditional probability distribution defines a potential for variable X_i and its parents. A Bayesian network determines a joint probability distribution:

$$p(\mathbf{X} = \mathbf{x}) = \prod_{i \in N} p_i(x_i | \Pi(x_i)) \quad \forall \mathbf{x} \in \Omega_{\mathbf{X}} \tag{1}$$

Probability trees [8] have been used as a flexible data structure that enables the specification of *context-specific independencies* (see [4]) as well as using exact or approximate representations of potentials. A *probability tree* $\mathcal{T}$ is a directed labeled tree, in which each internal node represents a variable and each leaf represents a non-negative real number. Each internal node has one outgoing arc for each state of the variable that labels that node; each state labels one arc.

A probability tree $\mathcal{T}$ on variables $\mathbf{X}_I = \{X_i | i \in I\}$ represents a potential $p : \Omega_{\mathbf{X}_I} \to \mathbb{R}_0^+$ if for each $\mathbf{x}_I \in \Omega_{\mathbf{X}_I}$ the value $p(\mathbf{x}_I)$ is the number stored in the leaf node that is reached by starting from the root node and selecting the child corresponding to coordinate x_i for each internal node labeled X_i. A subtree of $\mathcal{T}$ is called a *terminal tree* if it contains only one node labeled with a variable, and all the children are numbers (leaf nodes).

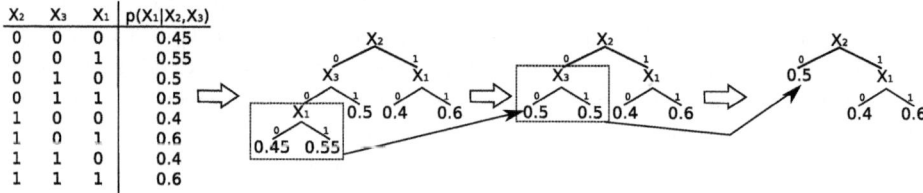

Fig. 1. Potential p, its representation as a probability tree and its approximation after pruning various branches (those rounded with a rectangular box)

A probability tree is usually a more compact representation of a potential than a table. This is illustrated in Fig. 1, which displays a potential p and its representation, using a probability tree. It can be seen that the values in the potential are independent of X_3 in the *context* $\{X_2 = x_2^2\}$. This context-specific independence is reflected in the tree in Fig. 1: it contains the same information as the table, but only requires five values rather than eight. Furthermore, trees enable even more compact representations in exchange for loss of accuracy. This is achieved by pruning certain leaves and replacing them with the average value, as shown in the right tree in Fig. 1.

If $\mathcal{T}$ is a probability tree on $\mathbf{X}_I$ and $\mathbf{X}_J \subseteq \mathbf{X}_I$, $\mathcal{T}^{R(\mathbf{x}_J)}$ (probability tree restricted to the configuration $\mathbf{x}_J$) denotes the *restriction operation* which consists of returning the part of the tree which is consistent with the values of the configuration $\mathbf{x}_J \in \Omega_{\mathbf{X}_J}$. For example, in the left probability tree in Figure 1, $\mathcal{T}^{R(X_2=x_2^1, X_3=x_3^1)}$ represents the terminal tree enclosed by the dashed line square. This operation is an important part of both combination and marginalization operations and is used for conditioning potentials to a given configuration. The basic operations (*combination, marginalization*) in potentials can be performed directly in probability trees [8].

3   Recursive Probability Trees

Recursive probability trees are a new data structure for representing potentials. As explained in previous section, probability trees make possible to reduce the size of the representation of a potential taking advantage of the context-specific independencies within the potential. *Recursive probability trees* generalize probability trees. With this new structure it is possible to represent context-specific independencies, as well as specifying a potential in a factorized form. However, in case of potentials without any context-specific independencies that can not be decomposed into several factors, using recursive probability trees as its representation probably will not offer any extra benefit.

It can be said that a potential is decomposed into a set of factors, if the product of the factors is equal to the original potential. For example, a Bayesian network specifies a joint probability distribution by means of a set of factors: the conditional probability distributions of each variable. In general, a factorized potential need less space than the original one. There are several inference algorithms for Bayesian networks that work with lists of potentials (factorization of potentials), instead of single potentials, reducing the complexity of probability propagation. For example, *lazy propagation* [9], *lazy-penniless* [10], *variable elimination* [11] and *mini-bucket* [12]. Some inference algorithms directly provide the factors of each potential, but in other ones, potentials must be explicitly decomposed into several factors. Martínez et al. [5,6,7] use probability trees to represent each factor. They give algorithms to decompose probability trees into two or more factors in exact and approximate ways, and then they take advantage of the factorizations in several inference algorithms for Bayesian networks.

A recursive probability tree $\mathcal{RT}$ is a directed tree. Now there are two kinds of internal nodes in the tree: *Split* nodes (N_S) and *List* nodes (N_L). There are also two kinds of leaf nodes: *Value* nodes (N_V) and *Potential* nodes (N_P). From now on, suppose $\mathcal{RT}$ is a recursive probability tree representing a potential $p^{\mathcal{RT}}$ defined on $\mathbf{X}_I$. A *Split* node represents a variable $X_i \in \mathbf{X}_I$. It has an outgoing arc for each $x_i \in \Omega_{X_i}$; each state labels one arc. A *List* node is used to list the factors in which a potential is decomposed. It has as many outgoing arcs as factors in the decomposition. Each child of a list node is again a recursive probability subtree that represents a potential (a factor) for a subset of variables $\mathbf{X}_J$, $\mathbf{X}_J \subseteq \mathbf{X}_I$. A *Potential* node stores a potential. This potential can be internally represented as a table, a probability tree or any other alternative representation. Finally, a *Value* node stores a non-negative real number. For example, the left side of Fig. 2 shows a possible recursive probability tree representing the factorization given by the network in the right one. Note that the branch enclosed with the dashed line represents a single potential for X_2, X_3, X_4 and X_5. The reader must notice that there could be different recursive potential trees factorizing the same set of potentials, being equivalent among them. Probability trees can be seen as a particular case of recursive probability trees where inner nodes are always *split* nodes and leaves nodes are *value* nodes.

Formally, a recursive probability tree $\mathcal{RT}$ defined on a set of variables $\mathbf{X}_I = \{X_i | i \in I\}$ represents the potential $p^{\mathcal{RT}} : \Omega_{\mathbf{X}_I} \to \mathbb{R}_0^+$ for the set $\mathbf{X}_I$, if for each $\mathbf{x}_I \in \Omega_{\mathbf{X}_I}$ the value $p^{\mathcal{RT}}(\mathbf{x}_I)$ is the number obtained with the following recursive procedure:

- If the root of $\mathcal{RT}$ is a value node labeled with the number r, then $p^{\mathcal{RT}}(\mathbf{x}_I)$ is r.
- If the root of $\mathcal{RT}$ is a potential node representing a potential p_i for $\mathbf{X}_J \subseteq \mathbf{X}_I$, then $p^{\mathcal{RT}}(\mathbf{x}_I)$ is $p_i(\mathbf{x}_I^{\downarrow \mathbf{X}_J})$.

- If the root of $\mathcal{RT}$ is a split node labeled with X_i then $p^{\mathcal{RT}}(\mathbf{x}_I)$ is the value $p^{ch_i(\mathcal{RT})}(\mathbf{x}_I)$, where $ch_i(\mathcal{RT})$ is the child of the root of $\mathcal{RT}$ corresponding to the value of X_i in $\mathbf{x}_I$.
- If the root of $\mathcal{RT}$ is a list node with n children $ch_1(\mathcal{RT}), \ldots, ch_n(\mathcal{RT})$ then $p^{\mathcal{RT}}(\mathbf{x}_I)$ is $\prod_{i=1}^{n} p^{ch_i(\mathcal{RT})}(\mathbf{x}_I)$.

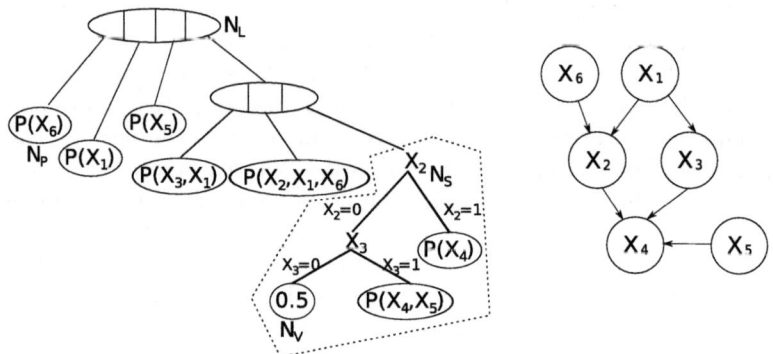

Fig. 2. A recursive probability tree representing a full bayesian network

4   Operations with Recursive Probability Trees

Recursive probability trees must be able to support the operations with potentials needed to perform inference algorithms on them, that are: *restriction, combination* and *marginalization*.

Let $\mathcal{RT}$ be a recursive probability tree and $\mathbf{x}_J$ a configuration for the set of variables $\mathbf{X}_J$, then $\mathcal{RT}^{R(\mathbf{x}_J)}$ ($\mathcal{RT}$ restricted to $\mathbf{x}_J$) is obtained with a simple algorithm: Prune every *Split* node which variable is included in $\mathbf{X}_J$, and restrict every *Potential* node in the tree to the given configuration $\mathbf{x}_J$. Therefore this operation acts on different ways depending on the kind of node where it acts: on N_L nodes the operation is sent to child nodes; on N_S nodes, if the node variable is contained in $\mathbf{X}_J$, then select the child corresponding to the value specified in the configuration; the potential contained in N_P nodes will be restricted to the given configuration if needed (the domain of the potential includes any of the configuration variables); and there is nothing to do on N_V nodes.

Figure 4 explains the restriction operation applied to the recursive tree presented in Fig. 3. The left part represents the recursive tree and the right one the set of potentials involved (in this case the potentials encoding the probability distributions defined by a Bayesian network). Suppose it is desired to get the value of the potential for the configuration $\mathbf{x} = \{X_1 = 0, X_2 = 1, X_3 = 0\}$. When the restriction operation $R(\mathbf{x})$ is invoked on the root node of the recursive tree the sequence of steps triggered by the operation are shown in Fig. 4. The final part of this figure shows the result of the operation: a node N_L containing three values. As the recursive tree supposes a multiplicative decomposition, the probability value for the configuration will be given by multiplying these values: 0.006.

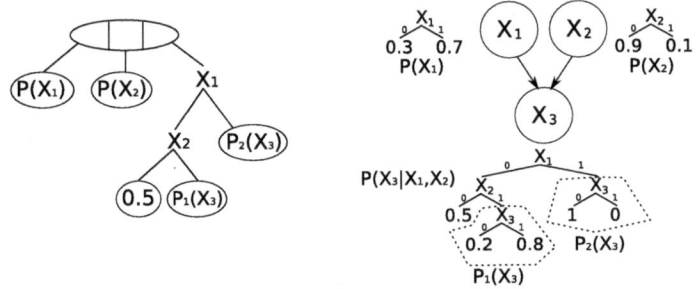

Fig. 3. Recursive potential tree encoding a Bayesian network

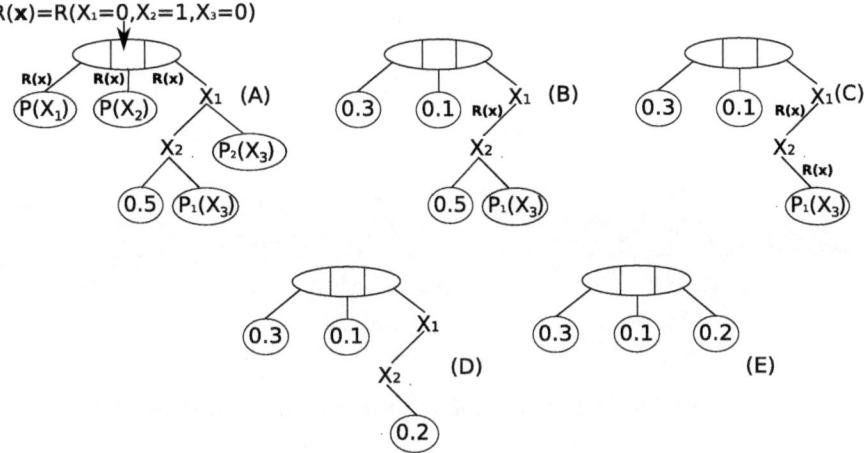

Fig. 4. Recursive potential restricted to a configuration

The *combination* of two recursive probability trees $\mathcal{RT}1$ and $\mathcal{RT}2$, being $\mathcal{RT}1 \otimes \mathcal{RT}2$, can be easily achieved by making the two recursive trees children of a new list node N_L. This definition is valid for combining a recursive potential tree $\mathcal{RT}1$ and a *potential Pot* or even a single *value Val*.

Given a recursive tree $\mathcal{RT}$ representing a potential p defined for a set of variables $\mathbf{X}_I$, let $X_\iota \in X_I$ be the variable to marginalize out. *Marginalization* obtains a recursive tree $\mathcal{RT}^{\downarrow \mathbf{X}_I \backslash \{X_\iota\}}$ for potential $p^{\downarrow \mathbf{X}_I \backslash \{X_\iota\}}$. The process of marginalization is divided into three steps:

- *DivideTree($\mathcal{RT}$)*: this operation consists of separating the original $\mathcal{RT}$ into two parts: one containing the variable of interest X_ι and another containing the rest of the recursive tree.
- *MultiplyVar($\mathcal{RT}, X_\iota$)*: combines all the potentials that contains X_ι
- *AddVar($\mathcal{RT}, X_\iota$)*: actually sums out X_ι. In the case of a recursive tree representing a single potential, *marginalization* can be performed just by applying *AddVar($\mathcal{RT}, X_\iota$)* directly.

The complete application of this operation is shown in Fig. 5. In this example the objective is to remove X_2 from the recursive tree.

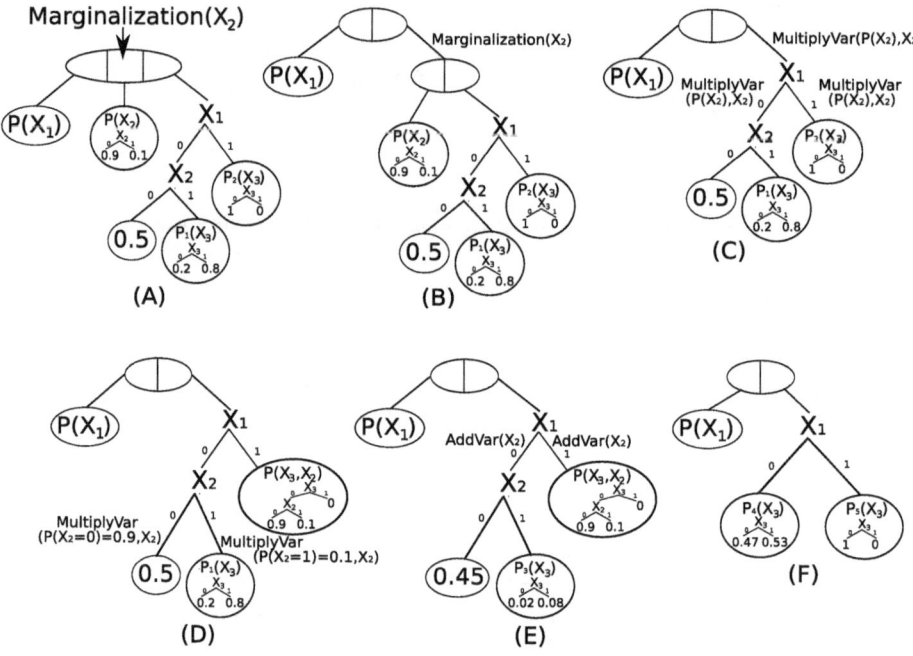

Fig. 5. Marginalization of recursive potential trees

The first step, see (B) in Fig 5, presents a recursive tree where the operation *DivideTree* has been performed: the left part of the tree contains a potential $P(X_1)$ and the right one contains all the potentials containing the variable to be removed, X_2, in their domains. The step represented by (C) has selected the potential $P(X_2)$ that will be multiplied with the tree under the split node for X_1. This is showed including it as an argument in the operation $MultiplyVar(P(X_2), X_2)$. In (D) the multiply operation reaches a split node for X_2 being needed to restrict the potential $P(X_2)$ passed as argument to the values of X_2. Therefore, the leftmost value in (D) must be multiplied by $P(X_2 = 0) = 0.9$. The child for $X_2 = 1$ will be given after multiplying $P_1(X_3)$ and $P(X_2 = 1) = 0.1$. Note the right child for X_1 split node: the result of multiplying $P(X_2)$ and $P_2(X_3)$ will be the new potential $P(X_3, X_2)$. Part (E) shows the result of multiplying $P_1(X_3)$ and $P(X_2 = 1) = 0.1$, producing $P_3(X_3)$. After that it is needed to remove X_2. This is showed in part (F). In X_2 split node this will be achieved by summing both children producing $P_4(X_3)$. In the right child of X_1 split node the operation will remove X_2 from $P(X_3, X_2)$ leading to $P_5(X_3)$.

5   Examples

As it has been explained before, recursive probability trees can be considered as a generalization of probability trees. This section contains an explanation of how to represent certain distributions using probability trees and recursive probability trees. For some of them, the representation with recursive probability trees will be more convenient or even the only solution.

Proportional values: Sometimes potentials present proportionality relations between several parts of the tree. In the simplest case, a part of the tree can be derived from another just by multiplying by a certain factor. This is the case of a probability tree encoding a joint distribution for X_1 and X_2 (see right part in Fig. 6): the potential for $X_1 = 0$ is proportional to the one corresponding to $X_1 = 1$. The second one can be obtained from the first one multiplying by 4). The left part of the figure shows the recursive probability tree for this potential. This recursive tree needs to store only 6 numbers instead of 8 (the savings could be important for potentials presenting proportionalities and defined over a big set of variables) and it is a much more compact representation. For example, an operation involving X_1 need not to work with the left part of the tree.

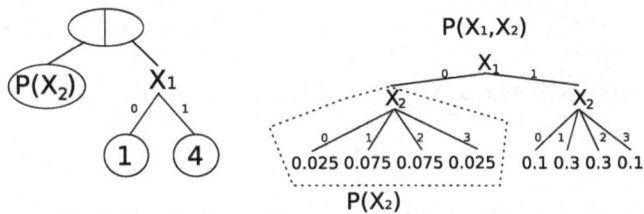

Fig. 6. Potential with proportional values

Tree splitting: When the distributions encode context specific independencies but certain values of the potential do not depend on the whole set of variables. Let us consider the tree in Fig. 7. The right part of the potential tree (right part of the figure) does not depend on X_2. This distribution can be represented with a recursive probability tree where the proportionalities and the independencies are clearly revealed, see left part in Fig. 7. Again recursive trees can ease posterior operations on the distributions. For example, a restriction operation to select a certain value for X_1 variable will actually operate on two nodes keeping the rest of the tree unaltered.

Multinets: An advantage of Bayesian networks is that they can specify dependencies only when necessary, leading to a significant reduction in the cost of inference. Bayesian multinets [13] further generalize Bayesian networks and can further reduce computation. A multinet can be thought of as a network where edges can appear or disappear depending on the values of certain nodes in the graph. Consider a network with four nodes X_1, X_2, X_3, X_4 where the conditional independencies properties among these variables depend on the values of X_4, a

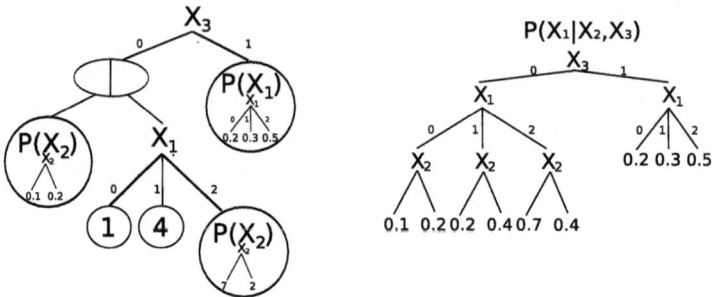

Fig. 7. Distribution with context specific independencies

binary variable. In fact this means the need to consider two different Bayesian networks, one for each state of X_4, (see Fig. 8, right part). The complete multinet can be represented with a recursive tree, as shown in the left part of the figure.

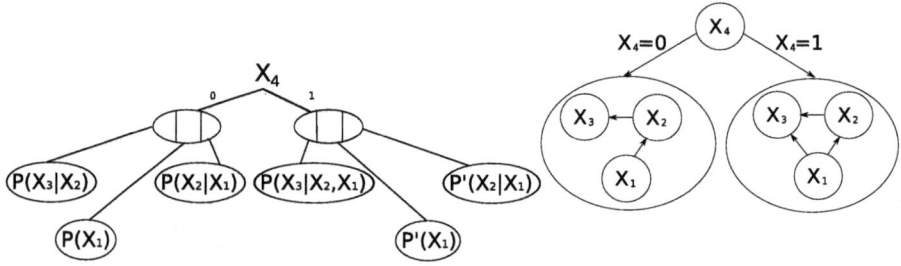

Fig. 8. Bayesian multinet and recursive tree representation

6   Conclusions and Future Work

In the present paper, a new data structure for representing the potentials in a Bayesian network has been introduced. In Section 5 several examples have been shown, illustrating some situations where recursive trees could take advantage over probability trees, getting smaller representations for potentials than probability trees. Section 4 has introduced how to make the basic operations with potentials directly with recursive trees. It seems possible to build more efficient propagation algorithms than those that use probability trees. About future directions of research, we plan to develop algorithms to automatically represent potentials as recursive trees, as well as adapting existing propagation algorithms to deal with recursive probability trees. Pruning recursive probability trees to achieve more compact representations is another of our goals. Also, we are studying how to learn recursive trees from databases, in the process of learning a Bayesian network. We expect that the ability for capturing context specific independencies and factorizing potentials is likely to be more faithful in representing the true underlying probability distributions, avoiding overfitting problems when learning from small data sets.

Acknowledgments. This research was jointly supported by the Spanish Ministry of Education and Science under the project TIN2007-67418-C03-03, the European Regional Development Fund (FEDER) and the FPI scholarship programme (BES-2008-002049). The authors have been also partially supported by the Andalusian Research Program under project P08-TIC-03717 and by the European Regional Development Fund (ERDF).

References

1. Pearl, J.: Probabilistic Reasoning with Intelligent Systems. Morgan & Kaufman, San Mateo (1988)
2. Cano, A., Moral, S., Salmerón, A.: Penniless propagation in join trees. International Journal of Intelligent Systems 15(11), 1027–1059 (2000)
3. Kozlov, D., Koller, D.: Nonuniform dynamic discretization in hybrid networks. In: Geiger, D., Shenoy, P. (eds.) Proceedings of the 13th Conference on Uncertainty in Artificial Intelligence, pp. 302–313. Morgan & Kaufmann, San Francisco (1997)
4. Boutilier, C., Friedman, N., Goldszmidt, M., Koller, D.: Context-specific independence in Bayesian networks. In: Proceedings of the Twelfth Annual Conference on Uncertainty in Artificial Intelligence (UAI 1996), Portland, Oregon, pp. 115–123 (1996)
5. Martínez, I., Moral, S., Rodríguez, C., Salmerón, A.: Factorisation of probability trees and its application to inference in bayesian networks. In: Proceedings of the First European Workshop on Probabilistic Graphical Models, Cuenca, Spain, pp. 127–134 (2002)
6. Martínez, I., Moral, S., Rodríguez, C., Salmerón, A.: Approximate factorisation of probability trees. In: Godo, L. (ed.) ECSQARU 2005. LNCS (LNAI), vol. 3571, pp. 51–62. Springer, Heidelberg (2005)
7. Martínez, I., Rodríguez, C., Salmerón, A.: Dynamic importance sampling in bayesian netwos using factorisation of probability trees. In: Proceedings of the Third European Workshop on Probabilistic Graphical Models, pp. 187–194 (2006)
8. Salmerón, A., Cano, A., Moral, S.: Importance sampling in Bayesian networks using probability trees. Computational Statistics and Data Analysis 34, 387–413 (2000)
9. Madsen, A.L., Jensen, F.V.: Lazy propagation in junction trees. In: Proceedings of the Fourteenth Annual Conference on Uncertainty in Artificial Intelligence (UAI 1998), pp. 362–369. Morgan Kaufmann Publishers, San Francisco (1998)
10. Cano, A., Moral, S., Salmerón, A.: Lazy evaluation in penniless propagation over join trees. Networks 39(4), 175–185 (2002)
11. Kohlas, J., Shenoy, P.P.: Computation in valuation algebras. In: Gabbay, D.M., Smets, P. (eds.) Handbook of Defeasible Reasoning and Uncertainty Management Systems. Algorithms for Uncertainty and Defeasible Reasoning, vol. 5, pp. 5–39. Kluwer, Dordrecht (1999)
12. Dechter, R.: Mini-buckets: A general scheme for generating approximations in automated reasoning. In: Proc. International Joint Conference of Artificial Intelligence (IJCAI 1997), Japan, pp. 1297–1302 (1997)
13. Geiger, D., Heckerman, D.: Knowledge representation and inference in similarity networks and bayesian multinets. Artificial Intelligence 82(1-2), 45–74 (1996)

Generating Saliency Maps Using Human Based Computation Agents*

Fidel Aznar, Mar Pujol, and Ramón Rizo

Department of Computer Science and Artificial Intelligence
University of Alicante
{fidel,mar,rizo}@dccia.ua.es

Abstract. This paper presents an agent system, which uses human based computation (HBC), that is able to calculate a saliency map for a specific image. This system will learn from human interaction to obtain a saliency map of the most important parts of an image. As we will see later, the maps generated using HBC are more robust than their classical counterpart, because they are less dependent on the group of features that exist in a given image.

1 Introduction

The most important part of the information received by human beings is visual, but not all this information is processed, in fact, the greatest part of this information does not excite us. It has been shown [1,2] that exists an information selection process, which helps us to look first on the most important parts of an image. This is a two ways job with a *bottom-up* process, that emerges from the image itself and a *top-down* process that represents the internal state of the being. More specifically, the *bottom-up* process is independent of the being, because only depends on a specific image and does not take into account the human internal state. Therefore, if a human gets visual information from the environment (without modulating it with their internal state), it will use a saliency map, that will be quite the same for all humans, and will contain the importance of each part of the image that is being processed.

Moreover, the biological plausibility of saliency maps has been demonstrated for mammals. We could find several models (both, biological and computational ones) for saliency map generation. Nowadays, saliency maps are an active research area with diverse applications such as: predicting eye-fixations in a given image, dinamical image resizing, or object recognition [3,4,5,6,7,8].

In this paper, a method for generating saliency maps, that uses human based computation (a kind of computation where humans are specially important and take part on the agent system) is presented. Using this kind of computation allows us to obtain saliency maps that take into account all the important features that human beings detect for a given image.

---

* This work has been supported by the Conselleria d'Educació de la Generalitat Valenciana, project GVPRE/2008/040, the University of Alicante, project GRE08P02 and by the Ministerio de Ciencia e Innovación of Spain, project TIN2009-10581.

P. Meseguer, L. Mandow, and R.M. Gasca (Eds.): CAEPIA 2009, LNAI 5988, pp. 252–260, 2010.

Moreover, the obtained maps will be compared with the saliency maps obtained with the model presented in [3,9], that for now on will be called classical model. As discussed below, many of the present systems designed to obtain saliency maps do not consider some of the most important features of an image.

The outline of this paper is as follows. First, we will review the state of the art of both, saliency maps and human based computation. Second, we will present a method to obtain this kind of maps, emphasizing the agent system used to specify our application. In addition, we will show the probabilistic formalization needed to fuse visual data and therefore, generate saliency maps. Next, the obtained maps will be reviewed and compared with classical maps. For this comparison the eye-fixation zones, obtained from both maps (classical and HBC) will be used. Finally, the advantages and the problems of this approximation will be commented, proposing some future lines of research.

2   On Human Based Computation and Saliency Maps

As it is commented in [6] the computational and psychological definition of saliency is well established and is related to the bottom-up distinctiveness of an object. It is a relative property, that depends on the relation between an object and the others that compose a scene.

There are many different physical qualities that can make an object more salient than other objects in the display, such as its color, orientation, size, shape, movement, ... Hence, it could be very complex to develop a model to mimic the biological process used to obtain a saliency map of a given image.

One of the most important research tasks in artificial vision is related to extracting important features from an image. On one hand, we can distinguish a wide range of artificial feature extractors, as commented in [10,7]. On the other hand, there are several biological based extractors for important features, such as [11,9]. Most of these systems are based on obtaining saliency maps that represent only a selected group of multiscale features combined using an aggregation function for obtain a single map.

One of the most used models with a biological basis is shown in [3]. In this model a set of multiscale features is extracted from a given image to generate a set of submaps (one for each feature). More specifically, intensity, color and orientation submaps are obtained. These submaps are normalized, centered and finally combined to a single saliency map.

The main idea of these biological models is to mimic the primates visual system. In fact, although they use a very simple architecture, the obtained saliency maps, when applied to natural images, are quite good [11]. However, their principal problem is related to specifying the most important features that must be selected to generate a saliency map. An image that has features that are not taken into account in the model will not generate a correct map. In addition, these models do not use any recurrence mechanism, so there are several human visual behaviors that cannot be reproduced (like contour completion and closure, which are important for certain types of human pop-out). It is mainly for these reasons that we decided to use human based computation to obtain an image saliency map.

Human based computation can be defined as a technique that performs computational problems requesting the resolution of certain steps of the problem to humans. In human based computation, the roles are often reversed: the computer asks a human (or several humans) to solve a problem, and then collects, interprets and integrates all the solutions.

Several of the most important applications related to the field of human based computation arise from the team directed by Luis von Ahn, who developed what he calls GWAPs (games with a purpose). To design this type of application and to make it more attractive to users, he has presented a guide to designing games [12], that should be referred to, and taken into account, by anyone wishing to develop a similar application.

Agents are commonly used with human based computation systems. On one hand, a social agent, that will be able to interact with other agents and also humans must be defined. On the other hand, the system must be pro-active and in this way, act not only as a response to the environment but also searching opportunities from it.

3   Proposed System

To obtain a saliency map we have developed an application, designed as a computer game, that can be used to extract the necessary data to compute the map. The application takes the form of a matching game in which users must select a fixed size window, extracted from an image, and click where it belongs in the main picture. We use a fixed-size window to maintain uniformity and playability of the game. The game uses several modification filters that are applied to the cropped image to highlight or hide certain features of the image. Using the matching information obtained from the users' game play, we obtain a saliency map that shows the zones that are most easily identified by humans.

In this way, we have defined a multi-agent system that is presented in figure 1b and is described below.

We define an agent called **SaliencyMap** that will generate a saliency map $M^k \in M$ for a given image $img_k \in Img$ from the image set Img. A human expert will use this agent to specify the images to work with and the priority of these images in the system. Moreover, this agent will obtain information from users which it will then filter, normalize and fuse to obtain a saliency map. Further information about this agent and the data fusion process used will be given in the next section.

SaliencyMap agent also communicates with other agent called **Dispatcher**. *Dispatcher* agent will provide to each *Request* agent the probability of showing a specific image to the user ($\Upsilon_{salmap} = P(Img)$). For each image a unique set of cropping zones will be defined, $\forall img_i \in Img \left(\exists! Z^i \subseteq Z \right)$. In the same way, for each cropping zone, there exists a unique features vector that describes it $\forall z \in Z^i, \exists! f_i^j \left(f_i^j = (a_1, a_2, ..., a_n, t_j) \right), f_i^t \in F, a_i \in \mathbb{R}, t_j \in T$, where T is the complete set of all the possible filters to be used in a specific zone. Agent *Dispatcher* also provides the cropping zone distribution for each image i, $\Upsilon_{zone} = P(Z^i)$, and the occurrence probability for each kind of filter that will be used in these zones $\Upsilon_T = P(T)$. This information is calculated using the requirements of an expert and then is sent to *Request* agents each time the game is started. The user information needed to generate the profile and pre-filter the data (to be used to generate the saliency map) is also obtained by this agent.

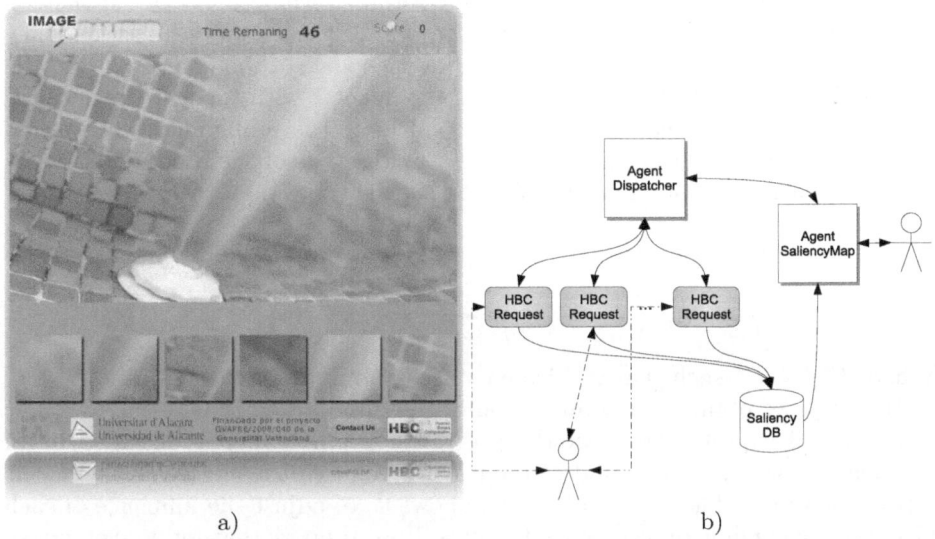

a)   b)

Fig. 1. a) Screenshot from *request* agent interface. This web application can be accessed by the following URL (http://www.i3a.ua.es/hbc/) b) System architecture. All the important interactions between agents and users are shown.

Request agents interact with users asking them for help to solve the matching problem. Users obtain gratification while playing the game, by competing to obtain the highest score (see figure 1a).

Firstly, *Request* agents communicate with agent *Dispatcher* to ask the images to be selected and the probability distribution to be followed to obtain the image crops. However, *Dispatcher* agent is not obliged to send this information (for example if we do not need to prioritize any image), giving more freedom to *Request* agent.

Secondly, these agents will query all image data from a specific database and will calculate the cropping zones for each image, applying a set of filters to it. The filters used are: rotation (indicating the angle to be applied), scale (indicating the factor), colour (eliminates the colour information transforming an image to greyscale) and gauss (applying a gaussian convolution with a given intensity).

Next, these cropping zones will be shown to users, so they must try to localize it. Once a stage is finished *Request* agents send to *Dispatcher* agents all the data related to the game play (that could be used to data filter) and the data related to the matching problem (the obtained cropping zones, the filters applied and the user matching). This information will be very important to calculate the saliency map for a given image.

4 Saliency Map Calculation with Bayesian Fusion

A saliency map $M^k \subseteq M$ of a given image k is defined as a set of cells where $m_i \in M^k$. Each cell is defined as a binary variable, where $m_i = m_i^+$ if there is important information inside this cell or $m_i = m_i^-$ if not. To obtain the saliency of a given cell i is equivalent to calculate for each zone of the image $Z^k \subseteq Z$ the probability that they are important given the image k with the features $F^k \subseteq F$ obtained until now, (that is, we want to calculate the probability distribution $P(m_i | F^k)$). We can group the features F^k by the type of the used modificators T, reformulating the previous distribution so that:

$$
\begin{aligned}
P(m_i | F^k) &= \\
&= \sum_{j=1..n} P(m_i, t_j | F^{k,j}) = \sum_{j=1..n} P(m_i | t_j, F^{k,j}) \times P(t_j | F^{k,j})
\end{aligned}
\tag{1}
$$

Where $F^{k,j} \subseteq F^k$ such that all elements of $F^{k,j}$ only use a kind of filter $t_j \in T$. In this way, we obtain a decomposition of the distribution that seems to follow a mixture of experts, where firstly, the saliency probability is obtained in an independent way for each kind of filter and secondly, it is aggregated with the rest of the filters. The term $P(t_j | F^{k,j})$ allows us to adjust the influence of each filter type depending on the image features. If we suppose that for a given image the saliency map M^k is approximated with the marginal distribution of image regions:

$$
\begin{aligned}
P(M^k | F^k) &= \prod_i P(m_i | F^k) = \\
&= \prod_i \sum_{j=1,,n} P(m_i | t_j, F^{k,j}) \times P(t_j | F^{k,j})
\end{aligned}
\tag{2}
$$

To calculate this probability distribution from a set of features F^k is a binary estimation problem with one state. In this way, to obtain the distribution from only one feature $\boldsymbol{f} \in F^k$, we will use a binary Bayesian filter. We will work with logarithms to avoid numerical problems:

$$
\begin{aligned}
l_i(x) &= l_i(x-1) + \varPhi - l(0) \\
\text{donde } \varPhi &= \frac{\displaystyle\sum_{j=1,,n} P(m_i | t_j, \boldsymbol{f}_x) \times P(t_j | \boldsymbol{f}_x)}{1 - \displaystyle\sum_{j=1,,n} P(m_i | t_j, \boldsymbol{f}_x) \times P(t_j | \boldsymbol{f}_x)}, \boldsymbol{f}_x \in F^{k,j} \\
l_i(0) &= \log \frac{P(m_i)}{1 - P(m_i)}
\end{aligned}
\tag{3}
$$

Finally, we need to specify how to calculate the distribution $P(m_i | t_j, \boldsymbol{f}_x)$, that is, we want to calculate the probability of a cell m_i being important knowing their features vector $\boldsymbol{f}_x$ (linked with zone $z_x \in Z$) and the filter used in this zone. If for a given feature vector a zone z_x is classified correctly [1] $\boldsymbol{f}_x^+$ then will assume that $P(m_i^+ | t_j, \boldsymbol{f}_x^+) = 0.6$ else $P(m_i^+ | t_j, \boldsymbol{f}_x^-) = 0.3$. Initially we will suppose that a zone has the same probability of being salient or not so $P(m_i^+) = 0.5$.

5 Experimentation

In this part of the paper, we will show the saliency maps obtained using the method presented in section 4. In this way we will show the designed experiments for map calculation and the comparison between classical and HBC maps.

5.1 Experiments Design

For this experimental section we have used the agent system, presented above, orientated to obtain a saliency map for each image of the system. More specifically, we have selected 70 images from a database, grouped in artificial (10 images), nature images (30 images) and animal/human faces (30 images). The artificial images are specially selected due to their complexity, so it is not easy to segment the artificial object from a given picture. Moreover, all images are taken in colour and share the same size of 600x337 pixels (this is needed to adapt the image to the game). We have 22,000 registers, which came from the interaction of different users of our application. In this way, we have around 300 registers for each image that we will combine to obtain a saliency map.

5.2 Saliency Maps Obtention

Obtaining saliency maps is based on applying the equation 3 to all game registers for each image. In figure 2a five images from the database with their associated HBC saliency map (2b) are shown. As we can observe, the more important zones of the image are usually related to brighter zones in the saliency map. The presented saliency maps are calculated assuming that $P(t_j | F^{k,j})$ is a uniform distribution, combining in this way all filter types with the same importance.

These maps reflect all the games played for each database image and show the unique features detected by human observers. As we will see in the next section, many of these zones match with classical saliency maps. However, some of these important features are not shown in their classical counterpart. The main differences between these kinds of saliency maps will be analyzed in next section.

---

[1] If we assume that when we apply all types of filters to a zone they have the same difficulty to be located then this distribution only depends on the data $\boldsymbol{f}_x$ and more specifically on the distance between the zone and the position where the user clicks in the main image if the zone is extracted from this click position. We use crop zones of 90x90 pixels, so we decided that a distance between the zone and the click position less than 54 pixels will be assumed as correct classification (54 pixels was chosen because it is the mean distance between the centre and the nearest/farthest points of the rectangle).

a)   b)   c)

Fig. 2. a) Selection of images from database. For each image, the first five visual fixations predicted by a classical map (triangles) and the HBC map (squares) are shown. b) Saliency maps obtained using HBC. The positive (triangle) and negative (star) votes are shown. The intensity of each position represents the importance of the zone (the brighter the zone the more important it is) c) Classical saliency map. This map has been normalized to use the same saliency scale as the HBC maps.

5.3   Comparing Saliency Maps

Once we have obtained the saliency maps for our image dataset we decided to compare these maps with the saliency maps obtained using the system proposed by Laurent Itti and Christof Koch [9]. This system is mainly used for predicting where the human eye will focus within a given image.

To compare both maps a *winner-take-all* (WTA) neuronal network has been implemented. [11] comments that when using this type of neural network the synaptic interactions among units ensure that only the most active locations remain, while all other locations are suppressed. We will use the same WTA network proposed in [11]. Applying this network, we obtained a set of fixation points for each type of saliency map. Furthermore, we have compared the five most important points for the two eye point fixation sets obtained from the WTA network (one set for each type of saliency map). This comparison is developed without taking into account the sequence of points obtaining a deviation between maps[2] around 18.82.

In figure 2c the most important fixations for each saliency map are shown (where stars represent the classic map and squares are used for the HBC map). We can observe that there are several positions highlighted in the HBC map that are not highlighted in the classical map. However, the first fixations in the HBC map are usually covered by the classical map for most of the image database.

Image type	Map deviation
Nature	8.11%
Faces	23.14%
Artificial	25.21%

Fig. 3. Deviation of the five most important fixations between HBC and classical saliency maps for each type of image

The most interesting results were observed when we compared the deviation between maps depending on the image types (see figure 3). The saliency maps obtained from faces or artificial images have more distance than natural images. We think that this difference of distance is obtained since classical saliency maps do not take into account important features in this kind of images, so they do not detect important zones that are perceived by humans. A good example can be seen in the first image of figure 2a. In this figure a traffic sign with a complex natural background is presented. The classical system does not distinguish the sign from the background and, therefore, does not consider it important enough. In contrast the HBC system highlights the importance of the sign with regards to the background.

6   Conclusions and Future Lines

In this paper, a method for obtaining saliency maps using human based computation is presented. The maps generated with HBC are able to fuse the important zones detected by independent human observers and, in this way, these maps will

---

[2] The deviation is calculated as $map_{desv} = \dfrac{\sum\limits_{i=1..|P^{hbc}|} \sqrt{\left(p_i^{hbc} - p_i^{cla}\right)^2}}{|P^{hbc}| \cdot d_{\max}}$ where $p_i^{hbc} \in P^{hbc}$ is the i point of the most important fixations (P^{hbc}) used in the HBC saliency map, p_i^{cla} is the i point of the most important fixations for the classical map and d_{max} is the maximum distance between two image points.

contain all the essential elements of the image and will not need to specify which features must be taken into account (in contrast with classical methods).

In addition, the saliency maps obtained with HBC, detect important features not always presented in classical systems, like faces or signs, but important for humans. However, generating HBC saliency maps is not a realtime process, because it needs a first step where the *request* agent asks the users for their participation.

We are now actively working to learn a model that mimics the extraction process of a saliency map from a given image. This task is very important to improve current saliency maps and to show the most important features (and their intensity) that are selected by human beings for creating a saliency map.

References

1. Bahmani, H., Nasrabadi, A.M., Hashemi Gholpayeghani, M.R.: Using weighted saliency map in visual attention for object recognition. In: 8th World Congress on Computational Mechanics (WCCM8), 5th European Congress on Computational Methods in Applied Sciences and Engineering, ECCOMAS 2008 (2008), http://www.iacm--eccomascongress2008.org/cd/offline/pdfs/a2180.pdf
2. Itti, L., Koch, C.: Feature combination strategies for saliency-based visual attention systems. Journal of Electronic Imaging 10, 161–169 (2001)
3. Itti, L.: Quantifying the contribution of low-level saliency to human eye movements in dynamic scenes. Visual Cognition 12(6), 1093–1123 (2005)
4. Le Meur, O., Castellan, X., Le Callet, P., Barba, D.: Efficient Saliency-Based Repurposing Method. In: IEEE International Conference on Image Processing, pp. 421–424 (2006)
5. Cheoi, K., Lee, Y.: Detecting perceptually important regions in an image based on human visual attention characteristic. In: Caelli, T.M., Amin, A., Duin, R.P.W., Kamel, M.S., de Ridder, D. (eds.) SPR 2002 and SSPR 2002. LNCS, vol. 2396, pp. 329–338. Springer, Heidelberg (2002)
6. Fecteau, J.H., Munoz, D.P.: Salience, relevance, and firing: a priority map for target selection. Trends in cognitive sciences 10, 382–390 (2006)
7. Moosmann, F., Larlus, D., Jurie, F.: Learning saliency maps for object categorization. In: ECCV International Workshop on The Representation and Use of Prior Knowledge in Vision (2006)
8. Siagian, C., Student Member, Itti, L., Member: Rapid biologically-inspired scene classification using features shared with visual attention. IEEE Trans. Pattern Anal. Mach. Intell. 29, 300–312 (2007)
9. Itti, L., Koch, C.: Computational modelling of visual attention. Nat. Rev. Neurosci. 2, 194–203 (2001)
10. Kadir, T., Brady, M.: Saliency, scale and image description. Int. J. Comput. Vision 45, 83–105 (2001)
11. Itti, L., Koch, C., Niebur, E.: A model of saliency-based visual attention for rapid scene analysis. IEEE Trans. Pattern Anal. Mach. Intell. 20, 1254–1259 (1998)
12. von Ahn, L., Dabbish, L.: Designing games with a purpose. Commun. ACM 51, 58–67 (2008)

A New Contiguity-Constrained Agglomerative Hierarchical Clustering Algorithm for Image Segmentation

Eduardo R. Concepción Morales[1] and Yosu Yurramendi Mendizabal[2]

[1] University of Cienfuegos, Faculty of Informatics, Cuatro Caminos, Cienfuegos, Cuba
econcep@ucf.edu.cu
[2] University of the Basque Country/EHU, Campus Guipuzcoa, Department of Computer Science and Artificial Intelligence, Donostia-San Sebastian, Spain
yosu.yurramendi@ehu.es

Abstract. This paper introduces a new constrained hierarchical agglomerative algorithm with an aggregation index which uses neighbouring relations present in the data. Experiments show the behaviour of the proposed contiguity-constrained agglomerative hierarchical algorithm in the case of medical image segmentation.

Keywords: contiguity-constrained clustering methods, agglomerative hierarchical classification, image segmentation.

1 Introduction

The goal of clustering, or unsupervised classification, is to partition a given set of data in homogeneous groups [1]. The main difference between supervised and unsupervised classification is considered the availability of information about individual data labels. However many different sources of knowledge might be available which could be integrated into the classification process. For example, proteins located in the same locations in a cell are likely to share common functionalities [2]; when clustering the succession of films scripts scenes the sequence might be taken into account [3].

In image segmentation pixels are classified in homogeneous clusters based on their appearance. When regular clustering algorithms are applied to this problem, the information about the two—dimensional structure of the image is not taken into account. In general, nearby pixels have similar characteristics and therefore should belong to the same cluster, i.e., that structure should be preserved as much as possible.

The spatial contiguity can be modeled defining for each pixel a set of neighbors. The idea of using neighborhood relations to model spatial interactions is similar to a Markov Random Field [4], where the classification of a pixel depends on the classification of neighboring pixels. The notion of spatial contiguity has been used also in the context of dimensionality reduction [5]. Extensive work has been done on incorporating different types of constraints into clustering methods [6-11].

Hierarchical clustering algorithms are widely used in clustering because they produce a set of nested partitions, and allow for a multiresolution or multiscale analysis

P. Meseguer, L. Mandow, and R.M. Gasca (Eds.): CAEPIA 2009, LNAI 5988, pp. 261–270, 2010.
© Springer-Verlag Berlin Heidelberg 2010

of the data. Even if the goal is to obtain a single partition of the data, an agglomerative algorithm provides a locally optimal or greedy way to do it.

Unconstrained clustering algorithms have been adapted to take into account several contiguity constraints. In this case, it has been shown that among classical agglomerative algorithms there are only two which do not give rise to inversions or reversals, i.e., non-monotonic variations in the criterion value. These are the contiguity-constrained complete link method and the contiguity-constrained single link method (with a different type of constraints) [12].

In this paper we introduce a new contiguity-constrained hierarchical agglomerative clustering algorithm which uses an aggregation function based on pairwise intercluster distances. It takes into account spatial interactions which are modeled by means of a contiguity relation. At each step only those clusters are considered to be merged which are spatially contiguous. When calculating intercluster distances we use those members of the clusters which are across the border and are contiguous. This contiguity-constrained method in the limiting case agrees with the classical average link method. We show that this contiguity-constrained average-like link method does not lead to inversions.

The algorithm is described in Section 2. Some experimental results are presented in Section 3 that show the behaviour of the proposed constrained algorithm for image segmentation. Conclusions and future work are presented Section 4.

2   Notation and Terminology

Let us consider a set $\Omega = \{\omega_1, \omega_2, ..., \omega_n\}$ of some abstract objects ω_i, $i = 1, ..., n$, and the data set $X = \{x_1, x_2, ..., x_n\}$ where x_i represents some measurements which describe the object ω_i. In the following we will also use indices to denote objects, i.e., i represents object ω_i. A connection matrix $A = [a_{ij}]$ is used where $a_{ij} = 1$ if objects ω_i and ω_j are contiguous or adjacent and $a_{ij} = 0$ otherwise. The neighborhood of an object is the set of adjacent objects according to the connection matrix. In the case of image segmentation the contiguity relation can represent the 4- or 8- adjacency, or an arbitrary neighborhood of radius r around any object consisting of all pixels which are at a (Euclidean) distance less or equal than r from a given pixel.

Assume we want to cluster these data into K disjoint clusters, i.e., we want to obtain a partition $P = \{P_1, P_2, ..., P_K\}$. Two clusters P_k and P_l are said to be contiguous if at least one member of P_k is contiguous to at least one member of P_l.

We will denote by n_{kl} be the number of related pairs of objects between contiguous clusters P_k and P_l, i.e., the number of links across the border of the two clusters. For a given cluster P_k the value n_{kk} is the number of connections inside the cluster. It is easy to note that

$$n_{kl} = \sum_{\omega_i \in P_k, \omega_j \in P_l} a_{ij} \tag{1}$$

In order to evaluate the quality of clustering several measures have been proposed [12]. Pairwise distances can define a global measure which favors certain properties such as low intra-cluster variability.

Let us first assume that for every pair of objects ω_i and ω_j, a dissimilarity measure $d(\omega_i, \omega_j)$ is available. We define an aggregation based on the concept of (average) heterogeneity of the clusters.

Definition 1: For any pair of neighboring clusters P_k and P_l, the dissimilarity between them, denoted by $d_{AH,}$ is defined as

$$d_{AH}\left(P_k,P_l\right)=\frac{1}{n_{kl}}\sum_{\substack{\omega_i \in P_k \\ \omega_j \in P_l}} a_{ij}d\left(\omega_i,\omega_j\right) \tag{2}$$

The dissimilarity defined in (**2**) measures the differences across the borders of contiguous clusters. Moreover, the dissimilarity is calculated taking into account only the neighbouring members of each cluster. We can think of d_{AH} as a measure of the average border split between two contiguous clusters.

With the idea of producing segmentations at various levels of resolution, an agglomerative hierarchical strategy is used. In the initial state of the algorithm every object is assigned to a cluster. The algorithm proceeds to select a pair of neighboring clusters with minimum dissimilarity and merge them. After this step, dissimilarities between the just created cluster and the rest of the adjacent clusters are updated.

After merging any two clusters, it is necessary to update the dissimilarities with the rest; this is the reduction step.

Property 1: Given a pair of neighboring clusters P_k and P_l, the dissimilarities between a newly formed cluster $P_k \cup P_l$ and any contiguous cluster P_m can be calculated as

$$d_{AH}\left(P_k \bigcup P_l,P_m\right)=\frac{n_{km}d_{AH}\left(P_k,P_m\right)+n_{lm}d_{AH}\left(P_l,P_m\right)}{n_{km}+n_{lm}} \tag{3}$$

The resulting method is similar to the average link method and will be called contiguity-constrained average-like link method. In the absence of structure, i.e., when every object is related to the rest, both methods coincide.

It can be proven that the problem of inversions or reversals in the series of agglomerations does not occur. Due to space limits we include without prove the following proposition.

Proposition 1: The cluster hierarchy obtained with the contiguity-constrained average-like link method dos not lead to inversions.

The former proposition guarantees that we can cut the hierarchy at any level to obtain an unambiguous partition.

As a result of the imposed contiguity constraint the number of needed comparisons can be significantly reduced. The running time is typically dominated by the time required for selecting the cluster pair to be merged. Efficient implementations can be obtained if we maintain a list of neighbouring clusters ordered by the dissimilarity for each cluster in the current set.

The contiguity-constrained average-like link method leads to contiguous clusters according to the neighbourhood relation defined. This means that a cluster can not be composed of two separate regions. This can be reasonable when segmenting an image into different objects. However if the same kind of object is present in different non-contiguous places in the image it might be spotted as different objects.

The next toy example illustrates this issue. Fig. 1a shows a sample image with two similar patterns in a black background. The hierarchy obtained with the proposed method, considering a 4 – adjacency relation, is shown in Fig. 1e. Cutting the dendrogram at level 10, a three-cluster partition is obtained (Fig. 1f). In this case the similar patterns correspond to two different non-contiguous clusters.

Figures 1g and 1h show the result when considering a neighbourhood of radius 3. In this case the two similar patterns are in the same cluster. The increase of the radius of the neighbourhood creates a link between two pixels of these patterns. This is prima facie evidence of the effect of the neighbourhood size in the results of the segmentation.

In Fig. 1b-1d we included the dendrogram obtained with the unconstrained average link method, a two-cluster partition, and a four-cluster partition, respectively. The two-cluster partition (Fig. 1c) obtained with a cut of the dendrogram at level 2 agrees with the one obtained in Fig. 1h. In Fig 1d a four-cluster partition obtained cutting the dendrogram at level 1.5 is shown. In this case the original image is recovered. Processing time savings are big: 90% and 75% with respect to the average-link method when using 4-adjacency, and a radius of 3 pixels, respectively.

The absence of link between two pixels is a hard constraint, namely, that those can not be merged unless all intervening pixels are also merged. For example, in Fig. 1f the two similar patterns can not be fused together without including the background. For that reason more clusters (three) are needed to make the solution comparable with the one in Fig. 1c.

3   Experimental Results

In this section we present some experiments with real MRI data provided by the Internet Brain Segmentation Repository (IBSR) of the Center of Morphometric Analysis (CMA) at Massachussets General Hospital available at http://www.cma.mgh.harvard.edu/ibsr/.

We obtained 20 normal MR brain data sets and their manual segmentations from IBSR. Manual segmentations were performed by trained investigators at CMA using a semiautomatic intensity contour mapping algorithm. While manual segmentations are not ground truth, they provide a reasonable way to compare segmentation methods. These 20 brain scans were chosen by IBSR because they cover a range of image quality.

The coronal three-dimensional T1-weighted spoiled gradient echo MRI scans were performed on two different imaging systems. Ten FLASH scans on four males and six females were performed on a 1.5 Tesla Siemens Magnetom MR System (Iselin, NJ) with the following parameters: TR = 40 msec, TE = 8 msec, flip angle = 50 degrees, field of view = 30 cm, slice thickness = contiguous 3.1 mm, matrix = 256x256, and averages =1. Ten 3D-CAPRY scans on six males and four females were performed on a 1.5 Tesla General Electric Signa MR System (Milwaukee, WI), with the following parameters: TR = 50 msec, TE = 9 msec, flip angle = 50 degrees, field of view = 24 cm, slice thickness = contiguous 3.0mm, matrix = 256x256, and averages = 1. We used the 8-bit scaled 3D MRI data files with brain regions only.

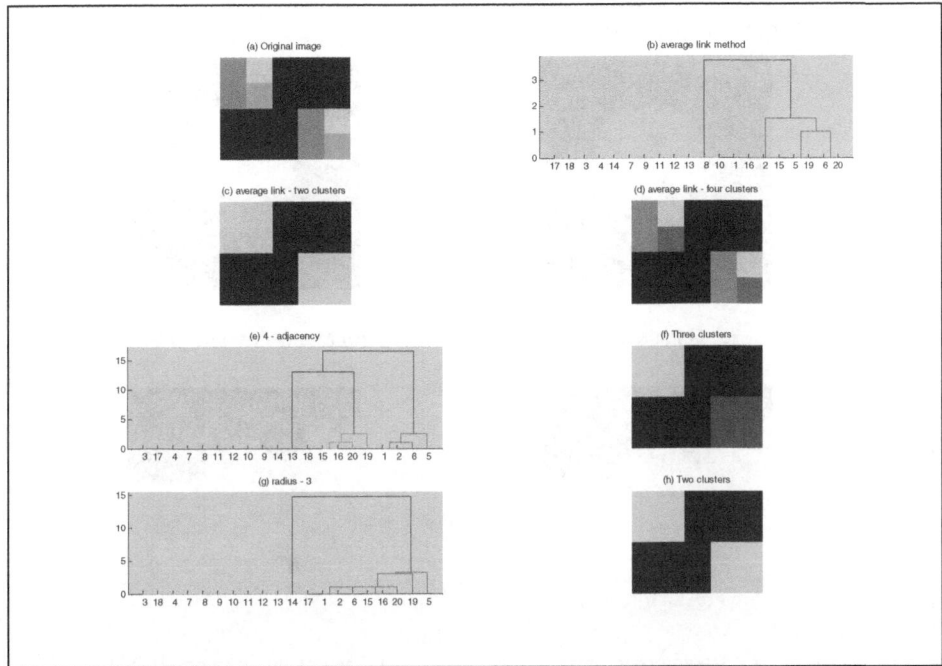

Fig. 1. Artificial example: (a) Original image with two similar patterns; (b) dendrogram obtained with the average link method; (c)-(d) two-cluster and a three-cluster partitions obtained with the average link method; (e)-(f) a three-cluster partition after segmenting considering 4 – adjacency; (g)-(h) a two-cluster partition when using a neighborhood of radius. 3;.

Our interest is mainly focused in the segmentation of the gray matter (GM) and white matter (WM) because they are the predominant tissues in the brain, together with the cerebrospinal fluid (CSF). Given a slice we first select a region of interest (ROI) where the main tissues are present. The rationale is that a small region requires less computer time to be processed. Moreover, in clinical settings users are normally interested in certain zones, e.g., the region where a tumor is located.

Figure 2 shows a sample (approximately central) slice of the volume and the corresponding manual segmentation. We applied our algorithm to the central slice of each volume. In each slice with segmented (approximately) the same region of interest.

Our main goal with experiments was to evaluate how well the obtained partitions agree with available knowledge (manual segmentations and results from other segmentation methods).

In order to compare results from automatic segmentations and manual segmentations, IBSR uses an overlap metric. This overlap metric is defined for given class as the number of pixels that the same class assignment in both segmentations, divided by the number of pixels where either segmentation has the class assignment, or equivalently, $|S_A \cap S_{Manual}| / |S_A \cup S_{Manual}|$. This is the same as the Jaccard coefficient [13]. This metric ranges from 1 for perfect agreement, to 0 for no agreement of classified pixels.

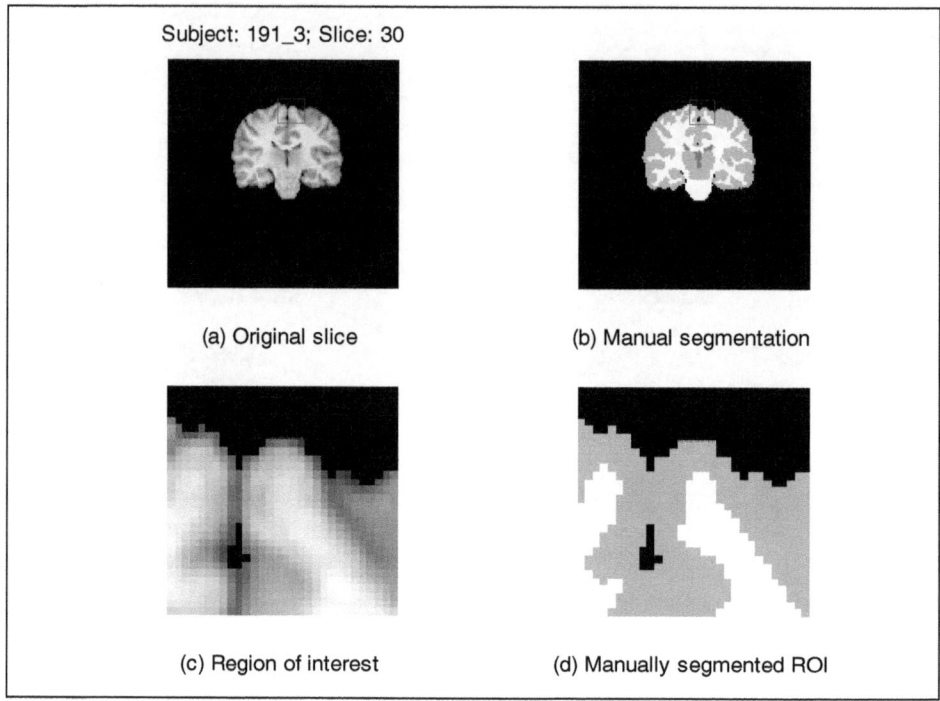

Subject: 191_3; Slice: 30

(a) Original slice   (b) Manual segmentation

(c) Region of interest   (d) Manually segmented ROI

Fig. 2. A sample slice (a), the corresponding manual segmentation (b); the selected ROI (c), and manually segmented ROI (d)

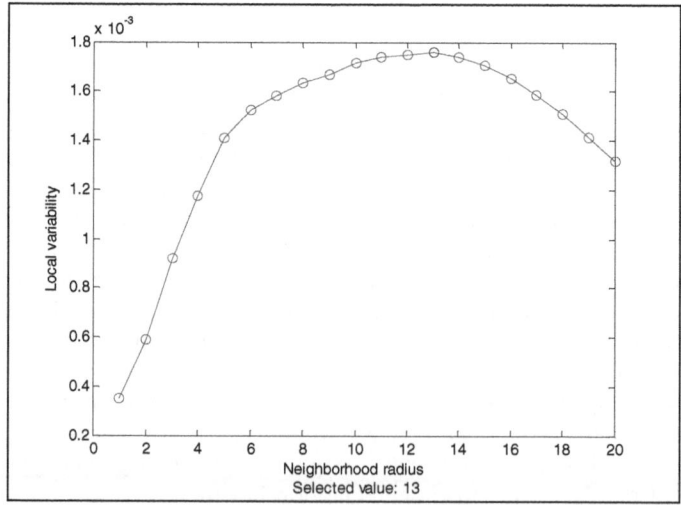

Fig. 3. Local variability values for different neighborhood radii

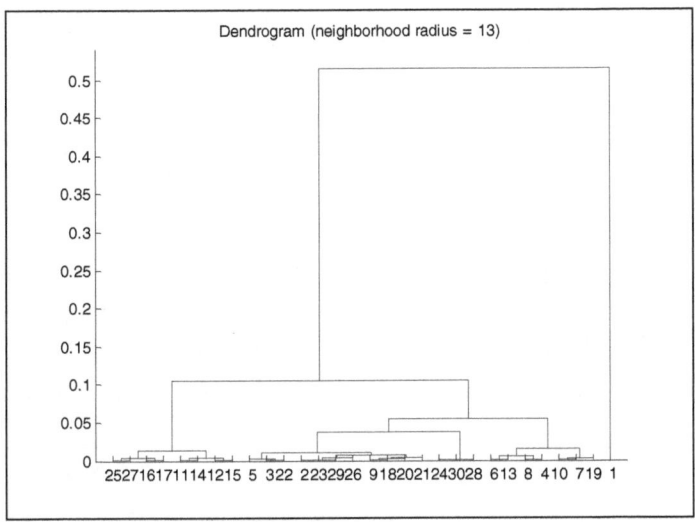

Fig. 4. Dendrogram obtained for a neighborhood radius of 13 pixels

Before applying the algorithm described above, a number of practical issues must be considered. We applied the algorithm without any preprocessing of the images. This decision has an impact in the results because image volumes have several artefacts such as noise and intensity inhomogeneity.

The dissimilarity between pixels was measured with the Euclidean distance between pixels intensities.

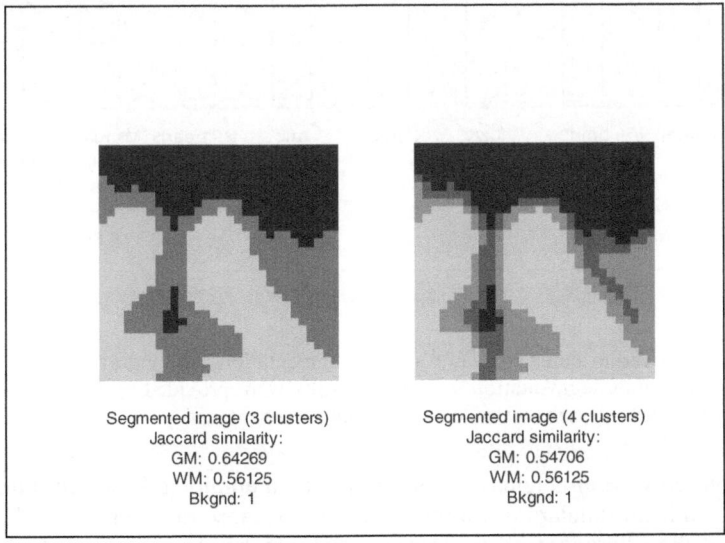

Fig. 5. Two segmentations obtained from dendrogram in Fig. 4

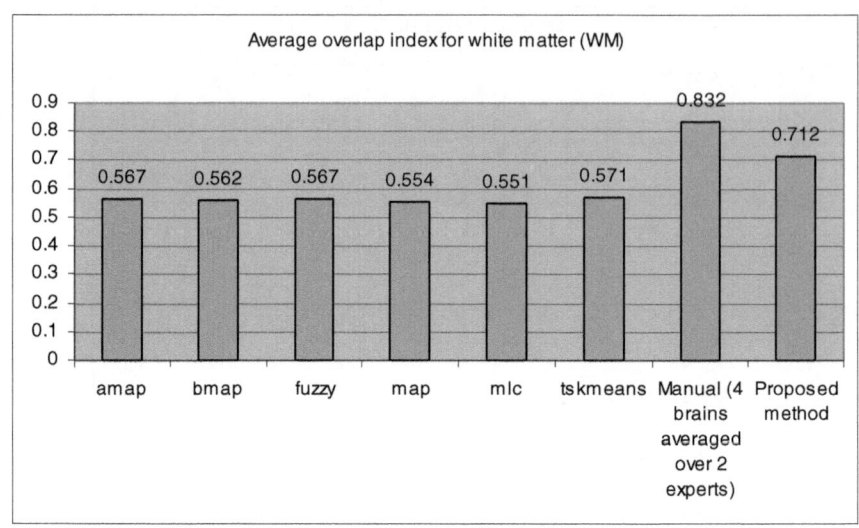

(a)

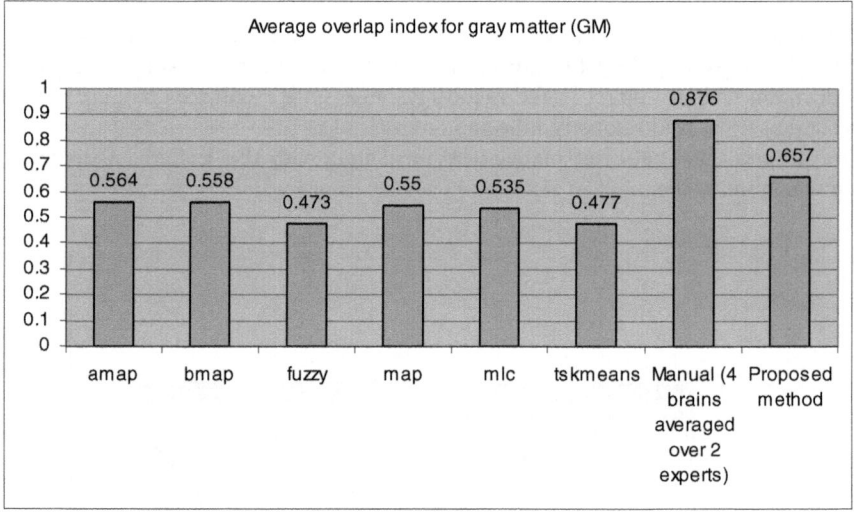

(b)

Fig. 6. Average overlap index for white matter segmentation, (a), and gray matter segmentation, (b), from various segmentation methods. Results were provided by IBSR. Results of the proposed method are averages over the selected regions of interest.

We explored several neighbourhood radii. On an empirical basis we found that after applying a local standard deviation texture filter, those radii for which the standard deviation of the filtered image is high give best results. The local standard deviation takes into account only neighbouring pixels [14]. The standard deviation of the filtered image gives a measure of the local variability of the image. Fig. 3. shows the results of this analysis for the example in Fig. 2. The peak of the local variability is obtained for a radius of 13 pixels. We observed that low neighbourhood radii tend to produce poor results in this data set. We set the minimum neighbourhood radius equal to 10 pixels.

After applying the proposed method to the original images, the obtained dendrogram is cut to obtain the desired segmentation.

Fig. 5 shows two segmentations obtained from dendrogram in Fig. 4, together with the overlap index for gray matter, white matter, and background. The three-cluster segmentation matches the manual segmentation (cf. Fig. 2). However, in the four-cluster segmentation a thin layer of cerebrospinal fluid between gray matter and background is identified. This is an interesting finding which shows the ability of the algorithm to view the data at different resolutions or scales. We noticed that experts did not identified cerebrospinal fluid in these regions. In the rest of the experiments we did not take into consideration this possibility because we can not measure the overlap of this class with respect to the manual segmentations in the selected regions of interest.

All twenty normal MRI brain datasets from IBSR were processed with the proposed method following the procedure described above using the brain-only datasets. Overlap index for white matter and gray matter was calculated in each case.

Fig 6 shows the average overlap index for white matter and gray matter segmentation on twenty normal brains from various automatic methods provided by IBSR: adaptive MAP, biased MAP, fuzzy c-means, Maximum A Posteriori Probability (MAP), Maximum-Likelihood, tree-structure k-means, and manual segmentations of 2 experts on 4 brains. The results of the proposed method are averages over the selected regions of interest. The automatic methods also used the brain-only data sets.

The average overlap index for the proposed method is 0.712 for white matter and 0.657 for gray matter. These values are higher than those from the six automatic methods, although they are lower than results on four brains averaged over two experts.

The values in Fig. 6 may appear low, but it must be taken into consideration that the data set contains images of different qualities. For that reason, these values must be considered valid only in the given context.

Other studies could be conducted (e.g., using data sets of better quality, or using other kind of images) for a more extensive evaluation of the proposed method.

4   Concluding Remarks and Future Work

In this paper a new contiguity-constrained agglomerative hierarchical clustering algorithm is presented which takes into account spatial relations present in the data. A new aggregation function is introduced, together with the update formula for the reduction step.

The resulting contiguity-constrained average-like link method is inversion free. This fact guarantees that unambiguous partitions can be obtained from the cluster hierarchy.

Experimental results in the case of medical image segmentation provide evidence of the behaviour of the proposed method in this particular task. Obtained results compare well with results from different automatic segmentation methods.

We plan to carry out additional experiments in order to evaluate the proposed method under different situations and contexts.

References

1. Jain, A.K., Murthy, M.N., Flynn, P.J.: Data Clustering: A Review. ACM Computing Surveys 31, 264–323 (1999)
2. Jensen, D., Neville, J.: Linkage and autocorrelation cause feature selection bias in relational learning. In: Proceedings of the 19th International Conference on Machine Learning (2002)
3. Murtagh, F., Ganz, A., McKie, S.: The structure of narrative: The case of film scripts. Pattern Recognition (2008), doi:10.1016/j.patcog.2008.05.026
4. Winkler, G.: Image Analysis, Random Fields and Markov Chain Monte Carlo Methods. Springer, Berlin (2003)
5. Roweis, S., Saul, L.: Nonlinear Dimensionality Reduction by Locally Linear Embedding. Science 290, 2323–2326 (2000)
6. Ferligoj, A., Batagelj, V.: Clustering with relational constraint. Psychometrika 47, 413–426 (1982)
7. Perruchet, C.: Constrained agglomerative hierarchical classification. Pattern Recognition 16, 213–217 (1983)
8. Murtagh, F.: A survey of algorithms for contiguity-constrained clustering and related problems. The Computer Journal 28, 82–88 (1985)
9. Gordon, A.D.: A survey of constrained classification. Computational statistics & Data Analysis 1, 17–29 (1996)
10. Wagstaff, K.L.: Value, Cost, and Sharing: Open Issues in Constrained Clustering. In: Džeroski, S., Struyf, J. (eds.) KDID 2006. LNCS, vol. 4747, pp. 1–10. Springer, Heidelberg (2007)
11. Davidson, I., Basu, S.: A Survey of Clustering with Instance Level Constraints. ACM Transactions on Knowledge Discovery from Data (2007)
12. Murtagh, F.: Contiguity-constrained hierarchical clustering. In: Cox, I.J., Hansen, P., Julesz, B. (eds.) Partitioning Data Sets. DIMACS, pp. 143–152. AMS, Providence (1994)
13. Jain, A.K., Dubes, R.C.: Algorithms for Clustering Data. Prentice Hall, Englewoods Cliffs (1988)
14. Lebart, L.: Contiguity Analysis and Classification. In: Gaul, W., Opitz, O., Schader, M. (eds.) Data Analysis, pp. 233–244. Springer, Berlin (2000)

Classifying Sleep Apneas Using Neural Networks and a Combination of Experts

Bertha Guijarro-Berdiñas, Elena Hernández-Pereira, and Diego Peteiro-Barral

Department of Computer Science, Faculty of Informatics, University of A Coruña,
Campus de Elviña s/n, 15071 A Coruña, Spain
{cibertha,elena,dpeteiro}@udc.es
http://www.dc.fi.udc.es/lidia

Abstract. *Objective:* The involuntary periodic repetition of respiratory pauses or apneas constitutes the sleep apnea-hypopnea syndrome (SAHS). This paper presents two novel approaches for sleep apnea classification in one of their three basic types: obstructive, central and mixed. The goal is to improve the classification accuracy obtained in previous works. *Materials and methods:* Both models are based on a combination of classifiers whose inputs are the coefficients obtained by a discrete wavelet decomposition applied to the raw samples of the apnea in the thoracic effort signal. The first model builds adaptive data-dependent committees, subsets of classifiers that are specifically selected for each input pattern. The second one uses a new classification approach based on the characteristics each type of apnea presents in different segments of the apnea. This model is based on the Error Correcting Output Code and its input coefficients were determined by a feature selection method (SVM Recursive Feature Elimination). In order to train and test the systems, 120 events from six different patients were used. The true error rate was estimated using 10 different simulations of a 10-fold cross validation. *Results:* The mean test accuracy, obtained over the test set was 85.20% ± 1.25 for the first model and 90.27% ± 0.79 for the second one. *Conclusions:* The proposed classifiers surpass, up to the author's knowledge, other previous results. Moreover, the results achieved are correctly enough to obtain a reliable diagnosis of SAHS, taking into account the average duration of a sleep test and the number of apneas presented for a patient who suffers SAHS.

1 Introduction

A sleep apnea is defined as a pause in breathing, or cessation of the airflow in the respiratory tracts, of at least 10 seconds in duration. The event is defined as a hypopnea when, rather than a complete cessation, a considerable reduction occurs in the airflow accompanied by a desaturation of oxygen levels in arterial blood. The involuntary periodic repetition of these respiratory pauses (until hundreds of times in one night) constitutes one of the most frequent sleep disorders: the sleep apnea-hypopnea syndrome (SAHS). The SAHS affects 4-6% of men, 2-4%

P. Meseguer, L. Mandow, and R.M. Gasca (Eds.): CAEPIA 2009, LNAI 5988, pp. 271–280, 2010.
© Springer-Verlag Berlin Heidelberg 2010

of women and 1-3% of children over the world (between five and eight million in Spain) although only between 5 and 9% of the patients are diagnosed.

Nowadays, the SAHS has no cure but an effective treatment improves symptoms and reduces the risk of mortality. The most effective method for the SAHS diagnosis is made on the basis of the analysis of a nocturnal polysomnogram, defined as a continuous and simultaneous recording during sleep of a set of variables including airflow in the upper air tracts, oxygen saturation in arterial blood (SaO_2) and respiratory effort (both abdominal and thoracic) [1]. Following conventional clinical criteria, the apneic episodes are detected in the airflow signal, using the information derived from the electrophysiological and oxygen saturation signals as context for interpretation. Later on, they are classified, independently to be an apnea or hypopnea, using the thoracic effort in three basic types of respiratory disfunctions [2]:

- Central apnea (CA) is a pattern characterized by a complete cessation of the respiratory movements (see Fig. 1, first column).
- Obstructive apnea (OA) is the most frequent pattern, characterized by the presence of thoracic effort for continuing breathing (see Fig. 1, second column).
- Mixed apnea (MA) is a combination of the previous two patterns, defined by a central respiratory pause followed, in a relative short interval of time, by an obstructive respiratory effort (see Fig. 1, third column).

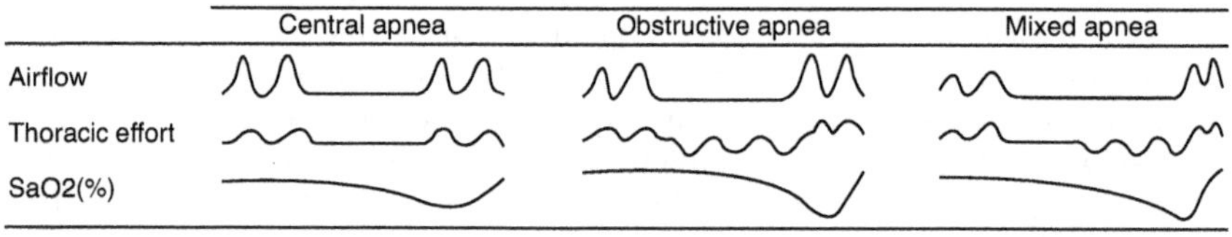

Fig. 1. The three basic types of apneic events and their representative signals

In the diagnosis, the prevalence of a certain type of apneic event determines the type of the syndrome of the patient: Obstructive Sleep Apnea-Hypopnea Syndrome (OSAHS), when most of the events are obstructive; or Central Sleep Apnea-Hypopnea Syndrome (CSAHS), when the great majority are the central ones. Mixed events rarely appear isolated and they are usually accompanied by central and obstructive events. The diagnosis offered for a patient who presents mixed events will be OSAHS when there is a predominance of obstructive events, or CSAHS if central events are the predominant ones [3]. The proper classification of the apneic events will determine the type of the syndrome and, consequently, the choice of the appropriate treatment. However, the manual analysis of the polysomnographic record implies the study of a considerable number of physiological variables during a prolonged lapse of time. For this reason, during the last years some computerized systems have been appearing with the aim of automatizing both the detection and the classification of sleep apneas [4,5].

Our contribution in the field of computerized diagnosis of SAHS is the intelligent monitoring system SAMOA [6,7]. SAMOA is an automatic system for respiratory analysis and sleep study, which makes a particularized diagnosis for the patient respect to the possible existence of the SAHS. For this system, regarding apnea classification, several different approaches have been tried [8] in order to improve the accuracy obtained by the original model. The best result [8], with an accuracy of 83.78%±1.90, was achieved by a feedforward neural network trained using the Bayesian framework whose inputs were the first level-5-detail coefficients, obtained from a discrete wavelet transformation of the samples of the thoracic effort signal. In this model, the main discrepancies appear between the obstructive and mixed classes and between the central and mixed classes. This is a logical result due to the fact that the mixed event is a combination of the other two. In order to overcome this problem and using a combination of neural networks [9], two new methods for classifying sleep apneas are presented in this paper.

The paper is structured as follows: section 2 reviews the materials and methods used, and sections 3 and 4 describe the two apnea classification models developed as well as the results obtained by each one. Finally, a comparison of the experimental results obtained and the conclusions drawn are presented in section 5.

2 Materials and Methods

In this section, the materials and methods used are presented. As in the previous work [8], a combination of feed-forward neural networks trained using the Bayesian framework [10] were used and, in order to fix the number of inputs to the classification model, a discrete wavelet transformation was applied to the raw samples of the thoracic effort signal segments where apneas were localized. The number of corresponding total wavelet coefficients is 16. Finally, for the development of the models, the software Weka [11] and Matlab [12] were employed.

2.1 Materials

In order to build the train/test data sets, six different recordings were available. The signals of these recordings were sampled with a frequency of 12.5 Hz and later analyzed by a medical expert who detected and classified the apneic events. A total of 339 apneas were found, being 217 obstructive, 40 central and 82 mixed. To obtain a balanced training set, as required by the classification models, 120 apneas were selected (40 of each class). All the central patterns were used while the other 40 events of the other classes were randomly selected. Finally, when working with artificial neural networks, data normalization is essential to avoid the saturation of the activation functions [13] and thus our data were normalized to have zero mean and standard deviation equal to 1.

2.2 Methods

To choose the best architecture the following method was employed:

1. For each model
   (a) Take the data set and generate 10 different 10-fold cross validation sets.
   (b) Train a model and obtain 10×10 accuracy measures over the test sets.
2. Apply a Kruskal-Wallis test [14] to check if there are significant differences among the accuracy means of the trained models for a level of significance $\gamma = 0.05$. The accuracy is obtained as $A = TP/(TP + FP)$.
3. If there are differences among the means, then apply a Tukey's multiple comparison procedure [15] to find the simplest model whose error is not significantly different from the model with the best mean accuracy rate.

3   Committees of Experts

It is well known that a combination of many different classifiers can improve classification accuracy. A variety of schemes have been proposed for combining multiple classifiers like: voting rules, belief functions, statistical techniques and other fusion schemes. The principle underlying these architectures is that certain estimators will be able to specialize to particular parts of the input space. The model developed in this work builds adaptive subsets of classifiers (committees), which are specific for each input pattern, in the way that, depending on an input pattern, different classifiers and a different number of them may be chosen to make a committee decision about the pattern [16]. To obtain such a committee of experts, each classifier uses different parts of the training set and, later, a prediction network selects the appropriate subset of classifiers for any given input. Fig. 2 illustrates the architecture of the model.

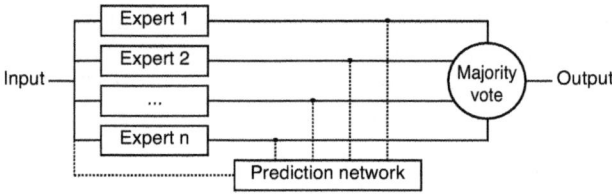

Fig. 2. Combination of experts architecture

The first step to train the model is to construct the set of classifiers. In this work, a *half&half bagging* method [17] was used, which is based on the general technique of manipulating the training examples to generate multiple hypotheses. The learning algorithm is run several times, each time adding a new classifier to the committee which is training on a different subset of the training examples. The basic idea of *half&half bagging* is to use purely random sampling to form a new training set that is half full of examples misclassified up to the present, and half full of correctly classified examples. Once the set of classifiers is trained, the next step is to train the prediction network which, for L classifiers, consists of L output neurons, which each output neuron assigned to an individual classifier, and receives the same inputs as the individual classifiers.

The number of hidden nodes is to be determined in the experimental stage. Then, it is necessary to determine the optimal threshold value that the output of a neuron has to surpass in order to include the corresponding classifier into the committee. Finally, the selected networks are aggregated into a committee decision according to majority vote. The complete description of the algorithm to build the committee used can be found in [16,17].

Results

In this work, a homogeneous set of classifiers has been used, i.e. all classifiers have the same architecture and use the same learning algorithm. In order to build the committee, several options for the many different parameters involved were tried as it is described below:

- Number of individual classifiers: from 2 to 35.
- Ratio of the original training set used to train each individual classifier: 40, 50 and 66% [16].
- Input coefficients for each classifier. Experimentally, in [8] it was determined that the first 13 coefficients obtains the best apnea classification results.
- Number of hidden neurons for the classifiers: from 2 to 4 [8].
- Number of hidden neurons for the prediction network: from 5 to 20.
- Threshold for the prediction network to include classifiers into the committee: from 0.1 to 0.9, step 0.1.

Following the method described in Section 2.2, a set of 9 individual classifiers trained using the 66% of the original training set for each one and a committee-inclusion threshold of 0.4 was selected. The number of hidden neurons for the individual classifiers and the prediction network were 3 and 6 respectively. Using this model, the mean test accuracy obtained was $85.20\% \pm 1.25$. Also, the mean accuracy obtained for each one of the classes was 90.19% (obstructive), 86.49% (central) and 79.20% (mixed). The corresponding confusion matrix is shown in Table 1.

4   A New Combination of Neural Networks Experts

The model presented markedly increments the complexity of the classifier while only slightly improves the classification accuracy achieved in previous works.

Table 1. Confusion matrix over 120 input patterns using a 10-fold cross validation and 10 experiments

			Predicted	
		Obstructive	Central	Mixed
	Obstructive	33.91 ± 1.66	0.70 ± 0.79	5.39 ± 1.10
Actual	Central	0.59 ± 0.88	36.42 ± 0.84	2.99 ± 0.71
	Mixed	3.10 ± 0.84	4.99 ± 0.85	31.91 ± 1.32

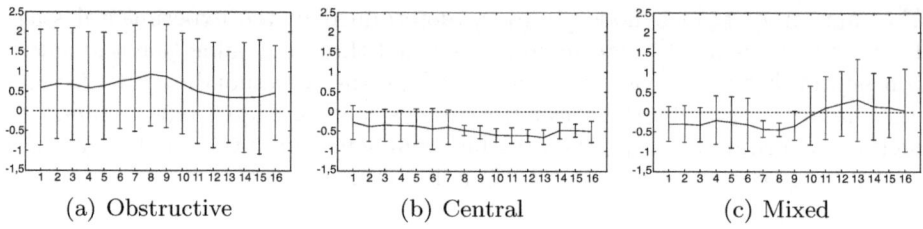

| (a) Obstructive | (b) Central | (c) Mixed |

Fig. 3. Mean and standard deviation of the coefficients of the wavelet transformation

For this reason, to find a more efficient model is still necessary. The model explained in this section is based on a new classification overview related with the characteristics that each apnea presents in different segments of the signal. According to the definition of the mixed events, Fig 3 shows that the beginning of the central and mixed patterns (approximately coefficients from 1 to 9) is similar, as well as the ending of the obstructive and mixed ones (approximately coefficients from 9 to 16).

Therefore, using the previous facts, the classification of the three types of apneas would be possible by identifying whether the beginning and the ending parts of the input pattern present the behavior of an obstructive or central apnea. Table 2 shows the classification based on this two characteristics. Using this approach, an obstructive beginning and a central ending is not a valid type of apnea and thus this situation should be taken into account.

Table 2. The new classification approach based on the pattern characteristics

		Characteristics	
		Beginning	Ending
	Obstructive	Obstructive	Obstructive
Classification	Central	Central	Central
	Mixed	Central	Obstructive

The new classification model presented has two stages: a feature selection stage that establishes the main inputs for classification and the classification model itself. First, it is necessary to determine with more accuracy which coefficients compose the beginning and the ending parts of the input pattern. Later, several classifiers will be developed to label each of the two mentioned parts of an apnea coefficient set and to establish a final classification based on Table 2. Both the feature selection and the classification stages will be described below.

Feature Selection Stage

To select the coefficients which define the beginning and the ending parts of the input pattern a Support Vector Machine Recursive Feature Elimination method (SVM RFE) [18], implemented in the software Weka [11], was employed. This method has been used twice: to specify the beginning coefficients it will be necessary to consider the mixed apneas as central (as the beginning of the pattern is common between them), and in the same way the mixed as obstructive for determining the ending coefficients. However, the number of possible combinations of coefficients which can be generated from these two lists would be intractable (for example, coefficient 1 for beginning and coefficient 9 for ending, or coefficients 1 and 2 for beginning and the rest for ending, etc.). For this reason, it will be necessary to establish some restrictions and two criteria were used:

- Select for each list a group of continuous coefficients.
- Select groups as small as possible (to reduce the complexity of the classifiers) but sufficiently representative to contain the necessary information.

Classification Stage: Error Correcting Output Code

Once the feature selection was made and the coefficients that form the beginning and the ending parts of the pattern were established, the method used for the classification stage is the Error Correcting Output Code (ECOC) [19]. ECOC builds a set of classifiers manipulating the desired outputs which indicate the classification of each pattern in the training set. This method will create new learning tasks by randomly dividing the different classes into two subsets A and B. After that, a classifier is trained to distinguish between these two subsets. By repeating this process L times, a combination of L classifiers is generated. The complete algorithm can be found in [19]. Table 3 shows the maximum number of possible divisions into subsets A and B for the sleep apnea domain.

Table 3. ECOC application to sleep apnea domain for training stage

	A_i	B_i
$i = 1$	{obstructive}	{central, mixed}
$i = 2$	{central}	{mixed, obstructive}
$i = 3$	{mixed}	{obstructive, central}

The sets obtained can be interpreted in an interesting way by focusing on the properties of mixed apneas mentioned at the beginning of this section (see Table 2): the first classifier, trained using A_1 and B_1, will learn to discriminate between obstructive and central or mixed characteristics, and thus, it will be applied to the beginning part of the input pattern. In the same way, the second classifier, trained using A_2 and B_2, will learn to discriminate between central and obstructive or mixed characteristics at the ending part of the input pattern. The application of these two classifiers to an apnea allows to label each part of the apnea as obstructive or central and thus, by using Table 2, it is also possible to identify whether the apnea is of the mixed type. Therefore, A_3 and B_3 sets will not be used for the development of the model but the two classifiers will be integrated to reach a final decision about the apnea classification. This way, the proposed model explicitly avoids mixed patterns classification as the classifiers

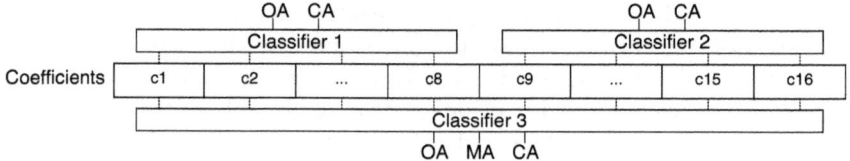

Fig. 4. Structure of the proposed classification method

developed so far have problems identifying mixed events. However, a third 3-class classifier (OA, MA and CA) will be used to solve the invalid result (see Table 2) formed by an obstructive beginning and a central ending pattern that might appear. To simplify the model, SVM RFE was also applied to this third classifier. Fig. 4 shows the generic architecture for the proposed model.

Results

First column in Table 4 shows the list of coefficients ordered by decreasing relevance obtained by the SVM RFE for each of the three classifiers. The initial set of inputs used for each classifier was shown in the second column of this table.

Table 4. Results of coefficient selection for each classifier

	Ranking list	Initial set
Classifier 1	9, 8, 7, 10, 5, 14, 12, 6, 3, 4, 2, 15, 16, 13, 11, 1	{8, 9}
Classifier 2	13, 10, 12, 11, 8, 15, 9, 16, 14, 3, 6, 4, 2, 5, 1, 7	{12, 13}
Classifier 3	9, 8, 13, 10, 7, 12, 11, 5, 14, 15, 6, 16, 3, 2, 4, 1	{8, 9, 10, 11, 12, 13}

According to the two criteria previously mentioned (to select a group of continuous coefficients as small as possible), several models were trained by starting with the initial set of coefficients shown in the second column of Table 4 as inputs

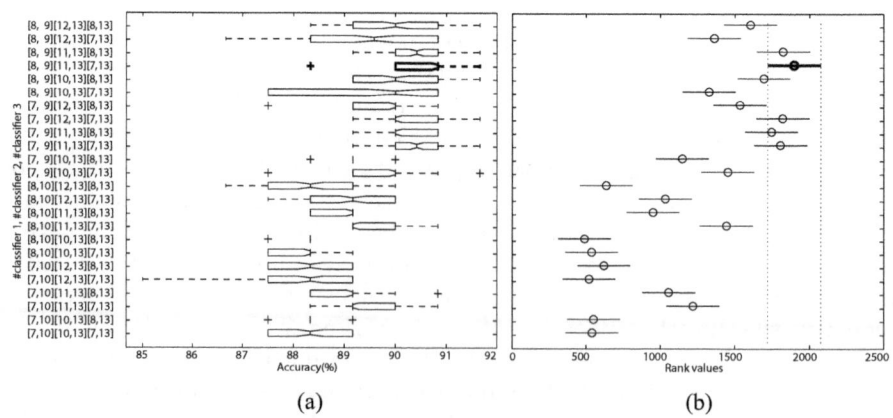

(a)   (b)

Fig. 5. Box-whiskers and multiple comparison procedure plots

Table 5. Confusion matrix over 120 input patterns using a 10-fold cross validation and 10 experiments

		Predicted		
		Obstructive	Central	Mixed
	Obstructive	35.85 ± 0.66	0.03 ± 0.17	4.12 ± 0.61
Actual	Central	0.19 ± 0.53	35.59 ± 0.59	4.22 ± 0.63
	Mixed	2.12 ± 0.41	1.00 ± 0.00	36.88 ± 0.41

and adding each time new coefficients. Fig. 5 (a) shows the box-whisper plot for each input combination. The best accuracy is obtained by the shadowed model. Finally, following the method described in Section 2.2, a multiple comparison procedure was applied (see results on Fig. 5 (b)) and coefficients from 8 to 9, from 12 to 13 and from 8 to 12 were selected as inputs for the first, second and third classifier, respectively, as this approach is more simple and statistically equivalent than the best model (see Fig. 5 (b)). Using this model, the mean test accuracy obtained was $90.27\% \pm 0.79$. Also, the mean accuracy obtained for each one of the classes was 93.95% (obstructive), 97.19% (central) and 81.56% (mixed). The corresponding confusion matrix is shown in Table 5.

5   Conclusions

In this paper, two new methods for sleep apnea classification using a combination of experts have been proposed. The approach based on a committee of experts slightly improves the previous results at the expense of increasing the complexity of the model. However, the new combination of three experts dramatically improves the classification accuracy obtained up to 90.27%. Thus, the improvements achieved by each model were 1.42% and 6.49% with respect to the approach described in [8]. Moreover, the variability was also reduced from 1.90% to 1.25% for the first model, and to 0.79% for the second one. These results demonstrate the validity of the proposed models that, in the case of the second one, even improve other recent works [4,5].

Acknowledgements

This research was partially funded by the Xunta de Galicia by projects PGIDT-05TIC10502PR and PGIDT-08TIC012105PR.

References

1. American Academy of Sleep Medicine Task Force. Sleep-related breathing disorders in adults: Recommendations for syndrome definition and measurement techniques in clinical research. Sleep 22, 667-689 (1999)
2. Varady, P., Micsik, T., Benedek, S., Benyo, Z.: A novel method for the detection of apnea and hypopnea events in respiration signals. IEEE T Bio.-Med. Eng. 49(9), 936–942 (2002)

3. Thorpy, M.: Handbook of Sleep Disorders. Informa Healthcare (1990)
4. Lu, Y.N., Zhang, H., Zhang, W.T.: The application of hierarchical evolutionary approach for sleep apnea classification. Machine Learning and Cybernetics 6 (2005)
5. Senny, F., Destine, J., Poirrier, R.: Midsagittal Jaw Movement Analysis for the Scoring of Sleep Apneas and Hypopneas. IEEE T Bio.-Med. Eng. 55(1), 87–95 (2008)
6. Hernández-Pereira, E.: Técnicas de Inteligencia Artificial e Ingeniería del Software para un sistema inteligente de monitorización de apneas de sueño, Tesis Doctoral. Departamento de Computación. Facultad de Informática. Universidade da Coruña (2000)
7. Cabrero-Canosa, M., Castro-Pereiro, M., Graña-Ramos, M., Hernández-Pereira, E., Moret-Bonillo, V., Martín-Egana, M., Verea-Hernando, H.: An intelligent system for the detection and interpretation of sleep apneas. Expert Systems with Applications 24(4), 335–349 (2003)
8. Fontenla-Romero, O., Guijarro-Berdiñas, B., Alonso-Betanzos, A., Moret-Bonillo, V.: A new method for sleep apnea classification using wavelets and feedforward neural networks. Artificial Intelligence in Medicine 34(1), 65–76 (2005)
9. Dietterich, T.G.: Ensemble methods in machine learning. LNCS, pp. 1–15. Springer, Heidelberg (2000)
10. MacKay, D.J.C.: A practical Bayesian framework for backpropagation networks. Neural Comput. 4(3), 448–472 (1992)
11. Weka 3 - Data Mining with Open Source Machine Learning Software in Java, http://www.cs.waikato.ac.nz/ml/weka/
12. MATLAB - The language of technical computing, http://www.mathworks.com/products/matlab/
13. Bishop, C.M.: Pattern recognition and machine learning. Springer, New York (2006)
14. Hollander, M., Wolfe, D.A.: Nonparametric Statistical Methods. John Wiley, New York (1973)
15. Hsu, J.C.: Multiple Comparisons. Theory and Methods. Chapman & Hall, Boca Raton (1996)
16. Verikas, A., Lipnickas, A., Malmqvist, K.: Selecting neural networks for a committee decision. Int. J. Neural Syst. 12(5), 351 (2002)
17. Breiman, L.: Half&Half bagging and hard boundary points. Technical report (1998)
18. Guyon, I., Weston, J., Barnhill, S., Vapnik, V.: Gene selection for cancer classification using support vector machines. Mach. Learn. 46(1), 389–422 (2002)
19. Dietterich, T.G., Bakiri, G.: Solving multiclass learning problems via error-correcting output codes. Arxiv preprint cs.AI/9501101 (1995)

Expert System to Real Time Control of Machining Processes*

Francisco Jesus Martín-Mateos[1],
Luis Carlos González Valencia[2], and Rafael Serrano Bello[2]

[1] Computational Logic Group
Dept. of Computer Science and Artificial Intelligence
University of Sevilla
E.T.S.I. Informática, Avda. Reina Mercedes, s/n. 41012 Sevilla, Spain
[2] Dept. de Diseño Industrial
Instituto Andaluz de Tecnología, Parque Tecnológico "Cartuja 93"
c/ Leonardo da Vinci, 2. 41092 Sevilla, Spain

Abstract. Industrial machining processes use automated milling machines. These machines are connected to a control device that provides the basic instructions used to obtain a piece. However, these processes depend on the human decision to diagnose and correct in real time the inaccuracies that can occur. In this work we present an expert system to real time control of machining processes using the information provided by sensors located on the machine. This system has been implemented as a prototype in a Kondia 600 milling machine with a FAGOR 8025-MG control device.

1 Introduction

Industrial machining processes use automated milling machines. These machines are connected to a control device that provides the basic instructions used to obtain a piece. However, these controls are not capable of checking and correcting in real time the imprecisions that happen in the process; for its usual operation, the milling machines still depend on the human decision for the production and modification of its processes. This dependence implies a high consumption of technical resources, affects the quality of manufactured products and the manufacturing and fine tuning process time. All these circumstances motivate that the current work on optimization of industrial machining processes remains a partially solved problem. To deal with this limitation, it has been proposed as a solution the use of artificial intelligence techniques.

According to Kyung [6], Artificial Intelligence applications to machining processes can be grouped into the following categories: knowledge-based expert systems, neural networks, probabilistic inference methods and fuzzy logic and genetic

---

* This work has been developed under the INFAERO project, supported by the "Orden de Incentivos a los Centros Tecnológicos de la Consejería de Innovación, Ciencia y Empresa de la Junta de Andalucía".

P. Meseguer, L. Mandow, and R.M. Gasca (Eds.): CAEPIA 2009, LNAI 5988, pp. 281–290, 2010.

algorithms. The difference between these approaches is the way how to represent the knowledge base in the system and its inference engine.

Early work on rule-based expert systems to control the machining process come from the late eighties, as in the case of Bohez [2], who developed the first prototype of an expert system based on 500 rules. Today they are also successfully implemented rule-based expert systems with the genetic algorithms approach [5].

Unlike expert systems where knowledge is made explicit, systems based on neural networks generate their own knowledge from case studies of network training. This means that such systems build the knowledge base through learning, and do not require additional processes of acquiring knowledge [3].

The probabilistic approach uses an influence diagram model with a probabilistic reasoning engine. The influence diagram is developed for the representation of complex problems where the decision is based on incomplete information belonging to several sources [8].

Another line of research are the adaptive controls. The aim of these devices is to control the process input variables using another ones that show the state of the process and must be monitored at all times. However, this architecture can not act in general on external parameters of the machine.

In this work we present an expert system based on production rules to control machining processes. This system is integrated into an interface from which information is collected from the machining process control device itself and sensors on the machine. The system diagnoses the state of the machining process and decides corrective actions to keep it within optimal parameters. The system performs a separate treatment of each datum provided, this allows both deactivation, such as adding new data sources. The system design minimizes the number of changes between successive runs, thereby reducing its response time.

2   Pilot Implementation

The system showed here was implemented on a Kondia 600 milling machine. This machine has a table that can move horizontally in both directions of the XY plane, with a swing jaw to fix the block to be processed, and a spindle that moves vertically, where the cutting tool is placed. It is equipped with a control unit 8025-MG FAGOR from which the cutting instructions needed to process a piece are provided. The machining process instructions are provided through a machining program that is stored in the control unit. While the machining program can not be modified during processing, the behavior of the machine can be altered modifying the machining table motion (also knows as *feed*) and the spindle speed, indicating a reduction over the values provided by the machining program, or ultimately stopping the machine.

To capture real-time information about the process, the machining center has been equipped with several sensors: an infrared temperature sensor providing the cutting tool temperature; two vibration sensors that provide information about the spindle vibration in X direction and the milling table vibration in Y and Z directions; and a strength sensor located under the swing jaw, that provides information about the vertical strength exerted by the cutting tool on the block to be processed. This information is transmitted to the Sensor-IA application through a data acquisition system.

The neural center of the Sensor-IA application is a user interface implemented in Visual Basic from which data are received from the sensors. These data are sent to the expert system, which generates a set of actions to modify the behavior of the machining center. There are three kinds of actions: acting on the two speed controls of the control device (feed and spindle speed) and acting on a coolant flow directed to the cutting tool. Once generated the set of actions, the expert system returns the control to the interface that is responsible to enforce these actions, and waits for new data. We call an expert system *run* to the process of receive data from the interface, decide the actions and return them to the interface.

In the implementation of this expert system we have pursued the following objectives: A design based on production rules in a shell integrated into Visual Basic, to obtain a good degree of efficiency in processing large sets of rules. A separate treatment of each datum provided from the interface. In this way, the expert system behavior is as expected whether it receives only a datum, or several. This also facilitates the incorporation of new data sources (e.g. from new sensors), because they do not affect or are affected by the treatment of the other data. Finally, a design that minimizes the number of changes between successive queries to the expert system, reducing its response time.

3   Production Systems

A production system is a computational mechanism based on rules. This mechanism has two components: a set of *facts* (*database*) and a set of *rules* (*knowledge base*). The facts are data describing a concrete situation and the rules describe how this situation could change. Every rule has two parts, the *antecedent* and the *consequent*. The antecedent is a set of conditions about the data, mainly the existence or absence of some datum matching a given pattern. The consequent of a rule is a set of actions by means of which some existent data are deleted or new ones are included.

In every moment there are a set of *active rules*, that is rules with their conditions accomplished, obviously this depends on the state of the database. In every step of computation an active rule is selected using a *conflict resolution strategy* and its actions are executed, we say that the rule has been *fired*. The firing of a rule changes the state of the database and, as a consequence, the set of active rules. This process continuates until the set of active rules is empty.

There are several languages designed to define production systems and provide an inference engine in which a production system could be evaluated. A common reference point between all of them is CLIPS [7], used in this work.

3.1   Facts in CLIPS

Basic facts in CLIPS have the following syntax: **(name v1 ... vn)**, where **name** is a symbol identifying the fact and **v1**, ..., **vn** are the information stored in the fact. In this case we say that **name** is the *type* of the fact.

Facts represents information known in a concrete instant and can change at any time. The elimination of a fact would suggest that the information it represents is no longer relevant or true. In the other hand, new situations generate information represented by new facts.

3.2   Rules in CLIPS

As we have mentioned before, rules have two parts: antecedent and consequent. The antecedent is a set of conditions about the facts, establishing the existence or absence of facts matching a pattern. The consequent is a set of actions associated with the rule, the most common are the removal of existing facts and the inclusion of new ones.

The conditions of the antecedent of a rule are expressed by means of *patterns*. The syntax of these patterns is similar to the syntax of the facts, but we can use variables to specify unknown values and additional conditions about these variables. We can use two kinds of variables in a pattern fact: *simple* and *multiple*. Simple variables can store a simple value and have the syntax **?name**. Multiple variables can store a sequence, maybe empty, of values and have the syntax **$?name**. In both cases **name** is the *name* of the variable. When the value of a variable is not interesting, we can use the *unnamed variables* **?** or **$?**.

Actions in the consequent of a rule depend on the conditions in its antecedent. So in order to delete a fact, there should be a condition in the antecedent ensuring the existence of that fact. Furthermore, to include a new fact, the associated information must be provided in a explicit way, perhaps from the values of the variables used in the antecedent. It is also possible to use *global variables* in the consequent of a rule. Global variables have the syntax **?*name*** and must be previously declared. These variables are used to store values that do not change during the execution of the expert system. In our work, we use them as a communication channel between the expert system and the Sensor-IA application.

3.3   The Inference Engine in CLIPS

CLIPS uses a *forward chaining* inference engine, based on removing or deriving data from a set of facts, following the guidelines specified in the rules. This process has the risk of entering infinite loops of derivation: the simplest example is a rule without conditions or actions, this rule could be fired indefinitely. To avoid such situations, CLIPS exhibits a property called *refraction*, which prevents from firing a rule more than once for a specified set of facts. To improve performance in the rule pattern match stage, a optimized version of Rete algorithm by Forgy [4] is used: instead of testing the conditions of all rules to compute the active rules, it only checks changes in the rules that may be affected by the last rule fired.

4   Description of the Expert System

The expert system integrated into the Sensor-IA application receives as input a data set from the interface. As a result, it generates a set of actions on the manual controls of the control device. The objective of these actions is to safeguard the proper operation of the machine, and to fit it to a predetermined level.

The data provided from the interface are considered in the following stages: setting the data level; setting the data state; setting the actions associated with the data; and finally combining the actions associated with the data. In the first three stages the treatment is independent for each datum, and the latter is the only stage in which all the data provided are related in some way.

4.1   Setting the Data Level

The data received from the interface have the form: **(value ?datum ?v)** where **?datum** is a unique identifier for each datum and **?v** is the value of this datum in its range of values.

Since the range of values of each datum is very broad, we considered subdividing it into six intervals or numbered levels. Thus, the *level* of a datum is the number of the interval in which its value is located. The boundaries of these levels are stored as: **(risk-levels ?datum ?l1 ?l2 ?l3 ?l4 ?l5 ?l6 ?l7)** where **?datum** is the identifier of the datum considered and **?l1**, **?l2**, **?l3**, **?l4**, **?l5**, **?l6** and **?l7** are the boundaries of the six levels.

For every datum we take into account its evolution over the last 5 runs of the expert system. We call this information *history* of the datum and it is stored as: **(history-level ?datum ?n4 ?n3 ?n2 ?n1 ?n0)**, where **?datum** is the identifier of the datum considered, **?n0** is the current level of this datum, **?n1** is the level of the datum in the previous run of the expert system, **?n2** is the level of the datum two runs ago, and similarly **?n3** and **?n4**.

The expert system rules determining the data history (and of course, the data level) have the following form:

```
  | (defrule update-history-level-data-2
1 |    ?h1 <- (value ?datum ?v)
2 |    (risk-levels ?datum ? ?l2&:(<= ?l2 ?v) ?l3&:(< ?v ?l3) $?)
3 |    ?h2 <- (history-level ?datum ? ?n3 ?n2 ?n1 ?n0)
  |    =>
4 |    (retract ?h1 ?h2)
5 |    (assert (history-level ?datum ?n3 ?n2 ?n1 ?n0 2)))
```

This rule updates the history of a datum whose level is 2. Condition #1 gets the current value **?v** of a datum **?datum**. Condition #2 gets the boundaries of the levels established for the datum and checks that the value **?v** is in the second level (between the boundaries **?l2** and **?l3**). Condition #3 gets the history of the datum in the previous run of the expert system, where the current level (2) should be included in the last position and the oldest level (just the one after the datum identifier) should be removed. The actions of this rule are the elimination of the facts with the current value of the datum and the history of the datum in the previous run (action #4), and the inclusion of a fact with the history of the datum for the current run (action #5).

Once we have updated the information about the data history in the current run, the facts about the current values of the data provided from the interface are no longer needed and they are removed. The elimination of these facts avoids that they could be used several times in the update rules of the data history, in the same run of the expert system.

4.2   Setting the Data State

The *state* of a datum represents the last change of level in this datum over the last 5 runs of the expert system. This information is stored in independents facts (one for each datum) as: **(state ?datum ?v1 ?v0)**, where **?datum** is the identifier of the datum, the value **?v0** is the current level of this datum and **?v1** shows the trend of change of the datum in the last 5 runs of the expert system in the following way: if the datum comes from a lower level, then the value **?v1** is **?v0** minus 1; if the datum has been stable (that is, in the same level), then the value **?v1** is equal to **?v0**; and if the datum comes from a upper level, then the value **?v1** is **?v0** plus 1.

The state only changes when the current level of a datum is different from the previous one (in this case the state stores the current level and a value computed from it) or when the datum becomes stable in the same level over the last 5 runs of the expert system (in this case the state stores the current level repeated).

The rules to establish the state of a datum are two: the first one computes the changes of level of a datum in the last 5 runs and the second one the stability of a datum in the last 5 runs.

```
  | (defrule set-datum-state-1
1 |    (history-level ?datum ? ? ? ?v1 ?v0&~?v1)
2 |    ?h <- (state ?datum ? ?v1)
  |    =>
3 |    (retract ?h)
4 |    (if (< ?v1 ?v0)
  |         then (assert (state ?datum (- ?v0 1) ?v0))
  |         else (assert (state ?datum (+ ?v0 1) ?v0)))))
```

This rule starts with the history of a datum **?datum** where the current level **?v0** is different from the previous one **?v1** (condition #1). Condition #2 ensures that the state of the datum does not correspond to the current history and therefore it must be changed. Action #3 removes the incorrect state and action #4 inserts in the database the new state computed from the current level **?v0** and the previous one **?v1**.

```
  | (defrule set-datum-state-5
1 |    (history-level ?datum ?v0 ?v0 ?v0 ?v0 ?v0)
2 |    ?h <- (state ?datum ~?v0 ?v0)
  |    =>
3 |    (retract ?h)
4 |    (assert (state ?datum ?v0 ?v0)))
```

This rule starts with the history of a datum **?datum** where the level has been stable for the last 5 runs (condition #1). Condition #2 ensures that the state of this datum does not correspond to the current history because the values it stores are not equals. Action #3 removes the incorrect state and action #4 inserts in the database the new one.

These rules only change the data state when there are any modifications on it, this minimizes the number of changes between successive runs of the expert system, improving its performance.

4.3   Setting the Actions Associated with the Data

The actions associated with the data depends on the data state, the risk level assumed in the process and the status of the manual controls.

The risk level assumed in the process indicates the kind of use we want of the machine. We have considered three situations: *quality job mode*, where we focus on quality over time; *balanced job mode*, where we seek a balance between quality, time and half-life values of tools and equipment: and *time job mode*, where we focus on time over quality. This information is stored in facts as: **(assumed-risk ?v)**, where **?v** takes the values 1, 2 or 3, respectively.

The status of the manual controls indicates the degree of interference that has already been done in the machining program. These controls are the feed, the spindle speed and the coolant flow. This information is stored in facts as: **(control ?control ?v)**, where **?control** could take the values **feed**, **spindle** or **coolant**.

The rules establishing the actions associated with the data are the core of the expert system, constituting the 85% of it. An example of such rules, with medium complexity, is the following:

```
  | (defrule cut-strength-7[3]
1 |    (state cut-strength 4 4)
2 |    (assumed-risk 3)
3 |    (control spindle ?vs&:(< ?vs 105))
4 |    (control coolant ?vc)
  |    =>
5 |    (assert (action cut-strength 4 4 spindle (+ ?vs 5)))
6 |    (if (< ?vc 10)
  |         then (assert (action cut-strength 4 4 coolant (+ ?vc 5))))))
```

This rule establishes that if the cut strength is stable in the level 4 (condition #1), the assumed risk is 3 (condition #2), the level of the spindle control is less than 105 (condition #3) and the coolant flow level is **?vc** (condition #4), then the spindle control should be adjusted increasing in 5 units (action #5) and if the coolant flow level is less than 10 then it should be adjusted increasing in 5 unities (action #6).

The actions suggested by these rules are stored in facts as: **(action ?datum ?v1 ?v0 ?control ?value)** where **?datum** is the identifier of the datum in the state described by **?v1** and **?v0** that suggest the action, and **?control** is the control that must be adjusted in the amount indicated by **?value**.

While each datum suggests a single action by each of the controls, when the data set is considered, they can suggest several actions on the same control. These actions must be analyzed and combined to generate the effective action.

4.4   Combining the Actions

The effective action on a control is computed as a weighted sum of all the suggested actions on this control, where the weights of this sum depends on the highest level of the data generating actions on this control. The effective action is computed as follows:

First, we compute the highest level of the data generating actions on the same control, storing this information as **(effective-level ?control ?i)**. We also build a fact to store the partial weighted sum of the adjusting values suggested on this control: **(weighted-sum ?control 0 0)**.

```
  | (defrule effective-level
1 |   (action ? ? ?v1 ?control ?)
2 |   (not (action ? ? ?v0&:(< ?v1 ?v0) ?control ?))
3 |   (not (effective-level ?control ?))
  |   =>
4 |   (assert (effective-level ?control ?v1)
  |           (weighted-sum ?control 0 0)))
```

Next, we add up all the suggested actions on that control weighted according to a table of weights that depends on the effective level calculated in the previous stage. The function **(weight ?v1 ?v0 $?weights)** returns the weight corresponding to the state described by **?v1** and **?v0** within the weight vector **$?weights** obtained from the information about the weights stored as **(weights ?level $?weights)**.

```
  | (defrule weighted-sum
1 |   (effective-level ?control ?m)
2 |   (weights ?m $?weights)
3 |   ?h1 <- (action ? ?v1 ?v0 ?control ?v)
4 |   ?h2 <- (weighted-sum ?control ?n ?s)
  |   =>
5 |   (retract ?h1 ?h2)
6 |   (assert (weighted-sum ?control (+ ?n 1)
  |                       (+ ?s (* ?v (weight ?v1 ?v0 $?weights))))))
```

When the weighted sum is finished, the result must be divided by the number of actions and approximated in terms of the minimum increase of the control adjustment. The function **(aprox ?s ?n)** approaches the value **?s** in accordance with the minimum increase **?n**. The result is stored in a global variable through which communication is established with the interface. This is done for each control.

```
  | (defrule weighted-sum-coolant
1 |   ?h1 <- (effective-level coolant ?)
2 |   ?h2 <- (weighted-sum coolant ?n ?s)
3 |   (not (action ? ? ? coolant ?))
  |   =>
4 |   (retract ?h1 ?h2)
5 |   (bind ?*coolant* (aprox (/ ?s ?n) 5)))
```

At this point the execution of the expert system ends, though preserving the data structures used to store the rules and their partial activations. This is the starting point of the next run of the expert system, minimizing thus the number of checks to be carried out in each run. The global variables **?*feed***, **?*spindle*** and **?*coolant*** are read from the interface and are used to update the facts on the status of the controls at the beginning of the next run.

5   Experiments

The experiments developed consist in several XY rough cutting on a steel F114 block, with and without expert system, analyzing the behavior of the tool with respect to the temperature reached in the cutting tool and the vibrations in the spindle and the milling table. Let's see in more detail how they were developed and what results were obtained.

The test began with a vacuum machining (without material), for which the milling table vibration sensor gave values between 0.5 and 4 m/s^2 for spindle speeds between 500 and 3000 rpm. Machining steel without the expert system help, the vibration sensor detected values of 20 m/s^2 for machining process with 3000 rpm, 0.5 mm depth of cut and feed 200 mm/min. With these information it was determined the levels of the vibration sensor datum. The optimum vibration level that the expert system should maintain was defined between 6 and 9 m/s^2. Once these values were introduced into the system, the experiments were very positive, as it is show in the following figure:

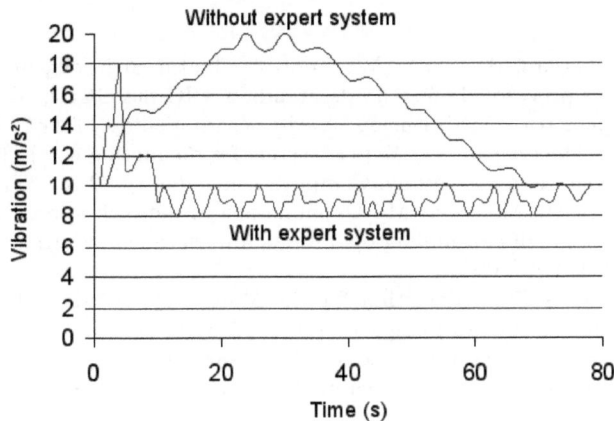

As we can see, the expert system tries to maintain the machining vibration into the optimal interval (6-9 m/s^2), getting this aim most of the machining time. In this state, the expert system reduces to 2700 rpm spindle speed and to 180 mm/min the feed. These changes obviously increase the process time, although this consequence is assumed in the risk level considered in the process (quality job), where the quality of the result is more important than the processing time.

6   Conclusions and Further Works

We have successfully designed and tested an architecture for the optimization of a machining process in real time by means of an expert system based on production rules. We have successfully achieved the goals outlined in the work: representation of the expert knowledge about the machining process by means of production rules; independent behaviour of the amount of input data provided to the expert system, allowing to activate or deactivate the sensors arranged in the machine or inserting new ones; and minimization of the number of changes between successive queries to the expert system, which reduces the response time.

The system can be deployed in any machining tool, whenever it is connected to a control device; can manage any information, internal from the device control or external from the sensors; and can act on serveral components of the machining process, internal as the feed or spindle speed or external as the coolant flow.

The next stage in the development of the expert system is the analysis of work sessions to adjust the rules that determine the actions associated with the data. From here there are some additional goals for the Sensor-IA system: the inclusion of new parameters in the system, such as type of material to be processed (steel, aluminum, etc.), the cutting tool, or new sensors; the automated correction of the rules from data stored about work sessions; or, in the longer term, the modification of the machining program.

References

1. Alique, J.R., Gajate, A., Novo, M.: Control adaptativo inteligente para la optimización de los procesos de fresado desatendido. CIC marGUNE, Centro de Investigación Cooperativa en Fabricación de Alto Rendimiento (2008)
2. Bohez, E.L.J., Thieravarut, M.: Expert system for diagnosing computer numerically controlled machines: a case-study. Computers in Industry 32(3), 233–248 (1997)
3. Cus, F., Zuperl, U., Milfelner, M.: Dynamic neural network approach for tool cutting force modeling of end milling operations. International Journal of General Systems 35(5), 603–618 (2006)
4. Forgy, C.: Rete: A Fast Algorithm for the Many Pattern/Many Objects Pattern Match Problem. Artificial Intelligence 19(1), 17–37 (1982)
5. Kuo, L., Yen, J.: Servo parameter tuning for a 5-axis machine center based upon GA rules. International Journal of Machine Tools and Manufacture 41(11), 1535–1550 (2001)
6. Park, S.K., Kim, S.H.: Artificial intelligence approaches to determination of CNC machining parameters in manufacturing: a review. Artificial Intelligence in Engineering 12(1), 127–134 (1998)
7. Riley, G.: CLIPS: A tool for building expert systems (2008),
   http://clipsrules.sourceforge.net/
8. Shachter, R.D.: Probabilistic inference and influence diagrams. Operations Research 36(4), 589–604 (1988)

A Flexible System for Document Processing and Text Transcription

Juan Miguel Vilar[1], María José Castro-Bleda[2], Francisco Zamora-Martínez[2],
Salvador España-Boquera[2], Albert Gordo[1,*], David Llorens[1], Andrés Marzal[1],
Federico Prat[1], and Jorge Gorbe[2]

[1] Departament de Llenguatges i Sistemes Informàtics
Universitat Jaume I
12071 Castelló, Spain
{jvilar,dllorens,amarzal,fprat}@lsi.uji.es, agordo@cvc.uab.es
[2] Departamento de Sistemas Informáticos y Computación
Universidad Politécnica de Valencia
46022 Valencia, Spain
{mcastro,fzamora,sespana,jgorbe}@dsic.upv.es

Abstract. STATE is a flexible system for document processing. It comprises a graphical front-end that can be easily connected to different text recognition back-ends. We comment here the front-end and two back-ends: one based on nearest neighbors and one based on Hidden Markov Models. Experimentation shows that if the back-end has a moderately low character error rate, productivity gains can be as high as 100% when compared to directly transcribing the text.

1 Introduction

STATE is a flexible system for document processing and text transcription. It comprises a graphical front-end that can be easily connected to different text recognition back-ends. This flexibility arises from the way the connection is achieved: the front-end and the back-end are separate processes, possibly in different machines, that communicate via HTTP.

We comment here the front-end and two back-ends: one based on nearest neighbors for printed text and one based on Hidden Markov Models for handwritten text. The initial version of the front-end, which has been greatly improved, and the first back-end were presented in [3]. In that paper, the focus was on the transcription of ancient documents. Here, we concentrate on transcription of handwritten texts from the IAM database [5]. For these texts, we use a different back-end, based on HMMs and neural networks.

The rest of the paper contains a description of the system. The following two sections describe the front-end and the two back-ends. After that, an experiment measuring productivity gains and the conclusions end the paper.

---

* Albert Gordo is currently with the *Centre de Visió per Computador, Campus UAB, 08193 Bellaterra, Spain.*

P. Meseguer, L. Mandow, and R.M. Gasca (Eds.): CAEPIA 2009, LNAI 5988, pp. 291–300, 2010.
© Springer-Verlag Berlin Heidelberg 2010

2   The Front-End

The front-end of STATE is designed to work with projects. Initially, a project is simply a set of images, one for each of the pages to be transcribed. As the user proceeds, more information is added to the project, including the image processing operations needed to clear the pages, their layout, and their transcription. For flexibility and ease of later processing, all this information is stored in an XML file.

The user selects one project and can open simultaneously as many different pages as needed. For each page, a pipeline of three stages is built: the Image Conditioner, the Layout Manager, and the Assisted Line Transcriber. In Figs. 1–3, screenshots of these stages can be seen. The stages are accessible through the tabs on the left of the window. The tabs on the top correspond to different pages while the buttons on the right control the overall aspects of the project and the application.

The order of the stage tabs is designed after the order of usual workflow on a page: first, the page is conditioned (a set of image processing tools are applied to it); then, its layout is detected; finally, the user transcribes each line in the page.

The Image Conditioner and the Layout Manager offer a similar interaction behavior: both show a view of the page and let the user act on it by executing commands. The Image Conditioner (Fig. 1) offers commands to remove noise and to enhance the text in the image. The Layout Manager (Fig. 2) offers commands to automatically detect and to interactively edit the layout (lines, blocks, and text flows). Finally, the Assisted Line Transcriber (Fig. 3) allows the user to obtain transcriptions of the lines using a recognition engine and to manually correct these transcriptions. If the user feels that certain samples (line images and their corresponding transcriptions) may help to improve recognition accuracy, she can send them to the recognition engine.

The user is free to alter this workflow: for instance, she could condition all the pages first, then detect the layout of the pages and, finally, proceed to transcribe them in any order. To keep track of the progress, the pages can be marked with status information (cleaned, layout found, etc.), this is graphically shown by a color code.

Now, we briefly describe the functioning of each stage and its interaction with the user.

2.1   The Image Conditioner

Scanned documents usually need to be enhanced in order to feed an OCR. This stage offers a comfortable interface for image cleaning and a set of tools to restore the text when needed, for instance in the case of ancient documents as they are usually in poor condition due to moisture, torn pages, fading ink, staining, etc. The screen is divided into several regions (see Fig. 1): on the left, the image of the page after the commands have been applied to it, this image has overlaid controls for zooming and selecting; on the right, an area divided into two parts: in the upper part, the available commands are arranged as a tree and in the lower part, a list shows the commands applied to the page.

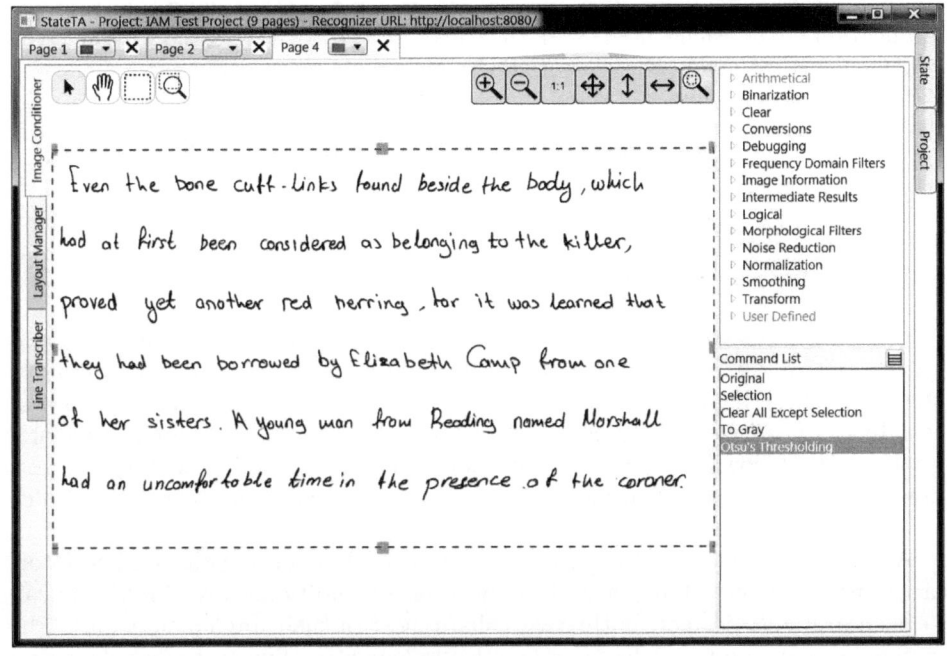

Fig. 1. The Image Conditioner

The command selection tree offers a hierarchical catalog of commands for image processing: binarizers, morphological operators, noise reducers, smoothers, etc. This set can be extended by defining new commands in C# that are compiled on the fly when the application starts.

At any moment, the user can add a command to the command list, which is executed with default parameters. The user can change the parameters at will. Undo and redo operations are simply executed by selecting a command in the list: the image view is updated to represent the result of the list up to the selected command. The command list can be edited by adding, deleting, or replacing commands.

For sophisticated actions, a stack of intermediate results is available (in fact, the image view simply shows the top of this stack). The stack can be manipulated to duplicate or swap some of its elements, eg to execute n-ary commands. For example, removing the background of an image by subtracting the windowed median at each pixel can be performed with this sequence of commands: 1) duplicate the image on the top; 2) pop the new top image, compute the windowed median of each pixel, and push the result; 3) swap the two topmost elements; 4) subtract the two topmost elements. The process takes one image and produces one image, but the stack contains several temporary results at some steps.

Since the system is interactive, a lot of effort has been put on responsiveness. For instance, when the parameters of some command have changed and the command list must be re-executed, only the commands actually affected by the parameter change are effectively executed. On the other hand, quitting the application saves cache images of the current state of the session. When the project is loaded again, the user immediately obtains a restored session state.

Once a page has been cleaned and enhanced, the user can reduce the time devoted to this task in other pages by copying the command list to them. Furthermore, the system gives the option to copy the current command list to every page in a given status as marked in its status information.

2.2   The Layout Manager

The Layout Manager offers a set of automatic layout detection commands and an interactive environment to edit the layout. A page layout is a hierarchical structure whose higher level component is the text flow, an ordered sequence of text blocks possibly continuing in other pages. For instance, the main text of a book is a text flow and the set of footnotes may be defined as a different text flow. Each text flow is identified with a user-defined label and contains zero or more blocks, each one containing zero or more lines.

Automatic layout detection tools usually need human assistance. The interfaces of the Layout Manager and of the Image Conditioner are similar, as can be seen in Fig. 2 (in fact, both stages share most of their implementation). The command selection tree offers commands implementing line and block detection algorithms, block editing operations (such as deletion and merging), etc. Some commands can also be introduced implicitly by user interactions with the mouse or stylus, for instance to redefine the limits of a line by moving its handles. The set of commands is also extensible with user-defined commands. The command list is linked to the command list in the Image Conditioner so changes in the conditioning of the page force the execution of the Layout Manager command list. Like in the case of the Image Conditioner, the user can copy the commands from the current page to others and save time. Once the user is satisfied with the page layout, she can proceed to transcribe the text by selecting the Assisted Line Transcriber tab.

2.3   The Assisted Line Transcriber

This stage helps the user to transcribe the lines in the text flows of a page. It uses a recognition engine available as a web service to provide automatic transcriptions that can be manually edited. The user can either start a (local) recognition engine or connect to a running one by giving its URL.

The Assisted Line Transcriber handles pen, keyboard, and mouse input. It can be comfortably used with a Tablet PC, digitizing tablet, or pen-sensitive screen. Figure 3 shows the GUI of the Assisted Line Transcriber. When the user selects a text flow (top left box), all its lines are shown on the right panel. The lines can be sent to the recognition engine to obtain a transcription. The user can also send a line and its corrected transcription to inform the engine that they can be used for improving the decoder.

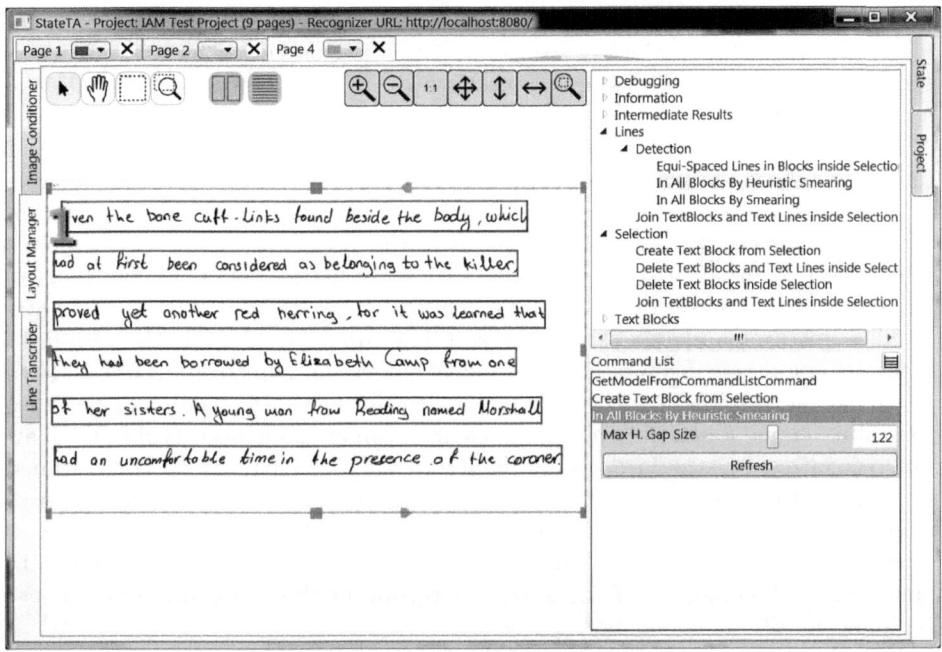

Fig. 2. The Layout Manager

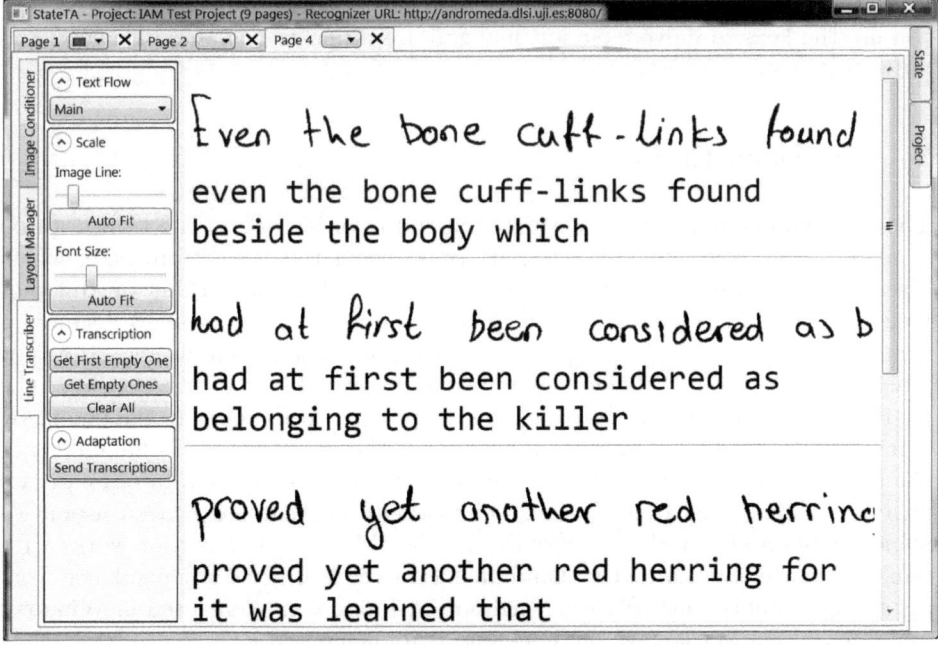

Fig. 3. The Assisted Line Transcriber

The transcription is stored in the project file as XML. It reflects the layout hierarchy: text flows, blocks, and lines. Each line is coded as a sequence of (possibly multi-character) symbols and stores its coordinates on the image as attributes.

In this stage, the text transcription is shown under the graphical view of each line, so validation is quick and easy. The user has at her disposal different ways of correcting the transcription. Direct writing over the transcription is handled by capturing electronic ink and feeding it to the Windows Vista recognition engine. The text or gestures so recognized are integrated in the transcription. For single character corrections, the user can employ our own pen input panel which handles gestures and ink. The Microsoft Ink Input panel from the .NET 3.5 platform could have been used, but we decided to build our own on-line isolated character recognition engine and input widget for the sake of flexibility and extensibility. Some fonts, like those in ancient documents, include glyphs which are not recognized by standard on-line handwritten text recognizers. For instance, in Spanish texts from the 16th or 17th centuries there are ligatures or special characters, such as ﬁ ("si"), q̃ ("que"), ﬅ ("st") or õ ("on"), which are not part of modern writing. Our pen-input panel could be adapted to new symbols by enriching its training set. A detailed description of this recognition engine can be found in [6].

Pen-based input is appropriate when the user is checking a transcription and must correct a few errors, but it can be tiresome if the user must provide a full transcription or there are many errors in the automatic transcription. To help in these cases, the pen-based input panel is also sensitive to keyboard. The user can use the keys to move a cursor, navigate from line to line, and also copy and paste text, etc.

3   The Back-Ends

The front-end communicates with a back-end in order to find the transcription of a line. This communication is performed using the HTTP protocol, which gives several advantages. First, it allows a team of users working on different pages of the same document or on documents with similar typographical conventions to share a single recognizer. This reduces the resources needed and it makes improvements of the engine immediately available to every user, too. The engine can be improved for instance by adapting it to the current document by using samples from it. A second advantage of the use of HTTP is flexibility, eg changing the recognizer can be done by simply changing a URL. In our case, we have a back-end based on Nearest Neighbor Search that has proven useful for ancient fonts and a back-end based in Hidden Markov Models that works with handwritten text. Finally, the communication via web gives independence from operating systems. Our Nearest Neighbor back-end is implemented in Windows and our Hidden Markov Model back-end is implemented in Linux.

The protocol of communication has been greatly simplified. The front-end sends a POST request to the specified URL. This request encodes in XML the image of the line from which a transcription is required. The back-end decodes the image, transcribes it, and sends the transcription, again as an XML string, in response to the request.

In the descriptions of our two back-ends, we center our attention in the actual process of transcription.

3.1   Nearest Neighbors

Our Nearest Neighbor back-end was presented in [3], here we give an overview. It works in a way reminiscent of the two-level architecture used in several speech recognizers. It can be globally described as a sequence of two steps: an initial classification of promising segments and a search for the optimum sequence using those segments.

The initial classification can also be split in two phases. The first one creates a heuristic over-segmentation of the line by analyzing the gray level of the columns and searching for local extrema, which define plausible segment marks. The second phase searches for the best glyph corresponding to each segment of an appropriate length. First, the segment is processed to eliminate character overlaps and to correct baseline deviation and then its Nearest Neighbor among the training samples is found.

Once each segment is so classified, the optimal transcription is found using a dynamic programming algorithm. Finally, white spaces are added to the transcription.

3.2   Hidden Markov Models

Hidden Markov Models (HMMs) are widely used in handwritten text recognition [1,8,9]. In our case, we have used the HTK toolkit [10] to train linear left-to-right HMMs with eight states and without skips. Emission probabilities are modeled by mixtures of 64 Gaussians in each state.

Slope and size normalization are achieved by classifying local extrema of text contours with Multilayer Perceptrons, as presented in [2]. The points classified as lower baseline are used for accurately estimating the slope and the horizontal alignment. Slant is also computed using Artificial Neural Networks. After slope and slant correction, the reference lines of the text are computed in order to normalize its size. Following [8], features are extracted by applying a grid to the image and computing three values for each cell of the grid: the normalized gray level and the horizontal and vertical gray level derivatives. A grid of square cells with 20 rows has been used, so every frame comprises 60 values.

The HMM recognizer was trained with offline handwritten text lines from the IAM database [5]. A writer independent text line recognition task has been considered. The subset of the IAM database used to train the HMMs consists of 6 161 training lines and 2 781 test lines, with a closed vocabulary composed of 8 500 words. Lexicon is modeled with 78 characters: 26 lowercase letters, 26 uppercase letters, 10 digits, 14 punctuation marks, the space, and a character for garbage symbols. A bigram language model trained with a subset of the LOB corpus [4] has been used in the test evaluation. The language model was trained with the SRI Language Modeling Toolkit [7] using the modified Kneser-Ney back-off discounting. Our HMM recognizer achieves comparative performance with state-of-the-art HMM systems: a word error rate of 35.3% and a character error rate of 17.7% on the test set.

4   Experimentation

In order to evaluate the increase in productivity attained by using STATE, we experimented with the IAM database [5]. This database consists in a collection of forms which contain texts extracted from the LOB corpus. The forms were given to different people to manually transcribe those texts. Later the forms were scanned and made publicly available as png files. In our experiments, only the handwritten part of the form was used.

We selected a random subset of 24 forms. These forms were divided into three blocks (B1, B2, B3). Three different writers participated in the experiment (W1, W2, W3) and three different approaches were used for transcribing: EditorOnly, the writer the writer transcribed the text in the form using only a simple editor; HMMEditor, the writer corrected the output from the HMM recognizer using only a simple editor; and HMMState, the writer corrected the output from the HMM recognizer using STATE. Each writer transcribed the three blocks using a different approach in each one, according to this table:

Writer	EditorOnly	HMMEditor	HMMState
W1	B1	B2	B3
W2	B2	B3	B1
W3	B3	B1	B2

This made writers use each approach on texts seen by them for the first time.

The time needed to complete each page was measured and divided by the number of lines of the page, since not all forms have the same length. A large correlation between the time per line and the character error rate (CER) of the HMM recognizer was observed. For instance, Fig. 4 is the plot of the time (in seconds) per line as a function of the CER when using the third approach.

Due to this, we decided to divide the data for comparison in three different groups: one for pages with a CER below 15% (12 pages), one for pages with a CER between 15% and 30% (6 pages), and a final one for pages with a CER equal or higher than 30% (6 pages). For each group, the average time saving was computed and the results are presented in Table 1. The first column represents the CER, the second column is the average time saving between using STATE and directly transcribing the page. For example, if the character error rate is below 15%, the average time saving is 51%, ie the time needed to transcribe the page is slightly less than half so a 100% productivity gain is achieved. The third column compares the second and third approaches, ie it shows the savings

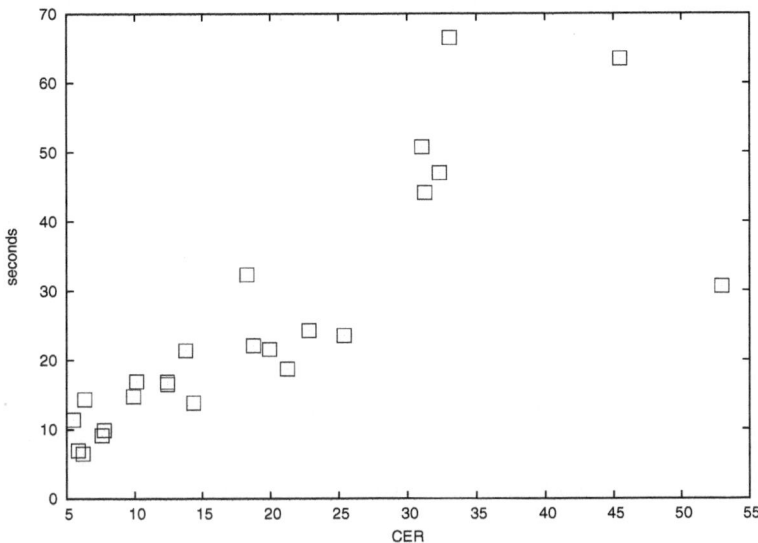

Fig. 4. Average correction time in seconds per line as a function of the CER of the page. Time is measured for users employing STATE to correct OCR output.

obtained when STATE is used against correcting the transcription of the OCR directly with an editor. From the table, it is clear that for moderate values of CER, STATE presents large time savings. Only when the CER is very high, using an editor for OCR output correction seems to be a better choice, since the writers preferred directly deleting completely wrong lines and retyping them with the editor, but still tried to correct them when using the STATE interface.

Table 1. Time savings when using STATE with respect to using only an editor (EditorOnly) and using an editor to correct OCR output (HMMEditor) as a function of the CER of the page

CER	Reference	
	EditorOnly	HMMEditor
CER < 15	51%	33%
15 ≤ CER < 30	31%	23%
30 ≤ CER	5%	-44%

5   Conclusions

The architecture of STATE divides the system into two parts: the front-end and the back-end. The loose coupling of these parts gives the system great flexibility and makes it suitable for very different transcription tasks ranging from ancient printed documents to handwritten text. The design of the interface and its adaptability to new fonts and writing styles allow great improvements in transcription times even in its current state of development.

Acknowledgments. Work partially supported by the Spanish *Ministerio de Ciencia e Innovación* (TIN2006-12767, TIN2008-06856, and *Consolider Ingenio 2010* CSD2007-00018), *Fundació Caixa Castelló-Bancaixa* (P1·1B2006-31), and *Conselleria d'Empresa, Universitat i Ciéncia, Generalitat Valenciana* (BFPI06/250 scholarship).

References

1. Bunke, H.: Recognition of cursive roman handwriting — past, present and future. In: Proc. 7th ICDAR, Edinburgh, Scotland, pp. 448–459 (2003)
2. Gorbe-Moya, J., España-Boquera, S., Zamora-Martínez, F., Castro-Bleda, M.J.: Handwritten text normalization by using local extrema classification. In: Proc. 8th International Workshop on Pattern Recognition in Information Systems, Barcelona, Spain, pp. 164–172 (2008)
3. Gordo, A., Llorens, D., Marzal, A., Prat, F., Vilar, J.M.: STATE: A multimodal assisted text-transcription system for ancient documents. In: Proc. 8th IAPR Workshop on Document Analysis Systems, Nara, Japan, pp. 135–142 (2008)
4. Johansson, S., Atwell, E., Garside, R., Leech, G.: The Tagged LOB Corpus: Users' Manual. Technical report, Norwegian Computing Centre for the Humanities, Bergen, Norway (1986)
5. Marti, U.-V., Bunke, H.: The IAM-database: an English sentence database for offline handwriting recognition. Journal on Document Analysis and Recognition 5, 39–46 (2002)
6. Prat, F., Marzal, A., Martín, S., Ramos-Garijo, R., Castro, M.J.: A template-based recognition system for on-line handwritten characters. Journal of Information Science and Engineering 25(3), 779–791 (2009)
7. Stolcke, A.: SRILM — an extensible language modeling toolkit. In: Proc. ICSLP, Denver, USA, pp. 901–904 (2002)
8. Toselli, A.H., Juan, A., González, J., Salvador, I., Vidal, E., Casacuberta, F., Keysers, D., Ney, H.: Integrated handwriting recognition and interpretation using finite-state models. International Journal of Pattern Recognition and Artificial Intelligence 18(4), 519–539 (2004)
9. Vinciarelli, A., Bengio, S., Bunke, H.: Offline recognition of unconstrained handwritten texts using HMMs and statistical language models. IEEE Trans. on Pattern Analysis and Machine Intelligence 26(6), 709–720 (2004)
10. Young, S.J., Woodland, P.C., Byrne, W.J.: HTK: Hidden Markov Model Toolkit V1.5. Technical report, Cambridge University Engineering Department Speech Group and Entropic Research Laboratories Inc. (1993)

Author Index